THE SALES AGENT'S GUIDE TO REAL ESTATE

GENERAL

A COURSE DESIGNED FOR REAL ESTATE LICENSING

Seventeenth Edition

Brian Swan, Esq.

Editor-in-Chief

Hannah Welch

Senior Editor

1

The Sales Agent's Guide to Real Estate General

Edition 17.1

Editor-in-Chief: Brian Swan

Senior Editor: Hannah Welch

Cover Designer: Julie Glenn

Cover Images:

© 9752864 | Dreamstime.com
© 24743512 | Dreamstime.com
© 39046671 | Dreamstime.com
© 40895874 | Dreamstime.com
© 46517595 | Dreamstime.com
© 4976996 | Dreamstime.com
© 6789479 | Dreamstime.com
© 33890612 | Dreamstime.com
© 44904071 | Dreamstime.com
© 33892285 | Dreamstime.com
© 42183118 | Dreamstime.com
© 34996167 | Dreamstime.com
© 4337324 | Dreamstime.com
© 38585597 | Dreamstime.com
© 30589662 | Dreamstime.com
© 56053199 | Dreamstime.com
© 50653893 | Dreamstime.com
© 45140294 | Dreamstime.com
© 40532746 | Dreamstime.com
© 51379397 | Dreamstime.com
© 24562155 | Dreamstime.com
© 46696206 | Dreamstime.com
© 13401066 | Dreamstime.com

Published in the United States by

Stringham Schools
635 W 5300 S
Murray, UT 84123

Visit us at stringhamschools.com

Books are available for purchase for professional and personal use. For information, call Stringham Schools at

(801) 269-8889.

4

Table of Contents

© Stringham Schools

Forward

The real estate career offers innumerable rewards. Many people see real estate as a lucrative industry where, with hard work, persistence, ethics, and good salesmanship an agent can transform their quality of life. For others, they see opportunity to help and bless the lives of others. And even still, there are some who view real estate in a completely different paradigm. Whichever way you look at real estate, and regardless of your reasons, there's an underlying commonality in all real estate agents as they pursue their own success: An unknowledgeable agent is an unsuccessful one.

When I went through Stringham nearly fifteen years ago, I used the same textbook that you now hold in your hands. The book was originally written by Stringham's founders, Arnold and Marti Stringham, who spent countless hours creating a textbook that became the industry's mark of a well educated agent. The Utah real estate industry and innumerable agents are indebted to them for their work. Since this book was originally written, the laws and principles of real estate have changed, so much so that the vast majority of the content within this text is now quite different than its original version. However, despite the fact that the content and presentation of this book is vastly new and different compared to the original, the Stringham's work is the foundation for what you now hold in your hands.

In this new edition of the Stringham textbook, the content is updated and current to reflect current law, regulation, and principles pertaining to real estate. The book has been restructured with two purposes in mind: (1) To help the prospective agent succeed on the state exam; and (2) to be a continual resource for the practicing agent. As an agent practicing in Utah, you may find yourself needing to reference or look up a particular law in a given situation. By finding a specific topic in the book, the practicing agent can use that concept's accompanying citation to find the exact governing statute or rule for which you then look up and act accordingly.

I hope you find this book helpful not only in preparing for the exam, but throughout your career. And remember, it is your duty as a licensed professional to keep abreast of the law and its changes. Because of this, I cannot stress enough how important it is for a licensed professional to have updated and current materials for which to stay sharp with.

As the President of Stringham Schools, we thank you for your trust as you enter the industry.

Learn. Pass. Succeed.

Brian Swan
Director of Stringham Schools

Introduction

Welcome to the remarkable world of real estate. It is here at Stringham Schools that you begin your journey into a new profession. As with any profession, the first sensible step must be education. What happens during this course will create your first view of this new occupation.

Since you are starting with us, we want to share our mission statement with you so you can be fully aware of how we approach our work.

Mission Statement

As Utah's premier real estate school, we provide excellence in real estate education. We encourage and empower our students to achieve their desired success in the real estate profession. This is accomplished through:

- Superior Instruction
- Up-to-Date Materials
- Integrated Technology
- Well-Managed Facilities
- Convenient Schedules
- Respected Faculty & Staff

Our primary concern is our students.

In order to make this statement a reality, we have set four goals for our school. We are committed in our instruction and interaction with students to:

- Care
- Be Professional
- Be Knowledgeable
- Be Funny

Important Information about Taking this Course

1. **HISTORY LETTER:** If you have been previously licensed in another state, you will need to furnish a history letter mailed direct from that state's real estate division to the Utah Real Estate Division before you can obtain your license.

2. **INTRODUCTION CLASS:** If you do not begin taking classes with the Introduction class, you should complete the class as soon as possible. It contains valuable information which will assist you as you progress through the course. The class is available online or in our computer labs where we can assist you.

3. **STUDENT COURTESY:** Please be on time for classes and in returning from breaks. It's very disruptive to the concentration of other students to have people wandering randomly into class during the first portion. Turn off all cell phones and other noisemaking devices during class, and do not use class time to pick up messages.

4. **SCHEDULE OF CLASSES:** We keep our schedule of live classes on our website www.stringhamschools.com for easy access. You may also have a schedule faxed or emailed to you by contacting us at (800)759-8889

5. **ACCELERATED SCHEDULE:** For those who want to finish as fast as possible, you will need to

take eight hours of classes per day. You can combine classes online to obtain classes not offered live when you want them. That gives you ultimate flexibility. (*Even though you could complete more than eight hours per day of classes by doing some online, state law prevents us from giving more than eight hours of credit in any one 24 hour period.*)

6.   **TOTAL FLEXIBILITY:** You can make up your own personal schedule by taking classes online anytime or live classes in the afternoon, or evening. You can mix and match – some live, some online.

7.   **COMPLETION OF THE COURSE:** The final two steps are the school exams and the State Test Prep class.

   A. The school exam is taken online. Our school exam is given in two parts: the general exam and the law exam. Each part is graded separately (as it is by the State), and if you fail a part, you only need to retake that part.

   B. Once you have passed our school test, you are ready for the State Test Prep class. It is available live in SLC and online. We recommend taking this class live. The advantage of the live review is that you can get immediate answers to your questions and clear up any misunderstanding you may have in the presence of a live instructor. This class is from 9 am – 4 pm, and is a required part of the course. It counts as part of your 120 hours. When it is over, we offer an optional hour of math review from 4:00 – 5:00 pm.

8.   **ONLINE ATTENDANCE:** Online attendance is automatically recorded for you. All classes are available online including reviews and testing.

9.   **LIVE ATTENDANCE:** Be sure to sign the class roster when attending live classes, this will ensure we update your record properly.   Use your student ID number if possible.

   Step 1 – Complete all classes.

   Step 2 – Complete the Course Reviews online.

      Review Test 1 & 2.

   Step 3 – Take your School Exam online. You need to pass each exam with 75%, if you don't pass, you only need to take the part not passed. Whether you pass or not, you will have an opportunity to review the questions you missed and make notes of the topics that gave you trouble so you'll know where to spend your study time. Any retakes must be done on a different day than the test was originally taken or reviewed.

   Step 4 – State Test Prep, Yeah!!! You've made it! Try to be here between 8:30 and 8:45 am to check in for the State Test Prep. Please remember it is all day from 9:00 am – 4:00 pm. We'll have a fun time together and you'll join the ranks of the many who say, "Boy, I saw so many items on the test that we covered during the State Test Prep." The State Test Prep class is also available online.

10. **STATE EXAM:** Don't forget to schedule your State Exam by calling Pearsonvue at 1-800-274-7292, the cost is $66.00 and the school code is 2300. The course completion date would be the date you complete the state test prep class.

Selecting a Broker

Introduction

There is probably nothing that will contribute more to your early success in the real estate business than the proper selection of a broker and an office. Each sales agent is different; therefore, the agent must individually seek a broker who will allow him/her to achieve the highest level possible. In most cases, it is wise to interview with several brokers before making a final decision. You will find that most brokers will be delighted to meet with you, and you should be equally grateful for the opportunity.

Approach the decision with these critical considerations: *Training, lead generation, listing services, and presentation.*

First and foremost is the need for excellent training. Make sure that you ask plenty of questions like: What are the results of those who have completed the training program? How often are courses offered? Who teaches them? What is the content? What are my costs?

Also, having access to quality lead opportunities is extremely valuable to new agents. Many statistics prove that if new agents have a closing within 60 days their likelihood of staying in the business dramatically increases. But be prepared to pay for quality leads. This is not a bad thing. If the company is benefiting because you successfully closed a transaction, then more leads will likely come your way. The same is true if another agent offers your lead opportunities.

Obtaining listings is the key to consistent production. The business is just easier when you have listings. So the questions directed to the broker should be: What are the reasons a seller would list with your brokerage? What services or tools would give me, as an agent, an advantage?

Presenting all of the benefits of the services you will provide to a client is another important piece of the puzzle. After all, what good are all of the amazing tools if no one knows about them? Consider looking at other agents' presentations. How do you like the design? Can customizations be done?

One more thing: Technologies are huge part of the modern day brokerage. Technologies can help in each of the points discussed above. The lack of cutting edge systems slows down the results and frustrates the process. So look closely at the kind of technologies the company and brokerage have invested in. You'll be glad you did.

Interview

1. Dress and groom yourself in the manner that you feel a real estate professional should. You want the broker to see how you will dress and present yourself when you are in the office.

2. Be relaxed, but speak confidently and properly. How you act in the interview reflects how you will act with clients and customers.

3. Interview the broker thoroughly, but leave him/her with the feeling that s/he is interviewing you . . . because s/he is.

4. Answer all questions honestly. Don't commit to things you will not be willing to actually do. When

information is offered, feel free to pursue the subject until you understand completely and your underlying questions have been satisfactorily answered.

5.   Ask your questions as they relate to the topics the broker is asking and talking to you about. Nevertheless, do not be reluctant to discuss commission splits or working conditions. S/He expects you to be interested in making a lot of money and knows that when you make money, s/he will make money. However, do not be overbearing.

Work Environment

The Broker:

1.   Do I like the broker? Will my personality and his/hers relate well? Am I comfortable with him/her? Do I like the broker's mannerisms? Do I agree with his/her philosophy of business and life?

2.   Is s/he a competing broker (a broker who takes on their own clients)? Is s/he actively engaged in working with buyers and sellers? If so, how much does the broker's success depend on the broker's own sales? In other words, will s/he have time for me, or will s/he be competing against me?

3.   Will the broker be able to motivate me?

4.   Exactly how will I interact with the broker? Will s/he be my direct supervisor?The Sales

Manager and Staff:

1.   Is there a sales manager (or equivalent)? If so, what will my relationship be with this person? What will be their role in relation to my own?

2.   What is the staff like?

3.   Will I like being among them?

4.   Are they professional?

5.   Are they busy?

6.   Do they have time for me?

7.   Are they successful and working together?

8.   Do I feel comfortable with them?

Office Location And Facility

1.   Is the location good for me? A location close to home is nice but not always necessary.

2.   Is the location good for the type of business I'll be doing (residential, commercial, leasing, etc.)?

3.   Do I like the decor and arrangement of the office? Does it reflect the type of atmosphere I would enjoy?

4.   Where, in the office, would I meet clients? (Conference, meeting rooms. etc.)

5.   What special equipment is available for my use, such as a copy machine. How much would I be allowed to use them and what restrictions are placed on their use?

6.   What will my personal work area be like? Do I have my own or will I share with others?

Earning Power and Office Policies:

1.   What is the beginning commission split? Is there a franchise fee?

2.   How does that commission increase and how much? Once I achieve certain levels, do I ever go back to a lower split, such as at the beginning of the month or year?

3.   Are there bonuses, contests, or other income possibilities?

4.   Is there an advantage if I sell an "in-house listing" (a listing held by the company you work for, but not one of your personal listings)?

5.   What is my commission split if I buy or sell property for myself? For my immediate family?

6.   Do I get the full bonus offered by other offices to the selling agent, such as "$1,000 to the selling agent," or "a trip for two to Hawaii for the selling agent"? Or will it also be split with the broker?

Expenses

1.   What start-up costs will I have?

$_____ Board of REALTORS'® initial fee

$_____ Board of REALTORS'® monthly fee

$_____ Real Estate License

$_____ Business Cards

$_____Business Apparel

$_____ Other _____

$_____ Other _____

$_____ Other _____

2.   How, when, and where does the office advertise listings? Who pays for the advertising? What if I want to advertise on my own, will the broker participate? Do they advertise regularly in the newspapers, magazines, etc.? What websites will my listings be found on? Are property photography services provided? What search applications are available? Are there relocation services?

One small parting thought: Not all of you who read this are the same, right? And thank goodness! So this advice may not fit everyone. There are differences in all brokerages. So, make sure you interview enough brokerages so that you can find what fits you best. You will know when you find it. As you go through the process of finding the right fit for you, you'll discover that most of brokerages really care about their agents and there is a lot of good in many of the companies out there!

REAL ESTATE OWNERSHIP

DEEDS AND TRANSFER

OWNERSHIP BASICS

OWNERSHIP PRINCIPLES

PROPERTY

PUBLIC & PRIVATE CONTROL

SURVEY & DESCRIPTION

16

Deeds & Transfer

I. **Definitions**

    A. **Deed**: The evidence of ownership of all the real property which is inside the property boundaries as defined by the property description in the deed. In a transfer of ownership or sale, the real property is that which exists on the property at the time the sales agreement is signed rather than the date of closing. A deed is considered corporeal, or tangible.

    B. **Title**: An abstract term denoting ownership of real property. An owner holds title and proves it by showing the deed. There is no actual document in real property called a title. Title is considered incorporeal, or intangible.

    C. **Alienation of Title**: A transfer of ownership in any of its forms is an alienation of title. The alienation may be voluntary or involuntary.

II. **Essential Elements of a Deed**

    When someone claims title to property, he must prove his ownership with a valid deed. The following are items which must be incorporated into the deed to make it valid.

    A. **Intent**: The intent of the grantor must be evident. In court, the judge will try to determine what the grantor was attempting to do with his property. The intent is established by each of the other items on this list.

    B. **Signature**: The deed must have the signature of the grantor.

    C. **Granting Clause**: It must contain a granting clause "I transfer," "I grant," "I convey," etc.

    D. **Names of the Parties**: Both grantor and grantee, must be written on the deed.

    E. **Description**: In Utah, all documents involving real estate must have a legally acceptable, or adequate, description. This would mean the description is adequate to separate the parcel in question from every other parcel on the face of the earth.

    F. **Consideration**: The deed must denote that consideration was exchanged for the deed. In most cases, the phrase "ten dollars and other good and valuable consideration" is used to hide the actual amount of consideration exchanged while still satisfying the legal requirement.

    G. **Written**: As required by the Statute of Frauds, a conveyance of an interest in real property must be done in writing (Note that this is different than the Statute of Frauds requirement that real estate contracts be in writing).

    H. **Delivery**: To be valid, a deed must be delivered to the grantee. Forms of delivery include:

        1. **Actual delivery**: The grantor actually hands or sends the deed to the grantee. If mailed it should be sent by registered mail.

        2. **Constructive delivery**: This is usually accomplished by having the deed recorded on the public records.

        3. **Third party delivery**: The grantor authorizes a third party to hold the deed in escrow or trust until some designated time, such as when the grantor dies. Then the deed is delivered

to the grantee. The third party must have written, acknowledged or notarized instructions to make this form of delivery valid.

Warranty Deed

Granting Clause:

I convey this property . . .

Property Description:

Lot 21, Block K, New Haven Su….

Names of the parties:

Grantor: Ezra L. Selor

Grantee: Ezekiel M. Bier

Consideration:

$10 and other good and val….

Warranties:

Seizin: Grantor has title & can convey it.

Against Encumbrances: No unrevealed liens, etc.

Quiet Enjoyment: No unexpected claims against the title

Further Assurance: Grantor will defend against adverse claims

Warranty Forever: Grantor will pay for losses.

Grantor

Quit Claim Deed

Granting Clause:

Quit claim of all interest of grantor, including releases and removal of various clouds on title.

Property Description:

Lot 21, Block K, New Haven Su….

Names of the parties:

Grantor: Ezra L. Selor

Grantee: Ezekiel M. Bier

Consideration:

$10 and other good and val….

Warranties:

No warranties or guarantees except that the grantor gives up all of his/her interest, which may legally be no interest whatsoever.

Grantor

III.   Non-Essential Elements of a Deed

The following items are not legally required but are used in most modern day conveyances:

A.   **Recording**: Though the most common form of delivery is recording, it is not the only form of delivery and therefore need not be used. Nevertheless, recording or constructive delivery is probably the safest form of delivery and is highly recommended. In the event a grantor wrongfully transferred the same property to two different parties, the one who recorded the deed first would be declared the owner, even if that deed had a later delivery date than one not yet recorded.

B.   **Acknowledgment** (notarized or witnessed):

1.   If the deed is not recorded, it does not have to be acknowledged in order to be valid. It is the signature of the grantor that is being notarized or witnessed (acknowledged), not the

actual content of the deed. Most county recorders require that the signature of the grantor be acknowledged before they will record the deed.

C. **Date**: Though a deed need not have a date to be valid, it is important and should not be neglected.

D. **Habendum Clause**: It is sometimes referred to as the "to have and to hold clause," the "Exceptions and reservations clause," or the "subject to" clause. It serves to define, lessen, enlarge, qualify, or affirm the extent of ownership the grantor is transferring. It must agree with the granting clause. For instance, if the grantor was selling all of his real property, except the mineral rights, he would note that exception in the habendum or exceptions and reservations clause.

IV. **Types of Deeds**

A. **Quit Claim Deed**: A quit claim deed performs the following:

    1. Conveys all interest, both ownership and non-ownership, without giving any guarantees.

    2. It is used most often in divorces, quick asset shifting, and to remove clouds on title such as misspelled names.

B. **Bargain & Sale Deed**: This deed is similar to the Quit Claim Deed except it implies that the grantor has an interest in the property. It is seldom used in Utah, but is utilized in other states.

C. **General or Full Warranty Deed**:

    1. The most complete transfer of ownership with the greatest protection.

    2. It includes the following five warranties:

        a. **Covenant of Seizin**: The grantor states that he/she holds title and has the right to convey it.

        b. **Covenant Against Encumbrances**: It is promised that there are no encumbrances against the property except those that have been revealed to the grantee and are accepted in the deed.

        c. **Covenant of Quiet Enjoyment**: The grantor guarantees that the grantee has rights to the property free of interference from acts or claims of third parties.

        d. **Covenant of Further Assurance**: Should anyone make a claim against the title after the transfer of the deed, the grantor promises to perform any acts necessary to perfect the title.

        e. **Covenant of Warranty Forever**: The grantor will bear the expense of defending the grantee's title if any person asserts a rightful claim to the property. If he is unsuccessful, the grantee may sue for damages up to the value of the property at the time of the sale. It covers the period of time from the conveyance back to the Patent Deed conveyed by the government.

D. **Special Warranty Deed**:

    1. Warrants only against defects arising during the period of the grantor's ownership.

    2. Gives only the Covenant of Seizin and Covenant Against Encumbrances.

E. **Grant Deed**: In some states, notably California, Idaho, and North Dakota, a grant deed is often used in place of a warranty deed. A grant deed gives less protection since it gives no guarantees relative to encumbrances that may have been created by owners previous to the grantor. These states have determined that title insurance gives adequate protection and a warranty deed is not necessary.

F. Deeds having to do with probate (the process by which a court transfers title of a deceased individual's property to his/her heirs):

    1. **Administrator's Deed**

    2. **Executor's Deed**

    These deeds are usually **Special Warranty Deeds**, which guarantees that the executor or administrator has not encumbered the property. Bargain and Sale Deeds are some times used.

G. Deeds having to do with foreclosure: These deeds usually take the form of Special Warranty Deeds or Bargain and Sale Deeds and are sometimes referred to as "Foreclosure Deeds." They include:

    1. **Sheriff's Deed**

    2. **Trustee's Deed**

    3. **Tax Deed**

H. **Gift Deed**: The conveyance of property for love and affection. If creditors could prove this was not a bona fide gift, but a way to avoid the property being used to satisfy a debt, the courts could order the property conveyed back to the grantor.

I. **Patent Deed**: This deed, sometimes called a "Public Grant," is used by the government to convey public property to private individuals.

V. **Transfer by Devise or Descent**

Death interrupts the ownership of property. Laws have been established by which a person can provide for the inheritance of his property if he so chooses, and then sets up the procedures for the distribution. Laws have also been established so that if the deceased did nothing to provide for the transfer of ownership, it can still be taken care of.

A. The following terms create the basis of the transfer of ownership after death.

    1. **Probate**: The process of validating a will with the court and carrying out the terms as set forth in the will.

        a. Each state has their probate code that governs how an estate will be administered and property distributed.

b. Some other states use Dower and Curtsey rights. Dower rights are the rights of the wife in her husband's estate. Curtsey rights are the rights of the husband in the wife's estate.

2. **Testate**: A person who dies leaving a will is said to have died testate.

3. **Intestate**: A person who dies and does not leave a will is said to have died intestate. Their assets will be distributed according to the State's intestate succession law (sometimes called the law of descent).

4. **Escheat**: When a person dies without a will and without heirs, the estate passes (escheats) to the state.

5. **Testator** (male) or **Testatrix** (female): A person who has made a will.

6. **Bequest or Legacy**: A gift of personal property given in a will.

7. **Devise**: A gift of real property given in a will. The testator is the "devisor," the one who receives the gift is the "devisee."

8. **Executor or Executrix**: A person or persons named in a will to carry out the terms of the will. In Utah, this person is called a Personal Representative.

9. **Administrator**: A person assigned by the court to carry out the terms of a will, since no executor was named in the will. Some states, Utah included, also refer to the Administrator as the Personal Representative.

10. **A Formal Witnessed Will**: A written document, usually prepared with the assistance of an attorney. It is considered the most valid form of a will and is least likely to be successfully challenged. If the signatures are notarized it is referred to as a self proving will. This type of will does not require the witnesses to appear in court if the will is challenged. If a notary public is not used, it is called a non-self proving will. A formal witnessed will requires:

    a. The signature of the testator in the presence of the witnesses (or a notary); and

    b. The signature of two witnesses present at the signing of the testator; or

    c. A notary public who is present at the signing and validates the signatures of the testator.

11. **Nuncupative Will**: An oral will, sometimes called a death bed will. The will must be written as soon as possible after the will has been spoken by the testator. Usually three witnesses, not beneficiaries of the will, must sign that the written document coincides with what they heard. A nuncupative will can only pass personal property. Not recognized in Utah.

12. **Holographic Will**: A handwritten will. It is written entirely in the handwriting of the testator and need not be witnessed. It should be dated, and it can pass both real and personal property.

13. A change or addition made to an existing will. The creation of a codicil must follow all of

the rules and formalities associated with creating the original will.

B. **Living Will**: This will allow the testator to donate body organs to science, give instructions relative to use of life support systems, etc. It is considered advisory and not binding.

C. **Trust**: A legal arrangement where legal title to real property and other assets is transferred by the grantor or trustor to the created trust to be held and managed by a named trustee for the well being of another person called the beneficiary. Because trusts provide for management of property and financial controls, as well as having some tax and estate planning advantages, this form of property ownership is growing in popularity. Trusts ordinarily take one of two forms:

1. **A living trust or inter vivos trust**: This trust takes effect during the life of its creator to make sure that assets are properly made available for the benefit of the beneficiaries. This also comes in two forms, both of which will provide for the avoidance of probate:

   a. **Revocable**: It can be changed by the trustor at any time. Since the trustor retains in control of the assets, it gives no protection from legal actions against the trustor.

   b. **Irrevocable**: Once this trust is set up, the trustor loses the right to change it. For instance, if a husband set up an irrevocable trust for his wife and children and later a divorce took place, the husband would lose all assets in the trust. However, this form of trust provides good protection from legal actions.

2. **A testamentary trust**: This trust takes effect after death. It does not allow one to avoid the probate process. It allows the trustor to give instructions as to how the assets are to bemanaged by the trustee, such as indicating how much and how often to pay the beneficiaries.

Caution – The laws governing wills, trusts, and other estate planning techniques are complex and change from time to time. Therefore it is essential to consult specialists in these fields when doing your estate planning.

Deeds and Transfer Terms to Know

- ☐ Acknowledge
- ☐ Actual Delivery
- ☐ Administrator
- ☐ Bargain and Sale Deed
- ☐ Bequest or Legacy
- ☐ Codicil
- ☐ Constructive Delivery
- ☐ Covenant Against Encumbrances
- ☐ Covenant of Further Assurance
- ☐ Covenant of Quiet Enjoyment
- ☐ Covenant of Seizin
- ☐ Covenant of Warranty Forever
- ☐ Descent
- ☐ Deed
- ☐ Delivery
- ☐ Devise (Devisor/Devisee)
- ☐ Exception and Reservations Clause
- ☐ Executor or Executrix
- ☐ Formal will
- ☐ General or Full Warranty Deed
- ☐ Gift Deed
- ☐ Grant Deed
- ☐ Grantee
- ☐ Grantor
- ☐ Habendum Clause ("Subject to" clause)
- ☐ Holographic will
- ☐ Intestate
- ☐ Nuncupative will
- ☐ Patent or Public Grant Deed
- ☐ Personal Representative
- ☐ Recording
- ☐ Quit Claim Deed
- ☐ Special Warranty Deed
- ☐ Testator
- ☐ Third Party Delivery
- ☐ Title

Deeds and Transfer Quiz

1. Jack and Jill have recently been divorced. The decree gave the house to Jill. Since there is no reason for Jack to give any guarantee of title, he will most likely pass his interest in the property with a:

    A. Special Warranty Deed

    B. Quit Claim Deed

    C. General Warranty Deed

    D. Patent Deed

2. Which of the following deeds would be most desirable as seen from the perspective of the buyer?

    A. Special Warranty Deed

    B. Quit Claim Deed

    C. General Warranty Deed

    D. Bargain and Sale Deed

3. When does title actually pass under a deed?

    A. On the day of the date written on the deed

    B. On the day the deed is executed or signed

    C. On the day it is delivered and accepted

    D. On the day it is acknowledged

4. A deed that the government uses to transfer government owned property to a private individual is known as a:

    A. Warranty Deed

    B. Patent Deed

    C. Quit Claim Deed

    D. Federal Land Deed

5. The most common use of a quit claim deed is to:

    A. Pass full title with all warranties to the grantee in a quick and timely manner.

    B. Pass title from the government to a private individual.

    C. Remove clouds from the title.

    D. Quit claim to all ownership and all liability for loans and other encumbrances on the title.

6. A property is sold at an estate sale and title is passed by the executor to the buyer. The executor's deed would be most like which of the following?

    A. Special Warranty Deed

    B. General Warranty Deed

    C. Quit Claim Deed

    D. Patent Deed

7. Which of the following describes the Covenant of Quiet Enjoyment?

    A. Freedom from distressing noise from an adjoining property owner.

    B. The seller must quietly relinquish possession.

    C. The purchaser shall not be disturbed in the peaceful possession of the property.

    D. All encumbrances have been recorded.

8. What clause means "to have and to hold" or "subject to" and defines the extent of a transfer of real property?

    A. Escalator clause

    B. Habendum clause

    C. Escheat clause

    D. Notice of Interest clause

9. Which of the following is NOT necessary to make a deed valid?

    A. Date of the transfer of ownership

    B. Property description

    C. Signature of the grantor

    D. Delivery of the deed to the grantee

10. Which of the following is NOT a valid means of delivering a deed from the grantor to the grantee?

    A. The grantor hands the deed to the grantee.

    B. The grantor tells the grantee that the grantee is to have the property after his death.

    C. The grantor gives written, notarized instructions to deliver the deed to the grantee after the death of the grantor.

    D. The grantor records the deed at the county recorder's office in the name of the grantee.

11. A handwritten will is:

    A. A nuncupative will

    B. A holographic will

    C. A bequest

    D. Invalid

12. A person appointed by the court to carry out the terms of a will is called a(n):

    A. Testator

    B. Executor or Executrix

    C. Administrator

    D. Devisor

13. If a person dies intestate, his estate would be distributed according to the law of:

    A. Holographic

    B. Devise

    C. Codicil

    D. Intestacy or descent

ANSWERS TO THIS QUIZ ARE FOUND IN THE "QUIZ ANSWERS" SECTION.

SEE TABLE OF CONTENTS

Ownership Basics

I. **The Bundle of Rights**

When real property is purchased, in addition to the physical property, rights of ownership are conveyed with the deed. The bundle of rights (sometimes called the "bundle of sticks") contains 11 property rights and includes the following:

A. **Possession:** These rights include the right to enter and occupy the property, to invite others to enter and/or occupy, and the right to exclude others (no trespassing).

B. **Use or Control:** These rights involve the purposes for which the property is used such as living, stores, farms, mining, or no use at all.

C. **Quiet Enjoyment:** The right of an owner or lessee to uninterrupted legal use of the property without interference or undue disturbance caused by defective title.

D. **Disposition:** The right to keep the property, sell it, lease it, give it away, etc.

II. **Freehold (Ownership) Estates**

If an individual has a freehold interest, he has an ownership interest in the property, but may or may not own it free and clear. The word ownership is a synonym for the word freehold. There are various forms of freehold interests. They include:

A. **Fee Simple:** This is the most complete form of ownership an individual can hold under the law. A fee simple estate is inheritable. Fee Simple is also known as:

   1. Fee Estate

   2. Fee Simple Absolute

B. **Fee Simple Qualified** or **Defeasible**: A defeasible fee has some condition or covenant involved that limits the extent of one's ownership. This is also an inheritable estate. Forms of a qualified or defeasible (defeatable) fee include:

   1. **Fee Simple Determinable:** Exists when there is a condition in effect after the conveyance of the property to the grantee. If that condition is violated, such as changing the defined use of the property, the property automatically reverts back to the original owner by right of reversion. Example: "A grants the property to B so long as the property is used as a school."

   2. **Fee Simple with a Condition Subsequent:** Is the same as Fee Simple Determinable except that there is no automatic right of reversion. If the condition is violated, the grantor may retake the property if the conveyance grants him/her the right to do so. Example: "A grants the property to B, but if the property is ever used for commercial purposes, then A has a right of reentry."

C. **Future Interests:**

   1. **Fee Simple with a Condition Precedent:** Title will not fully transfer to the grantee until a condition is met, such as a child reaching legal age.

2. Thus, the grantee holds a future interest—they will own the property in the future once the condition is satisfied. Example: "A grants the property to B 'if B graduates from college.'"

D. **Life Estate**: The life estate is a non-inheritable estate.

1. The fee simple owner conveys to the grantee the right to use a property as though the grantee owned it, so long as the grantee lives. The grantor has the **right of reversion**, and is a **remainderman** unless it has been specified that the final remainderman will hold the property fee simple.

2. The holder of the life estate has the right to sell, lease, or encumber his interest in the property (the life estate), but cannot will it. The life estate holder cannot commit "waste." In other words, he cannot damage or neglect the property and thereby diminish its value for when it is passed on to the remainderman.

3. A life estate can be used as collateral on a loan if all the parties (grantor, grantee, lender) agree and consent to the lender receiving the property fee simple upon default. In other words, a life estate can be mortgaged, but the reversion/remainder rights will be lost and the property will be foreclosed on by the lender who will then receive the property in fee simple.

4. The holder cannot convey an interest that extends beyond his life. For instance, if the holder of a life estate were to give a tenant a three year lease on his life estate, and then the holder of the life estate died before the lease expired, the lease would automatically terminate.

5. The grantor can create a series of life estates, e.g., Blackmore grants a life estate to Abel which is to be transferred to Baker when Abel dies.

    a. Abel is the holder of the life estate.

    b. Baker is a remainderman.

    c. The reversionary rights, if any, of the grantor are exercised after the death of both Abel and Baker.

6. In another instance, the grantor can create a series of life estates with title to be vested fee simple to the last individual in the sequence, e.g., Rose grants a life estate to Smith, which is to be transferred to Thomas when Smith dies. When Thomas dies it is to go to Wilson and be vested fee simple. In this case:

    a. Rose is the grantor, but not a remainderman.

    b. Smith is the initial holder of the life estate.

    c. Thomas and Wilson are remaindermen.

    d. Wilson will receive fee simple title after Smith and Thomas die. The grantor no longer has a right of reversion.

7. **Life Estate Pur Autre´ Vie** (on another's life): The life estate is based on the life of someone other than the holder of the life estate. For instance, Abel sells his life estate to Charles. Charles is the holders of the life estate pur autre vie. That is, Charles holds the life estate, but the extent of his ownership of the life estate is based on Abel's life. A life estate pur autre´ vie is inheritable as long as the person on whose life it is based is still alive.

8. Important rules:

    a. A basic life estate can be conveyed, sold, or gifted, but not inherited. If the life estate holder sells the life estate, the new owner owns the life estate pur autre' vie.

    b. A life estate pur autre' vie can be conveyed, sold, gifted, or inherited as long as the governing life is still alive.

    c. Unless a remainderman is created by the grantor, the grantor holds a reversionary interest, which can be inherited if the grantor pre-deceases the governing life.

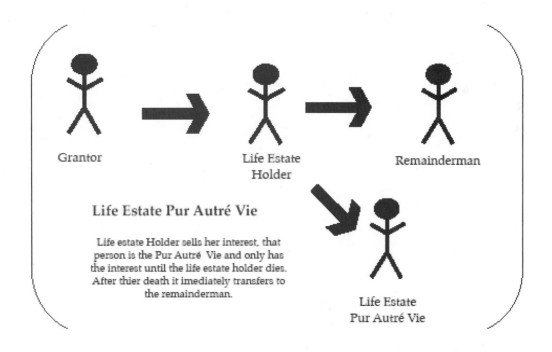

Grantor

Life Estate
Holder

Remainderman

Life Estate Pur Autré Vie

Life estate Holder sells her interest, that
person is the Pur Autré Vie and only has
the interest until the life estate holder dies.
After thier death it imediately transfers to
the remainderman.

Life Estate
Pur Autré Vie

29

Ownership Basics Terms to Know

- ☐ Bundle of Rights
- ☐ Defeasible Fee Estate
- ☐ Fee Estate
- ☐ Fee Simple
- ☐ Fee Simple Absolute
- ☐ Fee Simple Defeasible Estate
- ☐ Freehold Estate
- ☐ Holder of a Life Estate
- ☐ Life Estate
- ☐ Life Estate Pur Autre Vie
- ☐ Quiet Enjoyment
- ☐ Remainderman
- ☐ Right of Reversion

Ownership Basics Quiz

1. Which of the following is NOT a part of the Bundle of Rights?

    A. Use

    B. Disposition

    C. Possession

    D. Interest

2. The word or phrase that most accurately describes the word "Freehold" is:

    A. Owning free and clear

    B. Ownership

    C. Life Estate

    D. Pur Autre Vie

3. Don Meyers has the legal right to act as though he owns a property for the rest of his life, even though the property is actually owned by his father Ron Meyers. Don is a:

    A. Holder of a life estate

    B. Holder of a life estate pur autre vie

    C. Remainderman

    D. Holder of Rights of Reversion

ANSWERS TO THIS QUIZ ARE FOUND IN THE "QUIZ ANSWERS" SECTION.

SEE TABLE OF CONTENTS

Ownership Principles

I. **Forms of Property Ownership**

    A. **An Estate in Severalty** or **Sole Ownership**: Title is held by only one person, all others have been "severed" from the title. All other forms of ownership are classified as co-ownership or concurrent ownership.

    B. **Joint Tenancy**

        1. Requires that four unities be in place when the tenancy is created. If any of the unities are absent, joint tenancy cannot be created. The **four unities** (mnemonic = **PITT**) of joint tenancy are:

            a. **Possession:** Full and undivided rights of possession for all owners.

            b. **Interest**: Each of the owners hold an equal portion of ownership.

            c. **Time**: All grantees must become owners at the same time.

            d. **Title**: All must be named on the same instrument of title, i.e. the deed.

        2. **Full Right of Survivorship**: If Jason and Janice own their home as Joint Tenants, when one of them dies, the survivor automatically and without probate becomes the owner in severalty. If Jason, Janice, and Jessica owned a property as joint tenants, each would own a one-third interest. If one of them died, the two survivors would automatically own a half interest, still as joint tenants.

        3. One joint owner can sell his interest without the consent of other joint owners. If Jason, Janice and Jessica own as joint tenants and Jessica sold her interest to James, Jason and Janice would own two thirds as joint tenants and James would own one third as a tenant in common.

        4. There can be any number of joint owners.

        5. Joint tenancy takes precedence over a will. Joint tenancy takes effect "at death" while a will takes effect "after death." There is a legal instant between these two events causing the joint tenancy to take priority over the will.

        6. Under Utah law, if a deed says: "John Doe and Mary Doe, husband and wife . . ." with no indication as to how they are taking title, the law assumes it to be joint tenancy.

    C. **Tenants in Common**

        1. Each owner has a full and undivided right of possession regardless of his percentage of ownership. This is the only unity of joint tenancy which applies in tenancy in common.

        2. Owners can hold varying percentages of ownership. Interest must be stated in the deed or the law will presume that the owners each hold equal interest.

        3. Ownership can be taken any time (does not have to be taken at the same time).

        4. Each owner has his own deed.

        5. There is no right of survivorship, and the future estate is determined by will, trust, probate, etc.

        6. In many states, if two people are named on a deed with no indication of their being married, or of how they are taking title, the law will presume them to be tenants in common.

        7. In selling a portion of ownership in a commercial investment project, all the owners own

as tenants in common. This is defined in Utah law as an "undivided fractionalized long-term estate." In real life, it is commonly referred to as a "tenant-in-common interest."

D. **Tenants by the Entirety**

1. Its form is most nearly like joint tenancy, including the right of survivorship.

2. It pertains only to husband and wife.

3. The difference between this and joint tenancy is essentially that neither husband nor wife can sell, mortgage, or otherwise encumber the property without the agreement of the spouse.

E. **Community Property**

1. It applies only to husband and wife.

2. It is used only in a few states: among them, California, Idaho, Arizona, Texas, New Mexico, Louisiana, Wisconsin, Washington and Nevada.

3. It is based on the concept that husband and wife are "equal partners" each owning a half interest in any property obtained during marriage.

4. In community property states, separate property is that which is acquired before marriage, after dissolution of the marriage, or by gift or inheritance during the marriage. It can be owned in severalty or with other partners and not include the spouse.

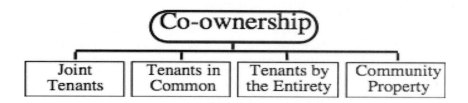

F. **Partition Action**. When co-owners disagree on whether or not to sell a property, the one(s) desiring to sell can bring a partition suit against the one(s) blocking the sale. This provides a way for people to free themselves of an unwanted common ownership. It can be used to invite the court to dissolve a joint tenancy or tenancy in common. If the property cannot be physically divided without prejudice to the parties, the court could order the property to be sold.

II. **Partnerships**

A. **Types of Partnerships**:

1. **General Partnership**: All partners have to be general partners.

2. **Limited Partnership**: There must be at least one or more general partners and there can be as many limited partners as desired.

B. **Types of Partners**:

1. **General Partner**: Has full financial liability and full right of decision making authority.

2. **Limited Partner**: Financial liability extends only to the amount of his investment and he has no decision making power.

C. A partnership is not considered a legal person, and the partners could be sued individually. A general partner can be sued for the full amount of the suit. Limited partners will not lose more than their investment.

III. Other Forms of Co-ownership

A. **Joint Venture**: Where two or more parties combine to carry out a single business project.

B. **Corporation**: A person or persons joined for business purposes.

1. It creates a single, legal person, rather than a natural person (real person), regardless of how many officers or agents may be in the corporation.

2. It creates some protection for personal assets.

3. Ownership is held in the form of stock.

4. A legal person and a natural person may own property together only as tenants in common. A corporation taking ownership alone would take ownership in severalty.

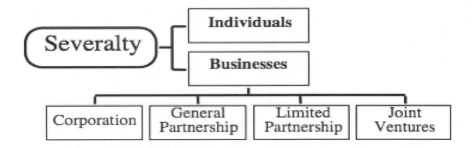

C. **Real Estate Investment Trust** ("REIT"): A REIT is a business trust that allows the investors to avoid double taxation if certain governmental requirements are met. Though the requirements change from time to time, currently a REIT must have, among other requirements, at least 100 shareholders and 90% of the profits must be disbursed to the shareholders as dividends each year.

IV. Dedication

A method by which a person can give real property as a gift. It is sometimes called a private grant. Dedication allows for transfer of real property from a private individual to the public (government) or a special interest group (church).

A. **Voluntary dedication**: Private individual gives real property as a gift for a park or church. The deeds often contain a clause specifying that the property must be used for the intended purpose or it reverts to the grantor, thus creating a defeasible fee.

B. **Statutory dedication**: Usually involves the dedication of streets and roads to the city or county when getting approval to develop a subdivision.

V. Adverse Possession

A. **Definition**: The right of adverse possession is based on the concept that land is too valuable to be left unattended for long periods of time. A person can enter and possess unused property and, after meeting the requirements for the statutory period of time, obtain title. You **cannot** acquire government property through adverse possession.

35

B. To make a valid claim of adverse possession of the property, the adverse possessor must be able to show that his possession was:

1. **Open and Notorious:** The owner or anyone else must be able to plainly detect the possession.

2. **Continuous** (not occasional): The owner uses it to the extent that any other owner would for the entire statutory period.

3. **Hostile**: This does not mean that the owner and the adverse possessor were fighting. It simply means that the adverse possessor is on the property without the owner's permission..

4. **Exclusive**: The adverse possessor must act as though he owns the property, which is to say that he/she holds the land to the exclusion of the true owner.

C. The ownership must be for the statutory period of time:

1. The statutory period ranges in the United States from three to 30 years

2. It is seven years in Utah. U.C.A. § 78B-2-214.

3. The adverse possessor is said to hold the property under color of title.

D. In some states, as in Utah, the property taxes must be paid by the adverse possessor, not the legal owner, during the period of adverse possession. If the owner is paying the property taxes, the adverse possessor will not be able to obtain title by adverse possession.

E. **Tacking**: A legal process of combining the rights of adverse possession of two or more successive adverse possessors. For instance, Mr. A adversely possesses a property for four years. He subsequently transfers his rights of adverse possession to Mr. B. After three more years, Mr. B can establish his right of adverse possession through a Quiet Title Action. Mr. A would transfer those rights with a Quit Claim Deed.

F. **Quiet Title Action**: A lawsuit used to clear title or to make a claim of interest and have title legally transferred to the adverse possessor.

Ownership Principles Terms to Know

- ☐ Adverse Possession
- ☐ Color of Title
- ☐ Community Property
- ☐ Corporation
- ☐ Dedication
- ☐ General Partner
- ☐ General Partnership
- ☐ Joint Tenancy
- ☐ Joint Venture
- ☐ Limited Partner
- ☐ Limited Partnership
- ☐ Natural Person
- ☐ Partition Suit
- ☐ Quiet Title Action
- ☐ Severalty
- ☐ Statutory Dedication
- ☐ Survivorship
- ☐ Tacking
- ☐ Tenancy by the Entirety
- ☐ Tenancy in Common
- ☐ Title
- ☐ Voluntary Dedication

Ownership Principles Quiz

1. Jason and Harriet Telford bought a home. The deed named them as grantees, but failed to indicate if they were tenants in common or joint tenants. Later Jason was killed in an accident. His will read that all of his real and personal property was to be divided equally between his children. Harriet claimed that she and Jason were joint tenants and therefore she should get all of the property. It ended up in court. How will the court most likely rule in this case?

    A. By Utah law, if the deed is ambiguous, the court will declare it to be joint tenancy between husband and wife. The kids have no claim.

    B. The court will always rule in favor of the wife and name her a joint tenant, thus giving Harriet the property.

    C. Since they were husband and wife in Utah, community property rules will take precedence and Harriet will get the property.

    D. The court will hold that they must duel it out. So the children must appoint a representative and that person will meet Harriet at dawn of the designated date. Then with pistols of their choice, they will each take ten paces, turn, fire, and settle this matter in a civilized manner.

2. When all partners are general partners, the organization is considered to be a:

    A. General Partnership

    B. Limited Partnership

    C. Joint Venture

    D. Corporation

3. Which of the following is a feature of a corporation?

    A. Personal assets are protected from law suits brought against the corporation.

    B. All partners are limited partners.

    C. Each member has full liability.

    D. Each owner has full right to make binding decisions on the corporation.

4. John and Lucy Mason own their home together. If one of them dies the other will automatically own the property. Therefore they own their property as:

    A. Tenants in Common

    B. Owners in Severalty

    C. Joint Tenants

    D. Tenants in Community Property

5.   Kyle and Bob own property as joint tenants. Bob dies. Kyle has Bob's name removed from the ownership. Kyle now:

   A. Owns the property as a tenant in common with Bob's heirs.

   B. Owns the property as a tenant in severalty.

   C. Has no ownership since his interest was dependent on the life of Bob.

   D. Bob's interest in the property will be part of his estate and must go through probate be fore anyone can own it.

6.   A little known fact about joint tenancy is that:

   A. One joint tenant cannot sell his interest in the property without the approval of the other joint tenants.

   B. Joint tenants cannot own unequal shares of the property.

   C. Joint tenancy applies only to husband and wife.

   D. Joint tenancy avoids probate only if the deceased has no will.

ANSWERS TO THIS QUIZ ARE FOUND IN THE "QUIZ ANSWERS" SECTION.

SEE TABLE OF CONTENTS

Property

I. **Real Property**

    A. **Allodial System**: A political/economic system that allows for the private ownership of real property is called an allodial system. The American Indian had a **non-allodial system**, but capitalism is an allodial system.

    B. Definition of **real property**: The land, all that is attached or appurtenant to the land; the subsurface to the center of the earth, and the air space to infinity.

        1. **Appurtenant**: Refers to things that are attached to the land or the deed. A fence is appurtenant to the land, whereas an easement would be considered appurtenant to the deed.

        2. Though the terms real property and real estate are used interchangeably by the most people, technically real property refers to intangible rights whereas real estate refers to the tangible or physical property. (The intangible rights referred to are discussed in detail in the Ownership class.)

    C. Water rights, mineral rights, and air rights are considered real property. **Water rights** for the state of Utah are discussed in more detail in the Real Estate Acts B class.

    D. Physical characteristics of real property

        1. **Immobility**: the land is immovable.

        2. Indestructibility: You can change the character of real property, but you still have the same amount of land. In other words, the property description remains unchanged; and, therefore, you have the same amount of real property.

        3. **Non-homogeneous**: No two parcels of real property are the same.

    E. Economic characteristics of real property

        1. **Scarcity**: There is a fixed amount of real property. Its scarcity adds to its value. Since there is no increase in the amount of land available, and since the population continues to grow, the law of supply and demand applies.

        2. **Improvements**: Land can be improved or modified, adding to the value of the real property. These manmade modifications are known as improvements. Property can be over improved, thus detracting from the value.

        3. **Location**: The location of the land affects its value. Location is referred to as "situs." Situs also refers to a personal preference for one location over another.

        4. **Residential Property**: Defined as real property consisting of, or improved by, a single-family one to four-unit dwelling.

    F. When a sale of real property takes place by the passing of a deed, the buyer obtains title to the real property, and the seller retains ownership of the personal property, unless both agree otherwise.

G.   **Lateral Support**: Support given to adjoining land, such as building a retaining wall.

H.   **Corporeal Property**: The term used to describe something which is physical or tangible. It could be real or personal property, such as a building, a car, etc. "Incorporeal" is the term for intangible assets such as an easement or leasehold right.

II.   **Addition To and Loss of Real Property**

There are several ways that real property can be added to or lost from that which already exists. They include:

A.   **Severance**: The process of turning real property into personal property by separating it from the real property. Thus, the personal property has been "severed." For example, a tree growing in a yard is real property. When it is cut down, it becomes personal property by severance.

B.   **Accession**: The opposite of severance. It is the process of adding to the real property by man (hauling in dirt, building a house) or nature (such as a mud slide or earthquake). Improvements is the term used to define additions made by man alone, such as buildings, utilities, roads, and landscaping.

III.   **Personal Property**

A.   Definition: That which is severed from real property.

B.   Synonyms: **Personalty, chattel**.

C.   Characteristics of personal property

1.   Any property that is not real property is personal property.

2.   Personal property is considered movable.

3.   It is temporary and considered a deteriorating or depreciating asset.

D.   The transfer or sale of personal property is documented with a "Bill of Sale."

IV.   **Fixtures**

A.   Definition: that which is attached to the real property without losing its identity.

B.   Fixtures are always considered real property.

C.   Whether or not an object is considered a fixture is determined by the intent of the parties. Following are the tests the court would use to determine if the item in question is a fixture:

1.   Manner it was attached to the real property (annexation)

2.   Whether the property is adapted around the item

3.   Intent of the owner

4.   If an agreement is in place that addresses a fixture issue, the agreement will control.

V.   **Trade Fixtures**

A.   Definition: that which is attached to a trade or business.

B.   Trade fixtures are always personal property.

C.   They may or may not be attached to the real property, but are sold as personal property. Any damage to the real property must be repaired after their removal.

VI.   **Emblements**

A.   Definition: Crops nurtured in the year of the sale or the lease.

B.   Emblements are considered personal property.

C.   When a property is sold during the growing season, the seller retains the right to harvest the crop, unless negotiated otherwise.

D.   A landlord cannot terminate the lease of a tenant farmer without giving the tenant the right to reenter the land and harvest his crops.

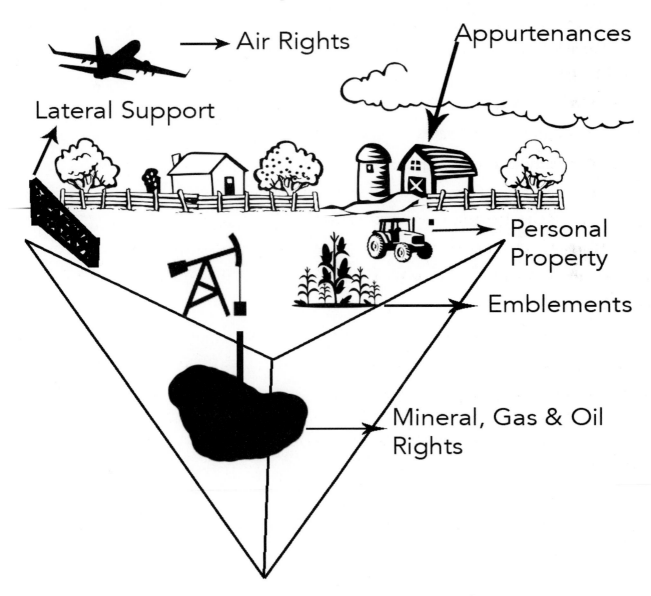

Property Terms to Know

- ☐ Accession
- ☐ Allodial
- ☐ Appurtenant
- ☐ Bill of Sale
- ☐ Chattel
- ☐ Corporeal
- ☐ Deed
- ☐ Emblements
- ☐ Fixture
- ☐ Improvements
- ☐ Incorporeal
- ☐ Lateral Support
- ☐ Mineral Rights
- ☐ Non-homogeneous
- ☐ Personal Property
- ☐ Personalty
- ☐ Real Property
- ☐ Severance
- ☐ Situs

- ☐ Trade Fixture

Property Quiz

1. Which of the following is NOT a test of a fixture?

    A. The intention of the person who attached it, as expressed in a listing agreement

    B. The cost of the item

    C. How the item was attached to the real property

    D. What was agreed to in the Real Estate Purchase Agreement

2. Situs refers to which of the following?

    A. Location

    B. Fixtures

    C. Emblements

    D. Lateral support

3. A display cabinet in a retail store would be considered:

    A. a trade fixture and real property

    B. a trade fixture and personal property

    C. a fixture and real property

    D. a fixture and personal property

4. If an item has been severed from real property, it would NOT be considered which of the following?

    A. Chattel

    B. Personalty

    C. Appurtenant

    D. Personal Property

5. When building a retaining wall, which of the following is the owner of the land providing?

    A. Lateral Support

    B. Emblement

    C. Accession

    D. Severance

6. "Attached to the land or the deed," defines:

    A. Accession

    B. Appurtenant

    C. Alienation

    D. Acceleration

7. Crops which have been nurtured in the year of the transfer are considered:
   A. Trade fixtures
   B. Appurtenant
   C. An example of severance
   D. Emblements

8. Water or mineral rights would be considered:
   A. Personal property
   B. Real property
   C. It depends on how they're used
   D. They are rights, not a kind of property

9. Which of the following is a true statement about trade fixtures?
   A. Attachment is not an issue one way or the other.
   B. The method of attachment is significant.
   C. Whether the business owns the property or is renting it is important.
   D. Only attached items are considered trade fixtures.

10. Which of the following would be considered chattel?
    A. Fence
    B. Water right
    C. Tractor
    D. Barn

11. "No two parcels of real property are exactly the same," is the definition of:
    A. A fixture
    B. An emblements
    C. Subterranean support
    D. Non-homogeneous

12. Which of the following is true?
    A. A bill of sale transfers ownership to real property only.
    B. A bill of sale can transfer ownership to real property and/or personal property.
    C. A deed transfers ownership to real property only.
    D. A deed typically transfers ownership to real property, but can transfer ownership to personal property if provided for in the Real Estate Purchase Agreement.

13. The process of nature adding to the real property is called:

    A. Situs

    B. Accession

    C. Severance

    D. Improvement

14. A barber's chair in a barber shop would be considered:

    A. A fixture

    B. A trade fixture

    C. Emblements

    D. Alluvion

15. When real property is detached from real property, it is a process called:

    A. Situs

    B. Severance

    C. Accession

    D. Appurtenant

ANSWERS TO THIS QUIZ ARE FOUND IN THE "QUIZ ANSWERS" SECTION.

SEE TABLE OF CONTENTS

Public and Private Control

I. **Encumbrance**

An **encumbrance** is a burden on the title, and includes any claim, right, lien, estate or liability that limits a fee simple estate. Anything that removes sticks from an owner's bundle of rights is considered an encumbrance.

   A. Encumbrances can be money encumbrances, such as mortgages or a trust deed and note; or a non-money encumbrance, such as an easement.

   B. Encumbrances can be voluntary, such as a mortgage or trust deed and note; or involuntary, such as a mechanic's lien, an encroachment, a judgment, or taxes.

   C. Encumbrances can be specific, such as property taxes and mortgages; or general, such as income tax liens or judgments.

      1. A specific lien is against one or more properties, as specified in the lien.

      2. A general lien is against the individual and whatever real or personal property, or other resources he may have, such as salary.

      3. There are four ways which government can control private property:

      Taxation

      Escheat

      Eminent Domain

      Police Power

PUBLIC CONTROL OF PROPERTY

II. **Escheat**

When an individual dies leaving no will and no heirs, ownership of his property escheats, or passes, to the state. The state cannot take ownership until the statutory period has passed (in Utah it is three years) giving ample time for heirs to come forth. When the state takes ownership, the property is deeded to the state for the benefit of the state school fund.

III. **Eminent Domain**

Eminent domain is the right of government to acquire private property for the public good. However, the government does not have the authority to simply take people's property from them.

   A. The Constitution protects the right of the individual to own real property without fear of government:

      1. The **5th Amendment** states, "...nor shall private property be 'taken' for public use without just compensation."

         a. This Amendment applies only to the federal government. The feds cannot take ownership, title or control of a private individual's property without paying fair market value for it.

      2. The **14th Amendment** states ". . . no individual shall be deprived or life, liberty, or

49

property, without due process of law."

      a.   The 14th Amendment imposes the same 5th Amendment restrictions on state governments. Therefore, the state, or any governmental authority under the state, may not take an individual's property without paying fair market value for the taking.

      b.   In addition to the 14th Amendment's proscriptions on State takings, each state has its own state constitution that mirrors or mimics the 5th Amendment of the federal constitution.

   3.   The "taking" of property is not always in the form of title, ownership, or control. The Supreme Court has held that when the government or State enacts regulations that limit the uses of private property to such a degree that the regulation effectively deprives the property owner of economically reasonable use or worth of the property to such an extent that it deprives them of utility or value of the property, a "taking" has occurred and just compensation is due even though the regulation does not formally divest the owner of title. Additionally, the Court has also held that a government entity can take private property and transfer the property to another private entity for economic redevelopment purposes. *See* Kelo v. City of New London, 545 U.S. 469 (2005).

B.   Purposes for acquiring private property:

   1.   Public schools, roads and highways, public buildings, railroads, airports, municipal hospitals, etc.

   2.   Urban renewal (discussed later)

C.   Condemnation Process:

   1.   The most common form of condemnation is when the government first attempts to purchase the property through normal negotiation processes.

   2.   If the required negotiations are unsuccessful, the government then files a "Condemnation Action" or suit for condemnation in court.

   3.   The government must prove:

      a.   The property is necessary for public good or use.

      b.   That it is necessary for them to obtain a/an:

         i.   "taking" (obtaining title)

         ii.   leasehold interest

         iii. easement

D.   Compensation:

   1.   The government must pay "just compensation," or fair market value, plus severance damages. They do not have to pay for loss of profits, loss of goodwill, inconvenience, etc.

2. Appeals must be accompanied by supplementary appraisals.

3. In June 2015, the U.S. Supreme Court held that when the government uses eminent domain to take personal property, just compensation must be given to the owner. Horne v. Department of Agriculture, 135 S.Ct. 2419 (2015) (holding that the government's physical appropriation of raisns from a raisn grower requires just compensation from the government).

E. **Inverse Condemnation**
Sometimes when the government takes property by eminent domain, the use to which it is put causes damage to neighboring properties. When that is the case, the injured party can sue the government, asking it to "take" their property as well. That process is called inverse condemnation.

1. A private individual initiates the inverse condemnation action.

2. Examples for which a suit of inverse condemnation might be won:

    a. Undue delay in taking the property.

    b. Property affected by noise at the end of an airport runway.

    c. Public works undertaken on private property without compensation.

3. Loss of profits is not an acceptable basis for a successful inverse condemnation suit.

F. **Urban Renewal**: A process of upgrading blighted neighborhoods through clearance and redevelopment, rehabilitation, the installation of new public improvements, or the modernization of existing ones.

IV. **Police Power**

The right of government to adopt and enforce laws and regulations to promote and support the public health, safety, morals and general welfare.

A. Police power does not include the right to take title to property. An exception would be drug seizures.

B. On the other hand, if the property is needed, it can be used without compensation.

C. Examples of the exercise of police power:

1. Licensing: Including a real estate license.

2. Emergency: Protection of property, e.g., in order to extinguish a fire on one property, another property is damaged by the fire trucks, flood plain controls

3. Zoning: Including the establishment and enforcement of building codes and furtherance of aesthetic beauty, such as:

    a. Restricting the use of signs in certain areas.

    b. Maintaining a certain design (e.g. Spanish architecture) in some areas.

V. **Zoning**

A right of government to regulate private property for the protection of the public. Zoning and planning commissions have been given the responsibility of protecting the health, welfare, safety, and morals of the public. Zoning laws divide land into districts and regulate such things as the property use, height and bulk of buildings, and number of persons they can accommodate. It can also control land development, ensuring adequate streets, sanitary and storm sewers, schools, parks, and utilities.

A. **Zoning** is a power of the state which through enabling acts delegates power to:

   1. Cities to zone incorporated areas.

   2. Counties to zone unincorporated areas. This is handled through the Board of County Commissioners.

B. **Board of Adjustment**: Created by most cities and counties to hear appeals from landowners desiring special exceptions to the zoning ordinances or variances from the existing zoning laws.

C. Some dimensions of zoning:

   1. Land use. Though there is some variation in the classification of land use, the following are generally accepted:

      a. A = Agriculture

      b. R = Residential

      c. C = Commercial

      d. M/I = Industrial, manufacturing

      e. S = Special purpose property, which is that property for which there is no zoning classification, such as churches, hospitals, government buildings, etc.

   2. **Structure (Building codes)**: Standards are established by individual zoning authorities as building codes. These involve almost every aspect of construction. Real estate agents should pay special attention to be sure either older homes, or remodeling situations, are in compliance with the code. Particular focus should be given to such things as electrical and plumbing systems.

   3. **Bulk zoning**: Controls density and overcrowding by regulating height, lot size, setback, side yard, and rear yard requirements, percentage of open areas, etc. The set back establishes how far from the street buildings have to be built. Side yard and backyard lines indicate how far from the boundaries buildings have to be. A party wall exists when there is a single wall on the lot line dividing two properties. It requires a zero lot line, or no side yard requirement.

   4. **PUD**: A planned unit development, or an area planned for high-density occupation. Twin homes, town homes, and condominiums are examples.

   5. Wetlands: These lands are regulated by the Corps of Engineers.

D. **Buffer zone**: A strip of land separating one land use from another. It is used primarily to protect the value of residential property by keeping commercial development from being built too close. It is sometimes used to prohibit any type of development being built next to property such as a chemical plant or military establishment.

E. Variations on Zoning requirements:

1. **Legal non-conforming use**: A permitted use of property established at the time of construction, even though the zoning requirements were later changed, since zoning changes are not retroactive.

    a. The use usually transfers with the deed upon sale.

    b. Substantial destruction may prohibit reconstruction of the non-conforming use.

    c. Even though the use can continue, it cannot be expanded.

2. **Variance**: Permission to vary from the prevailing zoning regulation for either building or use purposes. For instance, if a home owner wanted to build a two-car garage, but to do so would required that he build several feet over the side yard line, he could apply for a variance.

    a. A variance that allows a use, such as a mail order business in the basement, would be termed a conditional use permit. A conditional use permit is very restrictive and may be withdrawn.

3. **Spot zoning**: A provision in a general plan which benefits a single parcel of land by creating a different zone for use for just that parcel that is different from the surrounding properties in the area. For example, in a residential neighborhood zoned for single-family dwellings, the corner parcel is zoned commercial for a convenience store. Spot zoning is not favored since it smacks of favoritism.

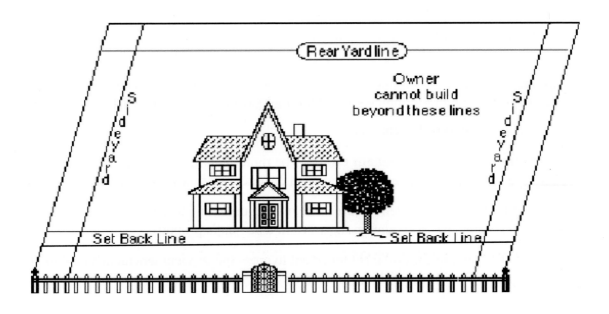

PRIVATE CONTROL OF PROPERTY

VI.   **Encroachments**

    A.   An unauthorized intrusion onto another person's property.

    B.   Examples would include: overhanging trees or shrubs, fences, garages, or sheds built across property lines.

VII.   **Private Restrictions or Deed Restrictions**

    A.   **Private restrictions** are usually created by a Uniform Declaration of Deed Restrictions. These restrictions are often referred to as CC&R's (covenants, conditions, and restrictions).

    B.   They are typically used to maintain value in a given area, subdivision, or condominium.

    C.   The **right of enforcement** typically is passed from the developer of a subdivision or condominium project to a homeowners' association, comprised of those who own the individual homes or units.

    D.   An **injunction** is obtained from the court and used to order those who violate the restrictions to stop doing so.

    E.   Restrictions can be terminated by:

        1.   Agreement of the majority of the home owners through the homeowners' association, or as specified in the CC&R's.

        2.   **Acquiescence** to violators by allowing the restriction to be violated several times without making an effort to stop the violators.

        3.   The passage of time, as set by the subdivider, the homeowners' association, or by state law.

VIII.   **Easements**

    A **non-possession right** of use or enjoyment of another's property. It usually involves a physical condition or use. There are two general types of easements

    A.   **Easement appurtenant**: An easement which runs with the land or the deed, such as a right-of-way.

    B.   **Easement in gross**: An easement granted to a specific person or created by a specific need, such as a utility easement or written permission for an individual to hunt or fish on private property.

IX.   **Special Terms Related to Easements**

    A.   **Dominant tenement or dominant estate**: The right of an individual to a specific use of another person's property. The dominant tenement is the one who holds the easement.

    B.   **Servient tenement** or **servient estate**: The obligation of an individual, created by an easement, to grant a specific use to another in the servient tenement's property.

    C.   **Ingress**: The right of the dominant tenement to cross the servient tenement's land to get to his own property. The holder of the easement has an ingress right of entry using the easement.

D.   **Egress** (the opposite of ingress): Is the right of the dominant tenement to leave his property and cross the servient tenement's property in the process.

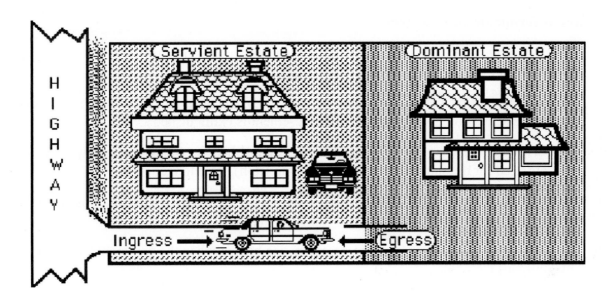

X.   **Ways of Creating an Easement**

A.   **Mutual agreement**: Both parties, grantor and grantee, agree to the easement. It would probably (but not necessarily) be an easement in gross.

B.   **Deed or Reservation in the Deed**: At the time of the purchase, the easement was created by the buyer and seller and noted in each deed affected by the easement. This would be an easement appurtenant.

C.   **Eminent domain**: If the government cannot prove a taking of title is required, or if they don't want ownership, they can nevertheless get an easement in gross by eminent domain, such as for utilities.

D.   **Implication**: The right of this type of easement is created by the act or acts of the individual who will become the servient tenement. An example would be Mr. A, who sells his property but retains the ownership of the mineral, oil, and gas rights. When Mr. A comes to claim the oil, the new owner of the property has most likely granted an easement by implication whether he likes it or not.

E.   **Necessity**: The most common example of this is the requirement to grant an easement appurtenant for ingress and egress to avoid the existence of a land lock.

   1.   A land lock occurs when the owner has no access to the property.

F.   **Prescription**: When an unauthorized right of use, sometimes called an adverse use, has been assumed and the use has continued for the statutory period, an easement by prescription may be created and the owner will be unable to force the discontinuance of its use. To avoid an

55

easement by prescription, the owner can either officially grant permission for the use, informing the user that it may be discontinued at any time, or he can put up "No Trespassing" signs and stop the use. The statutory period for a prescriptive easement in Utah is 20 years. <u>Cassity v. Castagno, 347 P.2d 834, (Utah 1959).</u>

XI. **Ways to Terminate an Easement**

A. **Mutual agreement**: The best way to accomplish anything is by agreement of the parties. Once the parties are in agreement, the easement can be released by a quit claim deed.

B. **Merger**: One of the parties purchases the property of the other party. Since a person cannot have an easement on his own property, the easement is extinguished.

C. **Prescription**: Once a prescriptive easement is established, it can later be lost by prescription. If it is not used for the statutory period (20 years in Utah), it no longer exists.

D. **Purpose no longer exists**: When the easement was created for a specific purpose, and that purpose no longer exists, the easement can be terminated.

E. **Improper use by the grantee**: The easement can be lost when the dominant tenement overburdens the right.

Public and Private Control Terms to Know

- ☐ Board of Adjustment
- ☐ Buffer Zone
- ☐ Building Codes
- ☐ CC&R's
- ☐ Condemnation Action
- ☐ Dominant Tenement
- ☐ Easement
- ☐ Easement Appurtenant
- ☐ Easement by Implication
- ☐ Easement by Necessity
- ☐ Easement by Prescription
- ☐ Easement in Gross
- ☐ Egress
- ☐ Eminent Domain
- ☐ Encroachment
- ☐ Encumbrance
- ☐ Escheat
- ☐ Ingress
- ☐ Injunction
- ☐ Inverse Condemnation
- ☐ Legal Non-conforming Use
- ☐ Merger
- ☐ Party Wall
- ☐ Police Power
- ☐ Servient Tenement
- ☐ Special Purpose Property
- ☐ Spot Zoning
- ☐ Uniform Declaration of Restrictions
- ☐ Urban Renewal
- ☐ Variance
- ☐ Zoning

Public and Private Control Quiz

1. When the state is able to take ownership of property because its original owner died and did not leave a will or have any heirs, it is called:

    A. Eminent domain

    B. Inverse condemnation

    C. Condemnation

    D. Escheat

2. Which of the following requires compensation by the government?

    A. Escheat

    B. Police Power

    C. Eminent Domain

    D. Zoning

3. An owner has three horses. During his ownership the zoning is changed from agricultural to residential and horses are not allowed. This owner is legally able to keep his horses. The right to keep the horses is called a(n):

    A. Legal conforming use

    B. Legal non-conforming use

    C. Variance

    D. Spot Zoning

4. When commercial development threatens to move close to a residential area and negatively affect the value of the homes, the planning and zoning commission might create a(n):

    A. Condemned area

    B. Variance

    C. Buffer zone

    D. Setback line

5. The main difference between police power and eminent domain is:

    A. Compensation

    B. Disregard for the law

    C. The creation of a variance

    D. The buffer zone

6. When an owner has no way to get to his property, his property is said to be:

    A. Negatively ingressed

    B. Without access in gross

    C. Road rotted

    D. Landlocked

7. The Johnson's built a new fence. It was later discovered that the fence was 3 feet onto their neighbor's property. This is an example of a(n):

    A. Encumbrance in gross

    B. Encroachment

    C. Easement appurtenant

    D. Ingress

8. The CC&R's in a subdivision require that the exterior of all homes be brick. When Mr. Kendall was building his home, it became apparent he was going to use aluminum siding. If the others who own homes wanted to stop him, they would go to the courts and obtain a(n):

    A. Injunction

    B. Encumbrance

    C. Cease and Desist Order

    D. There is nothing they can do.

9. Mr. Little has an easement on Mr. Biggs' property in the form of a right of way. Mr. Little would be considered the:

    A. Dominant tenement

    B. Tenement supreme

    C. Servient tenement

    D. Tenement in gross

10. School children have been walking across Mr. Walker's vacant lot for 40 years or more. When Mr. Walker begins to build on the lot in such a way that it would block the path of the children, the parents stop him claiming they have an easement by:

    A. Necessity

    B. Implication

    C. Mutual agreement

    D. Prescription

ANSWERS TO THIS QUIZ ARE FOUND IN THE "QUIZ ANSWERS" SECTION.

SEE TABLE OF CONTENTS

Survey and Description

I. **Public Land Survey System**

In the Western United States, the **Public Land Survey System** was implemented as a method to survey and identify unique real property for use in title work and deeds. Monuments are used to identify a specific geographic location on the earth. They are made of a durable material that often bear the markings of the surveyor and/or their license number who is responsible for its placement. Using the principal of triangulation, 2 or more reference points or benchmarks can be used to identify any one point on the earth or in space for that matter. Surveyors use the geometric principle of triangulation to fix these monuments which can reference things such as property corners or even the estimated level of water in a reservoir or river. Surveying has become more and more accurate with the application of technology to this industry.

A. Early on, much of the Western United States was divided using highly inaccurate means, in some cases by use of a wagon wheel and a handkerchief. Early surveyors would tie a handkerchief to a wagon wheel and count the revolutions to measure distance of either a township or section, place a valid marker and continue. Today, GPS (Global Positioning System), lasers, technology, and computer software has made the job of a surveyor much faster, easier, cheaper, and exponentially more accurate.

B. Although modern technology has made surveying more accurate, the information that is provided by GPS and modern software is only as good as the person who is inputting and interpreting information. This "human error" can and does occur, which is why those representing a real property transaction must be aware of what exactly they are selling/representing.

C. **Surveys** are useful to verify previous lot boundaries and to identify any possible encroachments that may have been created since the last legal survey. Sellers must be accurate in what they are selling and buyers need to do their homework. Builders need to be especially conscious of property boundaries as they will be held accountable to CC&R's (such as setbacks) and even local codes specific to the property that they are improving.

D. Surveys can be legally attached to a parcel of property. This happens when survey is recorded, usually at a local government office. Use of a recent and legal survey can allow title companies to eliminate survey exceptions that are typically added to title insurance policies.

II. **Land Description and the Real Estate Agent**

It is not fitting that a real estate professional not understand the standard practices of identifying land and being able to read a legal description.

A. The purpose of a **legal description** is to separate a particular parcel of land from every other parcel of land in the world by identifying its location and boundaries. A legal description is one that will accomplish that task in such a manner that, if challenged, the description will hold up under the scrutiny of the courts.

B. A common use of a property description that a real estate agent encounters, and which requires his professional knowledge of the use of that description, is the transfer of ownership. When ownership transfers, the grantee is to obtain all the real property inside the boundaries described in the Real Estate Purchase Agreement. When a buyer receives something less than he was supposed to receive, the real estate agent, as the agent of the seller, can become liable for the accuracy of the description and for any real property that has been removed or altered, except by agreement, between the time of signing the Real Estate Purchase Agreement and the date of possession.

1. When working with the title company, the real estate agent should be able to talk intelligently and even visualize in his mind the size and shape of the property.

2. When a deed is given from the grantor to the grantee, it transfers all of the real property that exists inside the property boundaries, unless exceptions are written in the Real Estate Purchase Agreement and, subsequently, in the deed.

C. The legal description does not describe the topography, or any improvements on the land.

D. There are five frequently used methods to describing property. They are:

1. Informal reference

2. Metes and bounds

3. Rectangular environment survey

4. Lot, block, and plat (map or subdivision)

5. Assessor's parcel number

III. **The Informal Reference**

A. Street numbers or coordinates and names or place names are typical. The following are examples:

> 715 East 3900 South
>
> 2157 Circus Circle
>
> Lazy Rocking J Ranch

OR

> 468 Walnut Plaza, Suite 104
>
> Yogi Yorgason's Place

B. The advantage of such property identifications is that they are usually easy to understand and equally easy for the average person to find.

C. The disadvantage is that they give very little information about property boundaries and they are changed from time to time. Ultimately, the purpose of a legal description is to specify the boundaries. An address or place name gives no information relative to width or depth of the property, or the placement of the boundaries. In other words, the legal description is not only designed to help a person drive to the property but to accurately identify the boundaries after he gets there.

IV. **Lot, Block, and Plat**

A. This is a relatively simple approach to land description. It is most often used in subdivisions, and often is combined with one or more of the other forms of land description.

B.   In the illustration above, the shaded lot would be described as, Lot 122, Block M, Blue Meadow Subdivision (Plat).

C.   This form of land description is often used when selling property in a subdivision or development, and sometimes as the land description on a property tax notice.

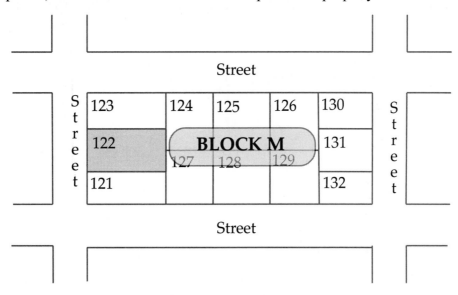

V.   Metes and Bounds

A.   This is the oldest method of land description. A typical metes and bounds property description in Utah, with the address of 512 South 450 East, might look like this:

Beginning at a point which is 688.00 feet South 0° 50' East along the Quarter section line and 218.34 feet South 89° 05' East along the South line of 500 South Street, Orem, Utah, from the North Quarter Corner of Section 23, Township 6 South, Range 2 East, Salt Lake Base and Meridian; thence South 89° 05' East 94.92 feet along the South line of said 500 South Street; thence South 0° 39.5' East 92.70 feet along the West line of 450 East Street; thence North 89° 05' West 94.72 feet; thence North 0° 47' West 92.70 feet to the point of beginning.

B.   Note: the above description is a combination of both Metes & Bounds and Rectangular Survey methods. Rectangular Survey is discussed in detail below.

C.   Drawn out, this description would look like this:

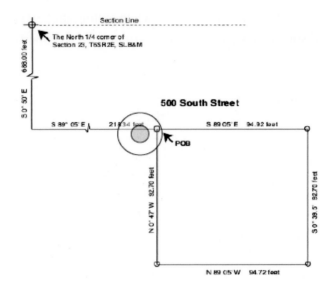

D.   In a metes and bounds description, metes stands for measures, and bounds stands for monuments. The monuments establish the corners and the metes gives the distance between the monuments.

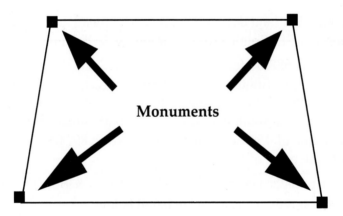

E.   Reading a metes and bounds description. Assume the first boundary line proceeding from the point of beginning looks like this:

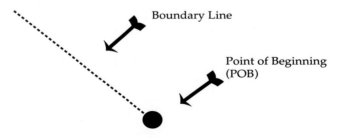

F. To describe it you would ask three questions. The first is, "Is the boundary line in the north or the south half of the circle?" As you can see in the illustration below, the answer is the North half. When that question is answered, two items of information are given. First, the answer "North" or "South" establishes zero degrees. Second, it provides the first word of the description. In this example, the answer is "North".

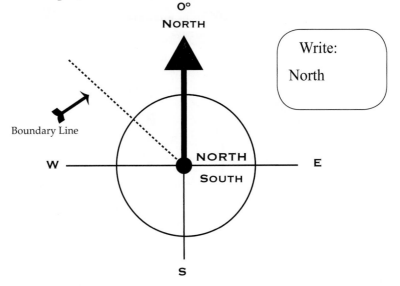

G. The second question is, "Is the boundary line to the East or West of North (or South)?" Obviously you can measure either to the east or west, or clockwise or counter-clockwise, and the answer has to be "East" or "West". In this situation, the answer is "West." Note the format. A blank is created between the words North and West. It will be filled in after answering the third question.

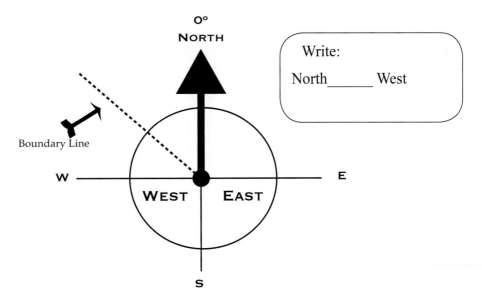

65

H.   H. The third question is, "How far West (or East) of North (or South) is the boundary line?" A surveyor answers this question in degrees, minutes, and seconds. There are 360° (degrees) in a circle, 60' (minutes) in a degree, and 60" (seconds) in a minute. The surveyor's answer to this question might be 40° 22' 14". For our purposes, 40° is adequate.

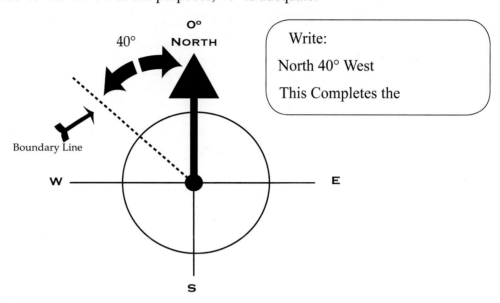

I.   See if you can write out a description of the boundary in the lot in the illustration below. The answer is given at the end of the chapter.

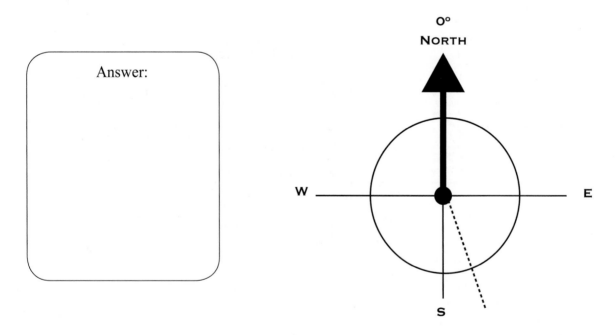

© Stringham Schools

VI. The Rectangular Survey or U.S. Government Survey

A. The **rectangular survey**, sometimes called the U.S. Government Survey, is not used in all states. However, it is used in Utah and in all of the states surrounding it.

B. The basis of the rectangular survey is two unseen lines established by longitude and latitude. The north-south line is called the Meridian and the east-west line is called the Baseline. As you can see in the illustration below, there are many of these scattered around the United States. Those states with no base or meridian lines do not use the rectangular survey system.

1. Utah has its own base and meridian lines which extend border to border in both directions.

2. The name of the principal base and meridian in Utah is the Great Salt Lake Base and Meridian. It is located on temple square in downtown Salt Lake City. From this point, almost all land in Utah is measured or described.

3. In Utah there is a secondary base and meridian. It is established on an old Indian reservation boundary and is known as the Uintah Base and Meridian. (See the United States map.)

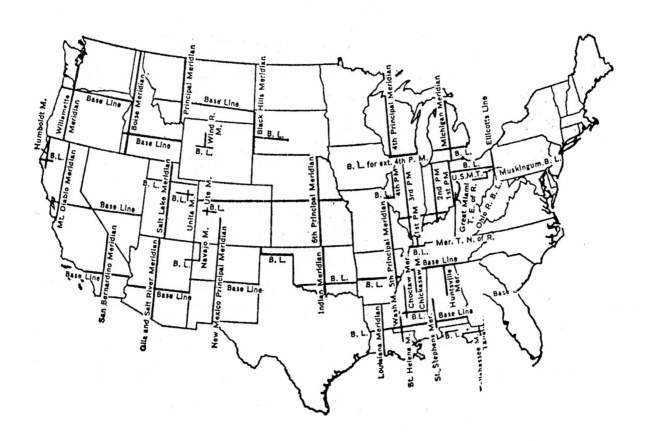

C. **Townships** are laid out along the base and meridian lines.

    1.   A township:

        a.   Is six miles on each side, making it a six mile square

        b.   Contains 36 square miles

        c.   Has a perimeter of 24 miles

    2.   A row of townships running East and West, which is counted from the baseline to the North or South is called a tier. The baseline is the zero point. The third layer of tiers north from the baseline is designated "Township 3 North" or "T3N." The fourth row of tiers south of the baseline is referred to as "Township 4 South" or "T4S."

    3.   A column of townships running North and South, which is counted East or the West from the meridian is called a range. The meridian is the zero point. The second column to the East of the meridian is designated "Range 2 East" or "R2E." The fifth column to the West of the meridian is referred to as "Range 5 West" or "R5W."

D. Townships are divided into **sections**. Each township has 36 sections which are numbered 1-36. Notice the serpentine way they are numbered. This permits each section to be next to the numbered section that sequentially precedes and follows it. For instance section 30 is bordered by both section 29 and section 3

E. A section:

    1.   Is one mile (5,280 ft.) on each side, making it one mile square.

    2.   Contains one square mile.

3. Has a perimeter of 4 miles.

4. Contains 640 acres. One acre is 43,560 square feet.

F. Sections are broken into smaller parcels by dividing them into halves or quarters.

1. There are two concepts that must be understood when reading this type of land description. First, when there is a description from which a map is to be drawn, the first thing drawn is determined by the last segment of the description.

2. Second, when the map exists and a description is to be written the first thing written is the beginning, or first, segment of the description.

3. This means that the first part of the description is the parcel of land being described.

4. To determine the number of acres in a parcel of land described in this manner, simply divide the number of acres in a Section, which is 640, by each of the denominators of the fractions given in the description. (The denominator is the bottom number: in 1/4, four is the denominator.) There is no need to draw out a map. For instance, if the description read: the Northeast 1/4 of the southwest 1/4 of the East 1/2 of section 29, (NE1/4 of the SW 1/4 of the E 1/2) the arithmetic would be:

$$640 \div 4 \div 4 \div 2 = 20 \text{ acres}$$

5. There are 43,560 square feet in an acre and 5,280 linear feet in a mile.

G. The datum marker is a reference point for vertical measurement based a mean sea level. Local vertical reference points set at calculated intervals from a datum are benchmarks.

VII. **VII. Property Tax Identification Numbers.**

Salt Lake City identifies **parcels** with a numbering system called **Sidwell numbers**. Sidwell numbers are also an alternative to place on the Real Estate Purchase Agreement in the blank that asks for further description of the property. Following is a breakdown of a Sidwell number.

16	27	476	025	0000
Area Number	Section Number	Block Number	Parcel Number	Encumbrance Number
A substitute number for tier and range	As described in the Retangular Survey	Each quarter of a section is given a number: NW 1/4 = 100 NE 1/4 = 200 NW 1/4 = 300 SE 1/4 = 400	The parcel number is assigned to the largest area of land under one owner	A special tax number where multiple tax records are required for the same physical parcel

VIII.   **Some interesting facts about Utah**

    A.   The legal description of Utah is:

Commencing with the intersection of the 42nd parallel of latitude with the 34th meridian of longitude West from Washington; running thence South on this meridian to the 41st parallel of latitude; thence East on this parallel to the 32nd meridian of longitude; thence South on this meridian to its intersection with the 37th parallel of latitude ; thence West upon this parallel of latitude to its intersection with the 37th meridian of longitude; thence North on this meridian to its intersection with the 42nd parallel of latitude; thence East on the 42nd parallel of latitude to the Point of Beginning. Salt Lake City is on approximately the same latitude as New York City and Madrid, Spain,

    B.   Utah contains 84,916 square miles or 54,346,240 acres. The land area is 52,721,550 acres and water covers 1,624,690 acres. Water is 3% of the total area.

    C.   Its highest elevation is 13,528 feet (Kings Peak), which is just a little short of Mt. Everest; 29,028 feet.

    D.   Its lowest elevation is 2,350 feet

    E.   Utah has 29 counties.

Answer for section V, letter I: South 20° East

Survey & Description Terms to Know

- ☐ Acre
- ☐ Baseline
- ☐ Lot, Block, and Plat
- ☐ Meridian
- ☐ Metes and Bounds
- ☐ Mile
- ☐ Monument
- ☐ Point of Beginning
- ☐ Range
- ☐ Rectangular Survey
- ☐ Section
- ☐ Tier
- ☐ Township

Survey & Description Quiz

1. The largest area of land used in the Rectangular Survey is:

   A. Acre

   B. Section

   C. Township

   D. Base and Meridian

2. A section contains:

   A. 640 acres

   B. 5,280 feet

   C. 36 square miles

   D. 43,560 square feet

3. Degrees are used in which of the following?

   A. Rectangular Survey

   B. Informal land descriptions

   C. Metes and Bounds

   D. Lot, Block, and Plat

4. Sections in a township are numbered from 1-36. Section number 1 would be in the:

   A. Northwest corner of the township.

   B. Northeast corner of the township.

   C. Southwest corner of the township.

   D. Southeast corner of the township.

5. A column of townships running North and South, and counted East and West from the meridian is called a:

   A. Range

   B. Acre

   C. Section

   D. Tier

6. How many acres are there in the parcel of land described below?

   1. The NW 1/4 of the SE 1/4 of the E 1/2 of Section 21.

   A. 1.13

   B. 20

   C. 165

   D. 1,361

7.   Herbert Landon, a surveyor, was standing in Section 14. Which direction would he go to get to Section 22?

    A. Northwest

    B. Northeast

    C. Southwest

    D. Southeast

Do questions 1 - 7; questions 8 - 11 are optional and not State exam type questions.

8.   Draw the following in the section below: the SW 1/4 of the NE 1/4 of the SE 1/4.

9.   Write the description for the lot below:

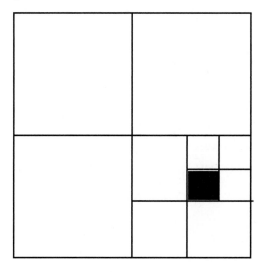

73

10. Describe the parcel below (You should be accurate to 10°):

    F. Line A:

    G. Line B:

    H. Line C:

    I. Line D:

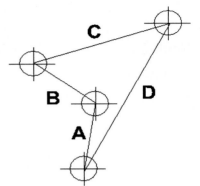

11. Draw this lot. From the Point of Beginning North 30° East, 120 feet, and thence South 60° East 210 feet, and thence South 20° West 130 feet, and thence North 60° West 230 feet back to the Point of Beginning.

ANSWERS TO THIS QUIZ ARE FOUND IN THE "QUIZ ANSWERS" SECTION.

SEE TABLE OF CONTENTS

LAW OF AGENCY

Agency A

An Introduction to Agency

Nothing is more important for real estate agents to understand than the law of agency as it applies to working with buyers, sellers, lessors, lessees, and customers. Most law suits brought against real estate agents originate from violation of agency relationships. Being a successful real estate agent requires a thorough understanding of this body of law as well as a high degree of personal honesty and integrity.

For the last 30 years, the law of agency in relation to real estate licensees has been subjected to a great deal of discussion and frequent changes. This text will address the forms of agency as practiced in the past, the various ways it is being applied today, and the applications being considered for the future.

I. **Agency – Definition**

    A.   An **agency relationship** exists when a person, called the principal, hires another to represent him/her; to act in the principal's best interest, and in everything that is said or done, to take care of the interests of the principal.

    B.   The agent's own interest or benefit is secondary to those of the principal.

    C.   In any negotiations, the agent should be seeking an outcome that achieves the best possible outcome for the principal.

    D.   If the agent represents the seller, and receives notice from the buyer, such as acceptance of an offer, the law regards that as the same as the notice being given directly to the seller.

II. **The Roles of the Parties**

    A.   **Principal** (client): This is the seller, buyer, lessor, or lessee. It is the individual who hires the agent to represent him/her.

    B.   **Agent**: This is the principal broker hired by the seller, buyer, lessor, or lessee. Only a **principal broker** can be hired as an agent for a member of the public in a real estate transaction.

        1.   There are two separate agency relationships involved in the practice of real estate.

        2.   The broker hires licensees (sales agents or associate brokers) to work for him/her and assist in meeting the needs of the principal broker's clients.

            a.   The broker is the principal in that relationship; and, therefore, is called the principal broker.

            b.   The sales agents or associate brokers are the agents of the principal broker. Their employing principal broker is the only person they can work for as a direct agent.

        3.   The buyers, sellers, lessors, or lessees hire a principal broker to assist and represent them in a real estate transaction.

            a.   The buyer, seller, lessor, or lessee is the principal in the agency relationship.

            b.   The principal broker is the agent.

      c.   The sales agents and associate brokers working under the principal broker's license are subagents to the principal (buyer, seller, lessor, or lessee).

C.   A written employment contract between the principal broker and his/her agents should be entered into, identifying the agents as independent contractors responsible for their own taxes. If a sales agent wasn't paying his/her taxes, in the absence of such an agreement, the broker could be held liable for the agent's unpaid taxes.

D.   **Subagent**: A subagent is a real estate licensee who agrees to work with the agent (principal broker) to achieve the objectives set forth by the principal (buyer, seller, lessor, or lessee).

      1.   Subagents could be sales agents or associate brokers working for the principal broker.

      2.   If the broker published an offer of subagency in the multiple listing service (MLS), and the selling principal broker accepted it, that broker and his/her agents would also be subagents to the seller. Though this is seldom done now, it still is allowed under the law. So a cooperating broker could be a subagent, representing the best interest of the seller. This could not be true if that broker had a contract with the buyer.

      3.   It might be helpful to think of subagents as "helper" agents. They help the actual agent – the principal broker – in representing the interests of the client.

E.   **Customer**: The other party directly involved in the transaction. If the seller is the principal, the buyer is the customer, or vice versa.

      1.   The distinction can clearly be discerned in this manner: the agent works for the client and works with the customer.

      2.   **Caveat emptor**: Latin for, "Let the buyer beware." Indicates that parties without an agent are responsible for protecting their own interests. However, this does not leave the unrepresented person without any protection:

            a.   A defect in the property must be open to observation or discoverable on reasonable inspection. That is, defects must not be covered up or concealed by the seller.

            b.   The buyer must have an unimpeded opportunity to examine the property.

            c.   All material defects in the property or in the principal's ability to perform must be disclosed.

            d.   The principal and the agent and all subagents must not engage in fraud.

            e.   An agent has a duty to the customer (general public) that he/she will be:

                i.   Honest

                ii.   Ethical

F.   **Limited agent** (sometimes referred to as dual agent): If one agent represents both parties in a transaction, the parties give up the right to undivided loyalty and confidentiality. The agent can only advance the interests of one party so long as they do not conflict with the interests of the other. Utah requires the informed consent of both parties in writing. Some states refer to the agent's duty in this instance not as a neutral duty, but one of a heightened duty because extra care must be taken to represent both parties in furthering their interests without misrepresenting either party. Thus, the heightened duty requires the agent to use the "utmost care and caution" in their actions. Lane v. Oustalet, 850 So.2d 1143, 1151 (Miss.App. 2002).

G. **Neutral negotiator**; facilitator, or transaction broker:

  1. There is no agency relationship involved.

  2. The real estate licensees are simply trying to bring a buyer and seller, or lessor and lessee, together in a win-win arrangement.

  3. Several states now recognize this concept in real estate transactions.

  4. Utah does not allow for transaction brokers. In Utah, the agent (principal broker) must represent a party to the transaction and have a written agreement with that party (the principal).

H. **Designated Agency**: The principal hiring an agent (seller, buyer, lessor, or lessee hiring a principal broker) may designate, or choose, which sales agent(s) or associate broker(s) affiliated with that broker they would like to have represent them.

  1. This is the opposite of a subagency agreement, which indicates that all sales agents and associate brokers in that company will represent the principal.

  2. Principals can designate that only the broker and chosen licensee(s) in the brokerage would be subagents to them. Licensees in other brokerages would always represent the other party (customer).

  3. Most offices are designated agency brokerages, but smaller companies often choose the subagency option.

  4. In-house sales could involve the listing agent acting as a limited agent: both the agent and the broker are limited agents.

  5. An in-house sale could have one agent representing the buyer, and one agent representing the seller. In this case, only the broker is a limited agent.

  6. In either case above (4 or 5) both buyer and seller must sign a Limited Agency Consent Agreement.

  7. With designated agency, there should be strict security policies to protect the confidentiality of all clients. For instance, the subagent of the seller should not have free access to the buyer's file and vice versa.

III. **Types of Agents**

The same term can apply to the person or to the agency relationship.

A. **Specific or Special agency**: The specific agent is hired to perform in a specified or limited way; e.g., listing the property or finding a particular type of property to buy. It is possible for the agent to be given a power of attorney, even in specific agency.

B. **General agency**: The general agent uses his/her expertise to fulfill the objectives set out by the principal; e.g., the agent seeks investment properties for an investor, or a licensee is hired as a property manager. The agents of the principal broker are general agents. General agency may or may not include a power of attorney.

C. **Universal agency**: The universal agent does all things for and in behalf of the principal; e.g., executor of an estate, guardian of a child, etc. Universal agency usually requires a general power of attorney.

D. **Power of attorney**: A written authorization to represent or act on a nother's behalf in private affairs, business, or some other legal matter. It comes in two forms:

   1. **General power of attorney**: Gives the agent power to sign for the principal in all things, such as a trustee.

   2. **Specific power of attorney** (limited power of attorney): Limits the agent to signing only in specifically designated and limited instances, such as signing the closing documents for an absent seller.

E. **Attorney in Fact**: The individual who has been given power of attorney. A principal appoints a competent person to sign for and in behalf of the principal.

F. A licensee can only sign or initial on behalf of the client with a duly executed power of attorney from the principal.

G. A copy of the power of attorney must be attached to any document signed or initialed by the licensee on behalf of the principal.

IV. **Types of Principals**

   The relationship of the principal (client) and the agent, as disclosed to the customer, determines the type of principal. There are three possibilities:

A. **Fully disclosed**: The customer knows there is both an agent and a principal, and knows the identity of both.

B. **Partially disclosed**: The customer knows there is an agent, and who the agent is. The customer also knows there is a principal, but doesn't know the identity of the principal.

C. **Undisclosed**: The agent indicates he/she is the principal, even though he/she is acting as an agent for someone else.

   1. To best learn this, it is critical to understand and make the distinction between a real estate agent and an agent. Remember, an agent can be any person acting for the principal; you do not have to be a real estate agent to be an agent. However, a real estate agent is a specific agent for a principal who wants to buy or sell real estate. In Utah, the Division of Real Estate has promulgated regulations that narrow the scope of general agency law as it applies to real estate agents and their conduct.

   2. In Utah, and in the context of real estate, an undisclosed principal is generally illegal if a real estate agent is involved in the transaction because a real estate licensee has a duty

80

to disclose his/her agency relationship in the transaction. Therefore, the real estate agent would be in violation of law if he/she acted as the principal while hiding the actual one. However, in general agency law, an undisclosed principal is legal.. See U.C.A. § 61-2f-401(10) and Utah Administrative Code R162-2f-401(a)(5)(c) and (9)(a) & (b).

3. Under Utah law, failing to disclose if the purchase is made for the agent, him or herself, or for a client of the agent, is grounds for revocation or suspension of your license. U.C.A. §§ 61-2f-401(10) & 61-2f-404(1)(a)(iii)(A).

V. Ways of Creating Agency

A. **Actual Appointment**: The parties to the agency create the agency relationship.

1. **Express appointment**: Words, oral or written, are specifically used by the parties to create the agency contract. Note, however, that in Utah, a listing agreement or buyer agency agreement must be in writing.

2. **Implied or ostensible appointment**, or **agency by implication**: This agency relationship is created by the actions of the agent and the principal. If customers are led to believe that the real estate licensee is their agent, the licensee will probably be considered by the courts to be their agent. When agents advise the customer in a manner detrimental to their client's best interest, they are creating agency by implication and, therefore, undisclosed limited agency.

3. **Ratification**: The agency relationship is approved by the principal after the agency service was created by implication. Payment would be a form of ratification.

B. **Appointment by Operation of Law**: This is where the agency is created through the force of law, such as a court order, rather than by the parties.

1. **Agency by Statute**: Examples could be a sheriff designated to conduct a foreclosure sale, or a court appointed administrator in a will. The agency is created by law, whether the parties like it or not.

2. **Agency by Estoppel**: The court stops a party to the relationship from denying that agency was previously created through implication.

VI. Termination of Agency

A. **Mutual consent**: The parties agree to terminate the agency relationship.

B. **Performance**: The contract has been fulfilled. When the sale of the house closes, the agent is no longer representing the seller. If the seller subsequently wants the agent's representation in buying a house, a new buyer agency contract will need to be executed.

C. **Abandonment**: The agent acts contrary to the best interest of the principal, or doesn't act at all.

D. Death of either party.

E. Insanity of either party, as determined by the courts.

F.   Destruction of the property: There must be a significant change of value.

G.   Bankruptcy: This is subject to the court. It may or may not terminate the agency.

VII.   Responsibilities of the Principal to the Agent

A.   **Compensate**: The principal must pay the agent for the services rendered.

B.   **Indemnify**: The principal must make up for losses sustained by the agent while following the instructions of the principal.

C.   **Perform**: The principal must:

     1.   Be honest in answering questions about the property and the transaction.

     2.   Assist the agent in performing his/her duties.

     3.   Keep promises; e.g., if the sellers say they will repair the roof prior to closing, they must do so.

Agency A Terms to Know

- ☐ Agency
- ☐ Agency by Estoppel
- ☐ Agency by Ratification
- ☐ Agency by Statute
- ☐ Agent
- ☐ Attorney in Fact
- ☐ Caveat Emptor
- ☐ Designated Agency
- ☐ Dual Agent (Limited Agent)
- ☐ Express Agency
- ☐ Fully Disclosed Principal
- ☐ General Agent
- ☐ Implied Agency
- ☐ Ostensible Agency
- ☐ Partially Disclosed Principal
- ☐ Power of Attorney
- ☐ Principal
- ☐ Specific or Special Agent
- ☐ Subagent
- ☐ Undisclosed Principal
- ☐ Universal Agent

Agency A Quiz

1. Howard and Betty Evers listed their home with Mac Miller, a sales agent. This makes Mac's principal broker the:

    A. Selling agent

    B. Listing agent

    C. Selling subagent

    D. Listing subagent

2. When a seller's agent suggests an offer amount that is less than the listed price, the agent might be creating:

    A. Agency by estoppel.

    B. Agency by ratification.

    C. Agency by implication.

    D. Agency by express consent

3. An agent who has authority to perform all lawful acts for a principal is referred to as a(n):

    A. Special agent

    B. Agent by estoppel

    C. General agent

    D. Universal agent

4. When the buyer does NOT enter into a buyer agency agreement with a broker, he is likely in a condition called:

    A. Ratification

    B. Estoppel

    C. Caveat emptor

    D. Lis pendens

5. When the agent is hired to use his/her expertise to fulfill certain objectives of the principal the agent is a:

    A. Specific agent

    B. Undisclosed agent

    C. Universal agent

    D. General agent

6. An offer is brought to a seller from a brokerage who did not take the listing. Assuming there is no buyer agency contract, and the MLS listing offered subagency, which best describes the agency relationships:

   A. The listing broker and his sales agents are the agents; brokers and agents from other offices are subagents.

   B. The listing broker and the selling broker are agents, and all sales agents from either office are subagents.

   C. The listing broker is the agent. All others, be they sales agents, associate brokers or principal brokers, are subagents.

   D. All brokers and sales agents involved in the transaction are agents, regardless of which office they work for.

7. Under a listing contract, the buyer is considered a:

   A. Principal

   B. Agent

   C. Client

   D. Customer

8. The seller became angry with the listing broker and refused to pay the commission, stating he didn't like the broker, so she was no longer his agent. The broker sued the seller and the court ruled in favor of the broker. The court ruled that the seller could not deny the fact that the agency was created in the listing. This is agency created by:

   A. Estoppel

   B. Implication

   C. Statute

   D. Ratification

9. A listing broker would be considered which of the following types of agent?

   A. General

   B. Specific

   C. Bilateral

   D. Universal

10. A property manager would be considered which of the following types of agent?

    A. General

    B. Specific

    C. Unilateral

    D. Universal

11. Mr. Zephyr employed a broker to make an offer to purchase Mr. Wilson's home. Mr. Zephyr instructed the broker to keep his (Mr. Zephyr's) identity concealed. When the broker filled in the buyer's name on the purchase agreement, he wrote, "Undisclosed principal." This would make Mr. Zephyr what kind of a principal in this transaction?

    A. Fully disclosed

    B. Partially disclosed

    C. Partially undisclosed

    D. Undisclosed

12. A broker who represents both the buyer and the seller, having fully disclosed his agency to each and obtained written permission from both, becomes a(n):

    A. Agent to the seller and a subagent to the buyer.

    B. Limited agent.

    C. Neutral mediator.

    D. Subagent to both the seller and the buyer.

13. Mr. Zingle listed his property with Jane Jacoby, the broker of Jacob & Jacoby Realtors®. He instructed Jacoby that he would offer subagency to no one except the agents of Jacob & Jacoby Realtors®. What agency does this create?

    A. Jacoby and her licensees are agents; other agents are buyer agents.

    B. Jacoby and her licensees are agents; other agents are subagents.

    C. Jacoby is the agent; all others are subagents.

    D. Jacoby is the agent, her licensees are subagents; and all others are buyer agents

ANSWERS TO THIS QUIZ ARE FOUND IN THE "QUIZ ANSWERS" SECTION.

SEE TABLE OF CONTENTS

it will be paid, and what happens in the event of the seller's default.

2. Paragraph 3 is where the protection period is detailed. This is also called the safety clause.

3. Paragraph 4 contains the seller's warranties and disclosures. This is kind of a preview, preparing the seller for what they will be agreeing to in the REPC.

E. In both documents (Buyer-Broker Agreement and Seller Listing Agreement mentioned immediately above), the following paragraph commonalities and importances should be understood:

1. The principal authorizes the agent or broker to appoint another agent from the company to also represent them, if the broker or designated agent is unavailable.

2. There is a detailed discussion of the possibility of limited agency with an in-house sale, educating the buyer or seller about that circumstance. An in-house sale is when a brokerage sells its own listing.

    a. The listing agent could represent both buyer and seller, and the broker would also represent both.

    b. One agent in the company could represent the buyer and a different agent represents the seller. These agents are single agents, and only the broker is a limited agent.

    c. In bold lettering at the end, it makes it clear that a separate document must be signed at the time the limited agency situation arises.

    d. The initials of the buyer or seller indicate they are/are not agreeable to the idea of limited agency. The initials do not create the limited agency.

3. Paragraph 9

    a. To eliminate the limitations of the Do Not Call law, the various ways of contacting the principal are filled in, and by signing the contract they agree to be contacted in the future.

    b. Buyer and Seller agree that the earnest money will be deposited in an interest bearing account, with the interest paid to the UARHOF fund (Utah Association of REALTORS® Housing Opportunity Fund) to assist in creating affordable housing.

4. Notice the title of each. They have two purposes:

    a. The contract between the principal broker and the buyer/seller

    b. Education and disclosure regarding agency

    c. These constitute the prior "disclosure" of agency relationships referenced in R162-2f-401a and discussed above.

    d. These agency relationships will be confirmed in the REPC, or with an addendum to a lease agreement.

F. Limited Agency Consent Agreement:

 1. Paragraphs 1 – 7 are education for the buyer or seller.

 2. Paragraph 8 should have the appropriate box marked to indicate which form of limited agency is applicable.

 3. Both buyer and seller sign the same page, each gets a copy and a copy should be in the listing file and in the buyer agency file.

G. For Sale by Owner Commission Agreement & Agency Disclosure: This would be used by a buyer's agent who's client is interested in a FSBO (property for sale by owner). It avoids limited agency.

 1. It discloses to the seller that the agent will be representing only the buyer.

 2. The seller agrees to pay a commission if that buyer purchases the property.

V. Code of Ethics

The National Board of REALTORS® has created a Code of Ethics. If you plan to join the National, State, and Local Boards of REALTORS® you should become familiar with the Code of Ethics. However, regardless of whether you join or not, an in-depth understanding of its principles will help you understand and conduct yourself within the laws of agency, as many of the provisions within that code echo and reinforce the law. A copy of the Code of Ethics is in the forms section of this textbook.

VI. Reducing Broker Risk

In order to reduce broker liability claims and lawsuits, it is necessary that principal brokers carefully plan and implement a strategy that will protect them should their licensees act improperly in carrying out their fiduciary duties.

A. A need for risk management exists from the smallest one-person office to the largest national multi-office companies. Agency liability is a fact of life today and cannot be ignored. Violation of agency rules and laws is one of the most frequent causes of law suits against real estate agents.

Agency B Terms to Know

- ☐ Code of Ethics
- ☐ Duty of Confidentiality
- ☐ Duty of Disclosure
- ☐ Duty of Reasonable Care & Diligence
- ☐ Fiduciary
- ☐ Rule of Loyalty
- ☐ Rule of Obedience

Agency B Quiz

1. Which of the following most accurately reflects the meaning of "fiduciary?"

    A. Estoppel

    B. Bankruptcy

    C. Trust

    D. Universal

2. Which of the following is NOT one of the fiduciary duties required of an agent?

    A. Informed consent

    B. Disclosure

    C. Loyalty

    D. Reasonable care

3. In looking for properties appropriate to show agent J's buyer, J finds one he would like to purchase. Which of the following is true as applied to this situation?

    A. It is impossible for J to purchase the property, since he is the buyer's agent.

    B. The client's interests always have to come before the agent's personal interest.

    C. J can make an offer on the one property, and show all the others to the client.

    D. Once J becomes the buyer's agent the law of caveat emptor applies.

4. L had listed a home through her brokerage. Later she wanted to offer to buy the home herself. What should she do?

    A. She should enter into a limited agency arrangement by having the seller sign a Limited Agency Consent Agreement.

    B. Under no circumstances can she purchase the home she has listed. It would conflict with her duties as the agent of the seller.

    C. She should have one of the other agents in the brokerage represent her with a buyer agency contract.

    D. She should withdraw from the agency. Another agent in the office would represent the seller and L would represent herself as the buyer.

5. The sellers had entered into an agency contract with a brokerage. Later, they signed consent to limited agency, as their agent was also representing the buyer. What fiduciary benefits are they giving up?

    A. Loyalty

    B. Confidentiality

    C. Reasonable care

    D. Obedience

6. Which of the following best describes a buyer brokerage?

    A. A company that never practices limited agency.

    B. A company that doesn't take listings.

    C. A company that, in addition to listings, also enters into buyer agency contracts.

    D. A full service company that represents all types of clients in all types of real estate transactions.

7. What is the purpose of Section 5 in the REPC?

    A. Create the formal agency relationship between buyer and agent.

    B. Create the formal agency relationship with the seller.

    C. Confirm agency relationships previously created.

    D. Provide notice of the two brokerages involved in the transaction.

8. Under what circumstances could a licensee in Utah use a buyer agency contract other than the one recommended by the UAR (Utah Assoc. of REALTORS®)?

    A. The attorney of the broker has created a different form for that purpose.

    B. The broker has created a different form for his/her agents to use.

    C. The buyers provided a contract they had drafted for this purpose.

    D. The sellers, at the time of listing, provided a form they wanted their agent to use.

ANSWERS TO THIS QUIZ ARE FOUND IN THE "QUIZ ANSWERS" SECTION.

SEE TABLE OF CONTENTS

Agency Practices 1*

*You should first complete the Agency A & B Classes before this class.

I. **Exclusive Right to Sell Listing Agreement**

   A. This contract is not a state approved form

      1. If the broker is a member of the Utah Association of REALTORS® ("UAR"), their recommended form may be used.

      2. Brokers can hire an attorney to draft a form for their brokerage.

      3. Larger companies have their own forms prepared by their attorneys.

      4. Reminder: Drafting contracts is legal work and the broker or owner of the brokerage cannot create, or draft, a contract.

   B. For purposes of these Agency Practices discussions, UAR forms will be used as examples. They are not to be copied or downloaded and used by any student. Those who are REALTORS® may freely download them from the UAR or MLS site.

   C. The discussion will start with the Designated Agency version of the contract.

II. **Addendum to Listing Agreement (subagency)**

   A. This replaces the wording in Section 5 AGENCY RELATIONSHIPS.

      1. The same wording is also in the addendum for the Buyer Broker Agency Agreement and the Non-exclusive Buyer Broker agreement.

      2. The purpose of the wording change is the shift from a Designated Agency relationship to a subagency relationship.

      3. In Designated Agency, only the named agent(s) represent the client, along with the principal broker. In subagency, all agents in the office represent the client, along with the principal broker.

      4. All other sections in the Designated Agency version of the contract remain the same.

III. **Unrepresented Buyer Disclosure**

   A. How much your brokerage uses this particular form will depend upon its policy relative to in-house sales.

   B. It is used only when a buyer, who has no agency representation, comes directly to the listing agent to see, negotiate for, or purchase a listed property.

      1. If the first choice is to get the buyer interested in your listing and have him/her sign a buyer agency contract, this form will not be used.

      2. If the buyer does sign a buyer agency contract, be sure to get buyer and seller to sign a limited agency agreement.

3. If the buyers say they don't need or want an agent, the unrepresented buyer agreement can be used.

4. This form avoids limited (or dual) agency.

C. The agent assists the buyer in completing the transaction, but only has a fiduciary duty to the seller.

Case Study: Broker Beth

Elizabeth works under Broker Beth of Beth's Realty. She recently took an exclusive right to sell listing for the Wilson's property. Beth's Realty uses the designated agency version of agency contracts. The Wilson's would only list if Elizabeth would hold open houses. She was sure this house would sell fast, so she said she would hold one open house per month, and the sellers signed the listing.

Unfortunately, Elizabeth wasn't keeping her calendar up to date and she found herself double booked for the time she had set for the Wilson's open house. They had cleaned like crazy and arranged to go away for the whole afternoon, so she didn't feel she could cancel without causing bad feelings. She asked Bob, another agent in the company, if he was available and would cover for her at the Wilson's open house. He wasn't too excited about it, but decided to look at it as an opportunity to pick up some buyers, so he agreed.

One of the couples who came through the open house was the Thompsons. They had just recently decided they were interested in buying a house, but didn't know anything about financing a purchase; if they would qualify or not, etc. As Bob talked with them about the whole buying process, they were very impressed with his knowledge and expertise and agreed to sign a buyer agency contract with him. They weren't particularly impressed with the Wilson's home, so Bob said he would do some research and find them some homes to match their parameters.

After looking at several homes over the next few weeks, they wanted to see the Wilson's home again. This time they saw it through new eyes, and decided to make an offer. Buyers and Sellers reached agreement and the sale closed as scheduled.

A few weeks later the sellers, the Wilsons, were talking with their old neighbors. The neighbors mentioned that the Thompsons had told them that Agent Bob had indicated there were some factors motivating the sellers to sell quickly, and that is why the Thompson's offer had been as low as it was.

The sellers are very upset, and are now considering what action to take. They feel Bob violated his fiduciary duty to them in sharing that information with the buyers. They wonder if they should get a lawyer and sue, or if they should complain to the Real Estate Division, or maybe even do both?

EXCLUSIVE RIGHT TO SELL LISTING AGREEMENT
& AGENCY DISCLOSURE
THIS IS A LEGALLY BINDING AGREEMENT - READ CAREFULLY BEFORE SIGNING
DESIGNATED AGENCY BROKERAGE

THIS EXCLUSIVE RIGHT TO SELL LISTING AGREEMENT & AGENCY DISCLOSURE ("Listing Agreement") is entered into by and between _____ (the "Company") and _____ (the "Seller").

1. TERM OF LISTING. The Seller hereby grants to the Company, including _____ (the "Seller's Agent") as the authorized agent for the Company starting on the Effective Date as defined in section 17 below, and ending at 5:00 P.M. (Mountain Time) on the _____ day of _____, 20____ (the "Listing Period"), the exclusive right to sell, lease, or exchange real property owned by the Seller, described as: _____ (the "Property"), at the listing price and terms stated on the attached property data form (the "Data Form"), or at such other price and terms to which the Seller may agree in writing.

2. BROKERAGE FEE. If, during the Listing Period, the Company, the Seller's Agent, the Seller, another real estate agent, or anyone else locates a party who is ready, willing and able to buy, lease or exchange (collectively "acquire") the Property, or any part thereof, at the listing price and terms stated on the Data Form, or any other price and terms to which the Seller may agree in writing, the Seller agrees to pay to the Company a brokerage fee in the amount of $ _____ or _____% of such acquisition price (the "Brokerage Fee"). The Brokerage Fee, unless otherwise agreed in writing by the Seller and the Company, shall be due and payable from the Seller's proceeds on: (a) If a purchase, the date of recording of the Closing documents for the acquisition of the Property; (b) If a lease, the effective date of the lease; and (c) if an option, the date the option agreement is signed. If within the Listing Period, or any extension of the Listing Period, the Property is withdrawn from sale, transferred, conveyed, leased, rented, or made unmarketable by a voluntary act of Seller, without the written consent of the Company; or if the sale is prevented by default of the Seller, the Brokerage Fee shall be immediately due and payable to the Company. The Company is authorized to share the Brokerage Fee with another brokerage participating in any transaction arising out of this Listing Agreement.

3. PROTECTION PERIOD. If within _____months after the termination or expiration of this Listing Agreement, the Property is acquired by any party to whom the Property was offered or shown by the Company, the Seller's Agent, the Seller, or another real estate agent during the Listing Period, or any extension of the Listing Period, the Seller agrees to pay to the Company the Brokerage Fee stated in Section 2, unless the Seller is obligated to pay a Brokerage Fee on such acquisition to another brokerage based on another valid listing agreement entered into after the expiration or termination date of this Listing Agreement.

4. SELLER WARRANTIES/DISCLOSURES. The Seller warrants to the Company that the individuals or entity listed above as the "Seller" represents all of the record owners of the Property. The Seller warrants that Seller has marketable title and an established right to sell, lease or exchange the Property. The Seller agrees to execute the necessary documents of conveyance. The Seller agrees to furnish buyer with good and marketable title, and to pay at Settlement, for a policy of title insurance in accordance with the terms of any real estate purchase contract entered into between buyer and Seller. The Seller agrees to fully inform the Seller's Agent regarding the Seller's knowledge of the condition of the Property. Upon signing of this Listing Agreement, the Seller agrees to personally complete and sign a Seller's Property Condition Disclosure form. The Seller agrees to indemnify and hold harmless the Seller's Agent and the Company against any claims that may arise from: (a) The Seller providing incorrect or inaccurate information regarding the Property; (b)The Seller failing to disclose material information regarding the Property, including, but not limited to, the condition of all appliances; the condition of heating, plumbing, and electrical fixtures and equipment; sewer problems; moisture or other problems in the roof or foundation; the availability and location of utilities; and the location of property lines; and (c) Any injuries resulting from any unsafe conditions within the Property.

© Stringham Schools

5.   AGENCY RELATIONSHIPS.
5.1   Duties of a Seller's Agent. By signing this Listing Agreement, the Seller designates the Seller's Agent and the Principal/Branch Broker for the Company (the "Broker"), as agents for the Seller to locate a buyer for the Property. The Seller authorizes the Seller's Agent or the Broker to appoint another agent in the Company to also represent the Seller in the event the Seller's Agent or the Broker will be unavailable to service the Seller. As agents for the Seller, they have fiduciary duties to the Seller that include loyalty, obedience, full disclosure, confidentiality, reasonable care, and any other duties required by law.
5.2   Duties of a Limited Agent. The Seller understands that the Seller's Agent and the Broker may now, or in the future, be agents for a buyer who may wish to negotiate a purchase of the Property. Then the Seller's Agent and the Broker may be acting as Limited Agents - representing both the Seller and buyer at the same time. A Limited Agent has fiduciary duties to both the Seller and the buyer as required by law. However, some of those duties are "limited" because the agent cannot provide to both parties undivided loyalty, confidentiality and disclosure. For this reason, the Limited Agent is bound by a further duty of neutrality. Being neutral, the Limited Agent may not disclose to either party information likely to weaken the bargaining position of the other – for example, the highest price the buyer will offer, or the lowest price the Seller will accept. However, the Limited Agent will be required to disclose information given to the agent in confidence by the other party if failure to disclose such information would be a material misrepresentation regarding the Property or regarding the ability of the parties to fulfill their obligations. The Seller is advised that neither the Seller nor the buyer is required to accept a limited agency situation in the Company, and each party is entitled to be represented by its own agent. In the event a limited agency situation arises, the Seller's Agent and the Broker, as applicable, may only act as Limited Agents based upon a separate Limited Agency Consent Agreement signed by the Seller and buyer.

6.   PROFESSIONAL ADVICE. The Company and the Seller's Agent are trained in the marketing of real estate. Neither the Company nor its agents are trained or licensed to provide the Seller or any prospective buyer with legal or tax advice, or with technical advice regarding the physical condition of the Property. The Seller is advised not to rely on the Company, or any agents of the Company, for a determination regarding the physical or legal condition of the Property. If the Seller desires advice regarding: (a) Past or present compliance with zoning and building code requirements; (b) Legal or tax matters; (c) The physical condition of the Property; (d) This Listing Agreement; or (e) Any transaction for the acquisition of the Property, the Seller's Agent and the Company strongly recommend that the Seller obtain such independent advice. If the Seller fails to do so, the Seller is acting contrary to the advice of the Company. Any recommendations for third-party services made by the Company or the Seller's Agent do not guarantee the Seller's satisfaction in the use of those third-party services and should not be seen as a warranty of any kind as to the level of service that will be provided by the third parties. The Seller is advised that it is up to the Seller in the Seller's sole discretion to choose third-party services that meet the needs of the Seller and not to rely on any recommendations given by the Company or the Seller's Agent.

7.   DISPUTE RESOLUTION. The parties agree that any dispute, arising prior to or after a Closing, related to this Listing Agreement shall first be submitted to mediation through a mediation provider mutually agreed upon by the Seller and the Company. Each party agrees to bear its own costs of mediation. If mediation fails, any other remedies available at law shall apply.

8.   ATTORNEY FEES/GOVERNING LAW. Except as provided in Section 7, in case of the employment of an attorney in any matter arising out of this Listing Agreement, the prevailing party shall be entitled to receive from the other party all costs and attorney fees, whether the matter is resolved through court action or otherwise. If, through no fault of the Company, any litigation arises out of the Seller's employment of the Company under this Listing Agreement (whether before or after a Closing), the Seller agrees to indemnify the Company and the Seller's Agent from all costs and attorney fees incurred by the Company and/or the Seller's Agent in pursuing and/or defending such action. This Listing Agreement shall be governed and construed in accordance with the laws of the State of Utah.

9.   ADVERTISING/SELLER AUTHORIZATIONS. The Seller authorizes the Company and the Seller's Agent to advertise the Property for sale through any printed and/or electronic media deemed necessary and appropriate by the Seller's Agent and the Company, including, but not limited to, each Multiple Listing Service (MLS) in which the Company participates. The Seller agrees that any advertising the Seller intends to conduct, including print and/or electronic media, shall first be approved in writing by the Seller's Agent. The Seller further agrees that the Seller's Agent and the Company are authorized to:

(a) Disclose to the MLS after Closing, the final terms and sales price for the Property consistent with the requirements of the MLS;

(b) Disclose to the MLS the square footage of the Property as obtained from (check applicable box): [   ] County Records [   ] Appraisal [   ] Building Plans [   ] Other (explain)_____

(c) Obtain financial information from any lender or other party holding a lien or interest on the Property;

(d) Have keys to the Property, if applicable;

(e) Have an MLS or local board of Realtors® approved/endorsed security key-box installed on the Property. If the Seller authorizes the Broker, or Seller's Agent, to install a non-MLS or local board of Realtors® approved/endorsed   security key-box on the Property, Seller acknowledges that it may not provide the same level of security as   the   MLS   or   local   board   of   Realtors® approved/endorsed security key-box;

(f) Hold Open-Houses at the Property;

(g) Place for sale, sold, or other similar signs ("Signs") on the Property (i.e., the only Signs on the Property shall be that of the Company);

(h) Order a Preliminary Title Report on the Property;

(i) Order a Home Warranty Plan, if applicable;

(j) Communicate with the Seller for the purpose of soliciting real estate related goods and services during and after the term of this Listing Agreement; and

(k) Place the Earnest Money Deposit into an interest-bearing trust account with interest paid to the Utah Association of Realtors® Housing Opportunity Fund (UARHOF) to assist in creating affordable housing throughout the state.

10.   PERSONAL PROPERTY. The Seller acknowledges that the Company has discussed with the Seller the safeguarding of personal property and valuables located within the Property. The Seller acknowledges that the Company is not an insurer against the loss of or damage to personal property. The Seller agrees to hold the Company harmless from any loss or damage that might result from any authorizations given in Section 9.

11.   ATTACHMENT. The Data Form is incorporated into this Listing Agreement by this reference. In addition to the Data Form, there **[   ] ARE [   ] ARE NOT** additional terms contained in an Addendum attached to this Listing Agreement. If an Addendum is attached, the terms of that Addendum are incorporated into this Listing Agreement by this reference.

12. FOREIGN INVESTMENT IN REAL PROPERTY TAX ACT ("FIRPTA"). The sale or other disposition of a U.S. real property interest by a foreign person is subject to income tax withholding under FIRPTA. A "foreign person" may include *a non-resident alien individual, foreign corporation, foreign partnership, foreign trust and foreign estate*. Seller warrants and represents to the Company and to the Seller's Agent, that Seller **[   ] IS [   ] IS NOT** a "foreign person" as defined in Section 1445 of the Internal Revenue Code and its associated regulations. If Seller is not a foreign person, Seller agrees, upon request, to deliver a certification to Buyer at closing, stating that Seller is not a foreign person.   This certification shall be in the form then required by FIRPTA. If FIRPTA applies to you as Seller, you are advised that the Buyer or other qualified substitute may be legally required to withhold 10% of the total purchase price for the Property at closing and remit that amount to the IRS. If Seller is a foreign person as defined above, and Seller does not have a US Taxpayer Identification number, Seller agrees to prepare to apply for a US Taxpayer Identification number.

13.   EQUAL HOUSING OPPORTUNITY. The Seller and the Company shall comply with Federal, State, and local fair housing laws.

14.   ELECTRONIC TRANSMISSION & COUNTERPARTS. Electronic transmission (including email and fax) of a signed copy of this Listing Agreement and any addenda, and the retransmission of any signed electronic transmission, shall be the same as delivery of an original. This Listing Agreement and any addenda may be executed in counterparts.

15.   DUE-ON-SALE. Certain types of transactions may trigger what is commonly referred to as a "due-on-sale" clause. A "due-on-sale" clause typically states that the Seller's lender or mortgagee may call the loan due and payable in full if the Seller participates in certain types of transactions. These types of transactions may include, but are not limited to, transactions where: (a) The sale of the property does not result in the underlying debt being paid in full; (b) The parties enter into a seller-financed transaction; (c) A lease option agreement is entered into; or (d) Any other unauthorized transfer of title to the Property has occurred without the lender's consent. The Seller understands that if any underlying encumbrances or mortgages on the Property contain a "due-on-sale clause," and the "due-on-sale" clause is triggered, the lender may call the entire unpaid balance of the loan immediately due.

16.   ENTIRE AGREEMENT. This Listing Agreement, including the Seller's Property Condition Disclosure form and the Data Form, contain the entire agreement between the parties relating to the subject matter of this Listing Agreement. This Listing Agreement may not be modified or amended except in writing signed by the parties hereto.

17.   EFFECTIVE DATE. This Listing Agreement is entered into and is effective as of the date: (a) The Seller and the authorized Seller's Agent or Broker have signed this Listing Agreement; and (b) The authorized Seller's Agent or Broker has received a mutually signed copy of this Listing Agreement (the "Effective Date").

THE UNDERSIGNED hereby agree to the terms of this Listing Agreement.

_____   _____   _____
(Seller's Signature)   (Address/Phone)   (Date)

_____   _____   _____
(Seller's Signature)   (Address/Phone)   (Date)

ACCEPTED by the Company

by: _____   _____
    (Signature of Authorized Seller's Agent or Broker)   (Date)

ADDENDUM TO LISTING AGREEMENT
(Subagency)

THIS IS AN ADDENDUM to the Listing Agreement entered into on the _____ day of _____, 20____, by and between _____ as Seller and_____ as the Company (a copy of the Listing Agreement is attached hereto) regarding the property more particularly described as follows:_____ (the "Property"). To the extent any term(s) of the Addendum conflict with or modify any term(s) of the Listing Agreement, the terms of this Addendum shall control. Seller and the Company agree as follows:

1.   AGENCY RELATIONSHIPS. Section 5 of the Listing Agreement is hereby deleted in its entirety and is replaced with the following language:

By signing this Listing Agreement, the Seller designates the Seller's Agent, the Principal/Branch Broker for the Company (the "Broker"), and every real estate agent affiliated with the Company (the "Affiliates") as agents for the Seller to locate a buyer for the Property. As agents for the Seller, the Seller's Agent, the Broker, and the Affiliates, have fiduciary duties to the Seller that include loyalty, full disclosure, confidentiality, and reasonable care. If the buyer that desires to acquire the Property is represented by another brokerage, then the Seller's Agent, the Broker and each of the Affiliates will continue to represent the Seller. However, if the buyer that desires to acquire the Property is also represented by the Seller's Agent, the Broker, or any of the Affiliates, then the Seller's Agent, the Broker, and each of the Affiliates, will, as a practical matter, be representing both the Seller and the buyer in the same transaction. Representing a buyer and seller in the same transaction is referred to as "Limited Agency". A Limited Agent has fiduciary duties to both the buyer and the seller. However, those duties are "limited" because the Limited Agent cannot provide to both parties undivided loyalty, full confidentiality and full disclosure of all information known to the Limited Agent. For this reason, the Limited Agent is bound by a further duty of neutrality. Being neutral, the Limited Agent may not disclose to either party information likely to weaken the bargaining position of the other – for example, the highest price a buyer will offer, or the lowest price a seller will accept. THE SELLER IS ADVISED THAT NEITHER THE SELLER NOR THE BUYER IS REQUIRED TO ACCEPT A LIMITED AGENCY SITUATION IN THE COMPANY, AND EACH PARTY IS ENTITLED TO BE REPRESENTED BY ITS OWN AGENT. If Limited Agency is agreed to below the Seller authorizes the Seller's Agent, the Broker, and each of the Affiliates to represent both the Seller and the buyer as Limited Agents when the Seller's Agent and the Broker also represent the buyer for the Property. **IF LIMITED AGENCY IS AGREED TO BELOW, THE SELLER AND BUYER WILL BE REQUIRED TO SIGN A SEPARATE LIMITED AGENCY CONSENT AGREEMENT AT THE TIME THE LIMITED AGENCY SITUATION ARISES. INITIAL APPLICABLE BOX: [   ] I AGREE TO LIMITED AGENCY; OR [   ] I DO NOT AGREE TO LIMITED AGENCY.**

ALL OTHER TERMS OF THE LISTING AGREEMENT not modified by this Addendum shall remain the same.

COMPANY   SELLER

_____   _____

DATE:_____   DATE:_____

 Utah Association of REALTORS®

UNREPRESENTED BUYER DISCLOSURE

 EQUAL HOUSING OPPORTUNITY

This disclosure form is not a contract. Signing it does not create any relationship between you and the real estate agent who has also signed.

NAME OF BUYER: _____ (the "Buyer")

NAME OF SELLER: _____ (the "Seller")

LOCATION OF PROPERTY: _____ (the "Property")

AGENT REPRESENTING SELLER: _____ (the "Agent")

BROKERAGE REPRESENTING SELLER: _____ (the "Company")

WHEN YOU ENTER INTO A DISCUSSION WITH A REAL ESTATE AGENT REGARDING A POTENTIAL REAL ESTATE TRANSACTION, YOU SHOULD, FROM THE OUTSET, UNDERSTAND WHO THE REAL ESTATE AGENT IS REPRESENTING IN THAT TRANSACTION. WHAT FOLLOWS IS A BRIEF BUT VERY IMPORTANT EXPLANATION REGARDING AGENCY RELATIONSHIPS AND THE REAL ESTATE AGENTS INVOLVED IN THIS TRANSACTION.

SELLER'S AGENT

A real estate agent who lists a seller's property for sale ("Seller's Agent"), acts as the agent for the seller only, and has fiduciary duties of loyalty, full disclosure, confidentiality and reasonable care to that seller. In practical terms, the seller hires a Seller's Agent to locate a buyer and negotiate a transaction with terms favorable to the seller. Although the Seller's Agent has these fiduciary duties to the seller, the Seller's Agent is, by law, responsible to all prospective buyers to treat them with honesty, fair dealing, and with good faith.

BUYER'S AGENT

A real estate agent that acts as agent for the buyer only ("Buyer's Agent") has the same fiduciary duties to that buyer that a Seller's Agent has to the seller. In practical terms, the buyer hires a Buyer's Agent to locate a suitable property and negotiate a transaction with terms favorable to the buyer. Although the Buyer's Agent has these fiduciary duties to the buyer, the Buyer's Agent is, by law, responsible to all prospective sellers to treat them with honesty, fair dealing, and with good faith.

AGENT OF BOTH BUYER AND SELLER

A real estate agent can, with the prior written consent of the buyer and seller, represent both the buyer and seller in the same transaction ("Limited Agent"). A Limited Agent has fiduciary duties to both the buyer and the seller, but the Limited Agent is also "limited" by a separate duty of neutrality in the negotiations between the buyer and seller.

CONFIRMATION OF AGENCY IN THIS TRANSACTION

The Property shown above is presently listed for sale through the Company. Consequently, the Company and the Agent are representing the Seller. BY SIGNING THIS UNREPRESENTED BUYER DISCLOSURE THE BUYER ACKNOWLEDGES AND AGREES THAT THE AGENT AND THE COMPANY WILL ONLY REPRESENT THE SELLER IN THIS TRANSACTION AS A SELLER'S AGENT. THE BUYER ACKNOWLEDGES THAT THE COMPANY AND THE AGENT HAVE ADVISED THE BUYER THAT THE BUYER IS ENTITLED TO BE REPRESENTED BY A BUYER'S AGENT WHO WILL REPRESENT ONLY THE BUYER. THE BUYER HAS HOWEVER, ELECTED NOT TO BE REPRESENTED BY A REAL ESTATE AGENT IN THIS TRANSACTION.

ACKNOWLEDGMENT

I/we acknowledge receipt of a copy of this Unrepresented Buyer Disclosure and understand and agree with the agency relationships confirmed herein.

_____   _____   _____   _____
(Buyer)   (Date)   (Buyer)   (Date)

The Company by: _____

(Authorized Agent)   Date

© Stringham Schools

Agency Practices 2*

*You should first complete the Agency A & B Classes before this class.

I. **Exclusive Buyer-Broker Agreement**

    A. This contract is not a state approved form

        1. If the broker is a member of the Utah Association of REALTORS® ("UAR"), their recommended form may be used.

        2. Brokers can hire an attorney to draft a form for their brokerage.

        3. Larger companies have their own forms prepared by their attorneys.

        4. Reminder: Drafting contracts is legal work and the broker or owner of the brokerage cannot create, or draft, a contract.

    B. For purposes of these Agency Practices discussions, UAR forms will be used as examples. They are not to be copied or downloaded and used by any students. Those who are REALTORS® may freely download them from the UAR or MLS site.

    C. The discussion will start with the Designated Agency version of the contract.

II. **Limited Agency Consent Agreement**

    A. A. This document would be used in either of the following cases:

        1. By contract, the listing agent is also the agent of the buyer. Therefore, both the agent and the broker/branch broker are limited agents.

        2. One agent in the office took the listing, and a different agent has the contract with the buyer. In this case, only the broker/branch broker is a limited agent.

    B. Before this agreement is signed, there should already be two signed agreements in the company files: A listing agreement with the seller; and a buyer-broker agreement with the buyer.

    C. In the listing and buyer-broker agreements, buyer and seller should have each initialed the box to indicate they agreed to future limited agency.

    D. In spite of the previous indication they would accept limited agency, it is still necessary that each signs an agreement for limited agency.

III. **Non-Exclusive Buyer-Broker Agreement**

    A. This form would rarely be used. We would all like to know we'll be paid if the buyer ends up purchasing a home, so it is most desirable to use an exclusive contract.

    B. It is only used when a buyer refuses to sign an exclusive contract.

        1. It gives the buyer the freedom to enter into a buyer contract with another agent.

        2. It doesn't bind buyers to an agent they don't really know or fully trust yet.

IV.   **For Sale by Owner Commission Agreement**

    A.   This form replaces the single party listing that used to be used with **for sale by owner** properties (FSBO's).

    B.   In cases where the agent already has a buyer contract, it avoids limited agency.

        1.   It does not create an agency relationship with the seller. In fact, it carefully discloses that the seller will not have agency representation.

        2.   It creates the obligation of the seller to pay a commission if the named buyers end up purchasing the property.

        3.   The agent will guide the sellers through the transaction process to closing, but it specifically states that those actions do not create agency.

 **Utah Association** *of* **REALTORS®**

LIMITED AGENCY CONSENT AGREEMENT

THIS IS A LEGALLY BINDING AGREEMENT - READ CAREFULLY BEFORE SIGNING

Name of Buyer(s):_____   Name of Seller(s): _____.

Agent Representing Buyer:_____   Agent representing Seller:_____.

Name of Brokerage: _____ (the "Company).

The Buyer and the Seller are both presently using the services of the Company in a possible real estate transaction involving real property located at:_____(referred to below as the "Property").

AS THE BUYER AND THE SELLER PROCEED WITH THIS TRANSACTION IT IS IMPORTANT THAT THEY EACH UNDERSTAND THEIR PROFESSIONAL RELATIONSHIP WITH THE REAL ESTATE AGENT(S) AND WITH THE COMPANY. WHAT FOLLOWS IS A BRIEF BUT VERY IMPORTANT EXPLANATION OF THE NATURE OF AGENCY RELATIONSHIPS BETWEEN THE BUYER, THE SELLER, THE COMPANY, AND THE REAL ESTATE AGENTS WORKING IN THIS TRANSACTION.

1. **Principal or Branch Broker.** Every real estate agent must affiliate with a real estate broker. The broker is referred to as a Principal Broker or a Branch Broker (if the brokerage has a branch office). The broker is responsible for operation of the brokerage and for the professional conduct of all agents.

2. **Right of Agents to Represent Seller and/or Buyer.** An agent may represent, through the brokerage, a seller who wants to sell property or a buyer who wants to buy property. On occasion, an agent will represent both seller and buyer in the same transaction. When an agent represents a seller, the agent is a "Seller's Agent"; when representing a buyer, the agent is a "Buyer's Agent"; and when representing both seller and buyer, the agent is a "Limited Agent".

3. **Seller's Agent.** A Seller's Agent works to assist the seller in locating a buyer and in negotiating a transaction suitable to the seller's specific needs. A Seller's Agent has fiduciary duties to the seller which include loyalty, full disclosure, confidentiality, diligence, obedience, reasonable care, and holding safe monies entrusted to the agent.

4. **Buyer's Agent.** A Buyer's Agent works to assist the buyer in locating and negotiating the acquisition of a property suitable to that buyer's specific needs. A Buyer's Agent has the same fiduciary duties to the buyer that the Seller's Agent has to the Seller.

5. **Limited Agent.** A Limited Agent represents both seller and buyer in the same transaction and works to assist in negotiating a mutually acceptable transaction. A Limited Agent has fiduciary duties to both seller and buyer. However, those duties are "limited" because the agent cannot provide to both parties undivided loyalty, full confidentiality and full disclosure of all information known to the agent. For this reason, a Limited Agent must remain neutral in the representation of a seller and buyer, and may not disclose to either party information likely to weaken the bargaining position of the other; such as, the highest price the buyer will pay or the lowest price the seller will accept. A Limited Agent must, however, disclose to both parties material information known to the Limited Agent regarding a defect in the Property and/or the ability of each party to fulfill agreed upon obligations, and must disclose information given to the Limited Agent in confidence, by either party, if the failure to disclose would be a material misrepresentation regarding the Property.

6. **In-House Sale.** If the buyer and the seller are both represented by one or more agents in the same brokerage, that transaction is commonly referred to as an "In-House Sale". Consequently, most In-House Sales involve limited agency because seller and buyer are represented by the same brokerage.

7. **Conflicts with the In-House Sale.** There are conflicts associated with an In-House Sale; for example, agents affiliated with the same brokerage discuss with each other the needs of their respective buyers or sellers. Such discussions could inadvertently compromise the confidentiality of information provided to those agents. For that reason, the Company has policies designed to protect the confidentiality of discussions between agents and access to confidential client and transaction files.

8. **Earnest Money Deposit.** Buyer and Seller agree that although the Company is authorized to act as a Limited Agent, Buyer and Seller authorize and direct the Principal Broker for the Company to hold and release the Earnest Money Deposit in accordance with the terms and conditions of the real estate purchase contract, or other written agreement entered into between the Buyer and the Seller.

9. **Authorization for Limited Agency.** The Seller and Buyer are advised that they are not required to accept a limited agency situation in the Company and that Buyer and Seller are each entitled to be represented by their own agent. However, it is the business practice of the Company to participate in In-House Sales. By signing this agreement, Buyer and Seller consent to a limited agency within the Company as provided below: (Check Applicable Box):

[   ]   A. One Agent. The Buyer and the Seller consent to: _____ (name of Agent);
and the Principal/Branch Broker representing both the Buyer and the Seller as a Limited Agent as described above.

[   ]   B. Two Agents. The Buyer and the Seller consent to:_____ (Seller's Agent) continuing to represent the Seller; and: _____(Buyer's Agent)continuing to represent the Buyer; and the Principal/Branch Broker acting as a Limited Agent as described above.

_____   _____   _____   _____
(Buyer)   (Date)   (Seller)   (Date)

_____   _____   _____   _____
(Buyer)   (Date)   (Seller)   (Date)

ACCEPTED by the Company:

by:_____   _____
          (Signature of Authorized Agent or Broker)   (Date)

EXCLUSIVE BUYER-BROKER AGREEMENT & AGENCY DISCLOSURE
THIS IS A LEGALLY BINDING AGREEMENT - READ CAREFULLY BEFORE SIGNING
DESIGNATED AGENCY BROKERAGE

THIS EXCLUSIVE BUYER-BROKER AGREEMENT & AGENCY DISCLOSURE ("Exclusive Buyer-Broker Agreement") is entered into between _____ (the "Company") and _____ (the "Buyer").

1.   TERM OF AGREEMENT.   The Buyer hereby retains the Company, including _____ (the "Buyer's Agent") as the authorized agent for the Company, starting on the Effective Date as defined in section 15 below, and ending at 5:00 P.M. (Mountain Time) on the _____ day of _____, 20____, or the Closing of the acquisition of a property, which ever occurs first (the "Initial Term"), to act as the exclusive Buyer's Agent in locating and/or negotiating for the acquisition of a property: (a) In _____ County, Utah; or (b) Located at _____ (property address). During the Initial Term of this Exclusive Buyer-Broker Agreement, and any extensions thereof, the Buyer agrees not to enter into another buyer-broker agreement with another real estate agent or brokerage.

2.   BROKERAGE FEE. If, during the Initial Term, or any extension of the Initial Term, the Buyer, or any other person acting in the Buyer's behalf, acquires an interest in any real property as referenced in Section 1 above, the Buyer agrees to pay to the Company a brokerage fee in the amount of $_____ or _____% of the acquisition price of the property (the "Brokerage Fee"). If the property acquired by the Buyer is listed with a brokerage, the buyer agent commission ("BAC") paid to the Company by the listing brokerage shall satisfy the Buyer's obligation for the Brokerage Fee shown above provided that the BAC is not less than the amount shown above. If the BAC is less than the amount shown above, Buyer will pay the difference at Closing. If the property is not listed with a brokerage, in the absence of a commission agreement with the owner of the selected property, the Brokerage Fee shown above shall be paid by the Buyer. Unless otherwise agreed to in writing by the Buyer and the Company, the Brokerage Fee shown above shall be due and payable on: (a) If a purchase, the date of recording of the Closing documents; (b) If a lease, the effective date of the lease; or (c) If an option, the date the option agreement is signed. If the transaction is prevented by default of Buyer, the compensation shall be immediately payable to the Company.

3.   PROTECTION PERIOD. If within _____ months after the termination or expiration of this Exclusive Buyer-Broker Agreement, Buyer or any person acting on the Buyer's behalf, enters into an agreement to purchase, exchange, obtain an option on, or lease any property, as referenced in Section 1 above, located for Buyer by Buyer's Agent or the Company, or on which Buyer's Agent negotiates in Buyer's behalf during the Initial Term, Buyer agrees to pay to the Company the Brokerage Fee referenced in Section 2.

4.   BUYER REPRESENTATIONS/DISCLOSURES. The Buyer warrants that the Buyer has not entered into any other Exclusive Buyer-Broker Agreement with any other brokerage that is still in force and effect. The Buyer will: (a) In all communications with other real estate agents, notify the agents in advance that the Buyer has entered into this Exclusive Buyer-Broker Agreement with the Company; (b) Furnish the Buyer's Agent with relevant personal and financial information to facilitate the Buyer's ability to acquire a property; (c) Exercise care and diligence in evaluating the physical and legal condition of the property selected by the Buyer; (d) Hold harmless the Company and the Buyer's Agent against any claims as the result of any injuries incurred while inspecting any property; (e) Upon signing of this Exclusive Buyer-Broker Agreement, personally review and sign the Buyer Due Diligence Checklist form; and (f) Disclose to the Buyer's Agent all properties in which the Buyer, as of the date of this Exclusive Buyer-Broker Agreement, is either negotiating to acquire or has a present interest in acquiring.

5.   AGENCY RELATIONSHIPS.
    5.1   Duties of a Buyer's Agent. By signing this Exclusive Buyer-Broker Agreement, the Buyer designates the Buyer's Agent and the Principal/Branch Broker for the Company (the "Broker"), as agents for the Buyer to locate properties as referenced in Section 1 above for Buyer's consideration and review. The Buyer authorizes the Buyer's Agent or the Broker to appoint another agent in the Company to also represent the Buyer in the event the Buyer's Agent or the Broker will be unavailable to service the Buyer. As agents for the Buyer, the Buyer's Agent and Broker have fiduciary duties to the Buyer that include loyalty, obedience, full disclosure, confidentiality, reasonable care, and any other duties required by law.
    5.2   Duties of a Limited Agent. The Buyer understands that the Buyer's Agent and the Broker may now, or in the future, be agents for a seller who may have a property that the Buyer may wish to acquire. Then the Buyer's Agent and the Broker may be acting as Limited Agents - representing both the Buyer and the seller at the same time. A Limited Agent has fiduciary duties to both the Buyer and the seller as required by law. However, some of those duties are "limited" because the agent cannot provide to both parties undivided loyalty, confidentiality and disclosure. For this reason, the Limited Agent is bound by a further duty of neutrality. Being neutral, the Limited Agent may not disclose to either party information likely to weaken the bargaining position of the other – for example, the highest price the Buyer will offer, or the lowest price the seller will accept. However, the Limited Agent will be required to disclose information given to the agent in confidence by the other party if failure to

Page 1 of 3   Buyer's Initials   [   ] Date_____

109

disclose such information would be a material misrepresentation regarding the Property or regarding the ability of the parties to fulfill their obligations. The Buyer is advised that neither the Buyer nor the seller is required to accept a limited agency situation in the Company, and each party is entitled to be represented by its own agent. In the event a limited agency situation arises, the Buyer's Agent and the Broker, as applicable, may only act as Limited Agents based upon a separate Limited Agency Consent Agreement signed by the seller and Buyer.

6.   PROFESSIONAL ADVICE. The Company and the Buyer's agent are trained in the marketing of real estate. Neither the Company nor the Buyer's Agent are trained or licensed to provide the Buyer with professional advice regarding the physical condition of any property or regarding legal or tax matters. The Buyer is advised not to rely on the Company, or any agents of the Company, for a determination regarding the physical or legal condition of the property, including, but not limited to: past or present compliance with zoning and building code requirements; the condition of any appliances; the condition of heating/cooling, plumbing, and electrical fixtures and equipment; sewer problems; moisture or other problems in the roof or foundation; the availability and location of utilities; the location of property lines; and the exact square footage or acreage of the property. As part of any written offer to purchase a property, the Company strongly recommends that the Buyer engage the services of appropriate professionals to conduct inspections, investigations, tests, surveys, and other evaluations of the property at the Buyer's expense. If the Buyer fails to do so, the Buyer is acting contrary to the advice of the Company. Any recommendations for third party services made by the Company or the Buyer's Agent do not guarantee the Buyer's satisfaction in the use of those third party services and should not be seen as a warranty of any kind as to the level of service that will be provided by the third parties. The Buyer is advised that it is up to the Buyer in the Buyer's sole discretion to choose third party services that meet the needs of the Buyer and not to rely on any recommendations given by the Company or the Buyer's Agent.

7.   DISPUTE RESOLUTION. The parties agree that any dispute related to this Exclusive Buyer-Broker Agreement, arising prior to or after the acquisition of a property, shall first be submitted to mediation through a mediation provider mutually agreed upon by the Buyer and the Company. Each party agrees to bear its own costs of mediation. If mediation fails, the other remedies available under this Exclusive Buyer-Broker Agreement shall apply.

8.   ATTORNEY FEES/GOVERNING LAW. Except as provided in Section 7, in case of the employment of an attorney in any matter arising out of this Exclusive Buyer-Broker Agreement, the prevailing party shall be entitled to receive from the other party all costs and attorney fees, whether the matter is resolved through court action or otherwise. If, through no fault of the Company, any litigation arises out of the Buyer's employment of the Company under this Exclusive Buyer-Broker Agreement (whether before or after the acquisition of a property), the Buyer agrees to indemnify the Company and the Buyer's Agent from all costs and attorney fees incurred by the Company and/or the Buyer's Agent in pursuing and/or defending such action. This Exclusive Buyer-Broker Agreement shall be governed and construed in accordance with the laws of the State of Utah.

9.   BUYER AUTHORIZATIONS. The Buyer authorizes the Company and/or Buyer's Agent to: (a) Disclose after Closing to each MLS in which the Company participates (consistent with the requirements of each such MLS), the final terms and sales price of the property acquired by Buyer under the terms of this Agreement; and (b) Communicate with the Buyer for the purpose of soliciting real estate related goods and services during and after the term of this Exclusive Buyer-Broker Agreement. The Buyer further agrees that in any transaction for the acquisition of any property, as referenced in Section 1 above, the Earnest Money Deposit may be placed into an interest-bearing trust account with interest paid to the Utah Association of Realtors® Housing Opportunity Fund (UARHOF) to assist in creating affordable housing throughout the state.

10.   ATTACHMENT. There **[   ] ARE   [   ] ARE NOT** additional terms contained in an Addendum attached to this Exclusive Buyer-Broker Agreement. If an Addendum is attached, the terms of that Addendum are incorporated into this Exclusive Buyer-Broker Agreement by this reference.

11.   EQUAL HOUSING OPPORTUNITY. The Buyer and the Company will comply with Federal, State, and local fair housing laws.

12.   ELECTRONIC TRANSMISSION & COUNTERPARTS. Electronic transmission (including email and fax) of a signed copy of this Exclusive Buyer Broker-Agreement and any addenda, and the retransmission of any signed electronic transmission, shall be the same as delivery of an original. This Exclusive Buyer-Broker Agreement and any addenda may be executed in counterparts.

13.   DUE-ON-SALE. Certain types of transactions may trigger what is commonly referred to as a "due-on-sale" clause. A "due-on-sale" clause typically states that the seller's lender or mortgagee may call the loan due and payable in full if the seller participates in certain types of transactions. These types of transactions may include, but are not limited to, transactions where: (a) The sale of the property does not result in the underlying debt being paid in full; (b) The parties enter into a seller-financed transaction; (c) A lease option agreement is entered into; or (d) Any other unauthorized transfer of title to the Property has occurred without the lender's consent. The Buyer understands that if any underlying encumbrances or mortgages on the Property contain a "due-on-sale clause," and the "due-on-sale" clause is triggered, the lender may call the entire unpaid balance of the loan immediately due.

14. **ENTIRE AGREEMENT.** This Exclusive Buyer-Broker Agreement, including the Buyer Due Diligence Checklist form, contains the entire agreement between the parties relating to the subject matter of this Exclusive Buyer-Broker Agreement. This Exclusive Buyer-Broker Agreement shall not be modified or amended except in writing signed by the parties hereto.

15. **EFFECTIVE DATE.** This Exclusive Buyer-Broker Agreement is entered into and is effective as of the date: (a) The Buyer and the authorized Buyer's Agent or Broker have signed this Exclusive Buyer-Broker Agreement; and (b) The authorized Buyer's Agent or Broker has received a mutually signed copy of this Exclusive Buyer-Broker Agreement (the "Effective Date").

THE UNDERSIGNED hereby accept the terms of this Exclusive Buyer-Broker Agreement.

_____   _____   _____
(Buyer's Signature)   (Address/Phone)   (Date)

_____   _____   _____
(Buyer's Signature)   (Address/Phone)   (Date)

ACCEPTED by the Company

by: _____   _____
    (Signature of Authorized Buyer's Agent or Broker)   (Date)

 Utah Association *of* REALTORS®

NON-EXCLUSIVE BUYER-BROKER AGREEMENT & AGENCY DISCLOSURE
THIS IS A LEGALLY BINDING AGREEMENT - READ CAREFULLY BEFORE SIGNING
DESIGNATED AGENCY BROKERAGE

THIS NON-EXCLUSIVE BUYER-BROKER AGREEMENT & AGENCY DISCLOSURE ("Non-Exclusive Buyer-Broker Agreement") is entered into by and between _____ (the "Company") and _____ (the "Buyer").

1.   TERM OF AGREEMENT. The Buyer hereby retains the Company, including _____ (the "Buyer's Agent") as the authorized agent for the Company, starting on the Effective date as defined in section 15 below and ending at 5:00 P.M. (Mountain Time) on the _____day of _____, 20____, or the Closing of the acquisition of a property, which ever occurs first (the "Initial Term"), to act as a non-exclusive Buyer's Agent in locating and/or negotiating for the acquisition of a property.

2.   BROKERAGE FEE. If, during the Initial Term, or any extension of the Initial Term, the Buyer, or any other person acting in the Buyer's behalf, acquires an interest in any real property on which: (a) The Buyer's Agent; (b) The Principal/Branch Broker for the Company (the "Broker"); or (c) Another real estate agent affiliated with the Company (an "Affiliate"), appointed to represent the Buyer as provided in Section 5 below, negotiates a transaction on the Buyer's behalf, the Buyer agrees to pay to the Company a brokerage fee in the amount of $_____ or _____% of the acquisition price of the property (the "Brokerage Fee"). If the property acquired by the Buyer is listed with a brokerage, the buyer agent commission ("BAC") paid to the Company by the listing brokerage shall satisfy the Buyer's obligation for the Brokerage Fee shown above provided that the BAC is not less than the amount shown above. If the BAC is less than the amount shown above, the Buyer will pay the difference at Closing. If the property is not listed with a brokerage, in the absence of a commission agreement with the owner of the selected property, the Brokerage Fee shown above shall be paid by the Buyer. Unless otherwise agreed to in writing by the Buyer and the Company, the Brokerage Fee shown above shall be due and payable on: (i) If a purchase, the date of recording of the Closing documents; (ii) If a lease, the effective date of the lease; or (iii) If an option, the date the option agreement is signed. If the transaction is prevented by default of Buyer, the compensation shall be immediately payable to the Company.

3.   PROTECTION PERIOD. If within _____ months after the termination or expiration of this Non-Exclusive Buyer-Broker Agreement, the Buyer or any person acting on the Buyer's behalf, enters into an agreement to purchase, exchange, obtain an option on, or lease any property on which, during the Initial Term: (a) The Buyer's Agent; (b) The Broker; or (c) An Affiliate was negotiating a transaction on the Buyer's behalf, the Buyer agrees to pay to the Company the Brokerage Fee referenced in Section 2.

4.   BUYER REPRESENTATIONS/DISCLOSURES. The Buyer will: (a) Furnish the Buyer's Agent with relevant personal and financial information to facilitate the Buyer's ability to acquire a property; (b) Exercise care and diligence in evaluating the physical and legal condition of the property selected by the Buyer; (c) Upon signing of this Non-Exclusive Buyer-Broker Agreement, personally review and sign the Buyer Due Diligence Checklist form; and (d) Disclose to the Buyer's Agent all properties in which the Buyer, as of the date of this Non-Exclusive Buyer-Broker Agreement, is either negotiating to acquire or has a present interest in acquiring.

5.   AGENCY RELATIONSHIPS.
    5.1   Duties of a Buyer's Agent. By signing this Non-Exclusive Buyer-Broker Agreement, the Buyer designates the Buyer's Agent and the Principal/Branch Broker for the Company (the "Broker"), as non-exclusive agents for the Buyer to locate properties for Buyer's consideration and review. The Buyer authorizes the Buyer's Agent or the Broker to appoint another agent in the Company to also represent the Buyer in the event the Buyer's Agent or the Broker will be unavailable to service the Buyer. As agents for the Buyer, the Buyer's Agent and Broker have fiduciary duties to the Buyer that include loyalty, obedience, full disclosure, confidentiality, reasonable care, and any other duties required by law.
    5.2   Duties of a Limited Agent. The Buyer understands that the Buyer's Agent and the Broker may now, or in the future, be agents for a seller who may have a property that the Buyer may wish to acquire. Then the Buyer's Agent and the Broker may be acting as Limited Agents - representing both the Buyer and the seller at the same time. A Limited Agent has fiduciary duties to both the Buyer and the seller as required by law. However, some of those duties are "limited" because the agent cannot provide to both parties undivided loyalty, confidentiality and disclosure. For this reason, the Limited Agent is bound by a further duty of neutrality. Being neutral, the Limited Agent may not disclose to either party information likely to weaken the bargaining position of the other – for example, the highest price the Buyer will offer, or the lowest price the seller will accept. However, the Limited Agent will be required to disclose information given to the agent in confidence by the other party if failure to disclose such information would be a material misrepresentation regarding the Property or regarding the ability of the parties to fulfill their obligations. The Buyer is advised that neither the Buyer nor the seller is required to accept a limited agency situation in the Company, and each party is entitled to be represented by its own agent. In the event a limited agency situation arises, the Buyer's Agent and the Broker, as applicable, may only act as Limited Agents based upon a separate Limited Agency Consent Agreement signed by the seller and Buyer.

6.   PROFESSIONAL ADVICE. The Company and the Buyer's Agent are trained in the marketing of real estate. Neither the Company, nor the Buyer's Agent are trained to provide the Buyer with legal or tax advice, or with technical advice regarding the physical condition of any property or regarding legal or tax matters. The Buyer is advised not to rely on the Company, or any agents of the Company, for a determination regarding the physical or legal condition of any property selected by the Buyer, including, but not limited to: past or present compliance with zoning and building code requirements; the condition of any appliances; the condition of heating/cooling, plumbing, and electrical fixtures and equipment; sewer problems; moisture or other problems in the roof or foundation; the availability and location of utilities; the location of property lines; and the exact square footage or acreage of the property. As part of any written offer to purchase a property, the Company strongly recommends that the Buyer engage the services of appropriate professionals to conduct inspections, investigations, tests, surveys, and other evaluations of the Property at the Buyer's expense. If the Buyer fails to do so, the Buyer is acting contrary to the advice of the Company.

Page 1 of 2   Buyer's Initials [   ]   Date _____

7. **DISPUTE RESOLUTION.** The parties agree that any dispute related to this Non-Exclusive Buyer-Broker Agreement, arising prior to or after the acquisition of a property, shall first be submitted to mediation through a mediation provider mutually agreed upon by the Buyer and the Company. Each party agrees to bear its own costs of mediation. If mediation fails, the other remedies available under this Buyer-Broker Agreement shall apply.

8. **ATTORNEY FEES/GOVERNING LAW.** Except as provided in Section 7, in case of the employment of an attorney in any matter arising out of this Non-Exclusive Buyer-Broker Agreement, the prevailing party shall be entitled to receive from the other party all costs and attorney fees, whether the matter is resolved through court action or otherwise. If, through no fault of the Company, any litigation arises out of the Buyer's employment of the Company under this Non-Exclusive Buyer-Broker Agreement (whether before or after the acquisition of a property), the Buyer agrees to indemnify the Company and the Buyer's Agent from all costs and attorney fees incurred by the Company and/or the Buyer's Agent in pursuing and/or defending such action. This Non-Exclusive Buyer Broker Agreement shall be governed and construed in accordance with the laws of the state of Utah.

9. **BUYER AUTHORIZATIONS.** The Buyer authorizes the Company and/or Buyer's Agent to: (a) Disclose after Closing to each MLS in which the Company participates (consistent with the requirements of each such MLS), the final terms and sales price of the property acquired by Buyer under the terms of this Non-Exclusive Buyer-Broker Agreement; and (b) Communicate with the Buyer for the purpose of soliciting real estate related goods and services during and after the term of this Non-Exclusive Buyer-Broker Agreement. The Buyer further agrees that in any transaction for the acquisition of any property, the Earnest Money Deposit may be placed into an interest-bearing trust account with interest paid to the Utah Association of Realtors® Housing Opportunity Fund (UARHOF) to assist in creating affordable housing throughout the state.

10. **ATTACHMENT.** There [ ] ARE [ ] ARE NOT additional terms contained in an Addendum attached to this Non-Exclusive Buyer-Broker Agreement. If an Addendum is attached, the terms of that Addendum are incorporated into this Non-Exclusive Buyer-Broker Agreement by this reference.

11. **EQUAL HOUSING OPPORTUNITY.** The Buyer and the Company will comply with Federal, State, and local fair housing laws.

12. **ELECTRONIC TRANSMISSION & COUNTERPARTS.** Electronic transmission (including email and fax) of a signed copy of this Non-Exclusive Buyer Broker-Agreement and any addenda, and the retransmission of any signed electronic transmission, shall be the same as delivery of an original. This Non-Exclusive Buyer-Broker Agreement and any addenda may be executed in counterparts.

13. **DUE-ON-SALE.** Certain types of transactions may trigger what is commonly referred to as a "due-on-sale" clause. A "due-on-sale" clause typically states that the seller's lender or mortgagee may call the loan due and payable in full if the seller participates in certain types of transactions. These types of transactions may include, but are not limited to, transactions where: (a) The sale of the property does not result in the underlying debt being paid in full; (b) The parties enter into a seller-financed transaction; (c) A lease option agreement is entered into; or (d) Any other unauthorized transfer of title to the Property has occurred without the lender's consent. The Buyer understands that if any underlying encumbrances or mortgages on the Property contain a "due-on-sale clause," and the "due-on-sale" clause is triggered, the lender may call the entire unpaid balance of the loan immediately due.

14. **ENTIRE AGREEMENT.** This Non-Exclusive Buyer-Broker Agreement, including the Buyer Due Diligence Checklist form, contains the entire agreement between the parties relating to the subject matter of this Non-Exclusive Buyer-Broker Agreement. This Non-Exclusive Buyer-Broker Agreement shall not be modified or amended except in writing signed by the parties hereto.

15. **EFFECTIVE DATE.** This Non-Exclusive Buyer-Broker Agreement is entered into and is effective as of the date: (a) The Buyer and the authorized Buyer's Agent or Broker have signed this Non-Exclusive Buyer-Broker Agreement; and (b) The authorized Buyer's Agent has received a mutually signed copy of this Non-Exclusive Buyer-Broker Agreement (the "Effective Date").

THE UNDERSIGNED hereby accept the terms of this Non-Exclusive Buyer-Broker Agreement.

_____   _____   _____
(Buyer's Signature)   (Address/Phone)   (Date)

_____   _____   _____
(Buyer's Signature)   (Address/Phone)   (Date)

ACCEPTED by the Company

by: _____   _____
    (Signature of Authorized Buyer's Agent or Broker)   (Date)

Page 2 of 2   Buyer's Initials [   ]   Date _____

ADDENDUM TO NON-EXCLUSIVE BUYER BROKER AGREEMENT
(Subagency)

THIS IS AN ADDENDUM to the Non-Exclusive Buyer Broker Agreement entered into on the _____ day of _____, 20____, by and between _____ as Buyer and_____ as the Company (a copy of the Buyer Broker Agreement is attached hereto) regarding the property more particularly described as follows:_____ (the "Property"). To the extent any term(s) of the Addendum conflict with or modify any term(s) of the Buyer Broker Agreement, the terms of this Addendum shall control. Buyer and the Company agree as follows:

SECTIONS 2 and 5 of the Non-Exclusive Buyer Broker Agreement are hereby deleted in their entirety and are replaced with the following language:

1. BROKERAGE FEE. If, during the Initial Term, or any extension of the Initial Term, the Buyer, or any other person acting in the Buyer's behalf, acquires an interest in any real property on which: (a) the Buyer's Agent; (b) the Principal/Branch Broker for the Company (the "Broker"); or (c) another real estate agent affiliated with the Company (appointed to represent the Buyer as provided in Section 2 below as an "Affiliate") negotiates a transaction on the Buyer's behalf, the Buyer agrees to pay to the Company a brokerage fee in the amount of $_____ or _____% of the acquisition price of the property. If the Property acquired by the Buyer is listed with a brokerage, the selling commission paid to the Company by the listing brokerage shall satisfy the Buyer's obligation for the brokerage fee show above provided that the brokerage fee is not less that the amount shown above. If the brokerage fee is less than the amount shown above, Buyer will pay the difference at closing. If the property is not listed with a brokerage, in the absence of a commission agreement with the owner of the selected property, the brokerage fee shown above shall be paid by the Buyer. Unless otherwise agreed to in writing by the Buyer and the Company, the brokerage fee shown above shall be due and payable on: (i) if a purchase, the date of recording of the closing documents; (ii) if a lease, the effective date of the lease, or (iii) if an option, the date the option agreement is signed. If the transaction is prevented by default of Buyer, the compensation shall be immediately payable to the Company.

2. AGENCY RELATIONSHIPS. By signing this Non-Exclusive Buyer-Broker Agreement, the Buyer designates the Buyer's Agent, the Principal/Branch Broker for the Company (the "Broker"), and every real estate agent affiliated with the Company (the "Affiliates") as agents for the Buyer to locate properties for the Buyer's consideration and review. As agents for the Buyer, the Buyer's Agent, the Broker, and the Affiliates, have fiduciary duties to the Buyer that include loyalty, full disclosure, confidentiality, and reasonable care. If the property the Buyer desires to acquire is listed with another brokerage, or is listed as "For Sale By Owner", then the Buyer's Agent, the Broker and each of the Affiliates will continue to represent the Buyer. However, if the property that the Buyer desires to acquire is listed with the Company, then the Buyer's Agent, the Broker, and each of the Affiliates, will, as a practical matter, be representing both the Buyer and the seller in the same transaction. Representing a buyer and seller in the same transaction is referred to as "Limited Agency". A Limited Agent has fiduciary duties to both the buyer and the seller. However, those duties are "limited" because the Limited Agent cannot provide to both parties undivided loyalty, full confidentiality and full disclosure of all information known to the Limited Agent. For this reason, the Limited Agent is bound by a further duty of neutrality. Being neutral, the Limited Agent may not disclose to either party information likely to weaken the bargaining position of the other – for example, the highest price a buyer will offer, or the lowest price a seller will accept. THE BUYER IS ADVISED THAT NEITHER THE BUYER NOR THE SELLER IS REQUIRED TO ACCEPT A LIMITED AGENCY SITUATION IN THE COMPANY, AND EACH PARTY IS ENTITLED TO BE REPRESENTED BY ITS OWN AGENT. If Limited Agency is agreed to below; (a) the Buyer authorizes the Buyer's Agent, the Broker and each of the Affiliates to represent both the Buyer and the Seller as Limited Agents when the Buyer's Agent and the Broker also represent the Seller of the Property the Buyer desires to acquire; (b) the Buyer further agrees that when another agent in the Company represents the Seller, that agent will exclusively represent the Seller, the Buyer's Agent will exclusively represent the Buyer, and the Broker will act as Limited Broker. **IN EITHER EVENT, IF LIMITED AGENCY IS AGREED TO BELOW, THE BUYER AND THE SELLER WILL BE REQUIRED TO SIGN A SEPARATE LIMITED AGENCY CONSENT AGREEMENT AT THE TIME THE LIMITED AGENCY SITUATION ARISES. INITIAL APPLICABLE BOX: [   ] I AGREE TO LIMITED AGENCY; OR [   ] I DO NOT AGREE TO LIMITED AGENCY.**

ALL OTHER TERMS OF THE NON-EXCLUSIVE BUYER BROKER AGREEMENT not modified by this Addendum shall remain the same.

COMPANY / DATE   BUYER / DATE

_____/_____   _____/_____

FOR SALE BY OWNER COMMISSION AGREEMENT & AGENCY DISCLOSURE
This is a legally binding agreement. If you desire legal or tax advice, consult your attorney or tax advisor.

1. **THIS COMMISSION AGREEMENT** is entered into on this _____ day of _____, 20___, between _____ (the "Company"), including _____ (the "Agent") as the authorized agent for the Company, and _____ (the "Seller") for real property owned by Seller described as follows: _____ (the "Property").

2. **BROKERAGE FEE.** The Seller agrees to pay the Company, irrespective of agency relationship(s), as compensation for services, a Brokerage Fee in the amount of $_____ or _____% of the acquisition price of the Property, if the Seller accepts an offer from _____ (the "Buyer"), or anyone acting on the Buyer's behalf, to purchase or exchange the Property. The Seller agrees that the Brokerage Fee shall be due and payable, from the proceeds of the Seller, on the date of recording of closing documents for the purchase or exchange of the Property by the Buyer or anyone acting on the Buyer's behalf. If the sale or exchange is prevented by default of the Seller, the Brokerage Fee shall immediately be due and payable to the Company.

3. **PROTECTION PERIOD.** If within _____ months after this Commission Agreement is entered into, the Property is acquired by the Buyer, or anyone acting on the Buyer's behalf, the Seller agrees to pay the Company the Brokerage Fee stated in Section 2. The Seller agrees to exempt the Buyer upon entering into a valid listing agreement with another brokerage.

4. **SELLER WARRANTIES/DISCLOSURES.** The Seller warrants that the individuals or entity listed above as the "Seller" represents all of the record owners of the Property. The Seller warrants that it has marketable title and an established right to sell, lease, or exchange the Property. The Seller agrees to execute the necessary documents of conveyance. The Seller agrees to furnish buyer with good and marketable title, and to pay at Settlement, for a standard coverage owner's policy of title insurance for the buyer in the amount of the purchase price. The Seller agrees to fully inform the Agent regarding the Seller's knowledge of the condition of the Property. The Seller agrees to personally complete and sign a Seller's Property Condition Disclosure form.

5. **AGENCY RELATIONSHIPS.** By signing this Commission Agreement, the Seller acknowledges and agrees that the Agent and the Principal/Branch Broker for the Company (the "Broker") are representing the Buyer. As the Buyer's Agent, they will act consistent with their fiduciary duties to the Buyer of loyalty, full disclosure, confidentiality, and reasonable care. The Seller acknowledges that the Company and the Agent have advised the Seller that the Seller is entitled to be represented by a real estate agent that will represent the Seller exclusively. The Seller has however, elected not to be represented by a real estate agent in this transaction. The Seller further acknowledges and agrees that all actions of the Company and the Agent, even those that assist the Seller in performing or completing any of the Seller's contractual or legal obligations, are intended for the benefit of the Buyer exclusively. This Commission Agreement does not require the Company or the Agent to solicit offers on the Property from the Buyer, nor does it authorize the Company or the Agent to solicit offers from any other person or entity.

6. **PROFESSIONAL ADVICE.** The Company and the Agent are trained in the marketing of real estate. Neither the Company, nor the Agent are trained to provide the Seller or any prospective buyer with legal or tax advice, or with technical advice regarding the physical condition of the Property. If the Seller desires advice regarding: (i) past or present compliance with zoning and building code requirements; (ii) legal or tax matters; (iii) the physical condition of the Property; (iv) this Commission Agreement; or (v) any transaction for the acquisition of the Property, the Agent and the Company STRONGLY RECOMMEND THAT THE SELLER OBTAIN SUCH INDEPENDENT ADVICE. IF THE SELLER FAILS TO DO SO, THE SELLER IS ACTING CONTRARY TO THE ADVICE OF THE COMPANY.

7. **DISPUTE RESOLUTION.** The parties agree that any dispute, arising prior to or after a closing related to this Commission Agreement, shall first be submitted to mediation through a mediation provider mutually agreed upon by the parties. If the parties cannot agree upon a mediation provider, the dispute shall be submitted to the American Arbitration Association. Each party agrees to bear its own costs of mediation. If mediation fails, the other procedures and remedies available under this Agreement shall apply.

8. **ATTORNEY FEES.** Except as provided in Section 7, in any action or proceeding arising out of this Commission Agreement involving the Seller and/or the Company, the prevailing party shall be entitled to reasonable attorney fees and costs.

9. **SELLER AUTHORIZATIONS.** The Company is authorized to disclose after closing the final terms and sales price of the Property to the following Multiple Listing Service: _____.

10. **ATTACHMENT.** There [ ] ARE [ ] ARE NOT additional terms to this Commission Agreement. If "yes", see Addendum ____ incorporated into this Commission Agreement by this reference.

11. **EQUAL HOUSING OPPORTUNITY.** Seller and the Company agree to comply with Federal, State, and local fair housing laws.

12. **FAXES.** Facsimile (fax) transmission of a signed copy of this Commission Agreement, and retransmission of a signed fax, shall be the same as delivery of an original. If this transaction involves multiple owners this Commission Agreement may be executed in counterparts.

13. **ENTIRE AGREEMENT.** This Commission Agreement, including the Seller's Property Condition Disclosure form, contain the entire agreement between the parties relating to the subject matter of this Commission Agreement. This Commission Agreement may not be modified or amended except in writing signed by the parties hereto.

THE UNDERSIGNED do hereby agree to the terms of this Commission Agreement as of the date first above written.

The Company:

_____
(Seller's Signature)

By:_____ By:_____
(Authorized Agent)   (Principal/Branch Broker)

_____
(Seller's Signature)

WHITE: Broker   **CANARY**: Agent   **PINK**: Seller

115

© Stringham Schools

Brokerage Types and Affiliations

I. **Brokerage Types**

There are different variations to Brokerages and there are advantages and disadvantages to each of them. It is important to thoroughly evaluate ALL of the different types of brokerages operating in the real estate industry.

A. The real estate industry is evolving continually; it attracts some of the brightest entrepreneurs with great ideas. Technologies are always changing the way we do business. New concepts and ideas on better ways to operate are constantly being explored. Any new concept should pass this simple test:

1. Do these concepts assist the public?

2. Produce good results?

3. Is ethical and good for the public as a whole?

4. Does it lower legal risk?

5. Is it lawful?

B. Occasionally, some real estate brokerage business models have harmed the public.

II. **Training**

Real estate is a complex field that changes often. Education and training are a key elements in the success of any agent. When considering a brokerage, all agents should evaluate the training offered by the brokerage. Some brokerages will have very formal training programs while others leave it up to the agent to obtain their own training. Some will take a "sink or swim" approach which can be very harmful to the agent and the client. Market conditions change, procedures change, new disclosure forms, and contracts are created to address new conditions.

III. **Your Value as a Real Estate Practitioner**

It is wise to invest in your ongoing education throughout your career. Outside of your brokerage there are many good programs and designations that are offered. Many of them will assist you in specializing in the different fields of real estate.

IV. **Compensation**

Compensation plans or commission schedules vary from company to company. Some will follow a traditional module of paying a certain percentage of the gross commission to the associate. Others are fee based, like a monthly fee and/or a transaction fee paid by the associate to the broker. Commission amounts are negotiable and are agreed upon between the broker and the principal (client).

A. **Independent Broker:**

1. Brokers who choose to NOT affiliate with any real estate franchise. These brokerage vary in size from one to two agents to multiple offices with hundred of agents. There could be more flexibility to customize a business model that the principal broker wishes to implement without having to follow the policies of a franchiser.

2. May also be considered by those who choose to work as a smaller organization. Typically the principal broker acts also as a listing agent and works with his/her own buyer-clients. This simplifies the process of selling property for the principal broker. More time and effort can be given to clients rather than to the managing of sales agents and office staff.

B. **Real Estate Franchises**:

Like other businesses the real estate industry also has franchises. The philosophies of these franchises vary greatly. It would be prudent for any agent to thoroughly investigate not just the benefits but the costs and fees associated with these franchises. The benefits are usually gained from the larger efforts of the franchiser. Agents and broker may take advantage of training as well as services for the clients that have already been designed and created. To put it simply every agent should ask themselves, "Do the benefits gained justify the expense?"

C. **Brokerage with Sales Associates**:

A principal broker may choose a business model that includes the recruiting, training, and support of sales associates. These brokerages sometimes grow to the point of requiring branch offices. Branch offices must be managed by an associate broker. The public may benefit from the large number of agents that know and understand and have client buyers. Marketing may be more cost effective when large groups of agents pool together.

D. **Cooperating Broker or MLS**:

Once licensed, an agent usually chooses to join the local MLS. The benefits from joining are many. The MLS provides access to data from current available property and the history of those that have sold. This information is essential for any real estate agent. Other benefits are: access to current, updated, and approved contracts; addenda and clauses; and training and networking. MLS's are entities that focus on technologies that bring information and   services to agents and brokers.

E. **Buyer Broker**:

A true buyer broker would be a principal broker who works and represents only buyers. The benefit for the public is their buyer broker will not be spending any time on marketing listings. Limited agency never happens with buyer brokers because they never have listing agreements.

F. **Referral Companies or 'Off Board Brokerages'**:

These Brokerages are designed to house agents that do not wish to be a part of the local REALTOR® Board. Typically these agents wish to avoid paying any fees. Agents in these brokerages may still operate as any other active real estate agent, but without the benefits or the services and information of the Board of REALTORS®. Many of these 'off board' agents choose to refer contacts, clients, or leads to agents in other brokerages. It should be noted that:

1. All agents in 'off board' brokerages must be off board.

2. Agents may not be entitled to commission offerings through the MLS by board brokers.

3. 3.Like any sales agent, agents must have a principal broker.

G. **Specialty Brokerages**:

There are many different types of properties and transactions in the vast world of real estate. Some companies have chosen to specialize in these different sub-markets.

1. Resort property: beach rentals, ski rentals, and sales.

2. Recreation property: mountain cabins

3. New construction: residential subdivisions

4. Condominium projects: urban living; high rises

5. Income property/ investment: investor oriented, multi- family, commercial

6. Residential leasing

7. Commercial leasing

8. Land development

9. Property management

V. **Brokerage Policies**

   A. Each Brokerage should have a comprehensive Policies and Procedures Manual. In these policies should contain information about what is expected and how the licensees are to work with different issues related to their business. Because the nature of the brokerage business is to profit from the collective revenue generated by the sales of licensees, it would be prudent to review the policies and procedures of any brokerage the licensee is considering affiliating with. Policies and procedures may include but are not limited to:

     1. Use of office facility

     2. Dress code

     3. The handling of signs calls

     4. The scheduling of showings

     5. Marketing costs

     6. Licensees' statements, payments, and billing

     7. Unacceptable behavior

     8. Referring lenders, loan officers, title companies, and home inspectors.

     9. Required documentation for each file in order to be paid a commission.

     10. All policies should be in line with State rules, such as providing copies of documents to the client.

     11. Brokerage should have procedures that verify rules and policies are complied with.

VI. **Real Estate Associations**

Associations provide a very valuable organization that protects the public by creating "Standards of Practice: and a "Code of Ethics" for all members to practice by. They also are a strong lobby group that seeks to protect property rights.

   A. **"The NATIONAL ASSOCIATION OF REALTORS®,** 'The Voice for Real Estate,' is America's largest trade association, representing 1.3 million members. Nar's 1 million members, including NAR's institutes, societies and councils are involved in all aspects of the residential and commercial real estate industries." – realtor.org/about-nar/

NAR's Mission and Vision:

Mission

"The core purpose of the NATIONAL ASSOCIATION OF REALTOR® is to help its members become more profitable and successful." – realtor.org/about-nar/mission-vision-and-history

Vision

"The NATIONAL ASSOCIATION OF REALTORS® strives to be the collective force influencing and shaping the real estate industry. It seeks to be the leading advocate of the right to own, use, and transfer real property; the acknowledged leader in developing standards for efficient, effective, and ethical real estate business practices; and valued by highly skilled real estate professionals and viewed by them as crucial to their success.

Working on behalf of America's property owners, the NATIONAL ASSOCIATION OF REALTORS® provides a facility for professional development, research and exchange of information among its members and to the public and government for the purpose of preserving the free enterprise system, and the right to own, use, and transfer real property."

–realtor.org/about-nar/mission-vision-and-history

B.   **UTAH ASSOCIATION OF REALTORS® ("UAR")**:

UAR Mission Statement

"The purpose of the Utah Association of REALTORS® is to serve its members and represent all facets of the real estate industry by providing programs and services to enhance members' freedom and ability to conduct successful business with integrity and competency and by using collective action to promote the preservation and extension of the right to own, transfer and use real property."

– utahrealtors.com/news-center/media-center/

Brokerage Types and Affiliations Terms to Know

- ☐ Buyer Broker
- ☐ Cooperating Broker
- ☐ Franchise
- ☐ Independent Broker
- ☐ Multiple Listing Service (MLS)
- ☐ National Association of REALTORS® (NAR)
- ☐ Referral Companies
- ☐ Utah Association of REALTORS® (UAR)

Brokerage Types and Affiliations Quiz

1. The compensation plans for Real Estate Agents can vary from company to company.

    A. True

    B. False

2. Specialty Brokerages might be all of the following EXCEPT:

    A. Property Management Company

    B. Land Development Company

    C. Commercial or Residential Leasing Company

    D. Referral Company

3. Brokers are responsible to insure that their agents record the necessary documents and file them accurately.

    A. True

    B. False

4. Brokerages Policies and Procedures have to be written according to the rules governed by the Utah Association of REALTORS®.

    A. True

    B. False

ANSWERS TO THIS QUIZ ARE FOUND IN THE "QUIZ ANSWERS" SECTION.

SEE TABLE OF CONTENTS

Minimum Service Requirements

I. **Minimum Service Requirements**

In 2005, the State of Utah, along with many other states, adopted minimum service requirements for real estate brokers and agents. These requirements were necessary to ensure that the public would not be left alone to address sensitive situations such as contractual offers and counter-offers. A small percentage of sellers selected brokerages that offered reduced services. The fees for listing a property were dramatically lower and, therefore, attractive to sellers. The results were not all positive. Many sellers became frustrated over the lack of assistance in dealing with the offer process and the many forms needed to complete transactions. Although many brokerages clearly disclosed this, it seems the public assumed that if they listed their property with a brokerage and agent, that certain standards would apply. Complaints against these agents and Brokerages resulted. The solution was to create a law requiring a minimum level of service that brokers and agents must perform.

Utah Code Annotated § 61-2f-308(2)(a):

A. "(2) (a) Except as provided in Subsection (2)(b), a principal broker subject to an exclusive brokerage agreement shall:

1. (i) accept delivery of and present to the client offers and counteroffers to buy, lease, or exchange the client's property;

2. (ii) assist the client in developing, communicating, and presenting offers, counteroffers, and notices; and

3. (iii) answer any question the client has concerning:

    a. (A) an offer;

    b. (B) a counteroffer;

    c. (C) a notice; and

    d. (D) a contingency.

B. (b) A principal broker subject to an exclusive brokerage agreement need not comply with Subsection (2)(a) after:

1. (i) (A) an agreement for the sale, lease, or exchange of the real estate, option on real estate, or improvement on real estate is signed;

2. (B) the contingencies related to the sale, lease, or exchange are satisfied or waived; and

3. (C) the sale, lease, or exchange is closed; or

4. (ii) the exclusive brokerage agreement expires or terminates.

C. (3) A principal broker who violates this section is subject to Section 61-2f-404 and 61-2f-405."

D. What should you do?

Rather than focus your business on the minimum service required, focus on what you can do above the minimum. How many businesses have been able to sustain success by only providing the minimum of service? Customers always remember what their agent did on their behalf, especially when it was above and beyond their expectation.

1. Thoroughly educate clients on offers and counter-offers by counseling with them about their options.

2. Be readily available to answer questions and keep clients updated.

3. Anticipate clients' concerns and be prepared to address them.

4. Understand ALL of the UAR and State approved forms used in the transactional process.

5. Provide a high level of service that you and your clients both deserve.

II. Additional Requirements

A. Settlement

Under state law, the broker and agent must review the Closing Disclosure to confirm its accuracy and to verify that it contains ALL of the monies related to the transaction.

1. Utah Administrative Code R162-2f-401c(1)(c)(i)(A)-(C): The principal broker is responsible for the content and accuracy of all closing statements regardless of who closes the transaction.

B. When verifying the accuracy of the settlement, review the offer (REPC), all addenda and any brokerage proceeds disclosures. Pay close attention to the following:

1. Sales price

2. Closing costs (paid by seller or buyer)

3. Home warranty costs

4. Earnest money deposit amount

5. Pre-paid fees

6. Rental deposits and rent proration

7. If a short sale, verify that the third party has agreed to allow payoffs for all liens.

C. Title companies work to gather information on the current balances on liens, such as first and second mortgage and home equity loans. Encourage the seller to verify these amounts and balances.

D. More Settlement Responsibilities:

The agent should work to communicate the parties intentions in regards to the occupancy. Agents should never allow a buyer access to property without the seller's permission. Does the Real Estate Purchase Contract ("REPC") indicate an agreement for occupancy? Does this still reflect the party's intentions? If not, a REPC addendum may be used to create, or change the occupancy agreement only as it relates to the language in section 4 of the REPC. NOTE: Use a separate lease agreement for extended time frames.

E.   Disclose all Material Defects:

Agents must disclose all physical defects in the property regardless of instructions from the seller. Pay close attention to those defects that are not clearly noticeable. (Note Section 10.2 of the REPC.) Encourage sellers to be honest and accurate when filling out the "Seller's Property Condition Disclosure." If conditions change during the listing period or while the transaction is under contract, instruct the seller to update the disclosure.

F.   Material Information must be disclosed:

Material Information is described as information that a buyer would want to know and should know. Information that may affect the outcome of the transaction or affect the seller/buyers ability to perform.

G.   Disclose Agency Rule: [Utah Administrative Code R162-2f-401a(8)]

1.   R162-2f-401a(2): A principal broker and a licensee acting on the principal broker's behalf who represent a seller shall have a written agency agreement with the seller defining the scope of the agency.

2.   Brokers and agents are required to disclose agency in writing. The UAR has created forms to help facilitate this requirement.

3.   The UAR has created forms to help facilitate agency disclosure.

   a.   Buyer Broker Agreement

   b.   Listing Agreement

   c.   Unrepresented Buyer Disclosure

   d.   Limited Agency Consent Form

H.   Disclose Relationships: [Utah Administrative Code R162-2f-401a(5)(c)]

Relationships such as: a relative, a past or current business relationship, ownership interest in any entity selling or purchasing property, owner or principal. If you question whether or not a relationship should be disclosed ask yourself if you were the seller/buyer would you want to know? Or do you think seller or buyer would want to know?

1.   Disclosure of Interest Addendum to the REPC.

III.   **Agency Disclosure Requirements**

A.   Explaining Agency to the Public: It is important for buyers and seller to understand who the agent or broker represents.

1.   At the first opportune moment every agent must disclose his or her agency relationship. R162-2f-401a(8). If they represent the seller they must disclose this verbally as soon as it is appropriate. If a buyer begins to ask questions about the price you should not answer until you have disclosed and discussed agency.

2.   In the beginning, the best way to educate the public on the differences in agency is to verbalize the definitions found on the agency disclosure form that is entitled "Unrepresented Purchaser." It is not necessary to have every party we come in contact with

sign an agency disclosure form, however, when the relationship or buying process elevates, it becomes required to obtain written disclosure. R162-2f-401a(2).

3.   It is important for agents to remember that R162-2f-401a(5)(c) requires a written agency disclosure prior to the buyer and seller entering into any binding contracts. Although such a disclosure is required before contracts are entered into, it is wise to discuss agency well before the offer process.

B.   Agency Options:

1.   Open House: You are showing the property to a potential buyer. First of all, as soon as there is a moment in the conversation you should introduce yourself as the seller's agent. Perhaps later on you will be able to go into more detail about what that means and answer any questions that they may have. If you are currently a seller's agent (listing agent) you may:

a.   Continue to represent the seller as long as you disclose this in writing (Use the Unrepresented Purchaser Disclosure form) AND you disclose and educate the buyer that they may choose to have their own representation.

b.   Enter into a Buyer Broker Agreement with the buyer and have both the seller and the buyer sign a Limited Agency Consent form. The seller should have preauthorized limited agency in the Listing Agreement then will have to re-agree in writing on the Limited Agency Consent form.

2.   In-House Sale:

a.   When an Agent within the same brokerage finds a buyer for a listing offered by their own brokerage, we refer to this as an "in-house sale." Additional levels of confidentiality and disclosure are required in these situations.

b.   Keep information that could weaken the client's ability to negotiate confidential.

c.   Complete the Limited Agency Consent form. Within a designated agency brokerage, the listing agent can continue to represent the seller, and the buyer's agent can continue to represent the buyer. The broker would be a limited agent.

C.   Educate the Public: When it becomes time to discuss agency options, agents must always educate the public on what their options are.

1.   Everyone has the right to hire their own agent to represent them. This may come at the expense of the buyer if it is determined that the new agent is not entitled to the commission offered by the listing broker through the MLS. Nevertheless, the buyer could choose to compensate the agent themselves.

2.   The buyer could choose to enter a "Buyer-Broker Agreement" and cause the listing agent to become a limited agent.

126

3.   The buyer could choose to simply have the listing agent continue to represent the seller and the buyer remain unrepresented.

Agents and brokers must educate the public on all of these agency options. It is also important to understand that although agents must disclose all options, the agent is not forced into limited agency or forced to agree to a Buyer-Broker Agreement.

APPROXIMATE SELLER'S PROCEEDS

Seller's Name(s): _____

Property Address:_____

Presented by: _____

Selling Price: $ _____

LESS-THE FOLLOWING REDUCTIONS:

Commission	$_____
First Mortgage Pay=off = Last Month's Interest	$_____
If FHA, Interest for Month of Closing	$_____
Second Mortgage Pay-off + Last Month's Interest	$_____
Lender Charges:	
Discount Points	$_____
Termite Inspection	$_____
Document Preparation	$_____
Tax Service Fee	$_____
Other Agreed-to costs	$_____
Title Charges:	
Escrow Closing Fee	$_____
Title Insurance Policy	$_____
Document Preparation	$_____
Express mail/Wire Fee	$_____
Reconveyance Fee	$_____
Special Recording Fees	$_____
(power of Attonery, certificate, Ect.)	
IRS Reporting Fee	$_____
Miscellaneous	$_____
Year-to-date Property Taxes	$_____
Home Warranty	$_____
Attorney's Fees	$_____
Tax Lien/Judgment Pay-offs	$_____
Final Utility Billing (Water/sewer)	$_____

TOTAL REDUCTIONS:	$_____	$_____
APPROXIMATE SELLER PROCEEDS	$_____	$_____

Minimum Service Requirements Quiz

1. When first discussing agency it is best to verbalize the language from what form?

    A. The Buyer Broker agreement

    B. Listing Agreement

    C. The Agency Open House Disclosure

    D. The Unrepresented Purchaser

2. Which of the follow is NOT required of a broker?

    A. To list the property on the local MLS

    B. To accept the delivery of an offer

    C. To assist in the completion of a counter offer

    D. To verify accuracy of the Closing Disclosure

3. Which forms are required when the agent is representing both parties in the transaction?

    A. Buyer Broker Agreement and Listing Agreement

    B. Limited Agency Disclosure

    C. Agency Disclosure

    D. Listing Agreement, Buyer Broker Agreement and Limited Agency Consent.

4. What things must an agent do when dealing with offers?

    A. Develop the offer

    B. Communicate the offer

    C. Present the offer

    D. All of the above

5. What year did the State of Utah adopt minimum service requirements?

    A. 2004

    B. 2005

    C. 2006

    D. 2007

ANSWERS TO THIS QUIZ ARE FOUND IN THE "QUIZ ANSWERS" SECTION.

SEE TABLE OF CONTENTS

CONTRACT LAW

CONTRACTS 1

CONTRACTS 2

ADVANCED CONTRACT LAW

LISTINGS & OPTIONS

NEW CONSTRUCTION CONTRACT

PROPERTY MANAGEMENT CONTRACT

REAL ESTATE FORMS 1

REAL ESTATE FORMS 2

SHORT SALE FORMS

Contract Law 1

I. **Definition of a Contract**

A legally enforceable agreement between parties who agree to perform or refrain from performing certain acts.

II. **Legal Terms & Types of Contracts**

A. **Express Contract:** A contract created by the words, oral or written, of the contracting parties.

B. **Implied Contract**: These contracts are created by the actions of the parties.

C. **Execution**: This refers to the placing of the signatures, thus putting the contract into effect. A person who signs a document is a signatory to the document.

D. **Executory**: The terms of an executory contract are not yet fully performed. The contract is in process of being carried out, and the contract is not in default.

E. **Executed**: The terms of an executed contract have been fully performed.

F. **Note**: A contract may be a executed by one party but still be a executory by the other party.

III. **Unilateral or Bilateral Contracts**

A. **Bilateral**: The exchange of a promise for a promise. Examples:

1. Real Estate Purchase Contract

2. Promissory Note

B. **Unilateral**: The exchange of a promise for a performance. Examples:

1. Reward poster

2. Employment agreement between a principal broker and a sales agent or associate broker.

3. An option contract for the purchase of real estate, until it is exercise

C. The difference between the two is that in a bilateral contract, the parties around bound to perform on the promises made. In a unilateral contract, The offeror of the promise is not bound to perform unless the offeree actually performs; and the offeree is not bound to perform whatsoever.

IV. **Essential Elements of a Contract**

A. **Mutual Assent**: The parties have come to a meeting of the minds.

1. Mutual assent occurs when there is an **offer** and **acceptance**.

2. An offer can be withdrawn any time prior to acceptance unless the offeree gives consideration to keep the offer open and alive; usually until an agreed upon deadline. If consideration is given to keep an offer open, this is called an option.

3. An offeree has three choices. The offer can be accepted, rejected, or a counter offer can be made. When a counter offer is made, the original offer is automatically rejected and the offeree then becomes the offeror in presentation of a new offer.

a. In the real estate profession, an addendum must be used for a counter offer or for any changes or additions to a contract. See R162-2f-401a(17)(a)(i)(A).

b. Lining out or whiting out preprinted provisions, or those previously entered in blank spaces is not allowed. R162-2f-401b(16).

4. Acceptance is usually governed by the contract. For instance, the Utah Real Estate Purchase Contract states that acceptance occurs only when the contract is signed to indicate acceptance and the agent or the client communicate that acceptance to the other party. However, if the contract is silent on how acceptance occurs, the courts will generally hold that acceptance occurs when a party manifests their intention (verbally or by conduct) to be bound to the contract.

B. **Consideration**: Each party must incur a legal detriment and/or receive a benefit. However, the exchange of consideration does not have to be of equal value.

1. **Valuable Consideration**: Includes money, real or personal property, services, or promises to act or not act.

2. **Good Consideration**: This includes love and affection, loyalty, friendship, et

a. Good consideration usually does not constitute sufficient consideration to bind a contract if it is not accompanied by valuable consideration.

b. The court typically feels that terms of a contract cannot give rise to love, et Therefore, the consideration is said to have pre-existed the contract and does not qualify as a sacrifice.

3. In order to conceal the actual amount of consideration involved in a contract, especially when the contract is being made public by recording, the phrase "$10 and other good & valuable consideration" is often use

C. **Capacity** or **Competency**: The premise is that each party is able to understand the terms of the contract and make a rational decision as to whether or not entering into it is desirable. Do the following have capacity or competency?

1. **Illiterate persons**: Yes, the contract can be read and explained to them and they can make their "mark" and have it witnessed or acknowledge

2. An **insane person**: No. To be insane, one must be declared so by the court. To become sane again also requires a declaration of the court.

3. An **alien**: Yes, except for an enemy alien or illegal alien.

4. A **deceased person**: They must be represented by an executor or an administrator.

D. **Legal Purpose**: This element protects the public from the contracting parties. All contracts must be in agreement with public policy or law. If the subject matter of a contract is unlawful, a court may either strike down the entire agreement or strike only the part(s) of the contract that exceeds legal boundaries. Examples of contracts which violate public policy:

1. A contract to lend and borrow money at an interest rate that exceeds the legally allowed interest rate. Charging such outrageous interest rates is called usury.

2. A listing contract to pay a commission to an unlicensed person.

3. A lease for a building to be used as an illegal gambling casino or selling drugs.

V. **Enforceability**

A. **Valid**: The contract contains all the essential elements of a contract and is binding on all parties.

B. **Void**: One or more of the essential elements are missing, and the contract is binding on none of the parties.

C. **Voidable**: One of the parties can challenge one or more of the essential elements and choose to affirm or disaffirm the contract. Four major items that create voidable contracts are:

1. **Duress**: The use of force or improper actions against a person to induce the party to enter into a contract.

2. **Menace**: The threat of duress.

3. **Undue influence**: Occurs when a person in a fiduciary capacity or in a position of authority misuses the trust or power to unfairly induce a party to enter into a contract.

4. **Lack of competency**: A contract entered into by a minor is one example.

D. **Unenforceable**: An unenforceable contract is one that may be a valid, but the court will not entertain disputes arising out of these agreements. Examples:

1. Oral contracts which fall under the statute of frauds.

2. Contracts barred by bankruptcy.

3. Contracts barred by the statute of limitations.

Contract Law 1 Terms to Know

- ☐ Bilateral Contract
- ☐ Communication
- ☐ Competency or Capacity
- ☐ Consideration
- ☐ Contract
- ☐ Counter Offer
- ☐ Duress or Undue Influence
- ☐ Enforceability
- ☐ Execute
- ☐ Executed Contract
- ☐ Executory Contract
- ☐ Good Consideration
- ☐ Legal Purpose
- ☐ Mutual Agreement
- ☐ Tender
- ☐ Valid Contract
- ☐ Valuable Consideration
- ☐ Void Contract
- ☐ Voidable Contract

Contract Law 1 Quiz

1.   Which of the following is NOT required for a contract to be valid?

    A. All parties agree to the contract

    B. All parties are competent

    C. All parties have a lawyer

    D. All parties have given consideration

2.   Jester offers orally to sell his office building to Sadier. Sadier accepts by handing Jester the full price of $250,000 in cash. Jester takes the money.

    A. This is a void contract.

    B. This is a voidable contract.

    C. Since there was nothing in writing, Jester can keep the money, declaring it to be a gift.

    D. This is an unenforceable contract.

3.   Mr. McDoddle agrees to lend Mr. Patriot $25,000 at 23% interest. After the contract is signed, Mr. Patriot learns that the legal limit on interest, as established by the state legislature, is 21%. This contract would now be considered:

    A. Void, because it lacked legal purpose.

    B. Void, because it lacked consideration.

    C. Void, because it is valid, but unenforceable.

    D. Valid

4.   A contract wherein each of the parties promise to do something would be a(n):

    A. Bilateral contract

    B. Unilateral contract

    C. Unenforceable Contract

    D. Voidable Contract

5.   When an offer is presented, the offeror can withdraw the offer:

    A. After the time extended to the offeree has expire

    B. Any time before acceptance of the offer, with the permission of the offeree.

    C. Any time prior to the acceptance

    D. Any time before the offeror actually receives the offer.

6.   A contract that is not fully performed, but it is not in default would be considered:

    A. Executed

    B. Executory

    C. Implied

    D. Contingent

7.   The use of duress, menace, or undue influence can cause a contract to be:

    A. Unenforceable

    B. Voidable

    C. Bilateral

    D. Unilateral

ANSWERS TO THIS QUIZ ARE FOUND IN THE "QUIZ ANSWERS" SECTION.

SEE TABLE OF CONTENTS

Contract Law 2

I. **Statute of Frauds**

    A.   Definition: Under the Statute of Frauds, certain contracts must be in writing to be enforceable included among them are:

        1.   Any contract for the purchase or sale of real estate.

        2.   Lease agreements that extend beyond one year.

        3.   Commission agreements between a real estate broker and the principal.

        4.   Any contract for the purchase or sale of personal property for more than $500.

        5.   Any contract that takes longer than one year to perform.

        6.   All changes to a contract governed by the Statute of Frauds must also be in writing.

    Every state treats real estate contracts differently under the State of Frauds. Generally, if a contract violates the Statute of Frauds, it is rendered unenforceable. In Utah, however, a contract that violates the statute is deemed void under the law. U.C.A. § 25-5 et seq.

    B.   The purpose of the Statute of Frauds is to prevent fraud.

    C.   The Statute of Frauds does not have anything to do with determining what fraud is or its respective penalties.

    D.   The **Parol Evidence Rule** states that testimony or other evidence that seek to modify the subject matter of a written contract will be inadmissible. In other words, when a written contract exists, all oral agreements concerning its subject matter, before or after the writing, have no legal significance in the eyes of the court. (However, this rule has some narrow exceptions.)

    E.   A real estate agent can modify a contract only when authorized in writing (Power of Attorney) by both parties to do so.

II. **Court Action**

    Terms are associated with court actions:

    A.   **Lis Pendens**: Is a required filing of constructive (public) notice that a legal action is pending on a property. Though property can be sold while a lis pendens is in place, the buyer accepts the property subject to the court action.

    B.   **Judgment**: The formal decision of the court in a legal action or suit.

    C.   **Attachment**: The legal process of seizing real or personal property of a defendant in a law suit by levy or judicial order, and holding it in the custody of the court as security for satisfaction of a judgment. An attachment creates a lien against a property before a case is resolved so the plaintiff is assured there will be property left to satisfy the judgment should the plaintiff win the case.

    D.   **Writ of Execution**: A court order directing an officer of the court to sell property of the defendant to satisfy a judgment.

III.   **Important Clauses**

    A.   **Contingency Clauses**: These clauses are known as "subject to" clauses.   They allow the parties to limit their liability if certain events occur or fail to occur and provide sufficient flexibility to accurately express their true intent. Contingency clauses must specify the contingency with definiteness and clarity so a reasonable person will know precisely what is expected. To make sure that happens, the Real Estate. Division has approved language for the most commonly used contingencies, referred to as the Standard Contingency Clauses, which are found in the Real Estate Forms chapter of this text. These clauses should be used word for word, thereby avoiding much potential liability that comes from drafting your own clauses. There should be a date indicated for performance. If the date is not met, the contingency may be automatically eliminated. For example:

        1.   This offer is subject to the buyer obtaining financing . . .

        2.   This offer is subject to a property inspection . . .

        3.   This offer is subject to the appraisal being at or above . . .

        4.   This offer is subject to approval by . . . (usually a wife, husband, or partner).

    B.   **"As Is" clause**: This clause usually refers to the buyer accepting the property in its present condition. However, that condition is "as it has been represented by the seller." If conditions have been hidden, the seller will be liable.

    C.   **"Time is of the Essence" clause**: This does not mean that everyone is to do things as quickly as they can. It means that all dates in the contract are firm; that a failure to adhere to a certain deadline constitutes a material breach of contract and will render the contract voidable by the non-breaching party.

    D.   **Abrogation**: The final documents executed at the closing abrogate, or nullify, the Real Estate Purchase Contract, except for the provisions that the parties specifically agree to extend beyond the closing date. It's a good idea to ask your client, "What requirements need to survive the closing?"

    E.   **Implied Covenant of Good Faith and Fair Dealin**g: This clause is not written into the contract but is implied into it by the law. The covenant requires that the parties to a contract do not do anything that obstructs or impedes the other party's ability to perform their obligations. Essentially, once a contract is made, the parties must be allowed to perform their duties without interference from each other.

IV.   **Types of Fraud**

    A.   **Intentional fraud**: The guilty person acted willfully with full intent to commit fraud. He intentionally misrepresented or used deception in order to induce someone to give up something of value. The penalties for intentional fraud include the awarding of damages or money, fines, and even imprisonment. There are two forms of intentional fraud:

        1.   **Positive**: Overt or deliberate misrepresentation. The guilty person openly and willfully lied or in other direct ways misrepresented the facts. For instance, a seller who has a basement that leaks during the rainy season, paints the basement to cover up all water

marks. When asked, the seller states that the basement does not leak.

   2. **Negative or Passive**: Covert, or hiding or omitting information. This differs from the example above only in the manner of deception. Using the example of the leaking basement, the buyer did not ask, therefore, the seller did not reveal the defect. The painting had done its job of deception. Even though the seller was not asked, he is just as liable for misrepresentation as if he had lied.

B. **Constructive fraud**: In this situation, the guilty party had no evil intent to misrepresent. Nevertheless, with reasonable care the fraudulent act could have been avoided. The penalty differs from intentional fraud in that fines and imprisonment cannot be levied.

C. **Puffing**: This is a gross exaggeration of opinion which is not considered misrepresentation. Example, an agent says to a buyer, "This is the most beautiful home in the city." It is easily recognized by a reasonable person as an exaggeration of opinion.

V. **Remedies for Breach of Contract**

   When a party commits a material breach of contract, there are several remedies that can be applied to benefit the harmed party.

A. **Rescission**: This is an annulment of the existing contract, sometimes expressed as a contract to end a contract. The idea is that all parties will return to their original position and it will be as though there had been no contract.

B. **Suit for damages**: The injured party is awarded a money adjustment. Because contracts contain results that the parties are expecting to occur, damages in contract law revolve around expectation damages – what was the injured party expecting? However, contract law also affords the options for reliance and restitutionary damages when the circumstances warrant them. Damages are particularly important. Even if a plaintiff can win his suit, he will not be awarded any damages or money if he cannot show actual losses. For instance, a lessee entered into a lease contract and then withdrew from the contract the next day. The day after that the lessor entered into a contract that would benefit him as much or more as the first lease. Then the lessor sued the original lessee for breach of contract. He will be able to show that the original lessee breached the contract, but will not be able to show damages and, therefore, will most likely not be awarded anything.

C. **Suit for specific performance**: The guilty party is ordered by the court to complete the contract as agreed.

D. **Liquidated damages**: In anticipation of a particular default, the default and its penalty are specifically and clearly stipulated in a liquidated damage clause in the contract. Examples:

   1. Late penalty in a loan.

   2. Penalty in a building construction contract for breaching the completion date.

   3. Forfeiting of earnest money if the buyer fails to perform on his agreement to purchase a property.

E. **Mediation**: Other options open to the parties in a dispute over a contract are mediation and arbitration. Section 15 in the Real Estate Purchase Contract deals with the issue of mediation.

F.   Other remedies may available according to the terms of the contract.

VI.   **Ways to Terminate a Contract**

    A.   **Performance** of the terms of the contract.

    B.   **Mutual release** (rescission).

    C.   **Assignment** (partial release): Most contracts are assignable, without the agreement of the other contracting party. While assignment does not terminate the whole contract, it shifts one party's contractual duties onto the assignee. Those contracts that are not assignable include, personal service or agency contracts (listings). The Real Estate Purchase Contract cannot be assigned unless the parties agree to amend the contract.

    D.   **Novation**: Substituting one obligor in place of another. This is referred to in real estate finance as a "qualified assumption." It requires the approval of "the other" contracting party and, if given, it releases the original party from further liability in the contract. Novation can also occur when the parties remain the same, but terms in the contract are changed and a new contract is created by mutual agreement.

    E.   **Impossibility of performance**: Something happens that neither party could have foreseen; and, therefore, the contract is terminated. For instance, Acton agrees in a Real Estate Purchase Contract to sell his home to Horton. Before the closing takes place, Acton's home burns down. He is no longer able to perform and the courts will order the contract declared void rather than order Acton to build a new home.

    F.   **Anticipatory repudiation**: If a party gives clear indication that they are about to breach a material provision of the contract, or otherwise refuse to perform, the "insecure" second party could terminate the contract before the breach occurs.

SUMMARY OF CONTRACT LAW

Classification of Contracts

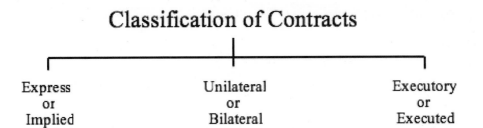

Express or Implied | Unilateral or Bilateral | Executory or Executed

Enforceability of Contracts

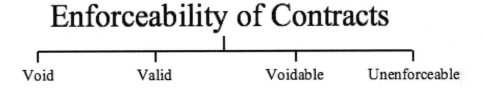

Void | Valid | Voidable | Unenforceable

Essential Elements of a Contract

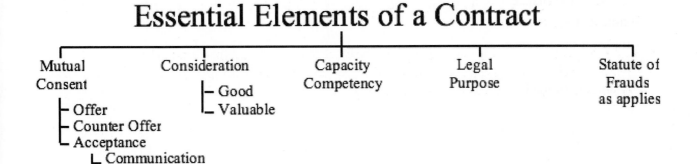

Mutual Consent | Consideration | Capacity Competency | Legal Purpose | Statute of Frauds as applies

- Good
- Valuable

- Offer
- Counter Offer
- Acceptance
  - Communication

Remedies for Breach of Contract

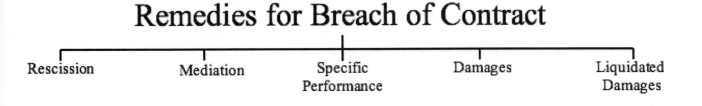

Rescission | Mediation | Specific Performance | Damages | Liquidated Damages

Terminating a Contract

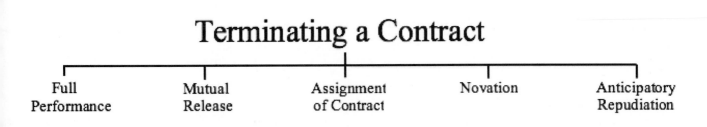

Full Performance | Mutual Release | Assignment of Contract | Novation | Anticipatory Repudiation

143

Contract Law 2 Terms to Know

- ☐ Abrogation
- ☐ "As Is" Clause
- ☐ Assignment of Contract
- ☐ Attachment
- ☐ Constructive Fraud
- ☐ Contingency Clause
- ☐ Damages
- ☐ Fraud
- ☐ Judgment
- ☐ Liquidated Damages
- ☐ Mediation
- ☐ Negative or Passive Intentional Fraud
- ☐ Novation
- ☐ Parole Evidence Rule
- ☐ Positive Intentional Fraud
- ☐ Rescission
- ☐ Specific Performance
- ☐ Statute of Frauds
- ☐ Time is of the Essence
- ☐ Undue Influence
- ☐ Unilateral Contract

Contract Law 2 Quiz

1. When Mr. Vegas, the buyer, asked Mr. Atlantic, the seller, about the condition of the basement, Mr. Atlantic replied that it was in perfect condition. All the while Mr. Atlantic knew the basement leaked when there were heavy rains. The courts would consider this an example of:

    A. Negative intentional fraud

    B. Positive intentional fraud

    C. Constructive fraud

    D. Puffing

2. If a seller is hiding defects in his property from the buyer:

    A. He will be protected by an "as is" clause.

    B. He will be protected by an "exceptions and exclusions" clause.

    C. He will be protected by a "contingency" clause.

    D. He would not be protected by any of those.

3. If a purchaser fails to complete the purchase of a property as has been agreed in a fully executed purchase agreement, he may have to forfeit the earnest money deposit because of this clause:

    A. Contingency

    B. Liquidated damages

    C. Constructive

    D. Statute of frauds

4. Mrs. Benackerly leased a property from Mrs. Castenelly for three years. During the middle of the third year, Mrs. Benackerly entered into a contract with Mr.Dippydo that he would take her place in the lease, move into the property and pay the rent for the remaining period of the lease. Though they informed Mrs. Castenelly, they didn't bother to get her approval. This would be an example of:

    A. An illegal transaction between Mrs. Benackerly and Mr. Dippydo.

    B. A simple, legal assignment of contract.

    C. A complex process of contract law known as a novation of contract.

    D. Pur autre vie.

5. The decision handed down by a court is referred to as a (an):

    A. Judgment

    B. Attachment

    C. Lis pendens

    D. Writ

Advanced Contract Law*

You should have completed Contracts 1 & 2, and Real Estate Purchase Contract A & B before taking this class

I. **Understanding Contracts**

What level of understanding of our approved contracts must a practitioner have?

A. As a licensed professional charged with safeguarding a client's interest in the transaction, the real estate agent should be well versed in the contract and able to explain its provisions with ease.

B. Agents should understand the line between explaining a contract and giving advice on the contract that affects client's rights. The latter requires a law license.

II. **Offer and Acceptance**

The party making the offer is the offeror. The party receiving the offer is the Offeree. The seller is the offeror when they counter the buyers offer.

A. **Acceptance**: Once the parties have a "meeting of the minds," the contract is formed when the offeree manifests his/her intent to be bound. The question then becomes, what does that manifestation look like?

1. If the offer is written, acceptance typically occurs when the **offeree** signs the offer in a location of the document that indicates acceptance. In some contracts, acceptance is specifically defined, which means that in order for the offeree to accept the offer, he/she must do exactly as the contract requires. Remember, the **offeror** has the power to dictate what constitutes acceptance.

2. If the offer is verbal, the above rule applies: the offeree must manifest their intent to be bound. Sometimes a verbal "acceptance" will create the contract, other times the offeree's actions will constitute acceptance.

B. In unilateral contracts, acceptance cannot occur until the performance is completed. In other words, completion of the condition constitutes acceptance, which then binds the offeror to perform on his/her promise.

C. Not reading a contract is no defense to the contract's enforcement. The law presumes the parties to know the terms of what they are agreeing to, regardless of whether they read the agreement or not.

III. **Termination of Offer**

A. **Withdrawal**: An offer can be withdrawn any time prior to its acceptance. Offers may be withdrawn in several ways, including a verbal revocation; however, the best practice in real estate is to always rescind an offer in writing.

B. **Counteroffer**: Each time a counteroffer is written, the initial offer is rejected and the counteroffer is an entirely new offer. Counteroffers should be clear and easy to understand. Even the most simple alterations or changes to an offer are still a counteroffer. When creating a counteroffer as a licensed real estate agent, it's not a good idea to change the boilerplate language of the contract. In some states, like Utah, changing boilerplate language to the Real Estate

Purchase Contract is unlawful. All counter offers should be written on an addendum.

1. When creating a counteroffer, specific and clear language is critical. While it may not be legally required to reference the contract provisions being countered, doing so creates clarity, and clarity helps mitigate problems.

2. The language of the offer itself may create a "self-destruct" provision where, if the offer is not accepted by a certain time, the offer becomes null and void. Therefore, by the offeree's inaction, the offer can be terminated. However, this applies mainly to those contracts that contain such a provision.

C. Counter Offer and Addenda Language:

1. The more complex the issue being addressed in a counteroffer or addendum, the more the real estate agent toes the line of practicing law without a license. As a result, always check to see if there's a standard supplementary clause already created and available for you to use. These supplementary clauses are typically available through the MLS or brokerage attorney. Not using supplementary clauses may result in disciplinary action state authorities.

2. If there is not a supplementary clause available for you, it would be wise for your broker to hire an independent attorney to draft the clauses you need. Remember, if the agent does it, he/she runs into two problems: (1) if the language is complex it could constitute practicing law; and (2) if the drafting is poor, it could create liability.

3. All addendum language should be clear, thorough, and specific.

D. **Rejection**: Terminates offer. When a Buyer or seller rejects an offer, they effectively terminate it. The offer is no longer alive.

1. Can a terminated offer be resurrected? Yes. If buyer and seller agree in writing, then a rejected offer can become an accepted offer.

2. The offeree can always counteroffer and extend the response time the offeror originally set. By extending the offer time, the offer will remain alive until the new response time expires or the offeree makes a formal acceptance on the offer.

E. Breaches

1. A breach of contract by one party does not necessarily discharge the non-breaching party of their obligations.

2. Only when there is a total breach of contract will a non-breaching party be discharged from performing on their end of the contract. What constitutes a total breach requires a legal analysis and in no event may a real estate agent render such a conclusion. An agent should always advise their non-breaching client to continue performance or consult with an attorney about their options.

IV.   **Dealing With Multiple Offers**

Occasionally there is more than one offer presented at once on the same property.

A.   The listing agent should be careful to not only treat each buyer and their agent fairly, but to also counsel with their seller appropriately. The UAR has created forms that should be used in these situations:

　　1.   The prudent agent will counsel with their seller and review the appropriate forms, then allow the seller to make their own decision.

　　2.   Agents should avoid making any predictive statements about which offer will turn out better than the others. Each possible choice comes with positive and negative consequences.

　　3.   Buyer's agent should remember that it is the listing agent's obligation to direct the method of presentation and response to offers. If the buyer's agent feels that their client is not being treated fairly, they should speak to their own broker and the broker of the listing agent.

B.   Sellers' Options With Multiple Offers

　　1.   They can simply choose the best offer and accept or counter that offer. The other offers can be "put on the shelf" until the results of a counteroffer is realized. Review the concept of "Time for Response" where offers automatically terminate once the time for response has expired. Do not avoid communication with the other buyers' agents.

　　2.   They could choose to notify each buyer that they are in competition with other buyers, then give each buyer the option to submit their best offer by a deadline set by the seller. Doing so provides an equal and fair chance to all buyers, but could also result in some or all of the buyers rescinding their offers to avoid a 'bidding war.'

　　3.   They could choose not to respond to any of the offers. Agents must present all offers,but sellers do not have to respond to offers. This can be frustrating for buyers' agents because they want to know their offers were, indeed, presented. So encourage your sellers to at least sign a rejection or provide written confirmation that they reviewed the entire offer.

　　4.   They could choose to counter all of the offers. It should be noted that it is possible to have more than one of the buyers accept the counteroffer. In that event, the seller is bound by both contracts. As a result, a carefully drafted counteroffer, written by an attorney or provided by the MLS, can allow the seller to counter and not by bound by the buyer's acceptance. Under that type of scenario, the seller may then choose and confirm which buyer's acceptance will have legal effect.

　　5.   After the acceptance of an offer, the seller may consider countering the next best offer with language that puts the second offer in a back up position. The backup offer would become the primary offer if the first offer fails.

C. UAR Recommended Forms:

1. **Addendum (Multiple Offers):**
   UAR form recommended when the seller has received multiple offers and wishes to send out multiple counteroffers at the same time. The key point to this form is that the seller reserves the right to notify which buyer will get the property, and until this notification is given, no binding contract is formed. This language prevents the seller from obligating themselves contractually to more than one buyer.

2. **Multiple Offer Disclosure**:
   UAR form used by listing agents to inform their sellers of their options in a multiple offer situation. Listing agents should review the contents of this form with their seller, as it provides different alternatives on how to handle multiple offers.

3. **Seller's Notice to Buyers of Multiple Offers**:
   UAR form used by sellers to notify competing buyers about the existence of multiple offers and to encourage them to submit their best and final offer.

Advanced Contract Law Terms to Know

- ☐ Counter Offer
- ☐ Multiple Offers
- ☐ Multiple Offer Disclosure
- ☐ Mutual Agreement
- ☐ Rejection
- ☐ Tender
- ☐ Withdraw

Advanced Contract Law Quiz

1. Susan wanted to buy Ray's prized coin collection, but she knew he would never sell it. Knowing Ray was renting his basement, she craftily drafted a contract for the coin collection purchase and labeled the contract, "Basement Lease Agreement." Putting his trust in Susan, Ray signed it without reading it. Now Susan wants to force the sale of the coin collection. Can she?

    A. Yes, all essential elements of a contract are present

    B. Yes, the contract is in writing

    C. Yes, unless the parties mutually agree to terminate the agreement

    D. No, Ray had no intention to be bound to that agreement

2. Listing agent Joe receives an offer on his client's property. The offer says, "for Seller to accept this offer, he must text 'I accept' to Buyer and sign this offer by 5:00pm." The seller signs the acceptance at 2:00pm, but is distracted for the next few hours. At 5:28pm, the seller texts, "I accept" to the buyer. The buyer responds, "I'm pursuing a different property." Can seller sue for breach of contract?

    A. Yes, the contract was signed and accepted before 5:00pm

    B. No, text messaging will not constitute acceptance of a contract

    C. No, the acceptance clause was not enough time for the seller to make an informed decision

    D. No, the seller never accepted the contract

3. Jane received three different offers on her home within an hour. She's upset that all of the offers are lower than what she wants. As a result, she decides not to respond to any of them. Her decision upsets her agent who insists that she must respond, but she is adamant that she'll ignore the offers. Must Jane respond to the offers?

    A. Yes, she must treat all buyers fairly and offer them all the chance to enter a bidding war

    B. Yes, she must respond to at least one of the offers

    C. No, she has no legal obligation to respond to the offers

    D. No, but she could be sued for violating the implied covenant of good faith

4. Jack is prepared for the settlement on his dream house. On the way to the title company, however, Jack's agent calls and tells him that the sellers are saying that they will not sell and will not be attending their settlement. Jack is heartbroken and nervous about signing papers when the seller won't be. He asks his agent if he should still go to his own settlement. What is the most appropriate response from Jack's agent?

    A. Either attend the settlement or consult with an attorney about it

    B. No, the seller is in total breach and it relieves Jack from performing

    C. No, because the seller is not closing, it's unreasonable to expect Jack to

    D. Yes, however, the settlement can now happen at a later date when the seller calms down

Listings and Options

I. **The Listing Contract**

    A.   A basic listing agreement is a unilateral agreement ('if you sell my house, then I'll pay you X% commission). However, when the agent promises to find a buyer, the listing agreement then becomes a bilateral contract ('I promise to pay you X% commission to sell my house; I promise to find a buyer').

    B.   An Exclusive Right-to-Sell listing has been held by the courts to be a bilateral contract because it implies a duty on the agent to use reasonable efforts to find a buyer.

    C.   In an Exclusive Right-to-Sell listing, the Seller agrees to:

        1.   Allow the agent to place the property on the market and seek a buyer.

        2.   Pay a commission if a ready, willing, and able buyer is found who offers the terms given in the listing agreement or agrees to other terms through an accepted Real Estate Purchase Contract.

    D.   In an Exclusive Right-to-Sell listing, the Broker agrees to:

        1.   Place the property on the market.

        2.   Make a reasonable effort to locate a ready, willing, and able buyer.

    E.   The seller, not the real estate agent, sells the property.

        1.   A listing is not an offer; rather, it is an invitation for offers.

        2.   Typically, the offer is initiated by the buyer in the form of a Real Estate Purchase Contract in response to the listing.

        3.   Depending on state law, the agent may have to present all received offers.

        4.   The seller can refuse any offer, even if it meets the terms stated in the listing.

        5.   The agent has *earned* a commission when a ready, willing, and able buyer is located and makes an offer that meets all the requirements specified in the listing agreement, regardless of whether the seller sells or not. The broker has also *earned* the commission when he produces a ready, willing, and able buyer at other terms the seller agrees to in the Real Estate Purchase Contract.

II. **Types of Listings**

    A.   **Open Listing**:

        1.   Non-exclusive – meaning the seller can list with as many brokers as he wants to.

        2.   Does not mean that *any broker* can find a buyer; only those who have signed listing agreements can do so.

3. The broker who finds the buyer is paid the entire commission and is not required to share with other brokers.

4. If the seller finds the buyer, no commission is owed to any of the listing brokers.

5. Typically open listings are not allowed in the data base of the Multiple Listing Service.

B. **Net Listing**:

1. The seller receives an agreed net amount from the sale. The broker receives everything over and above the net amount. For instance, if the seller wants $70,000 net from his home, and the agent sells the property for $95,000, then the seller would get the $70,000 and the agent would receive $25,000 as a commission.

2. Because the opportunity exists for agents to receive unconscionable commissions, and the possibility of artificially inflating market values, net listings are illegal (or prohibited) in Utah.

C. **Exclusive Agency Listing**:

1. The commission is paid exclusively to the listing broker and there can be only one listing broker.

2. The seller reserves the right to find a buyer himself, sell the property, and not pay a commission to the listing broker.

D. **Exclusive Right-to-Sell Listing**:

The listing broker has an exclusive right to the commission regardless of who locates a buyer, including the seller.

E. **Commissions**:

The listing broker can share the commission with other brokers through co-broker agreements. A co-broker agreement is when brokers from various brokerages agree that if a non-listing office, usually referred to as the selling office, finds the buyer, the listing broker will give a percentage of the total commission to the selling office. Principal brokers who join the national, state, and local Board of REALTORS® automatically enter into a co-broker agreement with all other principal brokers who are also members. Most boards require that all agents of a member principal broker also join the board. The cost is several hundred dollars, usually $400 - $500. Check your local board for exact costs. If a listed property doesn't get sold through the brokerage before a foreclosure sale is held, no commission will be earned by the brokerage.

III. **Miscellaneous Items**

A. **Single Party Exclusive Right-to-Sell Listing**:

This listing is exclusive to one broker for one specified buyer. It sometimes has a time-clause associated with it.

B. **Exclusive Right-to-Sell with Exclusions**:

The seller is allowed to exclude certain names from the listing. If one of the excluded parties purchases the property, the seller does not have to pay a commission. It sometimes has a time limitation placed on the exclusions. For instance, the listing may be for six months, but the exclusions are removed after 30 days.

C. Determination of who actually earns the commission. There is sometimes a dispute concerning which selling agent actually earned the commission. One of the following doctrines is used to settle such a dispute.

    1. **"To and Through"**: The agent who first takes the buyer to and through the property has the right to the selling portion of the commission if the buyer purchases the property.

    2. **Procuring Cause**: The agent who initiates an uninterrupted chain of events that ultimately leads to closing has the right to the selling portion of the commission. The uninterrupted chain of events usually begins with the broker introducing the buyer to the property, and the courts will weigh that factor heavily. *See e.g. Frederick May & Company v. Dunn*, 368 P.2d 266, 269 (Utah 1962). While, the courts tend to favor procuring cause, the Professional Standards Committee of the Board of REALTORS® considers both.

D. **Protection Clause**: To protect the real estate agent from a seller who might try to induce a potential buyer to wait until the listing has expired, the safety clause in a listing indicates that a commission is owed the agent if any buyer who was shown the property during the term of the listing purchases the property after the listing's expiration. This safety clause usually has a limited time frame (such as 120 days). To make the safety clause valid, the real estate agent must provide the seller with a list of protected names when the listing expires.

E. **Seller's Property Condition Disclosure**: This should be filled out by the seller at listing time. It should be reviewed and modified, if necessary, when an offer is accepted.

F. Be sure the listing information and Section 1.1-2 of the REPC are in agreement as to what's included in the sale.

G. When a seller and buyer are brought together, the one who sells or offers to sell is referred to as the "Vendor" and the one who buys or offers to buy is called the "Vendee."

H. **Estoppel certificate**: A legal instrument from the mortgagee setting forth the exact unpaid balance and other terms of a mortgage, such as its assumability. This document can be ordered by the court, but should be arranged for at the time a listing is taken. This is done by the mortgagor (borrower) signing a release form that allows the mortgagee (lender) to release loan information to the listing agent.

I. Listings are not assignable. A sales agent or associate broker cannot take his/her listings to the new office without the written rescission of the existing listing agreement which requires the signature of the listing broker and the seller.

IV. **Options**

An option is the purchased right of a buyer to purchase or not purchase a specified property during a

155

stated period of time and for predetermined price and terms.

A.   The seller is the "**Optionor**."

B.   The potential buyer is the "**Optionee**."

C.   The seller agrees to take the property off the market for the period of time stated in the option.

D.   The buyer agrees to pay non-refundable consideration for the option.

E.   An option is a unilateral contract until it is exercised, and it creates a contractual right. Once the option is exercised it becomes a bilateral contract.

F.   The seller must sell if the buyer exercises his right during the term of the option.

G.   The buyer does not have to purchase, but loses his consideration if he doesn't.

H.   An option must contain the:

1.   Term (time period) of the option.

2.   Proposed purchase price - the price can be expressed as:

a.   A dollar amount.

b.   An amount based on an appraisal at the time the option is exercised, etc.

3.   Essential terms of the purchase, such as agreement by the seller to carry a contract, limitations on interest rate, number of years of the contract, etc.

4.   Amount of non-refundable consideration for the option.

I.   **Uses for an option**:

1.   It may be used to secure the right to purchase a rental property that has not yet been completely built but is located next to a similar property that is presently being purchased. The buyer purchases the completed property with an option to buy the incomplete property when it is built.

2.   An option is used to lock-up a property while securing financing, zoning changes, other buyers, etc. If the optionee is unable to arrange things to his satisfaction, he simply lets the option period expire and forfeits the option money.

J.   **Lease with an Option to Purchase**: An option sometimes contains a clause that prohibits the owner from selling the property during the term of the lease. The lessee, on the other hand, can exercise the option to purchase the property during or at the conclusion of the lease, as agreed upon in the option portion of the contract.

K.   **Right of First Refusal**: A contractual stipulation that the owner must present all legitimate offers which the holder of the right of first refusal can then match or refuse until the property sells. This is an alternative for the same situations in which an option would be used.

Listing and Options Terms to Know

- ☐ Exclusive Agency Listing
- ☐ Exclusive Right-To-Sell
- ☐ Lease with an Option to Purchase
- ☐ Listing
- ☐ Net Listing
- ☐ Open Listing
- ☐ Option Contract
- ☐ Optionee
- ☐ Optionor
- ☐ Procuring Cause Doctrine
- ☐ Right of First Refusal
- ☐ Safety Clause
- ☐ To and Through Doctrine
- ☐ Vendee
- ☐ Vendor

Listings And Options Quiz

1.   Broker Bell entered into an agreement with Seller Samuels to market Samuels home and seek a buyer for him. The agreement stated that regardless of who found the buyer, Samuels would owe Bell a commission. What kind of a listing agreement is this?

    A. Exclusive agency listing

    B. Open listing

    C. Net listing

    D. Exclusive right-to-sell listing

2.   Under an exclusive right-to-sell listing, a broker has earned a commission when:

    A. The property is listed

    B. The purchaser hands the broker an earnest money deposit

    C. A purchaser is found who is ready, willing and able to buy the property on the seller's terms

    D. Title to the property is transferred at closing

3.   Which of the following listings are considered illegal or prohibited?

    A. Net listing

    B. Exclusive right-to-sell listing

    C. Exclusive agency listing

    D. Open listing

4.   The main difference between an exclusive right-to-sell listing and an exclusive agency listing is that with an exclusive agency listing:

    A. The listing broker cannot enter into a co-brokering agreement with another broker.

    B. The seller can find a buyer himself and sell the home without paying a commission.

    C. The listing broker cannot allow any of his sales persons to work on the listing.

    D. It is exactly the same as an exclusive right-to-sell; they are just two names for the same kind of listing.

5.   Jeff paid Mike $750 for the right to buy or not buy his property. They each signed a contract to confirm their intentions. This is an example of a(n):

    A. Right of first refusal

    B. Exclusive agency

    C. Listing agreement

    D. Option

6. An agent is protected from the seller and buyer waiting until the listing expires to reach an agreement by which clause:
    A. Exclusivity clause
    B. Protection clause
    C. Option clause
    D. Procuring clause

7. Which of the following types of listings gives the greatest protection to the agent:
    A. Exclusive agency
    B. Open listing
    C. Exclusive right-to-sell
    D. Net listing

8. If the seller will not agree to an option, it might be a good time to use a(n):
    A. Lease/option
    B. Exclusive right-to-sell
    C. First right of refusal
    D. Net sale agreement

9. In an option, the optionee is:
    A. Buyer
    B. Seller
    C. Agent arranging the option
    D. Broker of the agent.

10. The seller would like to list his home, but there are two parties he knows who might buy it. He doesn't want to pay a commission if either of these parties buy the home. This would be a good time for the agent to take a(n):
    A. Exclusive agency with exceptions
    B. Exclusive right-to-sell listing
    C. Net listing
    D. Exclusive right-to-sell with exclusions

New Construction Contract

I. **The New Construction REPC**

For convenience in this chapter, we'll refer to the Real Estate Purchase Contract for Residential Construction as the "NCREPC" (New Construction REPC).

A. This contract should be used for a residence that does not yet have a certificate of occupancy.

B. Some agents think that if the home is basically completed, it is just as well to use the regular Real Estate Purchase Contract ("REPC"). However, the substance of the two contracts is different and specifically designed for their own respective purposes.

II. **Agency Issues**

A. Utah law requires that licensees assisting a member of the public in the purchase or sale of real estate be an agent of the buyer or the seller, or a limited agent (agent to both of them). They can only function as a limited agent with informed consent of both parties (see the Agency chapter for details).

B. Utah law also requires a written agreement or contract between the licensee and the person he/she represents. Utah Administrative Code R162-2f-401a(2). If the licensee is a limited agent, there will be three documents involved:

   1. The contract with the seller/builder/developer

   2. The buyer agency contract

   3. A Limited Agency Consent Agreement

C. Agents hired by the developer are the agents of the developer, or in other words, the seller. Thus, they have a fiduciary obligation to obtain best price and terms for the developer. However, when potential buyers come to the model home, for instance, it is easy for a relationship to develop between the agent and buyer that quickly takes on the appearance of an agency relationship. Since there is no written agreement or disclosure at this point, an implied agency relationship could emerge and a double non-disclosure could occur. Therefore, it is important that disclosure take place very early in this situation. To handle this properly, the following things should be established:

   1. The broker and developer should have a clear and written agency agreement. This would include:

      a. The agency arrangement between the broker and the developer, which will likely be the broker being the agent of the developer.

      b. Whether or not the broker is allowed to created limited agency agreements with a buyer.

   2. Policies and procedures should be established that clearly define when disclosures should be made to the potential buyer.

   3. Policies and procedures should be defined for working with real estate agents from other companies, including payment of commission splits and interaction with the buyer relative

161

to decisions concerning construction.

    4.   Proper forms for contracts and disclosures should be provided.

D.   For a complete discussion of Agency, see the Agency chapter in the book and the two Agency classes, which are available as live instruction or online.

III.   Paying for the New Home

A.   **Fixed cost**: There is an agreed upon purchase price for the home up front. It cannot go higher except by mutual agreement. This is an advantage to the buyer. If the costs exceed what is expected, the builder must cover any overage. This option tends to favor the buyer.

B.   **Cost plus**: The buyer has agreed to pay the actual costs of construction, plus a certain amount or percentage on top of that. In this scenario, the builder has little incentive to keep costs down (shop for the best deal), as the buyer has all liability for cost overruns. This option is usually to the advantage of the builder.

C.   With either of these options, homes often end up costing more than the original contract amount. During construction buyers may go over their allowances for carpets, cabinets, lighting, etc., or they may want new features, or even change the basic design of the home. All these things increase the price, and the buyer must pay extra for them.

IV.   Financial Issues

A.   Lot ownership: Regardless of who owns the lot initially, the lender will want the same name on the deed for the lot as the name of the person getting the construction loan. The lot becomes security for the construction loan.

    1.   If the buyers own the lot free and clear, they may need to deed all or a portion of the ownership to the builder to facilitate the process of the builder obtaining the construction loan.

    2.   If the buyers own the lot, and it has a loan balance, the balance will be paid off with the first draw, thus ensuring the construction loan is a first mortgage rather than being in second position.

B.   **Construction loan**: This is a short term loan to cover the costs of the construction, and sometimes the cost of the land as well. Usually the buyer will have to qualify with the lender before the construction loan will be approved. Even if the long-term financing is not being obtained from the same lender, they still want to know the buyer is going to be able to qualify for a loan to complete the transaction.

    1.   Costs of construction involve more than the land, materials, and labor. They include, among other things, such items as:

        a.   Site preparation

        b.   Sanitary and storm sewers

        c.   Retaining walls

        d.   Taxes

e.   Fees

f.   Insurance

g.   Permits

2.   Construction loans are short term and usually at a higher interest rate, due to higher risks. These loans are open end loans with an established loan limit, similar to credit cards. The amount of the loan is created as money is taken for each phase of construction. These disbursements are called "draws."

3.   If the loan is in the buyer's name, the buyer will have to sign off on all draws. Checks and balances are built in to be sure the suppliers and subcontractors actually receive the money.

4.   A disadvantage to the buyers for having the construction loan in their name is that draws on that loan don't show up on the builder's records. This could allow the builder to overextend and exceed the statutory limit, thereby increasing the risk to the buyer.

C.   **Long term financing**: Once the construction is complete, an appraisal will be done and the permanent loan, which is obtained by the buyer ("take out loan"), is closed. Most homes appraise for more than the original contracted price, and this could enable the buyer to get a higher loan amount and, therefore, a down payment that is lower than originally planned.

D.   Both loans from the same lender: If both loans are obtained from one lender at the beginning, there may not be double origination fees, and the buyer can save money.

E.   Builder's recommended lender: Even though the builder may promote a certain lender and indicate there are financing concessions available, wise buyers will shop lenders to find the best deal for them.

F.   Buyer carries the construction loan:

1.   Lender will want application for both loans (construction and long term), and will usually want to approve the builder.

2.   Buyer must sign off on all draws. However, some builders use a waiver whereby the buyer agrees that this is not necessary. This does not mean the buyer has given up the right at any point if he/she has a reason to resume approving draws. This has several advantages to the buyer:

a.   The buyer knows what is being spent and for what.

b.   The buyer can withhold a signature as leverage against the builder.

c.   Loan interest may be deductible to the buyer (check with an accountant).

d.   The buyer can stop the draw at the bank if there is reason to question what's going on.

e.   If builder defaults, the buyer can terminate the contract and hire another builder.

163

3. Disadvantages to the buyer:

 a. Logistically signing off on draws can be a hassle.

 b. The buyer can't back out of the agreement. If they try, the builder just refers them to the lender.

G. Seller/builder obtains the construction loan:

1. Loan fees and interest are part of the builder's costs on production homes. With custom homes, the buyer usually pays fees and interest. Note: If the builder acquires the loan, there is added incentive to get the job done in a timely manner to save interest costs.

2. Caution to buyers: Sometimes buyers pick a particular builder because the bid was $10,000 lower than others. Subsequently, they discover that fees and interest on the loan are an additional cost to the buyers.

3. Advantages to the seller/builder:

 a. If the builder defaults, the land and the home in progress are part of the builder's assets and will be liquidated to pay the lender. If the builder goes into bankruptcy, they are the builder's assets and the buyer is stuck.

 b. The builder doesn't need the buyer's signature on draws.

 c. Builders often have credit lines established and can bend traditional loan ratios. They may be able to get the loan where the buyer could not.

V. **Differences Between NCREPC and Residential REPC include such topics as:**

1. Warranties
2. Required Disclosures
3. Conditions for Buyer's Right to Cancel
4. Home Design
5. Improvements
6. Method of Payment
7. Financing Condition
8. Substantial Completion
9. Walk-Through Inspection
10. Construction Access
11. Construction Compliance
12. Unavoidable Delay
13. Insurance
14. Protection against Liens and Civil Action

 Utah Association
of REALTORS®

NEW CONSTRUCTION
REAL ESTATE PURCHASE CONTRACT

This is a legally binding Real Estate Purchase Contract ("REPC"). If you desire legal or tax advice, consult your attorney or tax advisor.

OFFER TO PURCHASE AND EARNEST MONEY DEPOSIT

On this _____ day of _____, 20____ ("Offer Reference Date") _____ ("Buyer") offers to purchase from _____ ("Seller") the Property described below and **[ ] delivers to the Buyer's Brokerage with this offer, or [ ] agrees to deliver no later than four (4) calendar days after Acceptance (as defined in Section 25),** Earnest Money in the amount of $_____ in the form of_____. After Acceptance of the REPC by Buyer and Seller, and receipt of the Earnest Money by the Brokerage, the Brokerage shall have four (4) calendar days in which to deposit the Earnest Money into the Brokerage Real Estate Trust Account.

Buyer's Brokerage _____ Phone: _____

Received by: _____on_____(Date)
(Signature above acknowledges receipt of Earnest Money)

OTHER PROVISIONS

1. PROPERTY:

1.1 Location. The Earnest Money Deposit is given to secure and apply on the purchase of a new Residence (the "Residence") described below to be constructed by Seller on a parcel of real property (the "Lot") located at:_____ _____, in the City of _____County of _____ _____, State of Utah, more particularly described as Lot No._____ in the _____ _____ Subdivision/Development, or alternatively as follows:_____ _____ (collectively referred to hereinafter as the "Property").The Purchase Price for the Property **[ ] INCLUDES [ ] DOES NOT INCLUDE**, the Lot.

1.2 Home Design. Seller shall construct the Residence and related improvements described as the [ ] _____ model house plan; or [ ] custom design, in accordance with the Plans & Specifications as provided in Section 7(g) and 9.1 below, and any applicable plans, CC&Rs, and declaration of condominium.

1.3 Improvements. Seller represents that the Property will be connected to the utility service lines and serviced by the additional improvements identified below. **(check applicable boxes):**
(a) Utility Services
[ ] well [ ] public water [ ] private water [ ] natural gas [ ] propane [ ] electricity [ ] telephone [ ] cable
[ ] public sewer [ ] septic tank [ ] other (specify)_____
(b) Additional Improvements
[ ] dedicated paved road [ ] private paved road [ ] other road (specify)_____
[ ] curb & gutter[ ] rolled curb [ ] sidewalk
[ ] other (specify)_____

1.4 Permit Fees. Seller agrees to pay for building permit fees, impact fees, landscape bonds, and all connection fees except for the following: _____.

1.5 Water Service. The Purchase Price for the Property shall include all water rights/water shares, if any, that are the legal source of Seller's current culinary water service and irrigation water service, if any, to the Property. The water rights/water shares will be conveyed or otherwise transferred to Buyer at Closing by applicable deed or legal instruments. The following water rights/water shares, if applicable, are specifically excluded from this sale: _____

1.6 Survey. Seller shall ensure that the Lot corners have been staked by a licensed surveyor and that upon Substantial Completion of the Residence as defined in Section 12.2 below, the stakes are still in place. Any additional survey work shall be at the option of Buyer and shall be paid for by Buyer.

2. PURCHASE PRICE. The Purchase Price for the Property is $ _____. Except as provided in this Section, the Purchase Price shall be paid as provided in Sections 2.1(a) through 2.1(d) below. Any amounts shown in 2.1(c) and 2.1(d) may be adjusted as deemed necessary by Buyer and Buyer's Lender (the "Lender").

Page 1 of 8 pages Buyer's Initials_____ Date_____ Seller's Initials_____ Date_____
15. Contract Deadlines

165

2.1   Method of Payment. The Purchase Price will be paid as follows:

$_____   (a) **Earnest Money Deposit.** Under certain conditions described in the REPC, this deposit may become non-refundable.

$_____   (b) **Construction Deposit.** This amount shall be due and shall become **NON-REFUNDABLE** to Buyer as provided in Section 2.2 below.

$_____   (c) **Permanent Loan.** Buyer agrees to apply for a "Permanent Loan" on terms acceptable to Buyer as provided in Section 8.2(c) below. If an FHA/VA loan applies, see attached FHA/VA Loan Addendum.

$_____   (d) **Balance of Purchase Price in Cash at Settlement.**

$_____   **PURCHASE PRICE.** Total of lines (a) through (d). The Purchase Price may be increased if additional costs are incurred for any Change Orders as provided in Section 9.3. Such Change Orders shall be paid for as provided in Section 9.3.

2.2   Construction Deposit.

(a) **Delivery of Construction Deposit.** Provided Buyer has not cancelled the REPC pursuant to Section 8.1(b) below, then no later than the Pre-Construction Meeting, referenced in Section 9.2, or as otherwise agreed to in writing by Buyer and Seller, Buyer [ ] **WILL** [ ] **WILL NOT** deliver directly to the Seller a Construction Deposit. Seller may only use the Construction Deposit for the purpose of constructing the Residence and/or purchase of the Lot. The Earnest Money Deposit and Construction Deposit, if applicable, shall be credited toward the Purchase Price at Settlement as defined in Section 3.1 below.

(b) **Non-Refundable Construction Deposit.** Except as provided in Section 8, Buyer acknowledges that upon delivery of the Construction Deposit to the Seller, the Construction Deposit shall be **NON-REFUNDABLE** to Buyer unless Seller fails to close the transaction in accordance with the terms of the REPC. In such event, the remedies set forth in Section 17.2 shall apply.

3. SETTLEMENT AND CLOSING.

3.1   Settlement. Settlement shall take place no later than the Settlement Deadline referenced in Section 24(f), or as otherwise mutually agreed by Buyer and Seller in writing. "Settlement" shall occur only when all of the following have been completed: (a) Buyer and Seller have signed and delivered to each other or to the escrow/closing office all documents required by the REPC, by the Lender, by the title insurance and escrow/closing offices, by written escrow instructions (including any split closing instructions, if applicable), or by applicable law; (b) any monies required to be paid by Buyer or Seller under these documents (except for the proceeds of any Permanent Loan) have been delivered by Buyer or Seller to the other party, or to the escrow/closing office, in the form of cash, wire transfer, cashier's check, or other form acceptable to the escrow/closing office.

3.2   Prorations. All prorations, including, but not limited to, homeowner's association dues, property taxes for the current year, rents, and interest on assumed obligations, if any, shall be made as of the Settlement Deadline referenced in Section 24(f), unless otherwise agreed to in writing by the Buyer and Seller. Such writing could include the settlement statement. The provisions of this Section 3.2 shall survive Closing.

3.3   Special Assessments. Any assessments for capital improvements as approved by the HOA (pursuant to HOA governing documents) or as assessed by a municipality or special improvement district, prior to the Settlement Deadline shall be paid for by: [ ] **Seller** [ ] **Buyer** [ ] **Split Equally Between Buyer and Seller** [ ] **Other (explain)** _____
_____. The provisions of this Section 3.3 shall survive Closing.

3.4   Fees/Costs/Payment Obligations. Unless otherwise agreed to in writing, Buyer and Seller shall each pay their respective fees charged by the escrow/closing office for its services in the settlement/closing process. Buyer agrees to be responsible for homeowners' association and private and public utility service transfer fees, if any, and all utilities and other services provided to the Property after the Settlement Deadline. Utility service connection and hook-up fees shall however, be paid by Seller as provided in Section 1.4. The escrow/closing office is authorized and directed to withhold from Seller's proceeds at Closing, sufficient funds to pay off on Seller's behalf all mortgages, trust deeds, judgments, mechanic's liens, tax liens and warrants. The provisions of this Section 3.4 shall survive Closing.

3.5   Closing. For purposes of the REPC, "Closing" means that: (a) Settlement has been completed; (b) the proceeds of any new loan have been delivered by the Lender to Seller or to the escrow/closing office; and (c) the applicable Closing documents have been recorded in the office of the county recorder. The actions described in 3.5 (b) and (c) shall be completed within four calendar days after Settlement.

4. POSSESSION. Unless otherwise agreed to in writing, Seller shall deliver physical possession to Buyer upon Closing.

5. CONFIRMATION OF AGENCY DISCLOSURE. Buyer and Seller acknowledge prior written receipt of agency disclosure provided by their respective agent that has disclosed the agency relationships confirmed below. At the signing of the REPC:

Seller's Agent _____, represents [ ] **Seller**　[ ] both **Buyer and Seller as a Limited Agent**;

Seller's Brokerage _____, represents [ ] **Seller**　[ ] both **Buyer and Seller as a Limited Agent**;

Buyer's Agent _____, represents [ ] **Buyer**　[ ] both **Buyer and Seller as a Limited Agent**;

Buyer's Brokerage _____, represents [ ] **Buyer**　[ ] both **Buyer and Seller as a Limited Agent.**

6. TITLE / TITLE INSURANCE / LIENS.

　6.1　**Title to Property.** Seller represents that Seller has fee title to the Property and will convey marketable title to the Property to Buyer at Closing by general warranty deed unless otherwise agreed to in writing by Buyer and Seller. The Property will be delivered to Buyer at Closing, free and clear of mechanic's liens and claims for mechanic's liens. Buyer does agree to accept title to the Property subject to the contents of the Commitment for Title Insurance (the "Commitment") provided by Seller under Section 7(b), and as reviewed and approved by Buyer under Section 8.1(a). The provisions of this Section 6.1 shall survive Closing.

　6.2　**Title Insurance & Additional Coverage.** At Settlement, Seller agrees to pay for and cause to be issued in favor of Buyer, through the title insurance agency that issued the Commitment (the "Issuing Agent"), the most current version of the *ALTA Homeowner's Policy of Title Insurance (the "Homeowner's Policy")*. If the *Homeowner's Policy* is not available through the Issuing Agent, Buyer and Seller further agree as follows: (a) Seller agrees to pay for the *Homeowner's Policy* if available through any other title insurance agency selected by Buyer; (b) if the *Homeowner's Policy* is not available either through the Issuing Agent or any other title insurance agency, then the Seller agrees to pay for, and Buyer agrees to accept, the most current available version of an *ALTA Owner's Policy of Title Insurance* ("*Standard Coverage Owner's Policy*") available through the Issuing Agent.

　6.3　**Protection Against Liens and Civil Action.** Notice is hereby provided in accordance with the Residence Lien Restriction and Lien Recovery Fund Act of the Utah Code that an "owner" may be protected against liens being maintained against an "owner-occupied residence" and from other civil action being maintained to recover monies owed for "qualified services" performed or provided by suppliers and subcontractors as a part of this contract, if either section (1) or (2) is met: (1)(a) the owner entered into a written contract with an original contractor, a factory built housing retailer, or a real estate developer; (b) the original contractor was properly licensed or exempt from licensure under Utah Construction Trades Licensing Act at the time the contract was executed; and (c) the owner paid in full the contracting entity in accordance with the written contract and any written or oral amendments to the contract; or (2) the amount of the general contract between the owner and the original contractor totals no more than $5,000. (3) An owner who can establish compliance with either section (1) or (2) may perfect the owner's protection by applying for a Certificate of Compliance with the Division of Occupational and Professional Licensing.

7. SELLER DISCLOSURES. No later than the Seller Disclosure Deadline referenced in Section 24(a), Seller shall provide to Buyer the following documents which are collectively referred to as the "Seller Disclosures":

(a)　A Seller property condition disclosure form for the Lot and any improvements;

(b)　A Commitment for the policy of title insurance as referenced in Sections 6.1 and 6.2;

(c)　A copy of the recorded CC&R's, rules and regulations affecting the Property, and a copy of the recorded Plat for the Development, if any;

(d)　A copy of the most recent minutes, budget and financial statement for the homeowners' association, if any;

(e)　Written notice of any claims and/or conditions known to Seller relating to environmental, soil stability, drainage or other problems or other known defects in the Property that materially affect its value that cannot be discovered by a reasonable inspection by an ordinary prudent Buyer;

(f)　Evidence of any water rights and/or water shares referenced in Section 1.5;

(g)　Plans & Specifications for the Residence, or reduction copies thereof as defined in Section 9.1;

(h)　Name of contractor and contractor's license number;

(i)　If applicable and pursuant to 16 C.F.R., part 460 the type, thickness, and R-value of the insulation that will be installed in each part of the house;

(j)　Builder's Warranty (if different from Section 11); and

(k)　Other (specify)_____

_____

8. BUYER'S CONDITIONS OF PURCHASE.

8.1 DUE DILIGENCE CONDITION. Buyer's obligation to purchase the Property **IS** conditioned upon Buyer's satisfactory completion of Buyer's Due Diligence as defined in this Section 8.1 inclusive below. This condition is referred to as the "Due Diligence Condition." All of Buyer's Due Diligence shall be completed on or before the Due Diligence Deadline referenced in Section 24(b). Buyer's Due Diligence shall be paid for by Buyer and shall be conducted by individuals or entities of Buyer's choice. Seller agrees to cooperate with Buyer's Due Diligence. Buyer agrees to pay for any damage to the Property resulting from any inspections or tests during the Due Diligence.

(a) Due Diligence Items. Buyer's Due Diligence shall consist of the following:

(i) Buyer's review and approval of the Seller Disclosures referenced in Section 7 above, and

(ii) Any other tests, evaluations and verifications of the Property deemed necessary or appropriate by Buyer, such as: environmental issues or geologic conditions; setback requirements, utility easements, the costs and availability of homeowners' insurance and flood insurance, if applicable; water source, availability and quality; the location of property lines; regulatory use restrictions or violations; fees for services such as HOA dues, municipal services, and utility costs; convicted sex offenders residing in proximity to the Property; and any other matters deemed material to Buyer in making a decision to purchase the Property.

(b) Right to Cancel or Waive Due Diligence Condition. Buyer shall have the right to cancel the REPC or waive the Due Diligence Condition as provided below.

(i) Buyer's Right to Cancel or Resolve Objections. If Buyer, in Buyer's sole discretion, determines that the results of Buyer's Due Diligence are unacceptable, Buyer may either: (A) no later than the Due Diligence Deadline referenced in Section 24(b), cancel the REPC by providing written notice to Seller, whereupon the Earnest Money Deposit and the Construction Deposit, if applicable, shall be released to Buyer without the requirement of further written authorization from Seller; or (B) no later than the Due Diligence Deadline referenced in Section 24(b), resolve in writing with Seller any objections Buyer has arising from Buyer's Due Diligence.

(ii) Failure to Cancel or Resolve Objections. If Buyer fails to cancel the REPC or fails to resolve in writing any objections Buyer has arising from Buyer's Due Diligence, as provided in Section 8.1(b)(i), Buyer shall be deemed to have waived the Due Diligence Condition.

8.2 FINANCING CONDITION (check applicable boxes):

(a) Construction Loan. The obligations of the parties under the REPC [ ] ARE [ ] ARE NOT conditioned upon [ ] **Buyer** [ ] **Seller** obtaining a "Construction Loan" in the amount sufficient to construct the Residence.

(b) Failure to Obtain Construction Loan. Whether the Construction Loan is being obtained by Buyer or Seller, if the proceeds of that loan are not available for disbursement by the Construction Loan Funding Deadline referenced in Section 24(d), Buyer or Seller may cancel this REPC by providing written notice to the other party no later than four (4) days after the Construction Loan Funding Deadline; whereupon the Earnest Money Deposit and the Construction Deposit, if applicable, shall be released to Buyer without the requirement of further written authorization from Seller.

(c) Permanent Loan. Buyer's obligation to purchase the Property [ ] IS [ ] IS NOT conditioned upon Buyer obtaining the Permanent Loan as referenced in Section 2.1(c) above.

(d) Cash Purchase/Proof of Funds. If Buyer's obligation to purchase the Property **IS NOT** conditioned upon Buyer qualifying for the Construction Loan and/or the Permanent Loan as referenced in 8.2 (a) and (c) above (the "Applicable Loans"), Section 8.3 below shall not apply. If Buyer is paying cash, then no later than the Due Diligence Deadline referenced in Section 24(b), Buyer shall provide to Seller a current financial statement ("Proof of Funds"), evidencing Buyer's financial ability to close the purchase of the Property. If Seller, in Seller's sole discretion, is not satisfied with the Proof of Funds provided by Buyer, Seller may cancel the REPC by providing written notice to Buyer no later than seven (7) days after the Due Diligence Deadline. In such event, the Earnest Money Deposit, and Construction Deposit, if applicable, shall be released to Buyer without the requirement of further written authorization from Seller, and neither party shall have any further rights or obligations to each other under the REPC or otherwise. If Seller does not cancel the REPC as provided in this Section 8.2(d), Seller shall be deemed to have waived any objection to Buyer's Proof of Funds.

8.3 APPLICATION FOR LOAN.

(a) Preferred Lender. Buyer shall obtain a "Pre-Qualification Letter" from _____ (the "Preferred Lender"). Notwithstanding the requirement for Buyer to obtain a Pre-Qualification Letter from the Preferred Lender, Buyer is not required to obtain a loan from the Preferred Lender and may additionally apply for and obtain a loan from any mortgage lender of Buyer's choosing (the "Alternate Lender").

(b) Application. No later than seven (7) days after Acceptance of the REPC by Buyer and Seller as defined in Section 25 below, Buyer shall apply for any applicable loans from the Preferred Lender and, if applicable, the Alternate Lender in order to obtain a Pre-Qualification Letter. Buyer shall pay all loan application fees as required by the Preferred Lender. Buyer will promptly provide any documentation required by the Preferred Lender.

(c) Pre-Qualification Letter. No later than the Due Diligence Deadline referenced in Section 24(b), Buyer agrees to provide to Seller a Pre-Qualification Letter from the Preferred Lender and, if applicable, the Alternate Lender. Buyer agrees to diligently work to obtain the Pre-Qualification Letter.

(d) Right to Cancel. If the Preferred Lender or, if applicable, the Alternate Lender fails to provide Buyer with a Pre-

Qualification Letter, or if the Pre-Qualification Letter contains conditions unacceptable to the Buyer or Seller, Buyer or Seller may cancel the REPC by providing written notice to the other party no later than four (4) days after the Due Diligence Deadline; whereupon the Earnest Money and Construction Deposit, if applicable, shall be released to Buyer without the requirement of further written authorization from Seller. If the REPC is not canceled as provided in this Section 8.3(d), Buyer and Seller shall be deemed to have waived any objections regarding the lack of, or any conditions contained in the Pre-Qualification Letter.

8.4 FAILURE TO OBTAIN PERMANENT LOAN.

(a) **Failure to Obtain Permanent Loan.** If after expiration of the Settlement Deadline referenced in Section 24(f), Buyer fails to obtain the Permanent Loan, meaning that the proceeds of the Permanent Loan have not been delivered by the Lender to Seller or to the escrow/closing office as required under Section 3.5 of the REPC, then Buyer or Seller may cancel the REPC by providing written notice to the other party; whereupon the Earnest Money Deposit and the Construction Deposit if applicable, shall be retained by the Seller.

(b) **Seller's Exclusive Remedy.** In the event of a cancellation based on the Buyer's failure to obtain a permanent loan as described in Section 8.4(a), Seller agrees to accept as Seller's exclusive remedy, the Earnest Money Deposit and the Construction Deposit, if applicable, as liquidated damages. Buyer and Seller agree that liquidated damages would be difficult and impractical to calculate, and the Earnest Money Deposit and the Construction Deposit, if applicable, is a fair and reasonable estimate of Seller's damages in the event Buyer fails to obtain the Permanent Loan.

9. PLANS & SPECIFICATIONS / PRE-CONSTRUCTION MEETING.

9.1 Plans & Specifications. The Plans & Specifications contain descriptions of the type of materials to be used in finishing the Residence, a dollar allowance for specific items, and copies of the floor plans and elevations for the Residence and any Change Orders as described below. Buyer's selection of color, grade and type of finishing materials (including appliances, floor coverings, fixtures, cabinets, etc.) may differ from the Plans & Specifications, and may change the Substantial Completion Deadline and the Purchase Price. Seller agrees to construct the Residence in substantial compliance with the Plans & Specification and to place the Residence within the approved building area on the Lot as permitted by the local municipal authority. Buyer acknowledges that the Residence, upon Substantial Completion, may vary from the exact dimensions shown on the Plans & Specifications.

9.2 Pre-Construction Meeting. Prior to the Pre-Construction Meeting Deadline, Buyer and Seller shall meet to review the Plans & Specifications and plot plan, and sign a *Change Order Addendum* which itemizes and identifies any changes to the Plans & Specifications for the Residence. Any payments and/or fees as required by the REPC and any *Change Order Addenda* shall be paid in full at the conclusion of the Pre-Construction Meeting, unless a separate payment schedule is otherwise agreed to in writing by Buyer and Seller. To the extent that a choice of color, grade, or type of material is still required after the Pre-Construction Meeting, Buyer shall notify Seller in writing of such selections no later than [ ] 10 days, or [ ] ___ days after receipt of Seller's written request for such selections. If Buyer has not notified Seller in writing of such selections, Seller shall have the right to make said selections, at Seller's sole discretion, to avoid delay in Substantial Completion of the Residence.

9.3 Change Orders. No change will be made to the Plans & Specifications except by a written *Change Order Addendum* signed in advance by Buyer and Seller. Any *Change Order Addendum* shall set forth: (a) the changes to   be made; (b) any adjustment in the Purchase Price; and (c) any change in the Substantial Completion Deadline. Payments made by Buyer to Seller for any Change Orders may only be used for construction of the Residence. Buyer understands that any Change Orders requested may affect the appraised value of the Residence and the terms and conditions of available financing.

10. ADDITIONAL TERMS. There [ ] ARE [ ] ARE NOT addenda to the REPC containing additional terms. If there are, the terms of the following addenda are incorporated into the REPC by this reference: [ ] Addendum No._____
[ ] FHA/VA Loan Addendum [ ] Plans and Specifications [ ] Change Order Addendum No. ____ [ ] Other (specify)_____

11. SELLER WARRANTIES. Unless Seller is providing an alternate Builder's Warranty under Section 7(j) (in which case this Section 11 shall not apply) Seller DOES warrant the heating, cooling, electrical, plumbing and landscape sprinkler systems (including all gas and electric appliances), fixtures, and structural elements of the Residence (including the roof, walls, and foundation) against defects in material and workmanship for a period of one year after the Settlement Deadline. Seller further warrants that as of the date Seller delivers possession of the Residence to Buyer, any private well or septic tank serving the Residence shall have applicable permits and shall be in working order and fit for its intended purpose. The provisions of this Section 11 shall survive Closing.

12. WALK-THROUGH INSPECTION / SUBSTANTIAL COMPLETION / CONSTRUCTION COMPLIANCE

12.1 Walk-Through Inspection. Not less than [ ] 7 DAYS [ ] _____ DAYS prior to Settlement, Buyer may conduct a "walk-through" inspection of the Residence. If, as of Settlement, minor work remains to be completed, corrected or replaced on the Residence, then Buyer, pending completion of such work, may withhold in escrow at Settlement, a reasonable amount agreed to by Seller, Buyer and mortgage lenders , if applicable, sufficient to pay for completion of such work. If such work is not completed within [ ] 30 DAYS [ ] _____ DAYS after Settlement, the amount so escrowed may, at Buyer's option, be released to Buyer as liquidated and agreed damages for failure to complete. The failure of Buyer to conduct a walk-through inspection prior to Settlement shall not constitute a waiver by Buyer of the right to receive on the date of possession, the Property as required under the REPC.

12.2 Substantial Completion. The Residence shall be considered "Substantially Complete" when occupancy of the Residence is allowable under the rules, ordinances and laws of the appropriate civil jurisdiction in which the Residence is located. In the absence of such governmental regulations, Substantial Completion shall be when the Residence is ready for occupancy and only minor work remains to be completed, corrected or replaced. Subject to the exceptions referenced in Section 13, the Substantial Completion Deadline shall be as referenced in Section 24(e). Seller shall provide Buyer written notice of Substantial Completion of the Residence. Change Orders may extend the Substantial Completion Deadline.

12.3 Construction Access. Buyer agrees that during the period of construction Seller shall have the unrestricted right to access the Property for the purpose of construction of the Residence and any necessary subdivision improvements if applicable. Buyer shall have the right to reasonable inspection of the Property. However, Seller reserves the right to limit Buyer's inspection of the Property in order to not hinder, interfere, or delay the work. Buyer assumes all risks and liability associated with all such inspections.

12.4 Construction Compliance. Construction of the Residence shall be in accordance with the standards and requirements of all applicable Federal, State, and Local governmental laws, ordinances and regulations, and in compliance with restrictive covenants applicable to the Lot. The Residence shall be correctly situated on the Lot. Construction shall also be done in accordance with the site plan as previously agreed to by Seller and Buyer.

12.5. Regulatory Changes. If any regulatory requirements for construction of the Residence change during the course of construction and result in an increase in the costs of labor and/or materials, the Seller reserves the right to adjust the Purchase Price for the Property to correspond with such regulatory changes. In such event, the Seller shall provide the Buyer with a specific description of the regulatory change(s) and an itemization of the costs incurred to comply with the change(s).

13. UNAVOIDABLE DELAY.
In the event the Residence is not Substantially Complete by the Substantial Completion Deadline as referenced in Section 24(e) due to interruption of transport, availability of materials, strikes, fire, flood, weather, governmental regulations, acts of God, or similar occurrences beyond the control of the Seller, the Substantial Completion Deadline shall be extended for a reasonable period based on the nature of the delay. In such event, the Seller shall notify the Buyer of the delay.

14. AUTHORITY OF SIGNERS.
If Buyer or Seller is a corporation, partnership, trust, estate, limited liability company, or other entity, the person executing the REPC on its behalf warrants his or her authority to do so and to bind Buyer and Seller.

15. COMPLETE CONTRACT.
The REPC together with its addenda, any attached exhibits, and Seller Disclosures, constitutes the entire contract between the parties and supersedes and replaces any and all prior negotiations, representations, warranties, understandings or contracts between the parties. The REPC cannot be changed except by written agreement of the parties.

16. MEDIATION.
Any dispute relating to the REPC arising prior to or after Closing: [ ] SHALL [ ] MAY AT THE OPTION OF THE PARTIES first be submitted to mediation. Mediation is a process in which the parties meet with an impartial person who helps to resolve the dispute informally and confidentially. Mediators cannot impose binding decisions. The parties to the dispute must agree before any settlement is binding. The parties will jointly appoint an acceptable mediator and share equally in the cost of such mediation. If mediation fails, the other procedures and remedies available under the REPC shall apply. Nothing in this Section 16 prohibits any party from seeking emergency legal or equitable relief, pending mediation. The provisions of this Section 16 shall survive Closing.

17. DEFAULT.

17.1 Buyer Default. If Buyer defaults, Seller may elect one of the following remedies: (a) cancel the REPC and retain the Earnest Money Deposit and the Construction Deposit, if applicable, as liquidated damages; (b) maintain the Earnest Money Deposit in trust, retain the Construction Deposit if applicable, and sue Buyer to specifically enforce the REPC; or (c) return the Earnest Money Deposit to Buyer, retain the Construction Deposit and pursue any other remedies available at law.

Page 6 of 8 pages   Buyer's Initials _____ Date_____ Seller's Initials _____ Date_____

17.2 Seller Default. If Seller defaults, Buyer may elect one of the following remedies: (a) cancel the REPC, and in addition to the return of the Earnest Money Deposit and the Construction Deposit if applicable, Buyer may elect to accept from Seller, as liquidated damages, a sum equal to the Earnest Money Deposit; or (b) maintain the Earnest Money Deposit in trust and sue Seller to specifically enforce the REPC; or (c) accept a return of the Earnest Money Deposit and Construction Deposit, if applicable, and pursue any other remedies available at law. If Buyer elects to accept liquidated damages, Seller agrees to pay the liquidated damages to Buyer upon demand.

18. ATTORNEY FEES AND COSTS/GOVERNING LAW. In the event of litigation or binding arbitration to enforce the REPC, the prevailing party shall be entitled to costs and reasonable attorney fees incurred in the litigation and/or arbitration. However, attorney fees shall not be awarded for participation in mediation under Section 16. The REPC shall be governed by and construed in accordance with the laws of the State of Utah. The provisions of this Section 18 shall survive Closing.

19. NOTICES. Except as provided in Section 25, all notices required under the REPC must be: (a) in writing; (b) signed by the Buyer or Seller giving notice; and (c) received by the Buyer or the Seller, or their respective agent, or by the brokerage firm representing the Buyer or Seller, no later than the applicable date referenced in the REPC.

20. NO ASSIGNMENT. The REPC and the rights and obligations of Buyer and Seller hereunder, are personal to Buyer and Seller. The REPC may not be assigned by Buyer or Seller without the prior written consent of the other party. Provided, however, the transfer of Buyer's interest in the REPC to any business entity in which Buyer holds a legal interest, including, but not limited to, a family partnership, family trust, limited liability company, partnership, or corporation (collectively referred to as a "Permissible Transfer"), shall not be treated as an assignment by Buyer that requires Seller's prior written consent. Furthermore, the inclusion of "and/or assigns" or similar language on the line identifying Buyer on the first page of the REPC shall constitute Seller's written consent only to a Permissible Transfer.

21. INSURANCE & RISK OF LOSS
   21.1 INSURANCE. During the period of construction and until Closing, the Seller shall maintain in full force and effect, at the Seller's expense, a builders risk insurance policy for the full replacement value of all completed portions of improvements included in the Residence; and all construction materials located on-site; workmen's compensation insurance in accordance with Utah law, and public general liability insurance in an amount not less than [ ] $1,000,000 [ ] $_____ .
   21.2 RISK OF LOSS. All risk of loss to the Residence, including physical damage or destruction to the Property or its improvements due to any cause, except loss caused by a taking in eminent domain, shall be borne by Seller until the transaction is closed.

22. TIME IS OF THE ESSENCE. Time is of the essence regarding the dates set forth in the REPC. Extensions must be agreed to in writing by all parties. Unless otherwise explicitly stated in the REPC: (a) performance under each Section of the REPC which references a date shall absolutely be required by 5:00 PM Mountain Time on the stated date; and (b) the term "days" and "calendar days" shall mean calendar days and shall be counted beginning on the day following the event which triggers the timing requirement (e.g. Acceptance). Performance dates and times referenced herein shall not be binding upon title companies, lenders, appraisers and others not parties to the REPC, except as otherwise agreed to in writing by such non-party.

23. ELECTRONIC TRANSMISSION AND COUNTERPARTS. Electronic transmission (including email and fax) of a signed copy of the REPC, any addenda and counteroffers, and the retransmission of any signed electronic transmission shall be the same as delivery of an original. The REPC and any addenda and counteroffers may be executed in counterparts.

24. CONTRACT DEADLINES. Buyer and Seller agree that the following deadlines shall apply to the REPC:

(a) **Seller Disclosure Deadline** _____ (Date)

(b) **Due Diligence Deadline** _____ (Date)

(c) **Pre-Construction Meeting Deadline** _____ (Date)

(d) **Construction Loan Funding Deadline** _____ (Date)

(e) **Substantial Completion Deadline** _____ (Date)

(f) **Settlement Deadline** _____ days after the Buyer's receipt of written
                                  Notice of Substantial Completion

Page 7 of 8 pages   Buyer's Initials   Date   Seller's Initials   Date

171

25. ACCEPTANCE. "Acceptance" occurs only when all of the following have occurred: (a) Seller or Buyer has signed the offer or counteroffer where noted to indicate acceptance; and (b) Seller or Buyer or their agent has communicated to the other party or to the other party's agent that the offer or counteroffer has been signed as required.

26. OFFER AND TIME FOR ACCEPTANCE. Buyer offers to purchase the Property on the above terms and conditions. If Seller does not accept this offer by: _____ [ ] AM [ ] PM Mountain Time on_____(Date), this offer shall lapse; and the Brokerage shall return the Earnest Money Deposit to Buyer.

_____   _____
(Buyer's Signature)   (Offer Date)   (Buyer's Signature)   (Offer Date)

_____   _____
(Buyer's Names) (PLEASE PRINT)   (Notice Address)   (Zip Code)   (Phone)

_____   _____
(Buyer's Names) (PLEASE PRINT)   (Notice Address)   (Zip Code)   (Phone)

ACCEPTANCE/COUNTEROFFER/REJECTION
CHECK ONE:
[ ] ACCEPTANCE OF OFFER TO PURCHASE: Seller Accepts the foregoing offer on the terms and conditions specified above.
[ ] COUNTEROFFER: Seller presents for Buyer's Acceptance the terms of Buyer's offer subject to the exceptions or modifications as specified in the attached ADDENDUM NO. _____.
[ ] REJECTION: Seller rejects the foregoing offer.

_____   _____
(Seller's Signature)   (Date) (Time)   (Seller's Signature)   (Date)(Time)

_____   _____
(Seller's Names) (PLEASE PRINT)   (Notice Address)   (Zip Code)   (Phone)

_____   _____
(Seller's Names) (PLEASE PRINT)   (Notice Address)   (Zip Code)   (Phone)

Page 8 of 8 pages

New Construction Contract Terms to Know

- ☐ Construction Loan
- ☐ Cost Plus
- ☐ Fixed Cost

New Construction Contract Quiz

(You may refer to the contract to answer these questions)

1. The NCREPC (New Construction REPC) contains the following information regarding a warranty:

    A. The property can be warranted for one year.

    B. There is no specific warranty.

    C. It is warranted up to the day of possession.

    D. It comes with a home owner warranty from a third party provider.

2. When a licensee is sitting the model home for a builder/developer and a potential buyer comes in and asks questions, which of the following is true about agency?

    A. The agent represents the seller and the buyer automatically.

    B. The agent becomes a limited agent and should have the buyer sign a limited agency agreement.

    C. The agent will be acting only as the buyer's agent.

    D. The agent should disclose he/she is representing the seller and not the buyer.

3. With a fixed cost contract which of the following is NOT true?

    A. There is an incentive to the builder to have subcontractors work in a timely manner.

    B. If it ends up costing more than was originally projected, the added costs are passed on to the buyer.

    C. It benefits the buyer because he/she knows from the beginning what the end cost will be.

    D. This option is more favorable to the buyer than the seller.

4. Which is NOT a true statement about a construction loan?

    A. It is usually a higher interest rate.

    B. The full loan amount is obtained the day the footings are poured.

    C. The amount of the loan is paid in installments as work is done.

    D. It will be paid off when the long-term financing is obtained.

5. The NCREPC allows for the purchase price on the home to be increased if:

    A. The builder gives the buyer 10 days notice of the reason for and amount of the increase.

    B. The lumber costs are more than the builder anticipated.

    C. A written change order is signed in advance by the buyer.

    D. The buyer is given adequate notice and the notice is in writing.

6.   Which of the following is the best comparison of Section 5, Confirmation of Agency Disclosure between the standard REPC and the NCREPC?

   A. They both are exactly the same.

   B. The NCREPC has an additional line for the builder.

   C. The NCREPC assumes the agent is a limited agent.

   D. The standard REPC has a slightly different way of showing limited agency.

7.   According to the NCREPC, what happens if the buyer and seller can't agree upon the manner of resolving an objection of the buyer?

   A. It becomes a contract voidable by either party.

   B. There can be no disagreement as the seller has to fix anything not to the buyer's satisfaction.

   C. The buyer waives their right to cancel based on the due diligence provision

   D. The seller doesn't have to fix it, and it's voidable for the buyer only.

8.   Which of the following items is part of the Seller Disclosures in the NCREPC, but not in the standard REPC?

   A. Property Condition Disclosure

   B. Commitment for title insurance.

   C. A copy of the CC&R's

   D. Specifications for the residence

Property Management Contract

I. **Different Property Types**

    A. **Residential Property** has the following common conditions

        1. Shorter lease term, typically from 1 month up to one year. Month to month (periodic tenancy) is common.

        2. Pets are a common issue in residential leases.

        3. Many residential units are rented with some amount of furnishings.

        4. A gross lease is the most common form of lease.

    B. **Commercial Property**

        1. Longer term leases

        2. Tenant improvements are more common to meet the custom needs of commercial tenants.

        3. Net or triple net leases are used more often due to the longer lease term.

        4. Percentage rent leases are common when the tenancy is associated with a multi-tenant facility in which the landlord controls the tenant mix. The right tenant mix and the right anchor tenants can increase sales of other tenants. The percentage rent lease is targeted at this relationship.

    C. **Office Property**

        1. Long and short term leases

        2. Unit size adjustments are common. Many office structures are designed to have movable walls to adjust for tenant requirements.

        3. Gross and modified gross leases are used. The modified gross lease gives the landlord the ability to recover increasing cost of maintenance, taxes, or insurance through the use of an escalator clause based on a base year and increases in expense over a base year.

        4. Core loaded rents are very common in multi-story office buildings. The core is that section of each floor that includes stairs, elevators, and restrooms, and possible heating and cooling plants. The core cost is another way of sharing common area expense. The core is not included in the tenant square footage but is a surcharge on top of the square footage rents.

    D. **Industrial Property:** Differs from commercial property due to the emphasis on warehouse and/ or non-retail space.

        1. Long and short term leases could be used depending on the customization and configuration expenses of the tenant.

        2. Incubators to factories: An incubator space is a small office warehouse space typically under 2,000 square feet used for start up and growing enterprises.

3. Triple net and net leases are used primarily due to the longer term of rents, the uniqueness of each tenant.

E. **Condominium Property**: Property with common walls and/or structure, owners, and common ownership of common areas.

1. Homeowners association is an organization charged with the management of the common elements of the property and the relationships of owners to property and each other.

2. Air space is a reference to the owners' personally owned unit compared to the common area. The personal area could be between walls that are common to other units so airspace refers to the area between common walls.

3. Common area is that part of the condominium complex that is shared by all owners. It could include exterior building components, parking, landscaping, and amenities including, swimming pools, etc.

4. Covenants, Conditions and Restrictions (CC&R's) are the rules enforced by the Homeowners Association for the entire complex.

F. **Co-op Property**: Owned entirely by a single corporation. The occupants own the corporation.

1. Stock ownership. Each tenant owns shares of stock in the corporation.

2. Proprietary leases act as the equivalent to CC&R's in establishing rules and relationship criteria for the tenant/owners. These leases are referred to as proprietary because they are only available to stockholders.

3. Discrimination is available to Co-op corporations because the stock is not public but privately held and may be controlled as to whom it is offered. Protected classes are still protected against discrimination, but discrimination on the basis of any criteria not protected is possible, such as membership in trade organizations or churches, minimum balance sheet status, and many other criteria that is not protected.

4. Taxation for co-op stockholders is similar to real estate owners, though stock holders own personal not real property.

II. **The Contract**

The typical property management contract should address all of the following issues that apply to the contract relationship.

A. Agency: The property management contract is an agency agreement. It is generally considered as General Agency because property management includes many, if not, almost all duties related to a particular property, including entering into leases on behalf of the owner, collecting rents, enforcing contracts on behalf of the owner, etc.

1. Appointment: The contract must formally appoint the property manager as the owner's agent, subject to the contract terms.

2. Term: The length of the contract can be determined by the parties.

3. Renewal: The contract can be auto-renewing until cancelled or for a fixed term.

B.   Rent management:

  1.   Rent collection: The contract should designate the property manager as the owner's rental collection agent.

  2.   Market rents: Most owners want the property manager to keep them abreast of the market conditions and guide them in setting market rents.

  3.   Competition: Most owners want the property manager to be constantly aware of the competitive properties potential tenants could be exploring; their rental terms and their amenities.

C.   Maintenance management:

  1.   Contract out: Some maintenance tasks such as furnace repair is best done by contractors specializing in that trade. The property manager may be expected to identify an appropriate contractor and enter into agreements on behalf of the owner. The property manager would subsequently be expected to manage the relationship to protect the owner's interest.

  2.   Utilities: The property manager is sometimes expected to select, contract, and manage relationships with utility providers. Cable TV could be an example.

  3.   Periodic service of the property is performed by the property manager to reduce the need for repairs and prolong the property's life and serviceability.

  4.   The property manager may be expected to hire workmen to perform maintenance and repairs under the property manager's supervision, but at the owner's expense. This brings the requirement of payroll taxes, workers' compensations, and liability for supervision.

  5.   Repairs should be made promptly. Usually, delayed repairs mean increasing cost to the owner. The tenant is expected to bring repairs to the landlord's attention, but the blame for delays cannot compensate for the increased cost.

  6.   Maintenance: Should be scheduled so that important work is not neglected. A property owner should know what is needed in all property systems and ensure that the necessary maintenance is accomplished.

D.   **Crisis management**:

  1.   Property Managers should investigate tenant complaints aggressively and promptly, regardless of whether they involve other tenants or property conditions. Harm to the owner is caused by exposure to liability, and increased costs can occur by delays.

  2.   The property manager is the owner's eyes and ears on the property. Crisis usually means expense. It is rare that the owner does not want to know about a crisis as soon as possible so that they can be involved with the decisions and be forewarned about the consequences

  3.   Property managers need authority in the agency agreement to take emergency action even before the owner knows about the crisis.

4. The property manager needs authority to respond to municipal authority. Local authorities will expect it. Compliance with law and lawful orders by police, fire, and rescue personnel cannot be avoided or delayed.

E. Money management:

1. Utah law requires licensed real estate agents and brokers serving as property manager to keep complete records for a minimum of three calendar years. This includes copies of all leases, collections, disbursements, contracts with others and agency agreements. It is wise to keep a record of phone calls with the owner to document oral instructions.

2. Follow a budget - Most owners prefer and appreciate spending within a plan. A budget can build confidence in the property manager if the property manager helped develop it and strictly adheres to its limits unless specific authority is given to exceed its boundaries.

3. Report monthly: Most property manager prepare a full report of activity and financial transactions for the owner. Reports include: lease status, late rents, maintenance needed and performed, budget status, legal issues, etc.

4. Standard accounting practices: The standard of care when handling and accounting others money is the same standard of care for that of the accounting industry. Utah law requires that licensees comply with this standard. For this reason, some property managers have accountants perform the money handling and accounting tasks. Property managers are only expected to report financial transactions they are not expected to give legal and/or tax advice.

F. Unlicensed property management assistants may be used in all of the following tasks (R162-2f-401j(3)):

1. Providing a prospective tenant with access to a rental unit;

2. Providing secretarial, bookkeeping, maintenance, or rent collection services;

3. Quoting rent and lease terms as established or approved by the principal broker;

4. Completing pre-printed lease or rental agreements, except as to terms that may be determined through negotiations of the principals;

5. Serving or receiving legal notices;

6. Addressing tenant or neighbor complaints; and

7. Inspecting units.

G. Quality of management:

1. Services customary for proper maintenance.

2. Positive relations with tenants. Positive relationships are the grease that reduce friction between that owner and their tenants no matter what the situation. Happy tenants pay their rent, complain less, and adjust easier to an inconvenience due to an emergency.

3. Disclosure of market conditions. Property managers are expected to be aware and report changing market conditions.

H. Agent is not a bank: The agent is not expected by the law to advance the owner money or cover owner's expense. Sharing owner expenses even for a short time could create an implied partnership that could bring liability for the owner's expenses.

I. Government relations: The contract should permit the property manager to actively build positive government relations.

1. Maintain licenses and permits: Many communities require business licenses of landlords and almost all require building permits for certain types of repairs and structural alterations.

2. Compliance with law: Community codes could regulate the number of cars in a parking lot, that all cars be licensed on the property. All communities require compliance with health, fire, building and nuisance ordinances.

3. Good neighbor: The best way to keep city officials happy is to keep property neighbors happy. Good relationships with neighbors are worth the time they take.

J. Leasing and renewals: The property management agreement should define the property manager's role in lease and renewals. Some property owners separate the leasing duties from the property manager's duties.

1. Agent cooperation: Interaction with other licensees can complicate and accelerate the leasing process. The property management contract should specifically discuss the expected relationship with outside agents.

2. No state approved lease: Unlike the Real Estate Purchase Contract ("REPC"), the state does not have an approved lease form. Each owner must decide the lease form they will use.

3. Use owner's lease form: If the licensee is involved with the selection of a lease form the licensee should recommend that the owner have the form reviewed by legal counsel.

4. Authority to sign lease: Authority for the property manager to sign leases effectively binding the owner to the lease agreement must be granted by a special power of attorney (R162-2f-401a(19)(a)) and brings full liability for consequences of bad acts to both the property manager and the owner.

5. **Duty to disclose**: Licensees must disclose their status as licensees acting under an agency agreement prior to executing a binding agreement with a prospective tenant. R162-2f-401a(5)(b)(c). The licensee is also required to disclose any material fact to prospective tenants and to the owner about a tenant. R162-2f-401a(1)(c)(i).

K. Management fees:

1. Percent of gross property income: A common method of computing property manager compensation is using a percentage of the total revenue collected.

2. Fixed fee.

3.   Extra-ordinary expenses are usually outlined in the contract as reimbursable by the owner.

4.   No undisclosed fees: All forms of compensation the property manager will receive for services in connection with the property manager's position as property manager must be outlined in the terms of the agency agreement. See R162-2f-403c(4)(b). This includes commissions and rebates form service suppliers to the property.

L.   Managing construction: Many property management contracts appoint the property manager as construction manager with duties to supervise all construction on the property. This occurs most frequently when the property is likely to be subject to tenant improvements. The expectation is that the owner's interests are best protected if the property manager is involved. Code compliance and changes could affect the integrity of the property or impact other tenant's rights under their lease.

M.   **Tenant improvements** are common in commercial and industrial leasing. Every retail store has its own personality. Major stores use floor plans to guide local outlets. The only question is who will pay for the change?

1.   Major repairs or changes could impact other tenants and be influenced by local building codes. Property managers need to protect the landlord's interests and prevent improper changes or additions that could affect the properties short and long term profitability.

2.   Compensation: The property manager should be included in the agency agreement because supervision of tenant improvements could become a time consuming duty.

3.   Liability: The owner could become liable for allowing illegal modification to occur. The Property manager would share in that liability.

N.   **Duty to confer**:

1.   What would the owner do? This is the question that will best guide decision making.

2.   Budget development can only be successful if you know the owners goals, objectives, and expectations.

3.   The maintenance schedule is a budget item as well as a value preservation tool.

4.   Tenant issues can sometimes be dealt with before they come up with good policies and procedures. Knowing the owner's philosophy is most valuable.

5.   Code compliance.

6.   Health and safety.

O.   **Indemnification**: An agreement to reimburse losses caused by another party. In the owner/ property manager relationship it is necessary that a contractual agreement exists to make liability insurance policies pay on behalf of their client to the other party in the property management agreement.

1.   By agent: The property manager could act or fail to act in a way that would make the owner liable for consequences.

2. By owner: Owners are typically liable for all action on or about their properties or by their employees or hired contractors and agents.

P. Insurance coverage:

1. **Liability insurance** pays others for the liability of the owner.

2. **Causality insurance** pays for property damage to the owner property.

3. Promptly investigating an accident or claim is necessary so that insurance investigators can be notified when it is possible that the claim will exceed the deductible. Failure to investigate could cause increased loss and even a loss of recovery rights.

4. **Co-insurance**: An extension of the insurance coverage to protect other parties.

    a. The agent/property manager wants to be included as a co-insured on the owner's policy so that the insurance company does not try to shift the liability to the property manager.

    b. Owner, & Owner's partners need to be covered by the basic policy.

    c. Mortgagee or lender also has an interest in being a co-insured to protect their collateral interest.

Q. Control of funds:

1. **Disbursement authority** should be outlined in the agency agreement.

2. Be auditable by keeping records in a form and complete so that a professional accounting audit could be performed. Good records demonstrate responsible management.

3. The paper trail needs to extend from beginning to end with all detail included, including notes of conversations.

4. Document everything.

5. Keep all record for a minimum of 3 calendar years for the Division of Real Estate, but, keep records for a minimum of 5 years of records for most tax audits. Keep property improvement and casualty record to define the adjusted basis for as long as the property is owned.

R. Termination:

1. Both parties can terminate the agreement by agreement of the parties. This can even occur when conflict arises.

2. Owner default would be a basis for termination actions by the property manager. If agreement cannot be reached then a court order would be necessary to formally terminate the agreement.

3. Agent default would be a basis for termination actions by the property manager. If agreement cannot be reached then a court order would be necessary to formally terminate the agreement.

Property Management Terms to Know

- ☐ Air Space
- ☐ Authority to Sign Lease
- ☐ Commercial Property
- ☐ Common Area
- ☐ Covenants, Conditions and Restrictions (CC&R's)
- ☐ Disbursement Authority
- ☐ Duty to Disclose
- ☐ Homeowners Association
- ☐ Indemnification
- ☐ Management Fees
- ☐ Net or Triple Net Lease
- ☐ Property Manager
- ☐ Residential Property
- ☐ Tenant Improvements
- ☐ Trust Account or Owners Account

Short Sale Forms

I. **Short Sale Defined**

   A. The term "**Short Sale**" is used in the real estate business to describe a situation where the current fair market value of the property is less than the debt owing against the property. The Seller can't sell the property unless the creditors ("Third Parties") agree to accept a payment that is less than (or "Short" of) the amounts actually owed to those Third Parties.

   B. The **Third Parties** may include mortgage lenders, mortgage insurers, bankruptcy trustees, and federal, state, and local taxing authorities (such as the IRS or State Tax Commission), or other lien holders.

II. **Short Sale Process**

   The seller decides to sell property. As part of the preparation for getting the property ready to sell, the agent and seller work together to provide the lender(s) with the information it needs. The combination of this information is referred to as a short sale packet. The agent and seller continue to work together to help the lender determine if the property qualifies. Qualification for a short sale is at the sole discretion of the lender(s). Many properties may never be approved for a short sale.

   A. Third Parties will research the market value of the property to determine the amount of the loss or any possible equity. This is usually accomplished by a **BPO** (Broker Price Opinion) or an actual appraisal.

   B. Must be an active broker, associate broker, or sales agent.

   Warning to Agents – List price should be reasonable and within actual market value. Do not intentionally encourage sellers to price property at levels well below the market value the lender would never approve.

III. **Third Party Guidelines**

   A. Lenders have guidelines to determine whether or not the seller (the current borrower) qualifies for a short sale. These guidelines vary from lender to lender.

   B. Loss and mitigation departments work with borrowers to collect as much as possible for the lender. They also work to lower the loss for the lender. These departments oversee and are heavily involved in the short sale process.

   C. **Mortgage insurance** is in place to protect lenders form defaulting borrowers. Lenders may be influenced whether or not to approve a short sale by the amount of claim that can be made.

   D. A lender may require that any person who is hired to work with the negotiations of short sales have an active real estate license.

   E. Short sale packet includes valuable information the lender will need to determine if the seller/borrower qualifies for a short sale. A prudent agent will make sure this information is thorough and accurate.

IV. **UAR Forms**

   A. Utah Association of Realtors attorneys have created forms to assist in the transactional process and to educate the buyers and sellers.

B.   Real estate agents and brokers have these forms at their disposal:

1.   Short Sale Disclosure

2.   Short Sale Addendum

3.   Secondary "Backup" Contract For Short Sale

4.   Exclusive Right To Sell Listing Agreement & Agency Disclosure (Short Sale)

C.   Seller may be required to continue to market the property even AFTER they have accepted an offer. This is an effort by the lender to insure the highest price is achieved.

D.   If the seller is not forced by the lender, the seller may choose to send only one offer at a time to the lender. This seems to work the best because it takes a considerable amount of time to get a buyer's offer approved for a short sale. Starting over every time there is a new offer may result in a longer processing time. Ultimately, this decision is one that falls to the seller. However, the seller would be wise to consult with an attorney.

V.   **Quick Facts about Contractual Terms in the Short Sale Forms**

• Buyer may choose to deposit Earnest Money AFTER Third Party Approval (Section 5 - of SS Addendum)

• Buyer or seller may cancel the REPC any time PRIOR to Third Party Approval by providing written notice. (Section 7 - of SS Addendum)

• The benchmark used as a time-frame for obtaining Third Party approval is 120 days from acceptance. (UAR Forms committee recommendation.)

• If Approval is not obtain by the "Third Party Approval Deadline" then the offer is AUTOMATICALLY canceled without any other requirement. (Section 4 - of SS Addendum.)

• Seller must submit the accepted offer to Third Parties within 4 calendar days. (Section 3 - of SS Addendum.)

• Seller may receive additional offers (Section 7 - SS Addendum, Section 1.3 Secondary "Backup" Contract For SS.)

• Seller may modify the terms of the "Prior REPC" even after accepting a Back up offer.

• Sellers Disclosures, Buyers Due Diligence, Financing and Appraisal and Settlement Deadlines can be set AFTER Third Party approval.

Short Sale Terms to Know

☐ Broker Price Opinion or Actual Appraisal

☐ Mortgage Insurance

☐ Short Sale

☐ Third Parties

 Utah Association *of* REALTORS®

SHORT SALE ADDENDUM NO. _____
TO
REAL ESTATE PURCHASE CONTRACT
Participating in a Short Sale may have negative legal or tax consequences. If you desire specific legal or tax advice, consult your attorney or tax advisor.

THIS IS AN [   ] ADDENDUM [   ] COUNTEROFFER to that REAL ESTATE PURCHASE CONTRACT (the "REPC") with an Offer Reference Date of _____ 20_____, including all prior addenda and counteroffers, between _____, as Buyer, and _____ as Seller, regarding the Property located at _____ (the "Property"). The terms of this Addendum are hereby incorporated as part of the REPC, and to the extent the terms of this Addendum modify or conflict with any provisions of the REPC, including all prior addenda and counteroffers, these terms shall control.

1. ACKNOWLEDGMENT OF SHORT SALE. This transaction is commonly referred to as a "Short Sale" because the Purchase Price for the Property is less, or "short", of the amount(s) owed to individuals/entities that have a financial interest in the Property (the "Third Parties"). Under the terms of the REPC, the Third Parties are being requested to accept less than what is owed to them. Therefore, Buyer and Seller agree that their respective obligations under the REPC are subject to Third Party Approval as defined in Section 2 below. For purposes of this Addendum, the term "Third Parties" may include, without limitation; institutional lenders, mortgage insurers, bankruptcy trustees, federal, state and local tax authorities, and private parties.

2. THIRD PARTY APPROVAL. For purposes of the REPC, "Third Party Approval" shall mean that the Third Parties, Seller, and Buyer have agreed in writing to the terms of a Short Sale as provided in Sections 2.1 through 2.3 below **AND** the Buyer and Seller have signed and accepted the *Acknowledgement of Third Party Approval Addendum*.

    2.1 Approval by Third Parties. The Third Parties have provided written approval of the terms and conditions of the Short Sale, including, if applicable, any modifications to the REPC required by the Third Parties ("Third Party Modifications to the REPC"). The Third Party Modifications to the REPC shall not however, be binding on Buyer or Seller unless they agree to such modifications by signing the *Acknowledgement of Third Party Approval Addendum* as referenced above. Consent may be withheld by Buyer and/or Seller in their sole discretion.

    2.2 Approval by Seller. Seller has entered into a separate written agreement with the Third Parties regarding any conditions of approval specifically required of Seller by the Third Parties, including, but not limited to any deficiency rights the Third Parties may retain against Seller, any requirements for a cash payment and/or promissory note from Seller to the Third Parties and any other Short Sale payoff criteria that represent a continuing obligation against Seller (collectively referred to as the "Additional Third Party Requirements"). Seller's consent to the Additional Third Party Requirements may be withheld by Seller, in Seller's sole discretion.

    2.3 Approval by Buyer. Buyer has agreed to any Third Party Modifications to the REPC and any Additional Third Party Requirements that require specific approval by the Buyer, by accepting the *Acknowledgement of Third Party Approval Addendum*. Buyer's consent to any Third Party Modifications to the REPC and/or any Additional Third Party Requirements may be withheld by Buyer, in Buyer's sole discretion.

3. DELIVERY OF REPC TO THIRD PARTIES. After Acceptance of the REPC by Buyer and Seller (as defined in Section 23 of the REPC) Seller agrees to submit the REPC to the applicable Third Parties, together with any additional documentation required by the Third Parties according to the Third Parties' instructions.

4. FAILURE TO OBTAIN THIRD PARTY APPROVAL. Seller and Buyer shall have until _____, 20 _____ ("Third Party Approval Deadline") to obtain Third Party Approval as defined in Section 2 inclusive above. If by the Third Party Approval Deadline, Third Party Approval has not been obtained, the REPC shall automatically be deemed cancelled whereupon any Earnest Money Deposit shall be released to Buyer without the requirement of further written authorization from Seller.

5. EARNEST MONEY DEPOSIT. Buyer agrees to deliver the Earnest Money Deposit to Buyer's Brokerage **(check applicable box): [   ]** as required in the first paragraph on page one of the REPC; **[   ]** no later than four (4) calendar days after Third Party Approval as defined in Section 2 above; or **[   ]** Other (specify) _____.

_____ .

Page 1 of 2   Buyer's Initials _____ Date _____   Seller's Initials _____ Date _____

6.   SELLER'S RIGHT TO ACCEPT BACK-UP OFFERS. Buyer agrees that at any time prior to Third Party Approval as defined in Section 2 above, Seller may: (a) continue to market the Property to other interested buyers; (b) continue to advertise the Property through the MLS showing any MLS status category (the MLS will allow) deemed necessary and appropriate by the Seller and/or the Third Parties; (c) accept additional backup offers for the purchase of the Property ("Backup Contracts") subject to the rights of Buyer under this contract; and (d) Seller may or may not submit any such Backup Contracts to the Third Parties for review.

7.   BUYER & SELLER'S RIGHT TO CANCEL REPC. Seller and Buyer acknowledge that there will be significant time delays in obtaining any response from the Third Parties to the terms of this proposed Short Sale; and because this is a Short Sale, Seller will need to obtain the highest and best terms for the sale of the Property. During this significant time delay, circumstances may change for both Seller and Buyer. The changes in circumstances may include, but are not limited to: (a) adjustments in available mortgage financing rates and terms; (b) modifications in the financial circumstances of Seller or Buyer; (c) the timing of the transaction may no longer meet Buyer or Seller's needs; (d) Buyer may find another property that better suits Buyer's needs; and (e) Seller may receive additional offers for the purchase of the Property that better address Seller's legal and financial needs. Based on the above, if at any time prior to Third Party Approval, or the Third Party Approval Deadline, whichever occurs first, the Buyer or Seller determines that their circumstances have changed and it is no longer in their best interest to pursue the sale/purchase of the Property, either Buyer or Seller may cancel the REPC by providing written notice to the other party. In such instance, the Earnest Money Deposit, if any, shall be returned to the Buyer without the requirement of further written authorization from Seller. Buyer and Seller acknowledge and agree that this mutual right of cancellation is fair and reasonable to both parties.

8.   CONTRACT DEADLINES. Unless otherwise agreed to as part of the Third Party Approval, Buyer and Seller agree that the Contract Deadlines in Section 24 of the REPC are as follows:

(a) Seller Disclosure Deadline   _____ days after Third Party Approval.

(b) Due Diligence Deadline   _____ days after Third Party Approval.

(c) Financing & Appraisal Deadline   _____ days after Third Party Approval.

(d) Settlement Deadline   _____ days after Third Party Approval.

(e) Buyer and Seller also agree that if any of the dates referenced in this Section 8 above fall on a Saturday, Sunday, or legal holiday, performance shall be required on the next business day.

ALL OTHER TERMS of the REPC, including all prior addenda and counteroffers, not modified by this ADDENDUM shall remain the same. **[ ] Seller [ ] Buyer** shall have until _____ **[ ] A.M [ ] P.M.** Mountain Time _____, 20_____ to accept the terms of this ADDENDUM in accordance with the provisions of Section 23 of the REPC. Unless so accepted, the offer as set forth in the ADDENDUM shall lapse.

_____   _____
[ ] Buyer [ ] Seller Signature   Date   Time   [ ] Buyer [ ] Seller Signature   Date   Time

ACCEPTANCE/COUNTEROFFER/REJECTION

CHECK ONE:

[ ] ACCEPTANCE of ADDENDUM: [ ] Seller [ ] Buyer hereby accepts the terms of this ADDENDUM/COUNTER OFFER
[ ] COUNTER OFFER: [ ] Seller [ ] Buyer presents as a counteroffer the terms of attached ADDENDUM No._____
[ ] REJECTION: [ ] Seller [ ] Buyer rejects the foregoing ADDENDUM/COUNTER OFFER

_____   _____
[ ] Buyer [ ] Seller Signature   Date   Time   [ ] Buyer [ ] Seller Signature   Date   Time

 Utah Association *of* REALTORS®

SHORT SALE DISCLOSURE

THIS SHORT SALE DISCLOSURE is provided by:_____ (the "Company") to:
_____ [   ] the Buyer [   ] Seller of the following property located at:
_____ (the "Property"). The following is an explanation regarding some of the practical and legal issues involved in Short Sales.

1.   SHORT SALE DEFINED. The term "Short Sale" is used in the real estate business to describe a situation where the current fair market value of the property is less than the debt owing against the property. In other words, the Seller can't sell the property unless the creditors ("Third Parties") agree to accept a payment that is less than (or "short" of) the amounts actually owed to those Third Parties. The Third Parties may include mortgage lenders, mortgage insurers, bankruptcy trustees, and federal, state and local taxing authorities (such as the IRS or State Tax Commission) or other lien holders.

2.   THIRD PARTY APPROVAL CONDITION. A Short Sale requires the written approval of the Third Parties. Consequently, the Seller of the property and any Buyer is advised that even if they reach an agreement with each other for the purchase and sale of the property the Buyer's obligation to purchase, and the Seller's obligation to sell, are respectively conditioned upon Third Party Approval of the Short Sale as defined in the Short Sale Addendum.

3.   THIRD PARTY REJECTION OR CHANGES TO THE PROPOSED SHORT SALE. Third Parties may reject a proposed Short Sale. If however, the Third Parties do not reject the proposed Short Sale, they will usually send to the Seller a list of requested changes to the proposed purchase contract ("Third Party Modifications"). The Third Party Modifications may affect the Seller; and others may affect the Buyer. For example, the Third Parties may not permit the Seller to pay for any of the Buyer's closing costs, or may require that the transaction close by a certain date. The Seller and the Buyer are not obligated to accept any of the requested Third Party Modifications – in which case, there will be no Short Sale. If, however, the Seller and Buyer agree upon the Third Party Modifications in an addendum to the REPC, then the Short Sale transaction may proceed to closing.

4.   DELAYS IN RESPONSE FROM THE THIRD PARTIES. Most purchase contracts for Short Sales impose a deadline for written approval by the Third Parties. The Third Parties may not meet that deadline or respond at all. The Seller and the Buyer should be prepared for significant delays in receiving any response from the Third Parties.

5.   RIGHT OF THIRD PARTIES TO ENCOURAGE ADDITIONAL OFFERS. As a condition to considering any proposed Short Sale, the Third Parties may require the Seller to keep the Property on the market even after the Seller and the Buyer have agreed to the terms of a proposed purchase contract. The Third Parties want to obtain the highest possible price for the property. Therefore, some Third Parties require the Seller to keep the Property on the market, and to promptly submit to the Third Parties any additional offers that the owner may receive from other Buyers. The Seller and the Buyer should understand that the Third Parties may not respond to a proposed Short Sale transaction until they have had an opportunity to compare that offer with other purchase offers. That process may also result in significant delays for all parties.

6.   RIGHT OF BUYER AND SELLER TO CANCEL. Seller and Buyer are also advised that at any time prior to the Third Party Approval Deadline or the Third Party Approval, whichever occurs first, as defined in the Short Sale Addendum, Buyer or Seller may cancel the proposed Short Sale transaction in accordance with the terms and conditions of the Short Sale Addendum.

7.   TAX AND LEGAL CONSEQUENCES. The undersigned is advised that participating in a Short Sale transaction may have negative legal or tax consequences. You are advised to consult your attorney or tax advisor if you desire specific legal or tax advice.

ACKNOWLEDGEMENT OF RECEIPT

The undersigned acknowledge that they have read and understand this document.

_____   _____   _____   _____
Signature   **Date**   **Signature**   **Date**

Buyer's Notice of Cancellation
of
Real Estate Purchase Contract

BUYER: _____

BUYER'S BROKERAGE: _____

SELLER: _____

SELLER'S BROKERAGE: _____

PROPERTY: _____

CITY _____, COUNTY _____, UTAH, ZIP_____

1. **NOTICE OF CANCELLATION OF CONTRACT.** Buyer hereby gives notice of cancellation of the Real Estate Purchase Contract (REPC) with an Offer Reference Date of _____, between Buyer and Seller regarding the above-described Property. The cancellation of the REPC is based on the following:

[ ] Due Diligence Condition - REPC Section 8.1(b)
[ ] Appraisal Condition - REPC Section 8.2(a)
[ ] Financing Condition - REPC Section 8.3(a)
[ ] Financing Condition - REPC Section 8.3(b)
[ ] Risk of Loss - REPC Section 20.2
[ ] Subject to the Sale of Buyer's Residence Addendum - Section 1.3
[ ] Secondary "Backup" Contract Addendum – Section 1.3
[ ] Short Sale Addendum – Section 7
[ ] Other (describe) _____
_____

2. **RELEASE OF EARNEST MONEY DEPOSIT.** By signing below Buyer acknowledges that the REPC is cancelled and hereby directs: [ ] Buyer's Brokerage; [ ] Other (describe) _____to release per the terms of the REPC, the Earnest Money Deposit(s) of $_____ to [ ] Buyer [ ] Seller.

_____   _____
Buyer Signature   Date   Time   Buyer Signature   Date   Time

 **Utah Association** *of* **REALTORS®**

SECONDARY "BACKUP" CONTRACT FOR SHORT SALE
ADDENDUM NO. _____
TO
REAL ESTATE PURCHASE CONTRACT

THIS IS AN [ ] ADDENDUM [ ] COUNTEROFFER to that REAL ESTATE PURCHASE CONTRACT (the "REPC") with an Offer Reference Date of _____ 20_____, including all prior addenda and counteroffers, between _____, as Buyer, and _____ as Seller, regarding the Property located at _____ (the "Property"). The terms of this Addendum are hereby incorporated as part of the REPC, and to the extent the terms of this Addendum modify or conflict with any provisions of the REPC, including all prior addenda and counteroffers, these terms shall control.

1. **BUYER ACKNOWLEDGEMENTS.** Buyer acknowledges that:
   1.1 **Short Sale & Third Party Approval.** The Property is currently being marketed as a "Short Sale" and is also subject to "Third Party Approval" as those terms are respectively defined in the attached Short Sale Addendum (the "Short Sale Addendum");
   1.2 **Prior REPC & Backup Contract.** Seller has previously accepted a purchase offer for the Property from another buyer (the "Prior REPC"), and therefore, this REPC from the above-referenced Buyer is a "Backup Contract";
   1.3 **Additional Backup Contracts.** Because Seller and the Third Parties desire to minimize their respective losses under a Short Sale, Seller has the right to accept additional Backup Contracts from other interested buyers ("Additional Backup Contracts");
   1.4 **Submission of Prior REPC.** Seller has submitted or will submit the Prior REPC to the applicable Third Parties for Third Party Approval;
   1.5 **Submission of Backup Contracts.** In reference to Section 3 and 6 of the Short Sale Addendum and based on the requirements of the Third Parties, Seller may or may not submit this Backup Contract and any Additional Backup Contracts to the applicable Third Parties for Third Party Approval. If this REPC is submitted to the Third Parties, Seller agrees to provide Buyer with written notice within four (4) days after submission to the Third Parties.
   1.6 **Modification of Terms.** Seller may, by mutual agreement with the Buyer under the Prior REPC, or the Buyer(s) under any Additional Backup Contract(s), amend or modify the terms of the Prior REPC and/or any Additional Backup Contracts, as applicable. In the event this REPC is submitted to the Third Parties for Third Party Approval, any modification of this REPC and this Addendum shall require the written consent of Buyer and Seller as required in the Short Sale Addendum.

2. **BUYER AND SELLER'S RIGHT TO CANCEL.** At any time prior to the Third Party Approval Deadline or Third Party Approval, whichever occurs first, Buyer or Seller may cancel this REPC in accordance with the terms and conditions of the Short Sale Addendum. If Third Party Approval of this REPC is not obtained by the Third Party Approval Deadline referenced in Section 4 of the Short Sale Addendum, this REPC shall automatically be deemed cancelled.

ALL OTHER TERMS of the REPC, including all prior addenda and counteroffers, not modified by this ADDENDUM/COUNTER OFFER shall remain the same. **[ ] Seller [ ] Buyer** shall have until ____ **[ ] A.M [ ] P.M.** Mountain Time _____, 20___, to accept the terms of this ADDENDUM/COUNTEROFFER in accordance with the provisions of Section 23 of the REPC. Unless so accepted, the offer as set forth in the ADDENDUM/COUNTER OFFER shall lapse.

_____
[ ] Buyer [ ] Seller Signature   Date   Time

_____
[ ] Buyer [ ] Seller Signature   Date   Time

ACCEPTANCE/COUNTEROFFER/REJECTION
CHECK ONE:

[ ] **ACCEPTANCE:** [ ] Seller [ ] Buyer hereby accepts the terms of this ADDENDUM/COUNTER OFFER
[ ] **COUNTER OFFER:** [ ] Seller [ ] Buyer presents as a counteroffer the terms of attached Counteroffer No.____
[ ] **REJECTION:** [ ] Seller [ ] Buyer rejects the foregoing ADDENDUM/COUNTER OFFER

_____
[ ] Buyer [ ] Seller Signature   Date   Time

_____
[ ] Buyer [ ] Seller Signature   Date   Time

ADDENDUM NO. _____
TO
EXCLUSIVE RIGHT TO SELL LISTING AGREEMENT & AGENCY DISCLOSURE
(SHORT SALE)

THIS IS AN ADDENDUM to that EXCLUSIVE RIGHT TO SELL LISTING AGREEMENT & AGENCY DISCLSOURE (the "Listing Agreement") entered into on the _____ day of _____,20_____, between _____, the "Seller"), and _____(the "Company"), regarding the Property located at:_____ (the "Property"). The following terms are hereby incorporated as part of the Listing Agreement, and to the extent these terms modify or conflict with any provisions of the Listing Agreement, these terms shall control.

1. **Acknowledgement of Short Sale Disclosure**. Seller acknowledges that Seller has received from the Company a form entitled Short Sale Disclosure (the "Short Sale Disclosure"). Seller acknowledges that Seller has read, understands, and agrees with the information contained in the Short Sale Disclosure.

2. **Third Parties Considerations**. Seller acknowledges that a Short Sale is subject to Third Party approval. Third Parties ("Third Parties") may impose conditions prior to approval of a Short Sale, including, but not limited to: (a) the Third Parties obtaining a broker price opinion or appraisal; (b) requiring Seller to demonstrate financial hardship; (c) requiring Seller to provide copies of tax returns, pay stubs, assets, and other financial information.

3. **Seller Authorizations.** Seller authorizes the Company to:
   (a) Advertise the Property as a Short Sale in all marketing materials prepared by the Company;
   (b) Advertise the Property as a Short Sale on the MLS (in accordance with the MLS rules and regulations);
   (c) Continue to advertise the Property for sale on the MLS (in accordance with the MLS rules and regulations) until approval of the Short Sale by the Third Parties;
   (d) Contact the Third Parties to obtain lien payoff amounts or other related information regarding the Short Sale;
   (e) Communicate directly with the Third Parties on Seller's behalf; and
   (f) Provide to the Third Parties such disclosures, information, and documentation requested by the Third Parties for the purpose of obtaining approval of the Short Sale.

4. **Seller Acknowledgements.** Seller acknowledges the following:
   (a) If the Third Parties agree to a Short Sale, then (i) Seller may not receive any sales proceeds at Closing; (ii) Seller may be required by the Third Parties to bring some of Seller's own funds to Settlement; (iii) the Third Parties may seek a deficiency judgment against Seller or pursue other collection efforts to recover any loss incurred by the Third Parties in accepting the Short Sale; and (iv) even if the Third Parties elect not to pursue a deficiency judgment, any Short Sale discount accepted by the Third Parties may be reported to the IRS by the Third Parties as taxable income to Seller;
   (b) If the Third Parties refuse to approve the Short Sale, the Property may go into foreclosure and Seller may lose all legal and financial interest in the Property;
   (c) A Short Sale transaction may have a negative impact on Seller's credit rating even if the foreclosure process has not officially begun, or once begun, is not completed;
   (d) Upon marketing the Property as a Short Sale, Seller may receive one or more offers for the purchase of the Property, but the Third Parties may require that only one offer be presented to the Third Parties for approval;
   (e) There are other legal and financial options that Seller may want to consider with legal counsel and tax advisors rather than a Short Sale, including, but not limited to: (i) negotiating a loan modification; (ii) refinancing; (iii) bankruptcy; (iv) foreclosure; or (v) a deed in lieu of foreclosure;
   (f) The Company has no control over the decision of the Third Parties to accept a Short Sale, or over the timing associated with that decision;
   (g) Seller agrees to hold the Company harmless from acts or omissions of the Third Parties;
   (h) If the Third Parties do not cooperate or fail to communicate with the Company, the Company may cancel this

Page 1 of 2

193

Listing Agreement by providing written notice to Seller;
(i) If the Property is conveyed to any mortgage insurer or lien holder during the term of this Listing Agreement, then in such event, Seller or the Company may cancel this Listing Agreement prior to its expiration by providing written notice to the other party;
(j) The brokerage fees referenced in this Listing Agreement are subject to the Third Parties approval; and
(k) Seller is advised by the Company to consult with legal counsel and other professionals as provided in Section 5 below.
(l) If the Listing Period referenced in Section 2 of the Listing Agreement expires prior to Third Party Approval, as defined in Section 2 of the Short Sale Addendum, Seller and the Company agree that the Listing Period shall automatically be extended until the Third Party Approval Deadline, as defined in Section 4 of the Short Sale Addendum, unless otherwise cancelled by the Company in accordance with the terms and conditions of the Listing Agreement.

5. Advice to Consult with Legal Counsel and Other Professionals. Seller has been advised by Seller's Agent and the Company that: (a) there may be significant legal and tax consequences, and negative credit rating impacts associated with entering into a Short Sale; (b) Seller is strongly encouraged by the Company and the Seller's Agent that before agreeing to a Short Sale, and entering into any agreement with the Third Parties, as defined in the Short Sale Disclosure, Seller should obtain and carefully evaluate professional advice from legal counsel and tax advisors to assure that Seller fully understands and accepts the legal and tax consequences of entering into an agreement and completing a Short Sale. Seller acknowledges and agrees that Seller is not relying on Seller's Agent or the Company regarding any interpretation of the legal and tax consequences of a Short Sale transaction.

ALL OTHER TERMS of the Listing Agreement, not modified by this ADDENDUM shall remain the same. Seller acknowledges that Seller has read, understands, and agrees to the terms of this Addendum.

_____   _____   _____   _____
(Seller Signature)   (Date)   (Seller Signature)   (Date)

ACCEPTED by the Company:

by: _____   _____
(Signature of Authorized Seller's Agent or Broker)   (Date)

© Stringham Schools

PROPERTY MANAGEMENT

LEASES

PROPERTY MANAGEMENT

Leases

I.   **Less than Freehold**

An estate in real property that does not involve actual ownership is called **less than freehold**. It could correctly be called a "less than ownership interest in real property." Rights that are **non-possessory rights** in real property such as easements, licenses, and the right to do something for profit are sometimes referred to as incorporeal rights.

II.   **License**

A **license interest** in real property is not an estate or right in land, but is a personal right or privilege. That privilege is limited, revocable, and non-assignable.

A.   Examples of license interests are: theater ticket, library card, or permission to hunt or fish on private property.

B.   A license ceases upon the death of either party and is revoked upon sale of the property.

III. **Profit**

A **profit interest** is a non-possessory right, given by agreement with the owner, to remove soil or products from the land (such as harvesting crops, fruit, or Christmas trees) in order to make a profit. Ordinarily there would be a written agreement to pay for this right.

IV.   **Lease**

A **lease** conveys the right of possession without transferring any right of ownership.

A.   The **lessor** is the owner or landlord

B.   The **lessee** is the tenant

C.   The **lessor** holds an estate in reversion.

D.   If a landlord, who owns the property fee simple, dies during the term of the lease, the lease is still binding on the heirs.

E.   If a landlord, who owns his property fee simple, sells his property during the term of the lease, the lease is binding on the new owner and the terms cannot be renegotiated until the current lease expires.

      1.   **Non-disturbance clause**: this is a clause in a mortgage wherein the lender agrees not to terminate the tenant's lease, or the services provided, in the event the lender must foreclose on the borrower's (owner's) property.

V.   **Leasehold Estates**

A.   **Estate or Tenancy for Years**: Its characteristics are:

      1.   It has a specific starting date and, more importantly, a termination date.

      2.   It is extended by renegotiation and renewal of the lease.

B.   **Periodic Tenancy**: Its characteristics are:

      1.   It automatically renews itself.

2.   It can be terminated by notice of either party.

3.   The legal term of notice in Utah is 15 days. Utah Code Annotated § 78B-6-802(1)(b)(i). This legal time period takes effect when there is no mention of the term of notice in the lease.

4.   The tenant and landlord may agree to whatever term of notice they want so long as it is written in the lease.

5.   Periodic tenancy is often referred to as month-to-month tenancy.

C.   **Estate or Tenancy at Will**: Its characteristics are:

1.   The lease is of uncertain or unspecified duration, meaning there is no termination date and the lease does not automatically renew itself.

2.   Either party may terminate the lease without advance notice. However, Utah statute requires a 5-day notice. Utah Code Annotated § 78B-6-802(1)(b)(ii).

3.   It is automatically terminated at the death of either party or the sale of the property.

4.   An agreement to stay in a motel or hotel is usually considered tenancy at will.

D.   **Estate or Tenancy at Sufferance**: Its characteristics are:

1.   The tenant is wrongfully holding possession after expiration of the lease.

2.   If the tenant had not previously held a legal right of possession through a lease, he would be considered a trespasser.

3.   If the landlord accepts rent, the tenancy changes to periodic tenancy and the lessee is called a holdover tenant.

VI.   **Landlord/Tenant Law**

Leases for residential property contain a written or implied warranty of habitability. Unless otherwise stated:

A.   The landlord is responsible for major repairs and maintenance. All leases, unless otherwise noted, contain a clause of habitability, written or implied. The landlord must keep the premises habitable.

1.   A lessee is released from the obligation to pay rent if the property in condemned for health reasons.

B.   The tenant is responsible for minor repairs and maintenance.

C.   **Estovers**: These are necessities allowed by law, such as the right of a tenant to use timber for fuel on a ranch.

D.   **Rent control** is a law that limits the lessor's ability to raise rents. This places the burden for inflation on the lessor rather than the lessee.

E.   If the landlord sells the property that has a valid lease in place, the lease remains valid and in force.

VII.　**Payment of Rent**

    A.　**Lease**: Refers to the contract, written or oral, between the lessor and the tenant. Rent is the money that is paid.

    B.　**Gross rent (straight lease)**: Tenant pays a fixed rent and the landlord pays the operating expenses, which are primarily the utilities.

    C.　**Net rent or lease:** Tenant pays a fixed rent plus his own operating expenses.

    D.　**Percentage rent or lease**: This is most often used on commercial or retail rental property.

        1.　The tenant is charged a percent of the gross or net income.

        2.　Sometimes the rent includes a minimum flat rate or flat lease plus a percent of net or gross profits over a given dollar amount.

    E.　**Escalator clause**: This clause in a lease allows the landlord to periodically increase the rents by a dollar amount or a percentage, as provided in the contract. Escalation clauses create a graduated lease.

    F.　**Participation clause**: This expense clause allows the landlord to pass along unexpected increases in property taxes, utilities, maintenance costs, etc. above the base year.

VIII.　**Special Leases**

    A.　**Ground lease**: The lessor owns and receives rent on the ground while the lessee pays for and owns the improvements.

    B.　**Rooftop lease**: Used mostly for rental of space for billboards, antennas, and satellite or microwave disks. The lessee leases only that part of the building he needs.

    C.　**Vertical lease**: These leases are used when more than the surface rights are involved and apply to:

        1.　Mineral rights, such as oil and gas rights; and

        2.　Air rights. For example, in Chicago and New York City, railroads have leased surface and air rights above downtown tracks for construction of high-rise office buildings.

    D.　**Proprietary lease**: A lease given to an owner of stock in a stock cooperative. In effect, it is an owner's lease.

    E.　**Reappraisal lease**: A lease wherein the rent is determined by a periodic appraisal of the property, and is sometimes called an interval market evaluation.

    F.　**Graduated lease**: This type of lease has an escalator clause that provides for periodic increases in the rent as specified. It requires increase of rent at regular intervals. For instance, the lease agreement may state that the lease will increase 6% at the end of the first six months and 4% each year thereafter.

    G.　**Index lease**: The rent is based on an index such as the consumer price index (CPI) and thus fluctuates, usually on an annual basis.

IX. **Assigning and Subletting**

    A.   Unless the lease specifically prohibits it, the tenant has the right to assign or sublet the property,

    B.   The tenant cannot assign or sublet more rights than he has. If he has a five year lease with two years remaining, he can only assign the remaining two years.

    C.   **Assignment** of lease:

        1.   The lessee is the assignor and though he has no primary responsibility, he does retain secondary liability. If the assignee defaults, the lessor can seek satisfaction from the assignor.

        2.   The assignee assumes primary liability and is responsible to pay rent directly to the lessor.

    D.   **Sublet**:

        1.   The lessee is the **sublettor**. He retains primary liability for the lease, and pays rent to the lessor.

        2.   The **sublettee** is responsible only to the lessee and pays rent to the lessee. He has no legal responsibility to the lessor. (See diagram below)

X. **Sale and Leaseback**

A technique often used in commercial properties, where an owner sells the property to an investor and, at the closing, leases it back. This provides benefits to both the seller/tenant and the investor/landlord.

    A.   Advantages to the seller/tenant:

        1.   He retains possession of the property while obtaining the full purchase price. In some cases he contracts the right to repurchase the property at the end of the lease. This is called a sale/leaseback/buyback. In other situations, he negotiates for the option to renew the lease at the time of expiration.

        2.   By selling, he gets his capital investment in the property back for use in other ways; perhaps to build another building and expand his business.

        3.   If it's investment property, he can claim the rent on his income taxes.

    B.   Advantages to the buyer/investor/landlord.

        1.   A secure lease with a reliable tenant.

        2.   A fair return on and of his investment.

        3.   A depreciable asset.

        4.   The property taxes and mortgage interest can be deducted on his income tax return.

XI. **Constructive Eviction**

Constructive eviction was created for the benefit of the lessee. The tenant has the right to terminate the lease and move out because the landlord has either acted or not acted in accordance with their legal duties to maintain or repair hazards within the premises. An example would be if the furnace stops working and the landlord refuses to fix it or delays fixing it. The tenant may then constructively evict themselves and terminate the lease. It's important to note that in order for the tenant to claim constructive eviction and be relieved of paying rent, the tenant must vacate the property. Barton v. MTB Enterprises, Inc., 889 P.2d 476, 477 (Utah Ct. App. 1995).

XII. **Actual Eviction**

A. There are several causes for eviction:

  1. Non-payment of rent.

  2. Nuisance, such as making too much noise or in other ways disturbing other tenants.

  3. Damage or destruction of the property.

B. Process of eviction in Utah:

  1. The landlord must give the tenant a three-day Notice to Pay or Quit, delivered to the lessee by actual delivery or certified mail to the tenant's last known address. U.C.A. § 78B-6-802(1)(c).

  2. If the tenant does not respond, the landlord files an "**Unlawful Detainer Action**" with the court. The word "action" means lawsuit.

  3. The tenant is notified of the action and given the opportunity to respond to the charges. If the tenant does not respond, the judgment is automatically in favor of the landlord.

  4. A judgment is given by the court.

  5. If the decision of the court was in favor of the landlord, the judge issues a "**Writ of Restitution**" or a "**Writ of Eviction**" to the Sheriff. A writ is an official court order. U.C.A. § 78B-6-811(1)(b).

  6. The sheriff puts the tenant out. U.C.A. § 78B-6-812(3)(a).

Frequently Asked Questions and the Answers About Leasing

1. What duties do I have as an owner to make repairs and how quickly must I respond to the renter's requests?

  A. Major structural repairs and the maintenance of common areas are generally the responsibility of the owner as well as repairs or alterations required by building and health codes. The renter has a duty to repair conditions caused by his fault or negligence and other duties as set forth in the lease. It is the duty of the owner to respond with reasonable diligence in making repairs which is of course dependent on the facts of each case.

2. Can the renter withhold rent as a means of forcing me to make repairs?

  A. Yes. If an owner fails to take corrective action for his/her obligated repairs, a tenant may, upon giving proper notice: (1) stop making payments, terminate the lease, and receive back their security deposit and a prorated refund for any prepaid rent; or (2) repair the condition themselves and deduct the repair cost from future rent. U.C.A. § 57-22-6(4)(a)(i)-(ii).

3. If the water is in the lessor's name and the tenant is behind on the rent can the lessor shut the water off to force the tenant out?

201

A. No, such actions would constitute a "forcible entry" by the owner and would subject him/her to a possible. See U.C.A. §§ 78B-6-801(3) & 78-B-6-807(1). An eviction either must be accomplished through the court process or through abandonment by the renter of the premises.

4. When I give a 15-day Notice do I have to give the tenant a reason?

A. None is required by law.

5. Who can serve 3-Day Notices?

A. The owner or manager or anyone designated by him who is over 21 years of age.

6. After I've filed my Complaint with the court do I still have to accept the tenant's rent?

A. If after receiving a 3-Day Notice to Pay Rent or Vacate, the renter gives you the money in full, you must accept it. After the summons has been served he must pay you the rent, together with court costs and attorney's fees if such fees are provided for in the lease. After a judgment has been taken the renter must pay off the full judgment to stay, but the owner, if he so chooses, can force the renter out, but should not accept a partial payment until the property has been surrendered to him.

7. Can I evict someone though small claims court and if not, what can I do in small claims court?

A. Small claims court has the power to grant monetary judgments only and cannot order a person evicted. However, Small Claims is a good place to take rent and damage claims under $1,000 where the tenant has already moved out.

8. Can the owner or manager serve a Summons?

A. No, because they are interested parties in the action and thus prohibited. Only persons over 21 years of age who are not parties to the action or interested in the action can serve court papers.

9. Do weekends count in computing a 3-Day Notice?

A. Yes. The notices to quit are based on calendar days. See generally § 78B-6-802.

10. How does the Sheriff evict people?

A. Armed with the court order, the Sheriff usually goes to the place of residence and posts or gives notice to the tenants to be out within three business days. He comes back a second time and meets the owner or his agent there and changes the locks and forces the people to move out at that time.

11. What do I do if the renters leave valuable items behind?

A. The law requires the owner to safeguard those items for 15 days before disposing of them if the tenant sends written demand to do so. However, the owner can demand his cost of moving and storage before returning the goods. U.C.A. §78B-6-816(3).

12. If a tenant owes rent, can the lessor hold his TV (or other furniture) until he pays?

A. Unless a written agreement allows, it would be improper. A court order wherein the Sheriff is directed to hold property is the correct way to proceed.

13. How can I collect a Judgment?

A. Garnish wages, garnish bank accounts, sell personal property such as cars, TV's and stereos.

14. If I get a bad check from a tenant, can I demand that future payments be made in cash or cashier's check?

   A. The Rental Agreement used by the Apartment Association provides that you can, and most courts would consider it reasonable where you have been burned, to allow you to make that request. It is a crime to write a bad check.

15. Where can I get forms and further information?

   A. The Apartment Association of Utah, 448 East Winchester Street Salt Lake City, UT 84107-8551 (801) 487-5619.

Leases Terms to Know

- ☐ Actual eviction
- ☐ Assignment of Lease
- ☐ Constructive Eviction
- ☐ Escalation clause
- ☐ Estate or Tenancy for Years
- ☐ Estovers
- ☐ Flat Lease
- ☐ Graduated lease
- ☐ Gross Lease
- ☐ Ground Lease
- ☐ Habitability clause
- ☐ Holdover tenant
- ☐ Incorporeal Rights
- ☐ Index Lease
- ☐ Lease
- ☐ Less Than Freehold
- ☐ License
- ☐ License Interest
- ☐ Net Lease
- ☐ Non-disturbance Clause
- ☐ Notice to Quit
- ☐ Percentage Lease
- ☐ Periodic Tenancy
- ☐ Proprietary Lease
- ☐ Reappraisal lease
- ☐ Rooftop Lease
- ☐ Sale/leaseback
- ☐ Sublease
- ☐ Tenancy at Sufferance
- ☐ Tenancy at Will
- ☐ Unlawful Detainer
- ☐ Vertical lease
- ☐ Writ of Restitution or Writ of Eviction

Leases Quiz

1. Henry, the owner, negotiates a three year lease with Sally, the lessee. Six months later he sells the property to Tom. What would happen to the lease in this case?

    A. Sally must negotiate a new lease with Tom or move out.

    B. Henry cannot legally sell the property to Tom until the lease expires.

    C. The lease would only be good for the remainder of the year in which the sale is completed.

    D. The lease continues to run and Tom is obligated to the lease until it expires.

2. Alice is the manager of Hillside Apartments. One winter she fails to provide heating to Martin's apartment unit. Martin moves out and refuses to pay rent. What is the legal basis of Martin's argument.

    A. Constructive eviction

    B. Actual eviction

    C. Escalation of lease

    D. There is no legal basis for his argument

3. Tim enters into an agreement with George that he will harvest George's wheat if he can keep one-third of the wheat. This agreement would be termed a less than freehold interest for:

    A. License

    B. Profit

    C. Lease

    D. Emblements

4. In a sublease, the sublettee owes rent to the:

    A. Sublettor

    B. Landlord

    C. Property owner

    D. No one

5. Norbert enters into a lease which is to begin October 1 and end March 1 of the next year. This lease would be considered:

    A. Tenancy at Will

    B. Tenancy at Sufferance

    C. Tenancy for Years

    D. Periodic Tenancy

6. Mike has a three year lease. During the second year, he assigns the remaining term of the lease to Sam. Which of the following is true?

    A. If Sam defaults, Mike will have to pay the rent.

    B. Sam is now out of the loop and has no more liability.

C. Mike is now out of the loop and has no more liability.

D. Mike cannot assign the lease.

7. Buy More for Less, a local general store, leases their building. As rent they pay a flat fee of $2,300 plus 2% of any gross income in excess of $250,000. This is which kind of lease:

    A. Participation lease

    B. Graduated payment lease

    C. Percentage lease

    D. Vertical lease

8. Helen had a one year lease. At the end of the year, Helen continued to send checks for the rent. Her landlord refused the checks and asked her to leave. She refused. Helen is now considered a:

    A. Tenant at will

    B. Tenant at sufferance

    C. Trespasser

    D. Periodic tenant

9. The legal court action to evict a tenant is called a(n):

    A. Legal eviction action

    B. Writ of habeus corpus

    C. Unlawful detainer

    D. Writ of eviction

10. A leasehold interest in real property conveys a right of:

    A. Fee simple

    B. Possession

    C. Defeasible fee

    D. Qualified possession

11. What happens to a lease when the property is sold?

    A. Nothing, the lease stays in force.

    B. The lease expires immediately.

    C. The lease expires in 30 days.

    D. The lease must be re-negotiated immediately.

Property Management

I.   **Property Management Profession**

A.   Definition: **Property management** is the process of achieving the goals of the owner of investment properties, especially in the areas of maximizing net income, caring for the property, keeping the property leased, and maintaining good relationships with tenants, employees, and outside providers of goods and services.

B.   Duties of the **Property Manager**: The property manager's job can be very complex and require a high degree of professional expertise. The property manager, depending on the type of property, can be required to be a leasing agent, maintenance engineer, accountant, advertising executive, market analyst, diplomat, and all sorts of other roles. It is a fast-growing profession that is requiring ever increasing expertise, especially with the exploding increase in applicable technology.

C.   Classification of Property:

   1.   Residential:

      a.   Single family

      b.   Multi-family

      c.   Cooperative, condominium, and subsidized property

   2.   Commercial:

      a.   Office

      b.   Retail

      c.   Industrial

II.   **Managing the Relationship with the Owner**

A.   Identify owner's objectives.

   1.   To extract every possible dollar from the property.

      a.   Wants frequent payment

      b.   Reluctant to make repairs

      c.   Pays bills and taxes at the last possible moment

      d.   Not a good objective for long-term income

   2.   To maximize income in both short and long term.

      a.   Obtain good tenants

      b.   Collect rents

      c.   Maintain the property

         i.   Make repairs

         ii.   Hiring and paying repair people

207

B. The management contract.

    1. The parties to the contract

    2. Beginning date

    3. Hours and schedule: days, hours, holidays

    4. Payment of manager: Property managers are normally paid on the basis of percentage of gross income or gross rents. Other terms could be:

        a. Hourly

        b. Monthly

        c. Commission

        d. Time of payment

    5. Additional agreements, terms, or amendments.

    6. Responsibilities.

        a. Rent collection policy

        b. Repair policy

        c. Maintenance policy

        d. Reporting policy

    7. Conduct market surveys.

    8. Termination of contract.

C. Ongoing owner/manager relations

    1. The agency arrangement – specific or general

        a. Agent is very limited in scope - specific

        b. Agent is given broader responsibility and authority – general

    2. Communication:

        a. Formal and scheduled

        b. Informal

III. **Preparation of the Business Plan**

A. Basic strategy:

    1. Be competitive

    2. Have satisfied tenants

    3. Build reputation

    4. Create an effective team

    5. Generate profits without sacrificing quality of operation

B.   Prepare an **operating budget:**

    1.   Sources of income:

        a.   Rent

        b.   Parking

        c.   Laundry

        d.   Vending machines

        e.   Cleaning services

        f.   Pet Services

        g.   Fax/copying/mailing services

    2.   Operating expenses:

        a.   Payroll

        b.   Utilities

        c.   Maintenance

        d.   Insurance

        e.   Taxes and licenses

        f.   Advertising

        g.   Management

        h.   Miscellaneous, i.e., office supplies, professional fees, service contracts, etc.

    3.   Computation of the budget:

        a.   Gross scheduled income (GSI)

        b.   Cost of vacancies, lost rents, etc.

        c.   Gross operating (effective) income (GEI or GOI) (a) minus (b)

        d.   Other income (such as washer/dryer quarters)

        e.   Adjusted gross income (c) plus (d)

        f.   Operating expenses

        g.   Net operating income (e) minus (f)

        h.   Capital expenses

        i.   Debt service

        j.   Cash flow (g) minus (h) and (I)

        k.   Monthly income to owners (k) divided by (12)

    4.   Adjust to reflect anticipated market trends

    5.   Calculate yearly operating costs

6. Establish necessary reserve funds

7. Predict anticipated revenue

8. Review the cash flow in light of the owner's objectives

9. Prepare a five-year forecast

IV. Lease Negotiations

  A. Qualifying the tenant

    1. Do not violate federal discrimination rules. The categories of race, color, natural origin, gender, familial status, handicapped, and religion are protected.

    2. Have a clear and consistent policy of screening potential tenants. Treat all applicants the same

      a. Only one application for a given type of property

      b. Credit check for one? Then credit check for all.

      c. Reasons for rejecting a potential tenant the same for everyone.

      d. If you check references for one, you check them for all.

      e. Be careful of subjective reasons for rejecting a potential tenant such as appearance, "gut feeling," etc.

    3. Important qualifying considerations

      a. When will you be ready to move in?

      b. Financial capability

      c. Number of people that will be living in the unit

      d. Pet and water bed policy.

  B. The lease contract: Remember, it is absolutely necessary that a standard contract form or one prepared by an attorney be used. Do not become guilty of practicing law without a license. Consider each of the following when filling in a contract.

    1. Identify the landlord and the tenant

    2. Give a full description of the property

    3. State the term of the tenancy and whether it is month-to-month or a fixed term.

    4. State limits or conditions on use and occupancy

    5. Payment of rent

      a. Amount

      b. Day of payment

      c. Form of payment

      d. Late charges

e. Penalties for returned check

6. Deposits, i.e., security, cleaning, pets, etc.

7. Utilities – who pays

8. Assignment or subletting the property

9. Tenant's responsibility for maintenance

10. Repairs or alterations by the tenant

11. Violation of laws

12. Causing disturbance

13. Pets

14. Right of the landlord to enter the premises

15. Extended absences by the tenant and the obligation of the tenant to inform the manager of such absences

16. Possession of the property. Tenant fails to take possession soon after signing or landlord fails to give possession.

17. Tenant rules and regulations

18. Disclosures about such things as environmental hazards

19. Grounds for termination of the lease

20. Rules of notice

C. Negotiating the terms:

1. The goal: negotiating a lease that is beneficial to both the owner and the tenant.

2. Avoid personality conflicts. They prolong and even terminate a transaction.

3. Secure agreement on basic terms and conditions such as rent, term, and policies

4. Concessions and/or inducements

    a. Factors that influence willingness to offer concessions or inducements

    b. Owner's financial and strategic position

        i. Competition

        ii. Urgency of prospect to find suitable space

    c. Concessions should always be offered reluctantly. Remember, a concession granted to one tenant has the potential to extend to all tenants, including existing tenants.

    d. Rent concessions

        i. Have a basic rent schedule which includes increases or decreases for elevation (higher floors), corner space (increased views), inside space (no windows), etc. Know which concessions are possible and which aren't.

  A. Deposits – First or second month, cleaning, security, pets, water beds, etc.

  B. Term and the effect on rent of shorter or longer terms

  C. Tenant alterations

  D. The escalation clause – typically related to long term leases

D. Signing the agreement:

 1. Closing the deal

  a. Question close

  b. Summary close

 2. Money to be paid at closing

 3. Authorized signatories

V. Maintenance

A. Basic maintenance procedures

B. On-site/resident manager

C. Contract services

D. Preventative maintenance

E. Replacement reserve analysis

F. Life cycle costing

G. Inspections

VI. Reporting

Once frequency has been established, a report might contain the following:

Conclusions and recommendations. Start at the end and then give the data to back it up. Or a report might take the opposite approach.

 1. Observations about the market

 2. Summary about the property or project

 3. Recommendations and suggestions

A. Market data:

 1. Photo and map of the area

 2. Competitive property survey and information

 3. New laws, trends, changing economic and/or political conditions

B. Property or project update:

    1. Changing or continuing tenant profiles

    2. Existing or proposed marketing strategy and programs

    3. Synopsis of rental activity

    4. Review of repairs made

    5. Current status of capital needs

C. Financial report (discussed elsewhere)

VII. **Risk Management**

A. Emergency and life safety issues:

    1. Fire extinguishers

    2. Smoke detectors

    3. Locks, selection, and changing

    4. Peep scopes

    5. Outside lighting

B. Environmental issues:

    1. Asbestos – disclosure

    2. Radon

    3. Lead based paint – disclosure, units built before 1978

C. Hazard control – protect yourself:

    1. Failure to meet building codes

    2. Negligence or unreasonable careless conduct

        a. Lighting

        b. Snow removal

        c. Hazardous objects

    3. Failure to make repairs

    4. Failure to keep premises habitable

D. Insurance:

    1. Fire – Review the value of the policy each time the premium comes due

    2. Liability – Acquire full and high coverage. $1,000,000 will probably cost little more than $100,000.

    3. Renters' insurance – Encourage tenants to obtain this type of insurance to cover their personal belongings.

VIII. **The Law**

Uniform Residential Landlord and Tenant Act: Some provisions of the act:

1. Unless otherwise stated, the lease will be month-to-month

2. If the landlord accepts a rent payment, the lease is considered binding even without the signature of the other party.

3. Leases cannot contain any provision wherein the tenant waives any rights or remedies that are protected under the Act.

4. The landlord must keep the property habitable.

5. Rents cannot be raised or services reduced because a tenant complains to a government agency or joins a tenant union.

6. Courts may refuse to enforce provisions in a lease that the court determines to be grossly unfair.

7. A tenant who abandons a unit remains liable for rent unless the unit is re-rented. The landlord must make a reasonable effort to rent the unit.

A. Utah Landlord/Tenant Law:

1. Abandoned Property (U.C.A. § 78B-6-816(1)):

   a. Owner may retake the premises and attempt to rent them at a fair rental value.

   b. The tenant owes the entire rent due for the remainder of the term (contract); or

   c. Rent accrued during the period necessary to re-rent the premises at a fair rental value, plus

   d. The difference between the fair rental value and the rent agreed to in the prior rental agreement, plus

   e. The cost to restore the rental unit to its condition when rented by the tenant less normal wear and tear, plus

   f. A reasonable commission for re-renting the property

2. The statutory requirements for notice:

   a. The contract, unless involving something illegal, will supersede the statutory requirements.

   b. When not mentioned in the contract, the statutory requirements are:

      i. (1) Periodic tenancy – 15 calendar days or more prior to the end of that month or period. U.C.A § 78B-6-802(1)(b)(i).

      ii. (2) Tenancy at will – 5 calendar days notice. U.C.A. § 78B-6-802(1)(b)(ii).

      iii. (3) Notice to Pay or Quit – 3 calendar days notice. U.C.A. §78B-6-802(1)(c).

iv. (i) The Notice to Pay or Quit is used for tenants who default on payments. All other notices are used to give notice that when the lease terminates, the landlord will not renew.

3. Deposits:

    a. The landlord must return all deposits upon termination of the tenancy or provide the tenant with written notice explaining why the deposit is being retained. U.C.A. § 57-17-1.

    b. The explanation must be sent within 30 days following termination. U.C.A. § 57-17-3.

    c. If a deposit was agreed to be "non-refundable" it must have been in writing and explained to the tenant when the deposit was taken. U.C.A. § 57-17-2.

    d. The penalty for improperly withholding a deposit is the full deposit, a $100 civil penalty, plus possible court costs. U.C.A. § 57-17-5(1)(a) & (2).

        i. (i) A renter will not be entitled to relief under § 57-17-5 if the renter fails to serve the landlord a notice demanding return of the deposit as required in § 57-17-3. U.C.A. § 57-17-5(3).

4. Eviction – See Leases, p. 22-4

Subject				Comparable 1		
	Units	Square Feet			Units	Square Feet
1 Bed		840		1 Bed	40	780
2 Bed	40	930		2 Bed	40	840
				3 Bed	25	900
Comparable 2				Comparable 3		
	Units	Square Feet			Units	Square Feet
1 Bed	112	950		1 Bed	9	525
2 Bed	112	1,070		2 Bed	0	0
3 Bed	32	1,190				
Comparable 4				Comparable 5		
	Units	Square Feet			Units	Square Feet
1 Bed	30	590		1 Bed	18	625
2 Bed	12	625		2 Bed	12	690

B. Rent for 1 bedroom apartments: $_____

C. Rent for 2 bedroom apartments: $_____

Property Management Terms to Know

- ☐ Abandonment
- ☐ Business Plan
- ☐ Management Contract
- ☐ Operating Budget
- ☐ Property Management
- ☐ Property Manager
- ☐ Uniform Residential Landlord and Tenant Act

Property Management Quiz

1. Which of the following would NOT be part of an operating budget?

    A. Operating expenses

    B. Property management trust account

    C. Rental income

    D. Other income

2. A management contract would NOT include which of the following?

    A. How the property manager is paid

    B. Reporting policy

    C. Rent collection policy

    D. Vacancy/lost rent percentage

3. Which of the following would reflect the true bottom line to the owner?

    A. Cash flow

    B. Net operating income

    C. Adjusted gross income

    D. Gross income

4. Which of the following is NOT a protected class so far as discrimination is concerned?

    A. Race

    B. Religion

    C. Familial status

    D. Motorcycle owners

5. Which of the following will the tenant, who has abandoned his lease before the expiration date, NOT have to pay?

    A. Commission to the manager for finding a replacement tenant

    B. Rent for the unused part of the lease

    C. Cost to restore the property to rentable condition

    D. The period prior to the expiration of the lease, but after the unit has been re-rented

6. The statutory period of standard notice to terminate periodic tenancy is:

    A. 5 days

    B. 10 days

    C. 15 days

    D. 30 day

7. The law suit for evicting someone is called:

   A. Restitution action

   B. Unlawful detainer

   C. Partition action

   D. Eviction order

8. When the type of tenancy is not clearly identified in the lease, the lease will be considered to be:

   A. Of no force

   B. Fixed term

   C. Month-to-month

   D. At will

9. When a deposit is not returned, the owner or property manager must:

   A. Immediately transfer the money to the operating account.

   B. Send notification and reasons to the Utah Real Estate Division.

   C. Send notification and explanation to the tenant within 30 days.

   D. Do nothing since the tenant already knows why they aren't getting it back.

10. Which of the following is illegal and unenforceable?

    A. The tenant joins a renters union

    B. The landlord inspects the property with proper notice and during reasonable hours

    C. A clause put in a lease requiring only 7 days notice for termination instead of the statutory 15.

    D. A clause in the lease says that all remedies against the landlord are forfeited when the tenant signs the lease

MATH SKILLS

MATH A

MATH B

*Must be taken together

Math A & B

SOME GENERAL GUIDELINES: Always use the percent key on your calculator. For those who have no percent key on their calculator, percentages must be converted into decimals. To translate a **percent into a decimal**, move the decimal two places to the left:

Example: 6% = .06, 21% = .21, 134% = 1.34 or 10.75% = .1075

To translate a **decimal into a percent**, move the decimal two places to the right:

Example: .08 = 8%, .11 = 11% or .125 = 12.5%

WATCH OUT FOR TWO INSIDIOUS PRINCIPLES:

1. _____

2. _____

LOAN PROBLEMS:

1. Interest is always expressed in what time frame?_____

2. How many days in a month?_____

3. How many days in a year? _____

NOTE: On the test, if you are asked to compute a payment, it will only be on a straight loan. You will not be asked to compute an amortized loan payment (P,I).

FORMULAS:

Area/square   = _____ X _____

Volume/cubic = _____ X _____ X _____

MEASUREMENT REVIEW:

1 yard = _____   1 Acre = _____ square feet

1 sq. yard = _____   1 Mile = _____ feet

1 cu. yard = _____   Section = _____ square miles

Section = _____ acres

CAUTION: Square Feet or Feet Square?

2'   [2' square figure]   A. This figure is a _____ foot square.

      2'   B. This figure contains _____ square feet.

A New Approach to Real Estate Math

Many real estate math problems involve percentages. You can use the "FRL" formula for all such problems, whether dealing with a commission, interest rates, cap rates, an owner's profit, a discount amount, etc.

    a.   THE FORMULA:

F $

R   %

L $

HOW IT WORKS:

F $	Known	When both knowns are above the line, the
R %	Known	rule is: You _____
L $	Unknown	

F $	Unknown	Known	When one of the knowns is below the line,
R %	Known or	Unknown	the rule is: You _____
L $	Known	Known	_____

F = _____

R = _____

L = _____

Six Guiding Questions

(to be used with the "FRL" formula)

    1. _____   The answer must not
contain a _____or the words _____or _
_____

2. _____

3. _____   (Only use a dollar ($) amount.)

4. _____

5. _____   (Only use a dollar ($) amount.)

6. _____   (Only use a (%)
percentage.)

THE MAGIC NUMBER!

_____is always equal to _____!!!

What Goes in the "R"?

1. J received a commission of 6% for selling a house. How much was the commission?

R = _____%

2. K sold his house for an 18% profit. How much profit did he make?

R = _____%

3. K sold his house for an 18% profit. What was the selling price of the house?

R = _____%

4. L sold his house and lost 18%. What was the selling price?

R = _____%

5. L sold his house and lost 18%. How much was his loss?

R = _____%

When you have an add (i.e. profit) or subtract (i.e. loss) word, you **ALWAYS** add or subtract from the magic 100% **UNLESS** the question asks for the add or subtract word.

When you have a number and a % that match, you have the R and the L.
If you don't have a match, create one if you can.

Math Worksheet

1. Clark Kent sold a property for $120,000. His commission was 5.5%. How much was he paid?

    F $

    R _____ %

    L $

2. Bruce Wayne made a commission of $1,960 on the sale of a $14,000 lot to Jack Joker. What rate of commission did Jack pay Bruce?

    F $

    R _____ %

    L $

3. After selecting $2,700 worth of computer equipment, Steve Jobs learned he would receive a discount of 35%. How much did the discount save Steve?

    F $

    R _____ %

    L $

16. The property taxes on A's home were $1,032 last year. If the tax rate is 8 mills and the property assessed at 80%, what is the value of the property?

A

A _____

A

T _____

T

17. J made $3,360 last month selling a home. J's split with the broker is 70%. The broker charges a 6% commission to the sellers. What was the selling price of the property?

F $

R _____ %

L$

F $

R _____ %

L$

Duplicate Math Worksheet

Complete this at home as soon after the math class as you can.

1. Clark Kent sold a property for $120,000. His commission was 5.5%. How much was he paid?

   F $ _____
   R _____ %
   L $ _____

2. Bruce Wayne made a commission of $1,960 on the sale of a $14,000 lot to Jack Joker. What rate of commission did Jack pay Bruce?

   F $ _____
   R _____ %
   L $ _____

3. After selecting $2,700 worth of computer equipment, Steve Jobs learned he would receive a discount of 35%. How much did the discount save Steve?

   F $ _____
   R _____ %
   L $ _____

4. Caitlin Jones realized a profit of $42,000, which represented 12% of her original investment. How much was her original investment?

   F $ _____
   R _____ %
   L $ _____

5. Caitlin Jones realized a 12% profit on her original investment of $350,000. What was the selling price of the property?

   F $ _____
   R _____ %
   L $ _____

6. Rip Roaring Realty (The Triple R) had a quarterly gross income of $140,000. If their operating expenses were 29% of gross income, what was their annual net operating income?

   F $ _____
   R _____ %
   L $ _____

7.   Minnie Mouser sold an investment property. At closing she paid a commission of 7% and $550 in other closing costs. She then received a check for the remaining $125,000. What was the selling price of the property?

         F $
         R _____ %
         L $

8.   Samson Strong sold his home to Phil Steiner for $86,000. Mr. Steiner made a 20% down payment, paid a 1.5% origination fee, and paid $825 for other closing costs. How much did Phil have to bring to closing?

         F $
         R _____ %
         L $

9.   Ms. Lisa Lovell borrowed $12,000 on a straight note for 125 days. Lisa paid $625 in interest. What rate of interest did she pay?

         F $
         R _____ %
         L $

10. Mr. Abner Little negotiated for a straight note of $69,000, at 9% interest. He ended up paying $13,972.50 in interest. How many months did the loan run?

         F $
         R _____ %
         L $

11. Quincy McQuaid wants to sell his farm and net $66,500. As his agent, you expect a 5% commission. What selling price would you set to make sure Mr. McQuaid nets $66,500 after you are paid your commission?

         F $
         R _____ %
         L $

12. Mr. Pigstiener developed a property. On it he built 32% straw homes and 16% stick homes. The remaining 78 homes were built of, you'll never guess... of brick. How many homes were in the entire project?

         F $
         R _____ %
         L $

13. Tom Quick subdivided 7.5 acres. He was required to use 35% of it for streets, utilities, etc. How many lots 150' by 120' could he build?

F $
R _____ %
L $

14. The lease on Mr. Pipeson's hardware store had the following terms. He paid a base rent of $3,200 per month on gross income up to $140,000. On gross sales over the $140,000 he paid 4%. If he paid a total of $5,700 in rent one month, what was his gross income for that month?

F $
R _____ %
L $

15. If the value of the property is $250,000 and the rate of capitalization is 9%, what is the property's net operating income?

F $
R _____ %
L $

16. The property taxes on A's home were $1,032 last year. If the tax rate is 8 mills and the property assessed at 80%, what is the value of the property?

A
A _____
A
T _____
T

17. J made $3,360 last month selling a home. J's split with the broker is 70%. The broker charges a 6% commission to the sellers. What was the selling price of the property?

F $
R _____ %
L $

F $
R _____ %
L $

MATH A & B QUIZ

1. An investment that is now worth $100,000 is expected to increase in value at a rate of 10% annually. What will its value be at the end of five years?

    A. $104,327.00

    B. $161,051.00

    C. $162,345.00

    D. $165,386.00

2. A broker splits the commission with her salespeople by paying three-fifths of the total commission. If one of her salespeople sold a property for $300,000 at 10% commission, how much did the salesperson receive?

    A. $12,000

    B. $13,000

    C. $15,000

    D. $18,000

3. A property has a net income of $8,500 per year. In order to earn 8% on his investment, how much would a person pay for the property?

    A. $ 64,500

    B. $ 85,000

    C. $106,250

    D. $110,250

4. A mortgage company agrees to lend an owner of a property an amount equal to 66% of its appraised value at an interest rate of 9% per annum. The first year's interest is $1,800. What is the appraised value, rounded to the nearest $100?

    A. $13,200

    B. $20,000

    C. $30,300

    D. $58,800

5. A residential investment property was sold and closed on the 18th of the month. If the rent was $500 per month, how would the rents be prorated on the closing statement?

    A. Seller owes buyer $200

    B. Seller owes buyer $300

    C. Buyer owes seller $200

    D. Buyer owes seller $300

6. An L-shaped lot was 85' by 190' and 55.9' by 120'. The lot was sold for $2.00 per square foot. The broker received an 8% commission. How much was he paid?

    A. $3,657.28

    B. $2.104.60

    C. $3,229.80

    D. $1,957.92

7. What was the annual rate on a $52,200 loan if the first semi-annual interest payment was $3,524?

    A. 3.4%

    B. 7.0%

    C. 7.41%

    D. 13.5%

8. A house sold for $60,000. The buyer paid $2,000 in closing costs. The loan amount was 97% of the first $25,000 and 95% of the balance, plus the lender agreed to finance 95% of the closing costs. What was the loan amount?

    A. $60,200

    B. $58,400

    C. $59,400

    D. $59,900

9. A home is appraised for $97,000. It had two rooms with very bad carpeting in them. One was 18'x 20' and the other was 10'x12'. The carpet was depreciated by $11.25 per sq. yard. How much did the carpet depreciate the values of the property?

    A. $600

    B. $660

    C. $550

    D. $40

10. The buyer closed on his new home on June 17. He assumed a loan for $50,000 which bore an interest rate of 9.5%. The buyer agreed to pay the interest for the day of closing. If the first payment is due on July 1, how much interest would the seller pay at closing?

    A. $184.72

    B. $211.11

    C. $395.83

    D. $580.56

SETTLEMENT

PROPERTY TAX & TITLE INSURANCE

RESPA

SETTLEMENT PROCEDURES

Property Tax and Title Insurance

I.   **Real Estate or Property Taxes**

A tax levied by government against real property.

A.   Real property is a favorite area of taxation because of its immobility and ease of assessing high value to increase the tax base.

B.   It is an exclusive right of state government to tax property. The federal government cannot tax real or personal property. The general real estate tax is made up of taxes levied on real estate by various governmental agencies and municipalities. These include the city, town, village, and county. Others allowed to participate include school districts, drainage districts, water districts, and sanitary districts.

C.   The tax is an **ad valorem tax**, which means that it is assessed according to the value of the property.

D.   Property value is usually set by the **County Assessor**.

E.   **Special assessments** are similar to property taxes, but are only charged to certain properties that will benefit from the improvements. For example, within a certain taxing district, only the properties on Main Street are having new street lights installed. The Main Street properties would be charged a special assessment in addition to their normal property taxes.

II.   **Property Tax in Utah**

A.   The tax period is a full calendar year: January 1 - December 31.

B.   Property taxes are due on November 30 and are delinquent on December 1.

C.   Property taxes become a lien on the property January 1.

D.   The period of redemption is four years, so the property cannot be sold until the fifth year.

E.   There is no period of redemption following the sale.

F.   The **Board of Equalization** is the resource available if someone wants to appeal the appraised value of their property. The appeal must be filed within 30 days of the mailing of the tax notice. The deadline date is printed on the notice. (See the forms section for a sample of the appeal form to be used.)

III.   **Methods of Computing**

A.   The basic formula:

> **Appraised Value**
> **x Assessed Rate**
> _____
> **Assessed Value**
> **x Tax Rate**
> _____
> **Taxes Due**

B.   The tax rate can be levied in one of three ways:

    1.   Dollars and cents per $100 of assessed value.

    2.   Dollars and cents per $1,000 of assessed value

    3.   The assessed value times a mill levy.

        a.   One mill equals one-thousandth of a dollar.

        b.   To change mills into a decimal amount, move the decimal three places to the left.

        c.   For instance, 21 mills = .021; 321 mills = .321; and 91.42 mills = .0914

C.   The following examples illustrate each of the ways to tax property. Assume the property is valued at $80,000 in each of the examples.

    1.   If the assessed rate is 28%, and the tax rate is $65.30 per $1,000 of assessed value, what would the taxes be? (See the previous page for formula.)

Appraised Value:	$80,000
x Assessed Rate:	x 28%
Assessed Value:	$22,400 / 1,000 = 22.4
Taxes Rate:	x $65.30
Taxes Due:	$1,462.72

If the assessed rate is 34% and the tax rate is $5.38 per $100 of assessed value = **$1,463.36**
Taxes due

Appraised Value:	$80,000
x Assessed Rate:	x 34%
Assessed Value:	$27,200 / 100 = 272
Taxes Rate:	x $5.38
Taxes Due:	$1,463.36

The appraised value is $80,000, the assessed rate is 60%, and the tax rate is .013256.
=$636.29 Taxes due

Appraised Value:	$80,000
x Assessed Rate:	x 60%
Assessed Value:	$27,200
Taxes Rate:	x .013256
Taxes Due:	$636.29

D.   When the property is sold, and the taxes are **prorated**, the seller must pay the buyer for the portion of the year the seller owned the property, including the day of closing. If the closing date was July 31 and the annual taxes were $756, the computation would be:

1. Seven full months X 30 days a month = 210 days to be prorated.

2. $756 ÷ 360 (days in a year) = $2.10 (taxes owed per day) X 210 (days to be paid for) = $441.00 the seller owes the buyer.

E. Property taxes are a debt of the property and are always in place. The only time there are not property taxes due is during December (if the taxes were paid when due.) If someone bought a property and there were two years taxes unpaid, they would purchase the property with the two years back taxes still due. The past-due tax lien would be an exception in the title insurance policy.

IV. **Title Insurance**

A. Under the standard Real Estate Purchase Contract, the seller represents that he/she is providing clear and marketable title to the buyer with a policy of title insurance. It is wise for every buyer and seller to make sure the title to the property is protected by title insurance. This is particularly true for the seller if a warranty deed is used to convey title.

B. An **Abstract of Title or Chain of Title** is a chronological summary or history of all recorded events that have affected the title to a particular parcel of property, thus showing a linkage from the present owner back to the original source of title.

C. An **Attorney's Opinion**, or **Certificate of Title**, is an evaluation of who the true owner of the property is. It usually carries no guarantees.

D. **Subrogation**: Title insurance functions under the process of subrogation. This is the substitution of a third party, the title company, in place of the grantor of the title. The title insurance company assumes the liability of the owner and/or exercises the owner's rights if a court case should become necessary.

E. In most sales, two title policies are obtained to close the sale.

1. The sellers obtain a policy to insure that they are passing clear and marketable title to the buyer as they committed to do in the Real Estate Purchase Agreement. The coverage is almost always for the full value of the purchase price.

2. The buyer/borrower obtains a policy to insure the lender that the property has no liens or encumbrances that would cause the lender to refuse to give the loan. This policy is usually limited in its coverage to the amount of the loan.

3. Both policies are paid for in full and take effect at closing.

F. Types of Title Insurance Policies

1. **Standard Policy**: A comprehensive examination of recorded documents to determine defects in the title.

    a. The amount of the policy is for the full sales price.

    b. It insures against all recorded defects that are not identified in the insurance policy.

  c. The insurance is good from the date of the policy backward in time to the patent deed.

  d. It insures that all parties are competent and that signatures are valid.

  e. It does not include an on-site inspection.

  f. Covers forgeries in a warranty deed.

2. **Lender's** or **ALTA Policy**: includes all of the coverage of a Standard Policy. However, it has some differences and some additional coverage.

  a. The policy is valid for only the amount of the loan, rather than the full value of the property.

  b. It covers defects that would be discovered by an on-site inspection of the property or a survey.

  c. A lender's policy is assignable to subsequent holders of that same loan.

3. **Extended Owner's Policy**:

  a. It is used by the buyer/borrower.

  b. An extended policy does not make exceptions for defects that could have been determined by an on-site inspection of the property.

  c. It covers encumbrances that are not recorded, such as prescriptive easements.

  d. This type of policy is non-transferable.

4. **Plain Language Policy**:

  a. Available since 1987

  b. Covers mechanic's liens

  c. Often costs no more than the standard policy

  d. As a buyer's agent, you should be sure the buyers know about and suggest they request this policy.

G. **Title insurance**, a one-time fee for both buyer and seller, is paid at the closing of the transaction.

Property Tax and Title Insurance
Terms to Know

- ☐ Ad Valorem Tax
- ☐ Alta or Lender's Policy
- ☐ Assessed Value
- ☐ Attorney's Opinion
- ☐ Board of Equalization
- ☐ Chain of Title or Abstract of Title
- ☐ Cloud on the Title
- ☐ Extended Coverage (Owner's policy) Title Insurance
- ☐ Plain Language Policy
- ☐ Property Tax
- ☐ Proration
- ☐ Special Assessment
- ☐ Standard Coverage Title Insurance
- ☐ Subrogation
- ☐ Title Insurance

Property Tax and Title Insurance Quiz

1. Ad valorem means:

    A. Taxes are "added to the value"

    B. Taxes are "not added to the value"

    C. Taxes are computed "according to value"

    D. It has no special meaning

2. The appraised value of a property for tax purposes is set by:

    A. A fee appraiser

    B. The county treasurer

    C. The tax commission

    D. The county assessor

3. Which of the following would give a buyer the greatest protection so far as title is concerned?

    A. Standard Title Policy

    B. Extended Title Policy

    C. Attorney's Opinion

    D. Abstract of Title

4. A lender, in order to make sure of the condition of a property he is using for collateral, will most often require a(n):

    A. ALTA Policy of Title Insurance

    B. Standard Policy of Title Insurance

    C. Attorney's Opinion

    D. Abstract of Title

5. Property taxes in Utah are due:

    A. January 1

    B. June 30

    C. November 30

    D. December 31

6. A property was purchased for $200,000 after obtaining a loan for $150,000. How much title insurance coverage did the buyer have to pay for?

    A. $200,000 of coverage, seller would pay the same

    B. $150,000; seller's policy would be $200,000

    C. 70% of the amount they financed

    D. None of the above

COMPUTE TAXES FOR THESE SITUATIONS:

7.   Property A is appraised at $68,000. The assessed rate is 34% and the tax rate is $8.76 per $100.

Answer: $ _____ .

8.   Property B is appraised at $105,000. The assessed rate 68% because it is residential property. The tax rate is .019468.

Answer: $ _____ .

9.   Property C is appraised at $314,000. The assessed rate is 28% and the tax rate is $64.72 per $1,000.

Answer: $ _____ .

10.   Property D is appraised at $1,200,000. The assessed rate is 24% and the tax rate is 98.674 mills.

Answer: $ _____ .

11. Mr. Allen ended up paying $1,789.00 in property tax. If his tax rate was 78.4 mills and the assessed rate was 32%, what was the appraised value of his home as determined by the county?

Answer: $ _____ .

Real Estate Settlement Procedures Act (RESPA)

I.   **Real Estate Settlement Procedures Act [**12 U.S. Code §§ 2601-2617 (1974)**; and** 12 C.F.R. § 1024.1 et. seq.] **Also known as Regulation X**

    A.   Passed in 1974, commonly referred to as **RESPA**

    B.   Administered and regulated by the **Consumer Finance Protection Bureau** ("CFPB").

    C.   The purposes of RESPA are to govern the real estate settlement process by:

        1.   Helping consumers become informed shoppers of settlement services through mandating specific disclosures to borrowers, including:

            a.   Accounting for all money associated with the transaction whether paid or received

            b.   All costs associated with settlement

            c.   Lender servicing practices

            d.   Escrow account practices

            e.   Business relationships between settlement service providers and other parties to the transaction

        2.   Prohibiting **kickbacks** and **referral fees** which unnecessarily increase the costs of settlement services and requiring full disclosure of all fees charged in connection with a loan.

    See generally 12 U.S.C. § 2601

    D.   RESPA applies to mortgage loans on one-to-four family residential properties, including (see generally 12 U.S.C. § 2602(1) and 12 C.F.R. § 1024.2(b)):

        1.   Home purchase loans

        2.   Refinances

        3.   Lender approved loan assumptions

        4.   Property improvement loans

        5.   Equity lines of credit

        6.   Reverse mortgages

        7.   Loans made or insured by an agency of the federal government

        8.   Loans intended to be sold by the originating lender to FNMA, GNMA, or FHLMC

    E.   RESPA does not apply to the following loans (12 U.S.C. § 2606 and 12 C.F.R. § 1024.5):

        1.   All cash sale

        2.   Sale where the individual home seller takes back the mortgage

        3.   Rental property transaction

4. Business purpose transaction

5. Construction loans from a lender other than the lender on the take out loan

6. Government transaction

7. Large parcels of land 25 acres or more

II. **Loan Application (**12 C.F.R. § 1024.2(b)**)**

A. A complete application includes the submission of a borrower's financial information in anticipation of a credit decision, whether written or computer generated, on a federally related mortgage loan.

B. If the submission does not identify a specific property, the submission is an application for pre-qualification and not an application for a federally related mortgage loan under this part.

C. The subsequent addition of an identified property to the submission converts it to an application for a federally related mortgage loan.

III. **Loan Estimate (**12 C.F.R. § 1024.7**)**

A. This is an estimate of the borrower's closing costs as they will appear on the **Closing Disclosure**.

B. The **Yield Spread Premium** (commission) must be disclosed on the Loan Estimate if the mortgage broker expects to receive it.

C. The **Loan Estimate** must be provided to the borrower upon application if the application is taken in person, or mailed to the borrowers within three business days if taken by telephone or mail. When receiving an application by internet, the originator may provide the Loan Estimate on line at the time of application or within three days by mail. An application must include, among other things, a specific property address in order to be considered an application. Borrowers who are asking for a preliminary evaluation of their ability to finance a future purchase are not required by RESPA to receive a Loan Estimate.

D. **Business day** means a day on which the offices of the business entity are open to the public for carrying on substantially all of the entity's business functions. Typically a business day is Monday through Saturday, but not holidays (State & Federal).

E. If the information in the Loan Estimate becomes incorrect:

1. No action is necessary if the change is related to reserves or escrow, daily interest charges, and/or homeowner's insurance. Good business practice would be to disclose this change but disclosure is not required by law.

2. Re-disclosure is necessary if:

   a. The costs for certain fees for services change 10% or more from when originally estimated. These fees include all lender required settlement services (the rule remains the same whether it is the lender or the borrower who selects the third party provider).

246

b. The cost of lender/broker fees, YSP, government recording and/or transfer taxes (where applicable) change at all.

c. Loan costs that are included in the original APR calculation increase so that the newly calculated APR increases by 1/8% or more.

3. If the lender exceeds the tolerances at closing that would require re-disclosure, the lender must redisclose with a new Closing Disclosure and the 3-day disclosure period starts over again.

F. For "no cost" or "no point" mortgages, a Loan Estimate must identify payments to third party vendors, such as underwriting, appraisal, credit, and title fees, as paid outside of closing ("POC").

IV. **Your Home Loan Toolkit** (12 U.S.C. § 2604 and 12 C.F.R. § 1024.6)

Information booklet produced by CFPB.

A. The booklet describes to borrowers, in laymen's terms, the most important steps a borrower needs to take to get the best mortgage for them; as well as the process to buy a home and the costs involved.

B. This booklet must be given to the borrower by the lender on all residential real estate purchases regulated under RESPA within 3 business days after the application is received.

V. **Kickbacks & Referral Fees: RESPA Section 8** (12 U.S.C. § 2607 **and** 12 C.F.R. § 1024.14)

A. RESPA prohibits anyone from giving or accepting a fee, kickback, or anything of value in exchange for referrals of settlement service business involving a federally related mortgage. One exception to this rule is when the lender discloses a loan rate together with a single guaranteed price for a package of settlement services (i.e. 7% int. and $4,500 GMP or guaranteed mortgage package).

B. Sharing of commissions and fees by multiple mortgage originators is restricted to only those persons who actually performed duties in connection with the transaction. The fee share must be proportionate with the task performed.

C. Giving or accepting any part of a charge for services that are not performed is prohibited. This is referred to as receiving unearned fees.

D. Marketing costs are not regulated so long as payments are not made to prohibited entities. Incentives given to buyers are not regulated.

E. **Penalties for violating** this section of the act are $10,000 and/or one year in prison for each violation.

VI. **Escrow Account Regulation** (12 U.S.C. § 2609 **and** 12 C.F.R. § 1024.17)

Lenders are prohibited from charging excessive amounts for an escrow account. **Aggregate Escrow Analysis** is used to reduce the amount being held in escrow or reserve accounts. The escrow or reserve account is established by the lender at settlement to collect payments to be held in reserve for the payment of homeowners' hazard insurance, property taxes and, if applicable, mortgage insurance.

247

A.   The amount the lender can hold in this account is limited to:

1.   1/12th of the total of all disbursements payable during the year.

2.   The lender may hold a cushion of up to an amount not to exceed 1/6th of annual disbursements.

3.   All accounts must be reviewed once every 12 months and any amount more than $50 above the cushion must be refunded within 30 days.

B.   The penalty for noncompliance is $50 per occurrence, up to $100,000 per year if unintentional; and $100 per occurrence, with no limit, if intentional.

C.   In the event of a shortage, the loan servicer may elect to:

1.   Do nothing.

2.   Spread the shortfall over 12 months.

3.   Require the borrower(s) to repay the deficiency over a two month period.

4.   Require a lump sum payment to bring the escrow account current. This can be done only if the shortfall is less than one month's worth of escrow deposits.

VII.   **Closing Disclosure** (12 U.S.C. § 2603)

A.   The Closing Disclosure is required on all federally related mortgage loans. It is not required for seller financing, cash transactions, or reverse mortgages.

B.   Its purpose is to account for all monies associated with the real property transaction.

C.   The "bottom line" indicates:

1.   What the buyers/borrowers have to bring to closing (or given at closing in some cases)

2.   What the sellers will realize from the transaction (or, occasionally, have to bring to close).

D.   All money must be disclosed even if it was **paid outside of closing** ("POC"). Items that are commonly POC are credit report fee, appraisal fee, and yield spread premium.

E.   RESPA stipulates the borrowers have the right to inspect the Closing Disclosure 3 business days prior to settlement time.

F.   Yield Spread Premium ("YSP") must be disclosed on the Closing Disclosure when the loan originator is a mortgage broker because it is a fee paid to the originator.

G.   The lender must retain the Closing Disclosure and related document for a period not less than 3 years after settlement.

H.   The Closing Disclosure must be issued to the borrower at least 3 days before closing (or settlement). If the Closing Disclosure has to be mailed to the borrower, it must be mailed at least 6 days prior to closing (or settlement).

VIII.   **Settlement and Other Services**

A.   When a loan originator allows a borrower to shop for third-party settlement services, the loan originator must provide the borrower with a written list of settlement services providers on a separate sheet of paper no later than the third business day after the consumer's application is received.. 12 C.F.R. § 1026.19(e)(vi)(C) (statutory provision effective August 1, 2015).

B. Settlement service providers includes and provider of a service in connection with real estate, including, but not limited to: title searches, title examinations, the provision of title certificates, title insurance, services rendered by an attorney, the preparation of documents, property surveys, the rendering of credit reports or appraisals, pest and fungus inspections, services rendered by a real estate agent or broker, the origination of a federally related mortgage loan (including, but not limited to, the taking of loan applications, loan processing, and the underwriting and funding of loans), and the handling of the processing, and closing or settlement. 12 U.S.C. § 2602(3).

C. **Affiliated Business Arrangements** ("AfBA") must be disclosed. An AfBA is an arrangement in which a person who is in a position to refer business incident to or a part of a real estate settlement service involving a federally related mortgage loan, or an associate of such person, has either an affiliate relationship with or a direct or beneficial ownership interest of more than 1 percent in a provider of settlement services; and either of such persons directly or indirectly refers such business to that provider or affirmatively influences the selection of that provider. 12 U.S.C. § 2602(7)(A)-(B). Thus, If a mortgage originator has a financial or ownership interest in a suggested service provider, that relationship must be disclosed prior to referral.

D. The mortgage originator can never require the use of certain providers, including:

1. Title Company.

2. Property inspectors, etc.

E. See 12 C.F.R. § 1024.14(f)(2); and 12 C.F.R. § 1024.14(b).

F. Section 9 of RESPA specifically prohibits a seller from requiring homebuyers to use the settlement services of a particular company as a condition of the sale.

IX. **Loan Servicing** (12 U.S.C. § 2605; and 12 C.F.R. § 1024.21)

A. Loan servicing involves receiving and distributing scheduled periodic payments from the borrowers including amounts to be held in escrow accounts. The servicer distributes payments of principal and interest to the owner of the loan or other third parties and makes payments as appropriate from the escrow account to taxing entities, insurance companies and others. In the case of a reverse mortgage, servicing includes making payments to the borrowers. These duties are typically carried out by the originating lender of the mortgage or mortgagee. The duties of servicing can also be sold or assigned to servicing companies. Often the originating lender packages and sells its loans to the secondary loan market while retaining the right and obligation to service the loan.

B. RESPA requires the following if lenders plan to sell all or a portion of their servicing functions:

1. The borrowers must be notified with a Servicing Disclosure Statement, the percentage of the loans sold and serviced by the lender.

2. This servicing disclosure must be provided to the borrowers within three business days of signing of 1003 application.

3. If servicing is transferred during the term of the mortgage, notice must be given to the borrowers not less than 15 days before the effective date of the loan servicing transfer.

C. The borrowers have the right to make payments to either lender during the 60 days following the effective date of the loan servicing transfer without suffering any negative implications, including credit reporting and, if applicable, late charges.

D. If a borrower sends a qualified written request to the mortgage servicer concerning the mortgage Section 6 of RESPA requires:

1. Servicers provide written acknowledgment within 20 business days of receipt of request.

2. Not later than 60 business days after receiving the request, the servicer must make any appropriate corrections to the account.

3. During the 60-day period, the servicer cannot provide any derogatory payment history information concerning the disputed period to consumer reporting agencies.

Real Estate Settlement Procedures Act (RESPA) Terms to Know

- ☐ Affiliated Business Arrangement (AfBA)
- ☐ Aggregate Escrow Analysis
- ☐ Business Day
- ☐ Buying Your Home, Settlement Costs and Helpful Information
- ☐ Closing Disclosure
- ☐ Kickbacks
- ☐ Fine for Violating Sec. 8 of RESPA
- ☐ Paid Outside of Closing (POC)
- ☐ Real Estate Settlement Procedures Act (RESPA)
- ☐ Referral Fee

Real Estate Settlement Procedures Act (RESPA) Quiz

True or False

RESPA applies to:

1. ___ Home purchase loans

2. ___ All cash sales

3. ___ Sale where the individual seller takes back a mortgage

4. ___ Refinance

5. ___ Rental Property Transaction

6. ___ Equity line of credit

7. ___ Property improvement loans

8. ___ Construction loans

9. ___ Reverse mortgages

10. ___ Lender approved loan assumptions

Fill in the blanks

11. One purpose of RESPA is to account for all the _____ associated with the transaction.

12. RESPA applies to loans on _____ - family, _____ properties.

Multiple CHOICE

13. The Federal consumer protection law passed in 1974, which requires lenders to provide the booklet "Settlement Costs and You" to borrowers is:

    A. Truth In Lending

    B. Real Estate Settlement Procedures Act (RESPA)

    C. Regulation Z

    D. HMDA

14. RESPA is administered by

    A. Federal Trade Commission (FTC)

    B. Federal Reserve

    C. Consumer Finance Protection Bureau

    D. U.S. Department of Commerce

15. RESPA governs all of the following EXCEPT:

    A. Costs associated with settlement

    B. Escrow account practices

    C. Title insurance premiums

    D. Kickbacks and referral fees

16. RESPA covers which of the following loans?

    A. Loans for businesses or commercial purposes

    B. Personal property loans

    C. Mortgages on one to four family residential properties

    D. Loans made to governmental agencies

17. Which of the following is a requirement under RESPA?

    A. A Loan Estimate of costs of borrowing

    B. Annual Percentage Rate box form

    C. Lock-in agreement

    D. Property taxes must be paid by the seller

18. Disclosure of the cost of borrowing must be given to the borrowers within:

    A. 30 calendar days of receipt of 1003 application

    B. At closing

    C. 3 days, but only if there are lender fees charged

    D. 3 business days of receipt of completed 1003 application

19. RESPA covers all federally related mortgages EXCEPT:

    A. Mortgages on properties of 25 acres or more

    B. FHA mortgages for residential

    C. VA mortgages for one-to-four family dwellings

    D. Conventional conforming loans

20. Mortgage originators can do all of the following EXCEPT:

    A. Give a real estate agent note pads with the lender's name on them

    B. Advertise with a real estate agent when the costs are prorated

    C. Offer something of value to a real estate agent for referrals

    D. Provide incentives to borrowers for doing business with them

21. According to RESPA, when can a lender collect higher fees then those actually charged by third party vendors for services rendered?

    A. If the third party vendor allows it.

    B. The borrowers agree in writing to such fees.

    C. They can never charge more than the actual costs.

    D. When the appropriate paperwork has been signed.

22. The RESPA required settlement document, accounting for all the monies in the transaction is called:

    A. Loan Estimate

    B. Closing Disclosure

    C. Reg. Z

    D. APR

23. RESPA stipulates that the borrower has the right to review the Closing Disclosure how long before the actual settlement?

    A. 3 business days

    B. 24 hours and upon lender request

    C. 24 hours upon borrower request

    D. 3 days after loan application

24. On the Closing Disclosure the escrow or reserve account can include all of the following EXCEPT:

    A. Property tax

    B. Hazard insurance

    C. Mortgage insurance

    D. Prepaid interest

25. According to RESPA how much of a cushion can a lender keep in the escrow account and how often must it be reconciled.

    A. 1/6th reconciled annually

    B. Zero to 2 months; reconciled annually

    C. 1/12th; reconciled annually

    D. 1 to 3 months; reconciled monthly

26. According to RESPA, which of the following statements is true?

    A. The mortgage originator cannot have a financial or ownership interest in the settlement provider.

    B. The mortgage originator need not disclose any financial or ownership interest in a settlement provider.

    C. The mortgage originator must supply the names of three settlement providers.

    D. The mortgage originator must supply a list of optional settlement providers.

27. If the mortgage lender intends to sell all or a portion of the mortgage servicing functions, according to RESPA, what must the mortgage lender do?

    A. Provide a specific servicing disclosure identifying the percentage of loans serviced.

    B. Provide the borrower with the option to not transfer the servicing.

    C. Offer a different loan program to the borrower.

    D. Provide the borrower with advance notice of the costs the borrower will face when the serving is transferred.

28. If loan servicing is transferred during the term of the mortgage, a loan servicing transfer disclosure must be made to the borrower within:

    A. Three calendar days before the loan servicing transfer

    B. 30 business days prior to the loan servicing transfer

    C. 15 days before effective date of the servicing transfer

    D. 45 days before the servicing transfer

Settlement Procedures

(The actual settlement and Closing Disclosure are governed by federal law. This course discusses the agent's duties under Utah law.)

I.   **Administrative Rules regarding SETTLEMENT [**Utah Administrative Code R162-2f-401c**]**

    A.   Although the lender holds federal liability to ensure the delivery of the Closing Disclosure, the principal broker must be sure that the BUYER/SELLER have received a Closing Disclosure showing all monies that have been received and disbursed.

    B.   The Principal Broker must ensure the settlement statements are reviewed for content and accuracy, regardless of who closes the transaction.

    C.   The Principal Broker must ensure delivery of the fully executed Closing Disclosure before commissions may be paid from the trust account..

    D.   The Closing Disclosure is used in both purchase and refinance transactions across the country.

    E.   It's strongly encouraged that all agents to attend settlement with the client they are representing.

II.   **Settlement vs. Closing**

    It is important to understand the difference between settlement and closing in Utah. You will find that many people use these words interchangeably. Below is a summary of section 3, Settlement and Closing, of the Real Estate Purchase Contract, which defines the two.

    A.   Settlement occurs when (2 things happen):

        1.   Buyer and Seller have SIGNED and delivered all required documents; and

        2.   Buyer and/or Seller has delivered all funds required (except loan funds) as "cleared funds." This means that personal checks are not accepted.

    B.   Closing occurs when (3 things happen):

        1.   Settlement has occurred

        2.   Loan funds have been authorized to be funded and dispersed; and

        3.   Applicable documents have been RECORDED.

    C.   The settlement agent/escrow officer will typically prepare the documents and settlement statements. The settlement agent's purpose is to assure that necessary documents are prepared, signed, recorded, and that all monies required are received and disbursed appropriately.

III.   **Understanding the Closing Disclosure**

    A.   The purpose of the Closing Disclosure is to account for all money involved in the closing.

        1.   If a person is charged for something it is called a COST.

        2.   If a person is receiving money that money will be indicated in sections that state "Due to" or "Paid Already."

        3.   It is not necessary for the buyer's side of the statement to balance with the seller's side. If

they do balance, that is merely a coincidence.

4.   The real estate agent should confirm that the necessary documents are in place and should check the amounts on the Settlement Statement. The agent should be able to answer any questions the buyer or seller might have about items appearing on the settlement statement.

IV.   **Review of Closing Disclosure**

A.   On the next page you will find a blank Closing Disclosure. Certain features and the "flow" of this statement will be discussed in class. As they are mentioned in class, you should make notes on the blank form to help you understand each section, it's importance and function.

B.   The page after the blank Closing Disclosure is a sample completed Closing Disclosure. During the class discussion specific items will be pointed out in terms of where they appear and why, and how it looks on a completed form. You might want to highlight and review these items later.

C.   PAGE 1: Contains the essential information and terms of the borrower's loan. The information is organized into three sections: loan terms, projected payments, and closing costs.

1.   **Loan Terms**. Under this section, the borrower will find the larger components of his/her loan: loan amount, interest rate, total monthly payment, prepayment penalty, and balloon payment. This section also informs the borrower of whether the terms of the oan can change over its life and whether a prepayment penalty and balloon payment apply to the borrower's loan.

2.   **Projected Payments**. Under this section, the borrower can see payment calculations based on the first seven years and the remainder of the loan. Payments are broken down to show the total principal and interest, mortgage insurance (if applicable), and escrow holdings. Thus, the borrower is given an estimated total monthly payment, along with an estimation of taxes, homeowner's insurance, and other assessments.

3.   **Costs at Closing**. Under this section, the borrower is given the total amount he/she needs to pay in order to close on the transaction. This section also indicates the amount of cash the borrower has agreed to pay as a down payment.

D.   PAGE 2: Contains disclosures of certain costs in itemized forms that are needing to be paid before closing can occur. The costs are generally broken down into two categories: loan costs and other costs. Within each of those categories, the costs are further broken down as labeled.

1.   The Loan Costs section includes the following:

a.   Section A: Origination charges are those incurred for the loan officer to find and broker the loan.

b.   Section B: The services the borrower did not shop for are costs still paid by the borrower, but are services that the lender and/or loan officer ordered throughout the application, origination, and underwriting period.

c.   Section C: The services the borrower did shop for are items that the borrower him or herself actually contracted for with the providers listed.

d.   Section D: The total costs of the above sections added together.

2.   The Other Costs section includes the following:

a.   Section E: Taxes and other government fees that must be paid on the property in order to close .

b.   Section F: The items that are to be paid by the consumer in advance of the first scheduled loan payment.

c.   Section G: Certain prepaid items can be disclosed as separate items in this section if a portion of their amount can be paid at a different time for a different purpose. For example, general property taxes assessed for January 1 to December 31 and property taxes to fund schools for November 1 to October 31 can be disclosed as separate items.

d.   Section H: Items disclosed under this section reflect costs incurred by the consumer or seller that were not required to be disclosed on the loan estimate, such as:

i.   Real estate brokerage fees,

ii.   Homeowner or HOA fees paid when the consumer becomes contractually obligated to pay on the loan,

iii.   Home warranties,

iv.   Inspection fees, and

v.   Others paid at closing byt not required to be disclosed anywhere wlse on the Closing Disclosure.

e.   Section I: This section totals the costs disclosed under the above sections.

f.   Section J: The total of all closing costs paid by the consumer, reduced by the lender credits, amounts to the total closing costs (borrower-paid). The total of items designated as "Borrower-Paid At or Before Closing," "Seller-Paid At or Before Closing," and "Paid by Others" are disclosed as Closing Cost Subtotals.

E.   Page 3: Contains disclosures of the total costs to close and those calculations, as well as an overall summary of the transaction.

1.   Calculating **Cash to Close**. This section breaks down the total amount of closing costs and the required amount that the parties are needing to pay at closing. This section includes such costs as the buyer's down payment and other deposits, along with the total costs from page 2.

2.   **Summaries of Transaction**. This section works with total costs already calculated from the prior pages. Here, the parties can see the overall amounts they owe and the amounts they are receiving or being credited for.

a.   Section K: Shows the total amount the borrower must pay, by way of loan and other means, to purchase the property and close on the transaction.

    b.   Section L: Shows the monies the borrower is receiving from the lender (if there is a loan to finance the purchase), as well as those the borrower has already deposited or receiving a credit for.

        i.   Sections K & L are then totaled to signal whether the borrower must bring any cash to closing or will be receiving cash back.

    c.   Section M: Shows the monies that the seller will be receiving from the transaction.

    d.   Section N: Shows the costs that the seller must pay in order to sell the property free and clear of all title defects and encumbrances. Such costs include, the seller's loans on the property, seller's portion of the property taxes, any assessments, etc.

        i.   Sections M & N are then totaled to signal whether the seller must bring any cash to closing or will be receiving cash back.

F.   Page 4: Contains additional loan disclosures for the borrow that include the following:

    1.   Information concerning future of the loan by a subsequent purchaser;

    2.   Whether the legal obligation contains a demand feature that can require early payment of the loan;

    3.   The terms of the obligation that impose a fee for late payment;

    4.   Whether the regular payments can cause the principal balance of the loan to increase, causing negative amortization;

    5.   The creditor's policy in relation to partial payments;

    6.   A statement that the consumer is granting a security interest in the property; and

    7.   Information related to any escrow account held by the servicer.

G.   Page 5: Contains the disclosures of the loan calculations, service providers' contact information, other disclosures, and holds a receipt confirmation.

    1.   Loan Calculations. This section discloses the following:

        a.   The total of payments;

        b.   The finance charge;

        c.   The amount financed;

        d.   The annual percentage rate; and

        e.   The total interest percentage over the life of the loan.

    2.   Other Disclosures. This section discloses the following:

        a.   A statement related to the consumer's right in relation to any appraisal conducted for the property;

    b.   A statement concerning the consequences of nonpayment, what constitutes default, when a creditor can accelerate maturity, and prepayment rebates and penalties;

    c.   A statement of whether state law provides for continued consumer responsibility for any liability after foreclosure;

    d.   A statement concerning the consumer's ability to refinance the loan; and

    e.   A statement concerning the extent that interest on the loan can be included as a tax deduction by the consumer.

3.   Contact Information. Contains the contact information for the lender, mortgage broker, real estate brokers who worked the deal, and the settlement agent.

4.   Confirm Receipt. The creditor, at its option, may include this line to confirm receipt of the Closing Disclosure. If no line is included, a statement to the Other Disclosures section must be added concerning Loan Acceptance that states: "You do not have to accept this loan because you have received this form or signed a loan application." 12 C.F.R. § 1026.38(s) (2) (2015).

V.   Prorations

Prorations occur when the charges or costs for something must be divided between two parties. This is not always between the buyer and seller.

A.   Key points about prorations:

1.   For prorations between Buyer and Seller, and unless otherwise agreed to, the seller is responsible for the day of settlement.

2.   Prorated items are shared costs, usually between buyer and seller, but sometimes buyer and lender.

3.   For prorations in class and on the test use a financial calendar: 360 day year/ 30 day months.

4.   PAID IN ADVANCE prorated items appear as a DEBIT to the BUYER and CREDIT to the SELLER

5.   PAID IN ARREARS prorated items appear as a CREDIT to the BUYER and DEBIT to the seller

6.   Rents collected by the seller for the settlement month will appear on the statement as a DEBIT to the SELLER and a CREDIT to the BUYER.

7.   Rental deposits that are refundable will appear on the Settlement Statement as a DEBIT to the SELLER, but nothing to the buyer. If it were shown as a credit to the buyer, then the buyer would be using "other people's money" to assist with their down payment. The rental deposits are merely noted in the comment line.

B.   Calculating prorations is split in to three simple questions. If you answer these questions in the exact order it will be easier to complete any proration:

　　1.　WHO OWES the MONEY and to WHOM DO THEY OWE IT?

　　2.　HOW MANY DAYS DO THEY OWE?

　　3.　HOW MUCH MONEY DO THEY OWE?

C.   Common situation that require proration on the Settlement State are:

　　1.　County property taxes

　　2.　Interest on an assumed loan

　　3.　Interest on a new loan

　　4.　Rents collected

　　5.　Homeowners Association dues

Closing Disclosure

This form is a statement of final loan terms and closing costs. Compare this document with your Loan Estimate.

Closing Information

Date Issued	4/15/2013
Closing Date	4/15/2013
Disbursement Date	4/15/2013
Settlement Agent	Epsilon Title Co.
File #	12-3456
Property	456 Somewhere Ave
	Anytown, ST 12345
Sale Price	$180,000

Transaction Information

Borrower	Michael Jones and Mary Stone
	123 Anywhere Street
	Anytown, ST 12345
Seller	Steve Cole and Amy Doe
	321 Somewhere Drive
	Anytown, ST 12345
Lender	Ficus Bank

Loan Information

Loan Term	30 years
Purpose	Purchase
Product	Fixed Rate
Loan Type	☒ Conventional ☐ FHA ☐ VA ☐ _____
Loan ID #	123456789
MIC #	000654321

Loan Terms

		Can this amount increase after closing?
Loan Amount	$162,000	NO
Interest Rate	3.875%	NO
Monthly Principal & Interest *See Projected Payments below for your Estimated Total Monthly Payment*	$761.78	NO
		Does the loan have these features?
Prepayment Penalty		YES • As high as $3,240 if you pay off the loan during the first 2 years
Balloon Payment		NO

Projected Payments

Payment Calculation	Years 1-7	Years 8-30
Principal & Interest	$761.78	$761.78
Mortgage Insurance	+ 82.35	+ —
Estimated Escrow *Amount can increase over time*	+ 206.13	+ 206.13
Estimated Total Monthly Payment	**$1,050.26**	**$967.91**

Estimated Taxes, Insurance & Assessments *Amount can increase over time* *See page 4 for details*	$356.13 a month	This estimate includes	In escrow?
		☒ Property Taxes	YES
		☒ Homeowner's Insurance	YES
		☒ Other: Homeowner's Association Dues	NO

See Escrow Account on page 4 for details. You must pay for other property costs separately.

Costs at Closing

Closing Costs	$9,712.10	Includes $4,694.05 in Loan Costs + $5,018.05 in Other Costs – $0 in Lender Credits. *See page 2 for details.*
Cash to Close	$14,147.26	Includes Closing Costs. *See Calculating Cash to Close on page 3 for details.*

Closing Cost Details

Loan Costs		Borrower-Paid		Seller-Paid		Paid by Others
		At Closing	Before Closing	At Closing	Before Closing	
A. Origination Charges		**$1,802.00**				
01 0.25 % of Loan Amount (Points)		$405.00				
02 Application Fee		$300.00				
03 Underwriting Fee		$1,097.00				
04						
05						
06						
07						
08						
B. Services Borrower Did Not Shop For		**$236.55**				
01 Appraisal Fee	to John Smith Appraisers Inc.					$405.00
02 Credit Report Fee	to Information Inc.		$29.80			
03 Flood Determination Fee	to Info Co.	$20.00				
04 Flood Monitoring Fee	to Info Co.	$31.75				
05 Tax Monitoring Fee	to Info Co.	$75.00				
06 Tax Status Research Fee	to Info Co.	$80.00				
07						
08						
09						
10						
C. Services Borrower Did Shop For		**$2,655.50**				
01 Pest Inspection Fee	to Pests Co.	$120.50				
02 Survey Fee	to Surveys Co.	$85.00				
03 Title – Insurance Binder	to Epsilon Title Co.	$650.00				
04 Title – Lender's Title Insurance	to Epsilon Title Co.	$500.00				
05 Title – Settlement Agent Fee	to Epsilon Title Co.	$500.00				
06 Title – Title Search	to Epsilon Title Co.	$800.00				
07						
08						
D. TOTAL LOAN COSTS (Borrower-Paid)		**$4,694.05**				
Loan Costs Subtotals (A + B + C)		$4,664.25	$29.80			

Other Costs		Borrower-Paid		Seller-Paid		Paid by Others
E. Taxes and Other Government Fees		**$85.00**				
01 Recording Fees	Deed: $40.00 Mortgage: $45.00	$85.00				
02 Transfer Tax	to Any State			$950.00		
F. Prepaids		**$2,120.80**				
01 Homeowner's Insurance Premium (12 mo.) to Insurance Co.		$1,209.96				
02 Mortgage Insurance Premium (mo.)						
03 Prepaid Interest ($17.44 per day from 4/15/13 to 5/1/13)		$279.04				
04 Property Taxes (6 mo.) to Any County USA		$631.80				
05						
G. Initial Escrow Payment at Closing		**$412.25**				
01 Homeowner's Insurance $100.83 per month for 2 mo.		$201.66				
02 Mortgage Insurance per month for mo.						
03 Property Taxes $105.30 per month for 2 mo.		$210.60				
04						
05						
06						
07						
08 Aggregate Adjustment		– 0.01				
H. Other		**$2,400.00**				
01 HOA Capital Contribution	to HOA Acre Inc.	$500.00				
02 HOA Processing Fee	to HOA Acre Inc.	$150.00				
03 Home Inspection Fee	to Engineers Inc.	$750.00			$750.00	
04 Home Warranty Fee	to XYZ Warranty Inc.			$450.00		
05 Real Estate Commission	to Alpha Real Estate Broker			$5,700.00		
06 Real Estate Commission	to Omega Real Estate Broker			$5,700.00		
07 Title – Owner's Title Insurance (optional) to Epsilon Title Co.		$1,000.00				
08						
I. TOTAL OTHER COSTS (Borrower-Paid)		**$5,018.05**				
Other Costs Subtotals (E + F + G + H)		$5,018.05				

		Borrower-Paid		Seller-Paid		Paid by Others
J. TOTAL CLOSING COSTS (Borrower-Paid)		**$9,712.10**				
Closing Costs Subtotals (D + I)		$9,682.30	$29.80	$12,800.00	$750.00	$405.00
Lender Credits						

Calculating Cash to Close

Use this table to see what has changed from your Loan Estimate.

	Loan Estimate	Final	Did this change?	
Total Closing Costs (J)	$8,054.00	$9,712.10	YES	· See **Total Loan Costs (D)** and **Total Other Costs (I)**
Closing Costs Paid Before Closing	$0	− $29.80	YES	· You paid these Closing Costs **before closing**
Closing Costs Financed (Paid from your Loan Amount)	$0	$0	NO	
Down Payment/Funds from Borrower	$18,000.00	$18,000.00	NO	
Deposit	− $10,000.00	− $10,000.00	NO	
Funds for Borrower	$0	$0	NO	
Seller Credits	$0	− $2,500.00	YES	· See Seller Credits in **Section L**
Adjustments and Other Credits	$0	− $1,035.04	YES	· See details in **Sections K and L**
Cash to Close	$16,054.00	$14,147.26		

Summaries of Transactions

Use this table to see a summary of your transaction.

BORROWER'S TRANSACTION

K. Due from Borrower at Closing	$189,762.30
01 Sale Price of Property	$180,000.00
02 Sale Price of Any Personal Property Included in Sale	
03 Closing Costs Paid at Closing (J)	$9,682.30
04	
Adjustments	
05	
06	
07	

Adjustments for Items Paid by Seller in Advance

08	City/Town Taxes	to	
09	County Taxes	to	
10	Assessments	to	
11	HOA Dues	4/15/13 to 4/30/13	$80.00
12			
13			
14			
15			

L. Paid Already by or on Behalf of Borrower at Closing	$175,615.04
01 Deposit	$10,000.00
02 Loan Amount	$162,000.00
03 Existing Loan(s) Assumed or Taken Subject to	
04	
05 Seller Credit	$2,500.00
Other Credits	
06 Rebate from Epsilon Title Co.	$750.00
07	
Adjustments	
08	
09	
10	
11	

Adjustments for Items Unpaid by Seller

12	City/Town Taxes	1/1/13 to 4/14/13	$365.04
13	County Taxes	to	
14	Assessments	to	
15			
16			
17			

CALCULATION

Total Due from Borrower at Closing (K)	$189,762.30
Total Paid Already by or on Behalf of Borrower at Closing (L)	− $175,615.04
Cash to Close ☒ From ☐ To Borrower	**$14,147.26**

SELLER'S TRANSACTION

M. Due to Seller at Closing	$180,080.00
01 Sale Price of Property	$180,000.00
02 Sale Price of Any Personal Property Included in Sale	
03	
04	
05	
06	
07	
08	

Adjustments for Items Paid by Seller in Advance

09	City/Town Taxes	to	
10	County Taxes	to	
11	Assessments	to	
12	HOA Dues	4/15/13 to 4/30/13	$80.00
13			
14			
15			
16			

N. Due from Seller at Closing	$115,665.04
01 Excess Deposit	
02 Closing Costs Paid at Closing (J)	$12,800.00
03 Existing Loan(s) Assumed or Taken Subject to	
04 Payoff of First Mortgage Loan	$100,000.00
05 Payoff of Second Mortgage Loan	
06	
07	
08 Seller Credit	$2,500.00
09	
10	
11	
12	
13	

Adjustments for Items Unpaid by Seller

14	City/Town Taxes	1/1/13 to 4/14/13	$365.04
15	County Taxes	to	
16	Assessments	to	
17			
18			
19			

CALCULATION

Total Due to Seller at Closing (M)	$180,080.00
Total Due from Seller at Closing (N)	− $115,665.04
Cash ☐ From ☒ To Seller	**$64,414.96**

Additional Information About This Loan

Loan Disclosures

Assumption
If you sell or transfer this property to another person, your lender
- ☐ will allow, under certain conditions, this person to assume this loan on the original terms.
- ☒ will not allow assumption of this loan on the original terms.

Demand Feature
Your loan
- ☐ has a demand feature, which permits your lender to require early repayment of the loan. You should review your note for details.
- ☒ does not have a demand feature.

Late Payment
If your payment is more than *15* days late, your lender will charge a late fee of *5% of the monthly principal and interest payment.*

Negative Amortization (Increase in Loan Amount)
Under your loan terms, you
- ☐ are scheduled to make monthly payments that do not pay all of the interest due that month. As a result, your loan amount will increase (negatively amortize), and your loan amount will likely become larger than your original loan amount. Increases in your loan amount lower the equity you have in this property.
- ☐ may have monthly payments that do not pay all of the interest due that month. If you do, your loan amount will increase (negatively amortize), and, as a result, your loan amount may become larger than your original loan amount. Increases in your loan amount lower the equity you have in this property.
- ☒ do not have a negative amortization feature.

Partial Payments
Your lender
- ☒ may accept payments that are less than the full amount due (partial payments) and apply them to your loan.
- ☐ may hold them in a separate account until you pay the rest of the payment, and then apply the full payment to your loan.
- ☐ does not accept any partial payments.

If this loan is sold, your new lender may have a different policy.

Security Interest
You are granting a security interest in
456 Somewhere Ave., Anytown, ST 12345

You may lose this property if you do not make your payments or satisfy other obligations for this loan.

Escrow Account
For now, your loan
- ☒ will have an escrow account (also called an "impound" or "trust" account) to pay the property costs listed below. Without an escrow account, you would pay them directly, possibly in one or two large payments a year. Your lender may be liable for penalties and interest for failing to make a payment.

Escrow		
Escrowed Property Costs over Year 1	$2,473.56	Estimated total amount over year 1 for your escrowed property costs: *Homeowner's Insurance Property Taxes*
Non-Escrowed Property Costs over Year 1	$1,800.00	Estimated total amount over year 1 for your non-escrowed property costs: *Homeowner's Association Dues* You may have other property costs.
Initial Escrow Payment	$412.25	A cushion for the escrow account you pay at closing. See Section G on page 2.
Monthly Escrow Payment	$206.13	The amount included in your total monthly payment.

☐ will not have an escrow account because ☐ you declined it ☐ your lender does not offer one. You must directly pay your property costs, such as taxes and homeowner's insurance. Contact your lender to ask if your loan can have an escrow account.

No Escrow		
Estimated Property Costs over Year 1		Estimated total amount over year 1. You must pay these costs directly, possibly in one or two large payments a year.
Escrow Waiver Fee		

In the future,
Your property costs may change and, as a result, your escrow payment may change. You may be able to cancel your escrow account, but if you do, you must pay your property costs directly. If you fail to pay your property taxes, your state or local government may (1) impose fines and penalties or (2) place a tax lien on this property. If you fail to pay any of your property costs, your lender may (1) add the amounts to your loan balance, (2) add an escrow account to your loan, or (3) require you to pay for property insurance that the lender buys on your behalf, which likely would cost more and provide fewer benefits than what you could buy on your own.

Loan Calculations

Total of Payments. Total you will have paid after you make all payments of principal, interest, mortgage insurance, and loan costs, as scheduled.	$285,803.36
Finance Charge. The dollar amount the loan will cost you.	$118,830.27
Amount Financed. The loan amount available after paying your upfront finance charge.	$162,000.00
Annual Percentage Rate (APR). Your costs over the loan term expressed as a rate. This is not your interest rate.	4.174%
Total Interest Percentage (TIP). The total amount of interest that you will pay over the loan term as a percentage of your loan amount.	69.46%

Questions? If you have questions about the loan terms or costs on this form, use the contact information below. To get more information or make a complaint, contact the Consumer Financial Protection Bureau at **www.consumerfinance.gov/mortgage-closing**

Other Disclosures

Appraisal
If the property was appraised for your loan, your lender is required to give you a copy at no additional cost at least 3 days before closing. If you have not yet received it, please contact your lender at the information listed below.

Contract Details
See your note and security instrument for information about
- what happens if you fail to make your payments,
- what is a default on the loan,
- situations in which your lender can require early repayment of the loan, and
- the rules for making payments before they are due.

Liability after Foreclosure
If your lender forecloses on this property and the foreclosure does not cover the amount of unpaid balance on this loan,

☒ state law may protect you from liability for the unpaid balance. If you refinance or take on any additional debt on this property, you may lose this protection and have to pay any debt remaining even after foreclosure. You may want to consult a lawyer for more information.

☐ state law does not protect you from liability for the unpaid balance.

Refinance
Refinancing this loan will depend on your future financial situation, the property value, and market conditions. You may not be able to refinance this loan.

Tax Deductions
If you borrow more than this property is worth, the interest on the loan amount above this property's fair market value is not deductible from your federal income taxes. You should consult a tax advisor for more information.

Contact Information

	Lender	Mortgage Broker	Real Estate Broker (B)	Real Estate Broker (S)	Settlement Agent
Name	Ficus Bank		Omega Real Estate Broker Inc.	Alpha Real Estate Broker Co.	Epsilon Title Co.
Address	4321 Random Blvd. Somecity, ST 12340		789 Local Lane Sometown, ST 12345	987 Suburb Ct. Someplace, ST 12340	123 Commerce Pl. Somecity, ST 12344
NMLS ID					
ST License ID			Z765416	Z61456	Z61616
Contact	Joe Smith		Samuel Green	Joseph Cain	Sarah Arnold
Contact NMLS ID	12345				
Contact ST License ID			P16415	P51461	PT1234
Email	joesmith@ficusbank.com		sam@omegare.biz	joe@alphare.biz	sarah@epsilontitle.com
Phone	123-456-7890		123-555-1717	321-555-7171	987-555-4321

Confirm Receipt

By signing, you are only confirming that you have received this form. You do not have to accept this loan because you have signed or received this form.

_____ _____ _____ _____
Applicant Signature   Date   Co-Applicant Signature   Date

SAMPLE PRORATION QUESTIONS

Remember to use the steps explained above.

1. The settlement date for the transaction was JULY 13. Property taxes for the previous year were $1234.56. Which of the following best describes the way the taxes will appear on the settlement statement?

    A. $617.28 charged to both buyer and seller

    B. $658.43 paid by seller, received by buyer

    C. $658.43 paid by buyer to seller

    D. $661.86 paid by seller to the buyer

2. The buyer made an offer of $119,000 for the property with a down payment of $18,500 and they plan to assume the seller's loan with its balance of $101,400. The interest rate on the loan is 9.5%. The settlement date is July 13. Which of the following is true about the interest proration?

    A. $347.86 debit seller, $347.86 credit buyer

    B. $347.86 debit buyer, $347.86 credit seller

    C. $321.10 debit seller, $321.10.86 credit buyer

    D. $321.10 debit buyer, $321.10 credit seller

3. The buyers are obtaining a loan of $115,000 in purchasing their new home. The interest rate is 8.25%. The settlement date is June 13, and the buyers have been told their first monthly payment is not due until August 1. Which of the following is a true statement?

    A. The September payment will cover interest for July and August.

    B. There will be a debit of $448.02 to the buyers for July Interest

    C. There will be a charge of $447.95 to the sellers for July Interest

    D. The September payment will be a balloon payment covering interest for July, August and September.

Settlement Procedures Terms to Know

- ☐ ¨Closing
- ☐ ¨Closing Disclosure
- ☐ ¨Credit
- ☐ ¨Debit
- ☐ ¨P.O.C.
- ☐ ¨Settlement

Settlement Procedure Quiz

1. Which of the following best describes the REPC's definition of "Settlement?"

    A. Recording of all necessary documents.

    B. Signing of all necessary documents

    C. The loan is funded.

    D. The sellers have received all funds coming to them.

2. Regarding debits and credits, which of the following statements is most accurate?

    A. Debit is what the buyer pays; credit is what the seller pays in prorations.

    B. Debit is like a debt, so the new loan for the buyers would be a debit for them.

    C. If a seller has a debit the buyer must have a corresponding credit.

    D. The person paying has a debit, the other one a credit, if applicable.

3. The main purpose of a Closing Disclosure is to:

    A. Reconcile the trust account for the closing of the transaction.

    B. Identify the form of funds the buyer needs to bring to close.

    C. Account for all monies involved in the transaction.

    D. Make sure the prorations are done accurately.

4. Who has the responsibility for the Closing Disclosure being completely and accurately filled out?

    A. The lender.

    B. The branch manager.

    C. The title officer or lawyer conducting the settlement.

    D. The real estate agent attending the settlement meeting.

Refer to the filled-in Closing Disclosure to answer the following:

5. The "bottom line" for the buyer's and seller's costs of closing appears where on the Closing Disclosure?

    A. Page 1

    B. Section J

    C. Section I

    D. Section D

6. The property taxes of $365.04 fit into which categories?

    A. A debit to both buyer and seller.

    B. A credit to the seller and a debit to the buyer.

    C. A credit to both buyer and seller.

    D. A debit to the seller and a credit to the buyer.

7. Which section indicates if the seller helped the buyer with loan costs?

    A. Section N

    B. Section M

    C. Section A

    D. Section K

8. Did the seller pay property taxes for the date of settlement?

    A. Yes

    B. No

9. Is the origination fee computed correctly?

    A. Yes

    B. No

10. Does this Closing Disclosure need to be revised?

    A. Yes

    B. No

11. Which line has the total cost to the seller to complete this transaction?

    A. Section D

    B. Section I

    C. Section J

    D. Section M

12. Where would the buyer's earnest money deposit appear on a Closing Disclosure?

    A. Section K

    B. Section L

    C. Page 1

    D. Page 2

13. How much was the title insurance to cover the lender's interest?

    A. $650

    B. $800

    C. $1,000

    D. $500

14. Did the seller contribute toward the buyer's loan costs?

    A. Yes

    B. No

IV. **Other Agencies and Institutions**

    A. **Federal Trade Commission** ("FTC"), originally established in 1914, has a primary mission of protecting consumers. The FTC enforces federal consumer protection laws, such as antitrust laws, telemarketing rules, Equal Credit Opportunity Act, and others. Some of the laws it once enforced are now under the jurisdiction of the Consumer Financial Protection Bureau.

    B. **Department of Housing and Urban Development** ("HUD") has a primary mission of increasing homeownership, supporting community development, and increasing access to affordable housing free from discrimination. HUD also oversees The Federal Housing Administration ("FHA") which provides an opportunity for home ownership for low to moderate level income earners. HUD also enforces RESPA procedures (www.hud.gov).

    C. **Department of Veteran Affairs** ("VA") guarantees loans for eligible veterans, enabling them to get mortgages with little or no down payment and limited closing costs (www.va.gov).

    D. **United States Department of Agriculture** ("USDA") is the federal agency in charge of executing government policy on farming, agriculture, and food. It is also engaged with assisting development and investment in rural communities.

    E. **Farmers Home Administration** ("FmHA") is part of the Department of Agriculture. It extends loans in rural areas, typically with populations of 10,000 or less for farms, houses, or possibly community property facilities

V. **Federal Reserve**

The **Federal Reserve** was created in 1913. Its purpose is to maintain sound credit conditions, help counteract inflationary and deflationary trends, and create favorable economic conditions. It manages the money supply available to consumers by regulating lending among banks.

    A. The "**discount rate**" is the rate the Federal Reserve offers its member banks when they need to borrow money. This rate is frequently in the news when the Chairman of the Federal Reserve holds a press conference announcing discount rate increases or decreases.

        1. The Federal Reserve raises the discount rate in an effort to reduce inflation and reduces the rate to encourage spending which causes inflation to increase.

        2. The only effect this rate has on mortgage interest rates is increasing or decreasing investor fears of inflation.

        3. If investors feel that inflation is under control and stable then long term rates remain stable.

        4. Fear of inflation causes long term interest rates, such as mortgage rates, to increase.

    B. The Federal Reserve has the power to increase or decrease the amount of cash a bank must keep on hand.

        1. Lenders are required by the Federal Reserve to keep a set amount of cash available for the protection of depositors.

        2. Since this money can't be used to earn money, interest rates must be adjusted upward to cover the costs of banking when the reserve requirement is high, or may allow interest rates to be lower if the reserve requirement is lowered.

3. Increasing the reserve could be done for the purpose of creating more security for depositors or to slow inflation.

C. The "**Prime Rate**" is the rate banks charge their lowest risk borrowers (their best customers.)

1. The Prime Rate is not determined by the Federal Reserve but by individual banks.

2. Since banking is competitive the rate from bank to bank is very close to the same.

VI. **Underwriting**

The **underwriter** is the person who reviews each loan application file and determines if the loan conforms to the lenders guidelines. Lenders that plan to sell their loans into the secondary or wholesale market will align their guidelines with the secondary markets requirements to be certain that the loan can be sold. The term conforming loan refers to loans conforming to FNMA or FHLMC guidelines.

VII. **Origination Fee**

Originating lenders who sold their loans, charged origination fees as compensation since the interest on the loan was a part of what was sold. The practice has become widely accepted by consumers so that now almost all lenders charge an origination fee whether they plan to sell their loans or not. The origination fee is usually charged as a percent of the loan. A 1% fee is computed by multiplying 1% times the loan amount. The fee is paid up front to the originating lender or mortgage broker.

VIII. **Loan Form Standardization**

Fannie Mae, Freddie Mac, FHA, and VA have agreed to use standardized forms. Many of the underwriting guidelines have also been standardized so that investors are more comfortable investing in any of these investment opportunities without confusion. Lenders that do not intend to sell their loans into the secondary market still have generally adopted much of the standardization just for simplicity sake.

IX. **Par Rate**

The par rate is the market interest rate for a mortgage loan.

A. Market interest rates are the result of competition and investor fear of inflation.

B. The investor wants investments to yield a return that compensates the investor for the risk of the investment in addition to keeping up with inflation.

C. Par mortgage rates reflect the investors' long term expectation of inflation.

D. There are many investment options to choose from. Mortgage rates have to compete for investor dollars among the other choices.

X. **Discount Points**

Discount points are a fee paid at closing to permanently lower the interest rate below par.

A. Example: If par was 8%, a lender might allow the borrowers to obtain a loan at a rate of 7.75% interest in exchange for two discount points (one discount point is equal to 1% of the full loan amount). Assume the loan was $100,000. By paying $2,000 (2%) at closing, the borrowers could obtain a 30 year loan for 7.75%, thus lowering the payment from $733.76 (principal and interest) to $716.41. That would save them $17.35 per month or $208.17 per year. They would get the $2,000 back in less than ten years and over the full term of the loan save a total of $6,245.19. However, if they sell the property and pay off the loan in two or three years, they might lose money.

B.   Why pay discount points? The borrower obtains a lower interest rate and lower monthly payment. This could allow a borrower to qualify for a loan that otherwise would not be available to them.

C.   The originating lender would want to charge discount points as a way to help the buyer qualify for the loan they need. The discount points become a bargaining chip for the originating lender to induce the wholesale market to buy the loan with an interest rate below Par (market).

D.   The secondary market views the points as prepaid interest that can be added to the return on the loan to increase the income or "yield." If the points are enough to offset the income lost by the below Par rate then the wholesaler would view the loan as comparable to other loans that are at par and be willing to buy it.

XI.   **Loan Buydown**

The term "buydown" sometimes is used to describe paying discount points. More recently the term has been used to refer to paying a fee to reduce the monthly payment for the early months of a loan.

A.   Buydowns are usually described using the change in interest rate used in calculating the lower payment.

B.   A 2/1 buydown computes the monthly payment for the first year using a rate 2% lower than the note rate and the second year payment by computing the payment based on a rate 1% less than the note rate.

C.   Someone (usually the builder) pays the difference in monthly payment to the lender up front leaving the borrower to make lower monthly payments temporarily.

D.   This practice has, in the past, allowed borrowers to qualify for a larger loan because of the lower payment in the early years. Most lenders now look past the buydown period to determine qualification.

XII.   **Locking Rates**

Borrowers face the risk of rates changing during the loan underwriting period which can sometimes take a few weeks. To protect them from the risk many lenders offer a "Rate Lock" option.

A.   For a slight premium in interest rate, the lender will "lock in" the rate as of the date of the loan application.

B.   If rates go up before the loan closes, as long as it closes within the specified time you receive the rate that was locked in.

XIII.   **Debt Service**

The term "debt service" refers to the payments that are made in accordance with the loan agreement for the payment of principal and interest.

A.   It does not include taxes, insurance, or mortgage insurance.

B.   A loan is seasoned if the debt service began on time and continued without default for a period of time long enough to indicate the borrowers intent to comply with the loan agreement.

XIV. **Discounting Loans**

Loans sold to a secondary money market are sometimes sold at a discount. They are referred to as a discounted note if they are sold for less than the "face" amount (remaining balance). A lender who wants to convert a loan to cash is sometimes willing to receive less than the face amount of the loan.

A. Lenders who have followed the secondary lender guidelines and priced the loan at Par do not need to discount a loan to sell it to the secondary market that the loan was prepared for. Uniformity of documents and similarity of underwriting guidelines followed by the major secondary market players make it easy to determine if loans eligible for FNMA may also be eligible for FHLMC.

B. **Seasoned loans** that do not meet secondary lender underwriting guidelines may still be sold. The sale price can be adjusted to provide a greater return to the investor to compensate for the added risk.

   1. Since the loan agreement is already in place the borrower is unaffected by the sale terms.

   2. The holder of the loan agreement may agree to a discount below the loan balance as a form of compensation for the unknown risk the loan buyer will face.

   Example: A seller made a loan of $25,000 to the buyer. The terms of the loan were $25,000 at 10% interest for a 15 year term with a monthly payment of $268.65. A buyer in the secondary money market might offer to buy the loan at a 30% discount. The secondary buyer would pay the seller $17,500 for the loan. Because the investment was only $17,500, but $25,000 is being paid back, along with the interest portion of the $268.65 payment (computed on the full $25,000) it increases the yield to the secondary lender to 16.95%.

C. Some loans are made above Par and follow lender underwriting guidelines. In this instance the lender may receive a premium above the loan amount as payment for the loan when sold.

XV. **Priority of Liens**

Mortgage loans use real estate as **collateral**. A lien is filed at the county courthouse indicating to the world that the lender is entitled to payment if default occurs. Property owners may agree to lien their property to more than one lender such as in a first mortgage and a second mortgage, or Liens may be imposed by courts or by statute. (law) The question then is who comes first?

A. To protect the public interest unpaid property taxes always come first regardless of recording date.

B. Priority for other liens is determined by which claim against the property was recorded first. First in time means first in line. The term "first mortgage," refers to the senior lien, the lien recorded first.

C. All other financing against the property are referred to as junior liens (those recorded after the first secured loan), and referred to as 2nd mortgage, 3rd mortgage, etc.

D. Liens imposed by court and by statute follow this same recording priority order.

E. **Mechanics liens** follow the recording order rule except the effective date is set not by recording but by law. They have a retro-active effective date that could leap ahead of some liens. Mechanics liens are discussed in the Utah Law – Real Estate Acts chapter.

F.   An agreement that allows a lender to take another lenders position in priority order is called a "subordination agreement." Subordination means to take a lower lien position.

Finance Basics Terms to Know

- ☐ Capital Mortgage Market
- ☐ Debt Service
- ☐ Department of Housing and Urban Development (HUD)
- ☐ Department of Veterans Affairs (VA)
- ☐ Discount Points
- ☐ Discounted Loan or Note
- ☐ Federal Home Loan Mortgage Corporation (FHLMC)
- ☐ Federal Housing Administration (FHA)
- ☐ Federal National Mortgage Association (FNMA)
- ☐ Federal Reserve
- ☐ Federal Trade Commission (FTC)
- ☐ Government National Mortgage Association (GNMA)
- ☐ Interest Rate
- ☐ Junior Lien
- ☐ Lien
- ☐ Loan Buydown
- ☐ Mortgage Broker
- ☐ Origination Fee
- ☐ Par (interest rate)
- ☐ Primary Financing
- ☐ Primary Mortgage Market
- ☐ Prime Rate
- ☐ Quai-Government
- ☐ Rate Lock
- ☐ Seasoned Loan
- ☐ Secondary Financing
- ☐ Secondary Mortgage Market
- ☐ Senior Lien
- ☐ Subordination
- ☐ Underwriter
- ☐ United States Department of Agriculture (USDA)

Finance Basics Quiz

1. Which of the following options would permanently lower the interest on a long term loan?

    A. 2-1 buydown

    B. Mortgage insurance

    C. Discount points

    D. Subordinating the loan

2. Which of the following is a junior lien?

    A. Secondary Money Market

    B. Second Mortgage

    C. Participation Mortgages

    D. Prime Rate Mortgages

3. A clause that allows two lenders to switch priority positions, such as the first mortgage becoming the second, and the second mortgage becoming the first mortgage is called a:

    A. Recordation

    B. Subordination

    C. Release

    D. Junior lien agreement

4. Mr. Boles goes to Last Chance Mortgage Company and obtains a loan. We would say that this loan originated in the:

    A. Primary Money or Mortgage Market

    B. Secondary Money or Mortgage Market

    C. Federal Reserve

    D. FNMA or Federal National Mortgage Association

5. This organization does not set interest rates, but because of the discount rate and the amount of money they require lenders to keep on reserve for depositors, they heavily influence the interest rate. The organization is the:

    A. FNMA (Federal National Mortgage Association)

    B. GNMA (Government National Mortgage Association)

    C. FDIC (Federal Deposit Insurance Corporation)

    D. Federal Reserve

6. K would most likely sell a discounted mortgage in which of the following markets:

    A. Primary Money Market

    B. Secondary Money Market

    C. Federal Reserve Market

    D. Private Mortgage Market

7. L&M Mortgages originated a loan between Centrum Lending and the borrower. L&M mortgage is an example of a:

    A. Secondary Market lender

    B. Mortgage Broker

    C. Savings and Loan

    D. Private Individual

8. An example of a quasi government lender is:

    A. Fannie Mae

    B. Commercial Bank

    C. Federal Reserve

    D. Ginnie Mae

9. Wilson Investments paid 80% of face value when it bought a loan. This is an example of a:

    A. Par rate

    B. Discount rate

    C. Discounted loan

    D. Loan Buydown

10. The loan origination fee is compensation paid to which of the following?

    A. Federal Reserve

    B. Fannie Mae

    C. Secondary Market

    D. Mortgage Broker

11. Which of the following actions would protect the applicant against rising market rates?

    A. Buyer pays discount points

    B. Federal Reserve lowers the Discount Rate

    C. Buyer pays a premium rate to lock the rate

    D. Broker imposes a Prime Rate

12. What is the discount fee for a 7.75%, 30 year, $100,000 loan, charging one discount point?

    A. .00775%

    B. $1000

    C. $2000

    D. $775

13. Debt Service is a term referring to the duties of the:

    A. Borrower

    B. Primary Lender

    C. Servicing Agent

    D. Secondary Market Lender

14. A seller takes a note back as partial payment when selling his home. The buyer has made many payments on the note. Which of the following would allow the seller to raise some quick cash?

    A. Demand the buyer pay Par

    B. Taking the note to the primary market

    C. Charging a origination fee to the buyer

    D. Discounting the loan to a secondary market investor

15. WT Investments is considering a proposal it received to buy a mortgage note. The discount points listed in the proposal will have which of the following effects on this potential investment if they accept the proposal?

    A. Raise the Par rate

    B. Become the discount rate

    C. Increase the yield

    D. Decrease the yield.

Application & Underwriting 1

I. **Leverage and Loan to Value Ratio**

Most buyers of real estate are unable or unwilling to use all their own money in the purchase of real estate. The purchase is more likely made up of some of the buyer's money, the down payment, combined with someone else's money, the loan.

A. **Leverage** is a relationship between the purchase price and the loan, or the percent of the lender's money involved in the purchase as compared to the percent of the borrower's money or down payment.

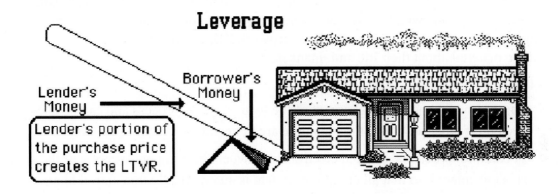

B. Formula for determining loan to value ratio:

$$L / V = R$$
Loan Divided by Value equals Ratio

C. **Equity**: The difference between the value of a home and the sum total of liens/encumbrances against it equals the equity.

For example:

Value	$180,000
(-) 1st Trust Deed of	$118,000
(-) 2nd mortgage	$ 12,000
(-) home equity loan balance	$ 8,000
The equity would be	$ 42,000

In this example, the combined debt equals $138,000 or 77% of value (LTVR.)

D. The lender views equity as a margin of safety. The unpaid debt plus foreclosure expenses could exceed the value recovered from the foreclosure sale if equity is low. Therefore if the equity is too small, the lender is at a greater risk of losing money in foreclosure.

287

E. Government loans feature a high LTVR. They also protect the lender from the high LTVR risk by government guarantee as in VA loans, or with mortgage insurance known as MIP (Mortgage Insurance Premium) on FHA loans. The part of the MIP due at settlement or the VA funding fee can be financed with the loan by adding it to the financed portion of the purchase price.

F. Usually no insurance is required in a conventional loan if LTVR is 80% or less.

G. Private Mortgage Insurance (PMI) is normally required on conventional loans when the LTVR exceeds 80%.

II. **Qualifying for a Loan (The 4 C's and a G)**

The **four C's**, Credit, Capacity, Capital, Collateral are used to compare a borrower to loan product Guidelines that determine which borrower qualifies for that lender's loans. The experience of qualifying for a mortgage can be stressful for borrowers. The borrowers are disclosing very private and sensitive material about their life and finances.

A. **Credit**

1. This can be the most critical aspect of the loan approval process and can be used as strength if other portions of the loan file are deficient.

2. A credit report can be ordered electronically when the computer version of the application is being entered, so that all credit report data is automatically transferred to a retrievable full report, and the debts automatically posted to the 1003 application. The credit report is normally valid for 60 days; after that, a new credit report needs to be ordered.

3. Credit bureaus assemble credit data on borrowers creating a risk model, called a credit score. The credit score is a quantitative risk value, with the sum of all values formulated into a single score based on many components about the borrower   including:

    a. Level of delinquencies

    b. Time since last delinquency

    c. Proportion of revolving balances to credit limits

    d. Bankruptcy

    e. Foreclosures

    f. Debt write-offs

    g. Recent inquires (may need to explain and/or verify that no new unreported debt has been obtained)

4. The statistical score known as the credit score is used by lenders to gauge the credit risk of borrowers

5. There are three credit bureaus:

    a. Equifax, www.equifax.com

    b. Experian (formerly TRW), www.experian.com

    c. Trans Union, www.transunion.com

288

6.   Each credit bureau issues a unique score using its own model. The three separate scores from the different bureaus will vary.

7.   An underwriter typically uses the middle score from the three bureaus for compliance to underwriting guidelines for the mortgage program requested.

8.   The higher the score, the better the credit, leading to more favorable underwriting and loan pricing guidelines.

9.   Although each credit bureau has their own scoring nuances, credit scores generally have a range of 300 to 850. (The following range break down is to be used as general reference only. Each lender will have their own definition for what they consider excellent, very good, etc.)

700-850 excellent

680-700 very good

639-680 generally acceptable

620-640 marginal

Below 620 caution

B.   Capacity

1.   Components of Loan Payments

Monthly payments could include all below, and are frequently referred to with the acronym of PITI (Principal, Interest, Taxes, Insurance).

a.   Principal is that portion of a payment that reduces the principal loan balance

b.   Interest is the payment of a rent-like fee charged by lenders for the use of borrowed money.

c.   The reserve account (also referred to as impound or escrow account) refers to an account where the lender stores the borrowers money collected monthly to be held by the lender for the payment of annual obligations.

d.   Property Taxes, which if not paid, can become a first lien on the lenders collateral subordinating the lender's position to a junior lien

e.   Hazard Insurance, which would repair the property if it was damaged by accident or act of God. Hazard insurance would also repay the loan if the improvements were destroyed entirely.

f.   Mortgage insurance, if applicable, could be included in the payment but is not referenced in the acronym PITI.

2.   Debt to Income Ratios

Front-end ratio or housing to income ratio (PITI) compares the housing payment to gross income.

The following is an example of a front-end calculation:

Proposed PITI payment $1,300 per month

Gross income ÷ $5,000 per month

Front-End Ratio 0.26 or 26%

a.   **Back-end** or **Total Debt ratio** is the sum of proposed housing expense (PITI) plus monthly recurring obligations reported on the credit report and court ordered debt, divided by the borrower's monthly gross income. Recurring obligations with 10 months or less left to be paid are not included in the back-end ratio. Utilities and health insurance are also never included in the debt ratios.

The following is an example of a back-end or debt ratio calculation:

Proposed PITI payment $1,300 per month

Add Credit Report and

Court Ordered Debt +$500 per month

Total Monthly Debt $1,800 per month

Total Monthly Debt $1,800 per month

Gross income ÷$5,000 per month

Back-End Ratio 0.36 or 36%

b.   Both front and back-end ratios must both be within guidelines in order to qualify. Even if the proposed PITI payment fits within the front-end limit, it still must not force the back-end ratio beyond its corresponding limit.

***Note that some conventional loans do not require taxes and interest to be made as part of the regular monthly payment and then would only require the principal and interest

3.   **Income**

a.   The lender considers the amount and stability of the borrowers' income to determine capacity for loan repayment.

b.   Income is verified from all sources. The key is to determine actual stable income of the borrowers which can reasonably be expected to continue for at least 3 years. Stable income is calculated by analyzing the borrower's Federal tax returns and, if necessary, business tax returns.

c.   Employed individual's income can be verified on the following forms:

i.   W-2: The W-2 reflects an employee's gross income. Salaried W-2 employees typically submit one month of pay stubs and the W-2 from the previous one or two tax years.

ii. Form 2106: An outside salesman could have business expenses that were not reimbursed by the employer. These are documented on Form 2106, Employee Business Expenses. If business expenses are not reimbursed, the value of the non-reimbursed expense is deducted from the employee W-2 income.

iii. Form 1099: Bonuses and other income that do not come on a monthly basis can be reported on form 1099 and, in some cases, on the W-2. It must be averaged over a 2 year period to show stability. Documentation from the employer must indicate that the income is likely to continue into the future.

iv. Verification of Employment (VOE): Printed form to be completed by the employer directly. Should never be in the hands of the borrower.

d. Self-Employment: Self-employed taxpayers must document their income using personal tax returns and business financial statements. Income is considered self-employment income if the borrower has an ownership interest in the employing entity of 25% or greater. The tax forms used in evaluating business income are:

i. Form 1040, Personal Income Tax Return

A. Schedule A. Itemized deductions

B. Schedule B. Interest and dividends

C. Schedule C. Profit and loss from business (Sole Proprietorship)

D. Schedule D. Capital gains and losses

ii. Form 1065 Partnership income tax return

E. Schedule D. Partnership gains and losses

F. Schedule K-1 Partners share of income

iii. Form 1099 statement of income paid from others. There are many 1099 forms used for the special types of income paid to individuals and companies.

iv. Form 1120 Corporate income tax return

G. Schedule D. Corporate gains and losses

H. 1099 Dividend on corporate stock

C. **Capital**

Requirements for down payment, closing costs, and reserves can vary among mortgage programs and products.

1. Borrower's funds must be sourced and/or seasoned.

2. **Sourced funds** are funds that are were not in your possession or you do not have a personal record over several months. Examples of funds that would need to be sourced might include:

    a. Grant money

    b. Money from the sale of an asset

    c. Gifted funds

    d. Tax refund

    e. Lottery winnings

    f. Cash under the mattress

    g. Secured or unsecured borrowings

3. **Seasoned funds** are funds that have been available to the borrower for a length of time and are shown on financial institution records for the required length of time. Gifted funds may also need to be seasoned as to the giver.

D. **Collateral**

1. The lender will want to determine if the property is good collateral for the loan by requiring such things as an appraisal, an inspection, a survey, and title work.

2. The goal is to determine whether or not the property could be sold to satisfy the obligation if the borrower were to default on the loan.

3. Property types are in the following categories:

    a. **Single Family Dwelling** ("SFD")

    b. **Planned Unit Development** ("PUD"): A master planned community that may or may not have common recreational areas maintained by a Homeowners Association ("HOA") and owners pay HOA dues.

    c. **Condominium** where owners, in fact, only own the air space in their unit and an undivided ownership in any common areas. Condominiums also pay HOA dues.

    d. **Cooperative** is real property owned by a corporation, whereby a prospective occupant will buy stock in the corporation for the privilege of occupying the real property. In turn, the occupant signs a proprietary lease with the corporation.

    e. **Leasehold** is a long-term lease, which entails no real property ownership interest. A leasehold is a property right and could have value if the value of the leasehold exceeds the cost of the lease.

4. Property evaluation ends with an appraisal of estimated value. Appraisals are typically

valid for 2-3 months. Lenders determine the appraisal "expiration date."

5. Property that was recently purchased within a year and have had little or no improvement before offering for sale again would typically be valued at its most recent sale price. Properties that have received significant improvement would be valued by the lender using a new appraisal.

E. Lender guidelines have been developed for use by loan originators to guide them in determining if the borrower will be acceptable to a particular lender. The four C's provide the information to compare the borrower to lender guidelines to determine if the borrower qualifies. Different lenders may have different guidelines. Lenders could differ in any of the following ways.

1. Credit score requirements

    a. Overall score

    b. Particular credit problem such as bankruptcy or recent foreclosure

2. Types of acceptable collateral

    a. Single family personal residence

    b. Investor owned rental property

    c. Commercial property

    d. Second homes

    e. Recreation property

    f. Land

    g. Multiple lots under one loan

3. Capital requirements

    a. Down payment requirements

    b. Reserves required

    c. Loan To Value

III. **Insurance**

A. **Homeowners insurance** protects the home owner against unforeseen hazard or peril. If an endorsement is added to the homeowner's policy the lender is also protected to the extent of their collateral interest.

1. Homeowner's insurance is a package policy covering two types of peril:

    a. **Hazard insurance** covers property damage caused by fire, wind, storms, and other similar risks. Typically earthquakes and floods are protected perils only by purchasing additional coverage.

    b. **Public liability** insurance coverage protects against claims alleging that one's negligence or inappropriate action resulted in bodily injury or property damage. (ex: My dog bit you; my tree fell on your car.)

2.   Homeowner's insurance is purchased as replacement or cash value coverage.

    a.   Replacement coverage restores the property to like-new condition, regardless of the cost, as long as the market value of the property was covered. Depreciation, wear and tear, and age are all ignored. New replaces old.

    b.   Cash value coverage pays only the market value of the property, which includes the effects of age, wear, and tear.

    c.   c.A lender's endorsement, also called a "mortgage clause," provides that the lender has primary protection from loss due to fire, theft, damage, or liability.

    d.   If the borrowers let the hazard insurance lapse, the lender may purchase a forced insurance policy to protect the lender's interest in the property improvements.

B.   **Flood insurance** is required, by law, if any portion of the property improvements is inside any flood zone beginning with an "A" or "V." Flood insurance is available to any property owner who desires it regardless of flood zone.

1.   Flood insurance is only required on the value of improvements at risk or 100% of the loan amount, whichever is higher.

2.   In "A" zones where no base flood elevation is determined, first floor areas and below could expect flooding and possible flood damage.

3.   FEMA (Federal Emergency Management Agency) flood maps are used to determine if a property is at risk.

4.   A third-party Flood Determination Certification is required on all loans. It is also typically noted on the appraisal.

5.   If flood insurance is required by a lender, it is required for the entire life, or term of the loan.

C.   **Private Mortgage Insurance** ("PMI") provides protection to the lender in the event of borrower default and foreclosure. The borrower pays the cost of the protection and the lender receives the protection. The advantage to borrowers is that they may receive financing which otherwise would not be available to them.

1.   Borrowers pay for coverage to offset the potential losses of a lender. Since lender loss begins at about the value of 80% of market value, the lender looks for a 20% down payment or insurance to offset the risk.

2.   Both FNMA and FHLMC will allow a portion of the mortgage insurance premium to be financed under certain conditions. Both will also consider buying loans when the lender has paid for the mortgage insurance out of lender funds.

3.   The amount of insurance charged varies by lender and is based on:

    a.   Credit

    b.   LTV

    c.   Loan Type (traditional or non-traditional mortgage)

4.   The major benefit of mortgage insurance to the borrower is that it reduces the down payment requirement on the purchase. Fannie Mae/Freddie Mac mortgage insurance requirements are:

    a.   PMI required on primary loans above 80% loan to value ratio.

    b.   PMI is not required on LTV's of 80% or less, even if combined loan to value ratio ("CLTV") higher than 80% (more than one loan).

    c.   Methods of payment

        i.   The standard PMI plan is the monthly payment plan. The benefit of the standard plan is that there is no upfront premium, requiring fewer funds at closing.

        ii.   The traditional plan has an upfront lump sum, and minimal monthly payments.

        iii.   There is a one-time lump sum premium payment plan.

D.   **Homeowners Protection Act ("HPA")**

1.   HPA, also known as PMI Cancellation Act was passed in 1998 and addresses homeowners difficulties in canceling PMI coverage.

2.   FHA insurance is not affected by this act.

3.   This act applies to:

    a.   Residential loan transactions

    b.   Acquisition, initial construction, or refinancing of single family dwellings that serves as the borrower's principal residence.

    c.   Lender must disclose at closing the cancellation date and the automatic termination date:

        i.   **Cancelation date** is the date the borrower may seek to cancel PMI

        ii.   Automatic termination date is the date the lender must terminate PMI even without borrower's request or notification.

4.   Borrower request. A borrower may initiate cancellation of PMI coverage by submitting a written request to the servicer. The servicer must take action to cancel PMI when the cancellation date occurs, which is when the principal balance of the loan reaches, or is first scheduled to reach, 80 percent of the "original value" based upon the initial amortization schedule (in the case of a fixed rate loan) or amortization schedule then in effect (in the

case of an adjustable rate loan), or any date thereafter that the borrower:

5.   Automatic termination. The act requires a servicer to automatically terminate PMI for residential mortgage transactions on the date that:

    a.   The principal balance of the mortgage is first scheduled to reach 78 percent of the original value of the secured property if the borrower is current; or

    b.   If the borrower is not current on that date, on the first day of the first month following the date the borrower becomes current;

    c.   The loan reaches it's amortization mid-point (example: the 1st day of the 181 month on a 360 month term mortgage);

    d.   High-risk loans reach 77 percent of their original value.

Application & Underwriting Terms to Know

- ☐ Capital
- ☐ Capacity
- ☐ Cash on Hand
- ☐ Debt to Income Ratio (DTI)
- ☐ Collateral
- ☐ Credit
- ☐ Credit Score
- ☐ Down Payment
- ☐ Equity
- ☐ FICO Score
- ☐ Hazard or Home Owner's Insurance
- ☐ Impound (also see Escrow Account or Impound Account)
- ☐ Lender Guidelines
- ☐ Leverage
- ☐ Loan to Value Ratio (LTVR)
- ☐ Mortgage Broker
- ☐ Mortgage Insurance Premium (MIP)
- ☐ Up Front Mortgage Insurance Premium (UFMIP)
- ☐ Planned Unit Development (PUD)
- ☐ Principal Interest Taxes & Insurance (PITI)
- ☐ Private Mortgage Insurance (PMI)
- ☐ Qualifying Ratio
- ☐ Reserves
- ☐ Single Family Residence (SFR)
- ☐ Seasoned
- ☐ Sourced
- ☐ Equifax
- ☐ Experian
- ☐ Trans Union
- ☐ Front End Ratio
- ☐ Back End Ratio
- ☐ Housing Ratio
- ☐ Total Debt Ratio
- ☐ Replacement Value
- ☐ Mortgagee Clause
- ☐ FEMA
- ☐ Homeowners Protection Act (HPA)

Application & Underwriting 1 Quiz

1. The difference between the total value of a property and the liens against the property is called:

    A. Equity

    B. Loan to value ratio

    C. Leverage

    D. Participation

2. If the purchase price was $75,000 and the loan was $48,000, what would the LTVR be?

    A. 156% LTVR

    B. 75% LTVR

    C. 64% LTVR

    D. 48% LTVR

3. The higher the LTVR, the greater the _____.

    A. Leverage

    B. Equity

    C. Discount Rate

    D. Usury

4. Private mortgage insurance will probably be required by the lender in which of the following situations?

    A. Two loans equaling 75% and 25% LTV respectively

    B. One loan that is 85% LTV

    C. Two loans equaling 60% and 30% LTV respectively

    D. Two loans equaling 80% and 10% LTV respectively

5. Which of the following most nearly describes the data used to compute the front end ratio?

    A. Principal, interest, taxes, insurance, PMI

    B. Principle, Interest, MIP

    C. Principle, interest, utilities

    D. Principal, interest, repairs

6. Which of the following is an example of cash on hand?

    A. Equity

    B. Business interest in a partnership

    C. Bank account

    D. Car that is paid off

7. Which of the following properties would likely have the lowest loan to value ratio requirement?

    A. Personal residence

    B. Investment property

    C. Vacant land

    D. Rental property

8. The back end ratio includes all of the following EXCEPT:

    A. PITI

    B. Any one time medical bills

    C. Mortgage insurance is required

    D. Long term debt payments

9. The lender will be most interested in which of the following conditions to determine if a self employed borrower will qualify for a loan?

    A. Stable income

    B. High gross Sales

    C. Low business expenses

    D. Monthly payments the business is obligated to pay

10. The loan qualifying process involves all of the following EXCEPT:

    A. Credit

    B. Capacity to repay

    C. Commissions

    D. Capital

11. One of the most critical items in the loan underwriting process that shows a borrower's payment behavior is:

    A. Marital status of the borrower

    B. Credit status of the borrower

    C. Location and form of collateral

    D. Amount of money in the retirement account

12. A mortgage qualifying ratio measures all of the following EXCEPT:

    A. Front or housing ratio of PITI

    B. Back or debt ratio of PITI + debt

    C. Maximum PITI allowable based on the lesser of front and back ratios

    D. Loan to value ratio

13. The three major credit bureaus include all of the following EXCEPT:

    A. Equifax

    B. Experian

    C. FTC

    D. Trans Union

14. The borrower risk model used by each of the credit bureaus to assess quantitative risk value is called a:

    A. Credit Score

    B. Good Faith Estimate

    C. Credit report

    D. Derogatory report

15. If the borrowers do not keep a hazard insurance policy in place, what can the lender do?

    A. Charge the borrower for a forced insurance policy

    B. Raise the reserve requirement

    C. Notify the borrows they have to get insurance

    D. Nothing

16. If a property is in a FEMA flood zone, what will the lender require the borrower to do?

    A. Build a retaining wall or other protective barrier

    B. Pay for an additional endorsement to the title insurance

    C. Buy flood insurance for the life of loan

    D. Include that stipulation in their hazard insurance

17. Mortgage insurance protects the:

    A. Borrowers in case of death

    B. Borrowers in case of loan default

    C. Lender in case of natural disaster

    D. Lender in case of borrower default

18. According to HPA, at what level must mortgage insurance on conventional loans automatically be removed?

    A. When the LTV reaches 78% of original value

    B. When the buyer requests it and the LTV is 80%

    C. When the lender obtains an appraisal to justify the 78% LTV

    D. Only if loan contains a prepayment penalty

19. The federal tax form an individual borrower must fill out, reflecting taxable income of any kind, is called a:

    A. 1003

    B. 1008

    C. 1040

    D. 2106

20. For a salaried employee, what federal tax form reflects gross income of the borrower?

    A. A. Year-to-date pay stub

    B. W-2

    C. K-1

    D. Schedule C

21. A self-employed individual borrower must submit what federal tax form to verify income?

    A. K-1

    B. Schedule C

    C. Form 2106

    D. Schedule F

22. What federal tax form reflects income and ownership percentage of borrowers receiving income from a partnership or a corporation?

    A. Schedule C

    B. Form 2106

    C. W-2

    D. K-1

23. When must borrowers submit business tax returns such as a partnership or corporation federal tax return in addition to individual tax returns?

    A. When borrowers' ownership exceed 10%

    B. Only if needed for qualification

    C. When borrowers' ownership exceeds 25%

    D. When borrowers' ownership is at least 50%

24. Income averaging must occur over what period of time for income other then W-2 salaried income?

    A. 2 years

    B. 36 months

    C. It is averaged if self-employed less than 2 years

    D. 12 months

Application & Underwriting 2

I. **Pre-Qualification**

A **mortgage loan officer** ("MLO") will often receive requests for qualification documentation from borrowers contemplating or in the process of purchasing a home. Once an application is complete and the MLO can evaluate the borrowing capacity, the following two types of letters can be requested:

A. **Prequalification letter**

1. Basic, unverified, information supplied by the borrowers is used

2. An estimate of loan amount is issued based on the information the borrowers supply

B. **Pre-approval letter**

1. Relies on verified information on borrowers

2. Normally

3. Underwritten and approved by lender

4. Usually only subject to appraisal and title report

II. **Qualifying Process**

A. The qualifying process is all about applying income against expenses (checking capacity), assessing usable assets or capital, checking credit, and verifying if the borrowers comply with the underwriting guidelines for the mortgage product applied for. The experience of qualifying for a mortgage can be stressful for borrowers. The borrowers are disclosing some of the most private and sensitive material about their life and finances. An MLO must make a sensitive and accurate assessment of borrowing capacity.

B. A skilled MLO will ask penetrating questions designed to uncover vital information, and do so in a diplomatic, compassionate way.

C. The Four "C's" of mortgage lending are:

1. Credit

2. Capacity to repay

3. Capital

4. Collateral

III. **Application Process**

A. Application: The standard application for a mortgage loan is referred to as the Uniform Residential Loan Application or the 1003 (Fannie Mae) or the Form 65 (Freddie Mac). They are identical and used interchangeably. The most commonly used is the 1003.

1. Uniform Underwriting and Transmittal Summary, also known as the 1008 form, along with the **Uniform Residential Loan Application**, provide a complete snapshot of the borrowing

capacity of the borrowers.

2. The loan application must be completed by the borrower. The information needs to be as accurate as possible. The borrower is going to certify the information to be true with signature and legal penalties for false statements.

3. Software: Most mortgage loan originators use software to create a loan application in electronic format. Paper is used but nearly always ends up being converted to electronic format. The electronic format is most usable because it allows for easy corrections and easy transmittal to the lenders underwriting software.

4. The MLO will provide a final copy of the application corrected with the final information used for loan approval at settlement for official signature.

5. The original application, however, should be kept in the loan file to document the information originally provided. Lenders, federal and state regulators do from time to time audit loan files.

    a. The MLO will want to be able to show the path followed to loan approval with full documentation from beginning to end, as a defense against charges of bad conduct if some portion of the file indicates loan fraud.

6. Once an application is complete, the MLO will evaluate the information in the application to determine which loan program from which lender the borrower qualifies.

    a. **Originators** who work for only one lender search their lenders products for a match.

    b. Originators who work for brokerage companies have the freedom to look at many lenders and their products to find a match.

7. The application is only submitted to the lender with the product that the originator believes will match up with the borrowers' application.

    a. Underwriting relies heavily on independent third-party information. The mortgage loan officer must:

        i.   Make an accurate assessment of borrowing capacity.

        ii. Review credit reports for issues that will allow or prevent the borrowers from qualifying for mortgage credit.

        iii. Have a reasonable knowledge of program guidelines in order to document and package the loan file so an underwriter can readily determine its integrity and eligibility.

B. **Loan Processor**: The loan processor follows procedures to verify that all information is true and correct. The processor position is not required and the MLO can perform this function. A loan processor is usually not licensed and is restricted to what they can do. Processors can follow up on requested information but may not directly request information.

1. The processor verifies that the lender's loan requirements have been met. The file is then packaged by the processor following lender instructions. The completed pack   age, including the appraisal and title report, is sent to the underwriting department.

C. **Underwriter:** Underwriting is the process of analyzing the loan package and signing approval on the bottom line.

　　1. The underwriter reviews the loan package to make sure it conforms to all the guide lines required for that loan product.

　　2. The underwriter also reviews the appraisal and title report and may do additional validation of employment, mortgage payments, credit, and anything else considered necessary to document the loan.

　　3. The underwriter has the authority to approve or deny the loan.

　　　　a. Computer automated underwriting is used almost exclusively today. The computer software makes an initial approval decision, after which the underwriter reviews the supporting documentation and the appraisal. The loan can be:

　　　　　　i.   Approved

　　　　　　ii. Conditionally approved. The conditions are sent to the originator to resolve.

　　　　　　iii. Denied

　　　　b. The advantage of computer automation of the process is speed with less documentation, and it allows lenders to be more accurate and consistent in making underwriting decisions on mortgage applications that have varying degrees of risk. Automated underwriting also allows lenders to approve more mortgages without increasing their risk.

　　　　c. Freddie Mac's underwriting software, Loan Prospector ("LP"), and Fannie Mae's underwriting program, Desktop Underwriter ("DU"), assess borrowers' eligibility and streamline the underwriting process for their particular loan products.

IV. **FHA Insured Loan Features**

A. FHA insured loans do not have prepayment penalties, and are assumable when approved by the lender, as stipulated in the promissory note.

B. Seller contributions are limited to 6% of the sales price for closing costs, not including dis count points.

C. Each FHA insured loan is assigned a case number, which must be posted on the FHA appraisal. To transfer the FHA insured loan to another lender requires transfer of the case number.

D. Eligible borrowers are:

1. Individuals, not companies or corporations

2. Co-signers cannot have a financial interest in the transaction, such as the seller, builder, or real estate agent.

3. Persons with legal residency, not illegal aliens

4. Legal age (18 or older) or married.

E. **Maximum allowable loan limits** are set on a county by county basis. Since these limits are subject to change, up-to-date information can be obtained at the <u>U.S. Department of Housing and Urban Development</u>.

F. Maximum loan amount is based on the lesser of:

1. Loan amount requested

2. Sales price

3. Appraised value

4. Repairs and improvements may, in certain cases, be added to the sales price before calculating the loan amount. The 203K mortgage program allows for rehabilitation of a home with a single loan. Under this program, a portion of the loan is used to purchase the home, and the remainder is placed in escrow and disbursed as repairs or remodeling is completed.

V. FHA Insured Loan Guidelines

A. Credit:

In general, FHA Insured loans are considered more flexible in regards to qualifying a borrower with a deficient credit history. This is due to the government insured nature of the loan.
Bankruptcy:

1. FHA guidelines to consider a loan for those that have bankruptcies and/or foreclosures can vary greatly depending on the circumstances.

2. Chapter 7 Bankruptcy: Generally a minimum of 2 years must have elapsed since the discharge date, but usually takes up to 4 years after discharge date for approval.

3. Chapter 13 Bankruptcy: Under extreme circumstances, consideration may be given for those individuals that have 1 year of satisfactorily making payments as stipulated in the chapter 13 discharge. Typically, FHA would prefer 2 years to have elapsed since the discharge date. The bankruptcy court trustee's written approval would be needed. A full explanation should accompany the application and the applicants must have re-established good credit.

4. Foreclosure: Three years must pass from the date of the foreclosure before FHA will consider granting loan approval. An exception to rule would be if the foreclosure was the borrower's main residence and an extenuating circumstance can be proven. Good credit must have been re-established to be considered.

5. Rental payment history, mortgage payment history, collections and judgments, and recent new debts all have significant impact on credit approval. They could make the borrower ineligible or, with appropriate explanation, could become qualified exceptions that will not disqualify the borrower. Most collections may be accepted if they are paid in full at or before closing.

6. Borrowers with delinquent federal debt are ineligible.

B. Capacity:

The FHA underwriter needs to be convinced that the borrower will have stable income for at least the first three years of the mortgage.

1. Employment gaps need to be explained.

2. The probability of continued employment is shown by employment history, qualifications for position held, previous training and education, and a statement from the employer as to the continued employment likelihood.

3. Frequent job changes indicate instability.

4. Overtime, part-time jobs, and commissions each need to be evaluated in terms of consistency and likelihood of continuance.

5. Unusual income or one time income such as capital gains income is not considered unless there is three years tax return history and predictable future gains. Capital gains income is income from the sale of an asset or investment.

6. Commission income must be averaged over the previous two years. The forms required might include:

    a. Form 2106

    b. Form 1040

7. Alimony and child support income require documentation showing its stability and continuance over the past 12 months using:

    a. A divorce decree or legal separation agreement

    b. 12 months of cancelled checks in consecutive order

8. Income that is non-taxable, such as social security income, may be adjusted before ratios are applied by multiplying the non-taxable income by 1.25%. This process is called "gross-up;" it is computing an estimated gross income as though the non-taxable income is taxable.

9. The housing expense (front end ratio) may not exceed 31% of gross income. The mortgage payment is defined for this calculation as PITI, plus the following, if applicable:

    a. Homeowners' association dues

    b. Ground rent

    c. Special assessments

10. The back-end ratio or debt to income ratio must not exceed 43% of gross income.

11. Compensating factors are issues that could be used to justify ratios that exceed the above limits. They are:

    a. 12- to 24-months' history of paying a housing expense equal or greater than the proposed amount.

    b. Down payment of 10% or more.

    c. Significant savings history.

    d. Credit history indicates the borrower can manage funds well.

C. Capital:

The borrower must have sufficient, verifiable funds for closing/down payment expenses. Verification of these funds requires contacting the financial institution for a **verification of deposit** ("VOD").

1. The report will include the amount of funds on deposit and the time frame of their current status (how long they have been on deposit.)

2. Seasoned funds must be held for three (3) months or more.

3. Unsecured, borrowed funds are typically not acceptable.

4. Liquid assets may include the following:

    a. Savings and checking accounts

    b. Sale of personal property

    c. Gifts may come from relatives and non-profit organizations with no repayment required, but never from the seller.

    d. Employer bonuses

5. Borrowers who have saved cash at home, and are able to demonstrate adequately that they pay their bills with cash, such as utility bills, car payments, insurance, etc, are permitted to use this cash as an adequate source of funds.

6. Sweat equity or trade equity are considered acceptable funds.

7. Grants from non-profit organizations.

8. Secured loans, including 401K's, if repayment is documented and used in qualifying ratios.

9. Seller contributions are limited to 6% of the sales price, including discount points, buy-downs, and prepaid items.

10. Statutory minimum down payment of 3.5% is required.

    a. Mortgage calculation example:

      i. Purchase price & appraisal $100,000

      ii. Minus down payment of 3.5% <$ 3,500>

iii. Base loan amount $ 96,500

    b. In certain circumstances the down payment can be contributed, utilizing state programs and by non-profit grants.

    c. Donations and contributions to the borrower's down payment funds may also come from:

        i. Domestic partners, which is defined as a person who has lived with the applicant for 12 months or more.

        ii. A qualified Employer Assisted Housing ("EAH") fund.

        iii. A person who will live in the property, such as a fiancé.

D. Collateral:

Property flipping: Sellers who plan to "flip" their property (sell soon after purchase) have a statistically higher likelihood of participation in loan fraud. This has caused FHA and most other lenders to become very cautious when financing property that is being flipped.

1. The seller must be the owner of record.

2. The transaction cannot involve any assignment of the sales contract.

3. The seller must have owned the property for more than 90 days for FHA to insure the buyer's loan.

4. If the seller has owned the property less than 180 days the buyer will need the appraisal used when the seller obtained the property and a separate second appraisal from a different appraiser.

5. If the seller has owned the property less than one year the buyer will have to document to the lender the details of the seller's purchase of the property, including justification for any increase in price over the seller's purchase price.

6. Occupancy of the borrower must be established within 60 days and continue for at least one year.

7. Property types

    a. Owner-occupied single family dwellings ("SFD")

    b. Condominium single units

    c. One to four-unit structures, with one unit occupied by the borrowers.

    d. Manufactured homes that have the red HUD certification attached.

8. The valuation/appraisal must be done by an approved FHA appraiser.

VI. **FHA Appraisal Unacceptable Practices:**

A. A **misleading report**.

B. A report based on discrimination. Discrimination is defined as basing value on membership in any protected class whether by association such as those in the neighborhood or directly.

C.   Misrepresenting physical characteristics. This could include failing to report or misreporting property conditions. If an appraiser never actually looking at the interior of the property, but relied on listing information, this error could occur.

D.   Failure to comment on negative factors. Negative factors include external obsolescence and waste of the property from any cause, easements, dissimilar neighborhood, etc.

E.   Failure to analyze the REPC. The transaction may include seller concessions, existing renters or any factor affecting value that could only be discovered by a thorough reading of the REPC and all addenda

F.   Using inappropriate comparables. This could occur by selecting property from another neighborhood that is experiencing different economic circumstances or from using properties as comparable and ignoring some of their features.

G.   Adjustments that do not reflect the market. Adjustments must be based on the market value of the difference, not the cost or any other factor.

H.   Using data provided by a financially interested party. This refers to the buyer, developer, agent, seller, lender, or any other entity that could benefit from the appraisal. Information from any of these parties must be independently verified and the sources named.

I.   Accepting a bribe in any form. Bribes could come in the form of a promise of repeat business, perks such as lunches, or free CE classes from an interested party to an appraisal.

J.   Other loan products such as FNMA and FHLMC have similar appraisal prohibitions.

VII.   **FHA Mortgage Insurance**

A.   The actual mortgage amount is calculated by adding the base loan amount to the upfront mortgage insurance premium ("UFMIP"). The loan origination fee can only be computed on the base loan before adding the UFMIP.

B.   UFMIP and the monthly mortgage insurance are used to offset costs and/or losses sustained by the FHA program. UFMIP can be as much as 1.75% for a purchase money mortgages or a full-credit qualifying refinance. Streamline refinances are charged 1.50%.

Total loan calculation including UFMIP example:

Base loan amount	$100,000
Current UFMIP 1.75%	* 1.0175 or 101.75%
Actual loan amount	$101,750

C.   Monthly mortgage insurance on an FHA loan is a minimum of 0.55% of the loan balance, paid monthly on the declining loan balance.

  1.   FHA's monthly mortgage insurance is a declining balance contract, which means the premiums decrease monthly as the loan balance decreases.

D.   Reverse mortgages have a maximum origination fee of 2% of the first $200,000 and 1% thereafter, with an overall cap of $6,000.

E.   Typically the allowable debt to income ratios are 31/43

VIII.   **Department of Veteran Affairs**

The Veterans' Administration ("VA") acts as a guarantor of loans. These loans are made by authorized lenders, and guaranteed by the Department of Veteran Affairs in the event the borrowers default. Program guidelines are similar to FHA loans in many respects; however, there are some differences.

A.   VA Loan Features:

1.   A VA loan is guaranteed to the lender, not insured, meaning it is guaranteed by tax monies. The guarantee is intended to motivate lenders to make loans to veterans who might not otherwise be approved

2.   No pre-payment penalty clause is allowed.

3.   The loans are assumable by qualified veterans. There is a $500 non-refundable fee to assume the loan. Pre-1988 loans can be assumed without qualifying, but the seller retains underlying liability.

4.   Seller contributions are limited to 4% of selling price.

5.   Discount points are negotiable and can be paid by the buyers or the sellers, within contribution limits.

6.   The allowable loan to value ratio is 100% of the appraiser's Certificate of Reasonable Value ("CRV").

7.   The CRV is the VA appraisal. If the purchase price is over the CRV, the borrower must make up the difference from his/her own pocket. If the purchase price is lower than the CRV, the loan will be based on the purchase price.

8.   Eligibility is determined by certificate.

9.   The veteran must obtain a Certificate of Eligibility from the Veterans   Administration in order to obtain a VA loan.

10.   VA loan limits are the same as the current conforming loan limit used by conventional lenders.

11.   VA charges a funding fee, which can be added to the loan amount. Factors such as service related disability, veteran special status, or paying a down payment can lower the fee. The actual loan amount is the loan amount plus a funding fee in lieu of mortgage insurance.

12.   This VA funding fee is not an insurance premium but a one-time charge.

13. Depending on eligibility, and based on the maximum loan allowable, the funding may vary as shown:

	Purchase And Construction Loans		
Type of Veteran	Down Payment	First Time Use	Subsequent Use for loans from 1/1/04 to 9/30/2011
Regular Military	None	2.15%	3.3%
	5% or more (up to 10%)	1.50%	1.50%
	10% or more	1.25%	1.25%
Reserves/ National Guard	None	2.4%	3.3%
	5% or more (up to 10%)	1.75%	1.75%
	10% or more	1.5%	1.5%

A. Example of funding fee:

Purchase price/base loan amount @100%	$160,000.00
Funding fee, 1st time, Active 2.15%	+ 3,440.00
Total loan amount	$163,440.00

B. Credit:

The VA program is similar to FHA in that loans are considered more flexible in regards to qualifying a borrower with a deficient credit history. This is due to the government guarantee of the loan.

C. Capacity:

Income analysis for VA loans utilizes a residual income formula which is:

1. Borrower's monthly income less monthly obligations determines borrower's residual income

2. This residual income must be equal to or greater than amounts set forth by VA under writing guidelines.

3. It typically equals an income qualifying ratio of 41/41.

D. Capital:

Liquid assets may include the following:

1. Savings and checking accounts

2. Sale of personal property

3. Gifts from relatives and non-profit organizations, with no repayment required, but never from the seller

4. Seller contributions are limited to 4% of the sales price for closing costs, not including discount points.

E. Collateral:

The maximum loan amount can go as high as 100% of:

1. Purchase price

2. CRV. Unlike a typical appraisal, a CRV is not intended to be an estimate of market value. The appraiser certifies that the veteran is paying a value that is reasonable in the market place.

IX. **Conventional Loans**

Conventional Loan programs are aslo known as Fannie Mae "FNMA" and Freddie Mac"FHLMC"

A. Credit:

Credit requirements are generally more stringent. Credit score is a large part of the determining factors in extending mortgage credit.

1. No collections or judgments within 24 months (medical is exception).

2. No public record of prior bankruptcy or foreclosure.

3. No mortgage delinquency within 24 months.

4. No revolving or installment delinquency within 12 months .

5. No more than one 30 day delinquency in 24 months.

6. Bankruptcies:

    a. Fannie Mae guidelines to consider a loan:

        i. Chapter 7 Bankruptcy: A minimum of 4 years must have elapsed since the discharge date.

        ii. Chapter 13 Bankruptcy: As little as 2 years must have passed since the discharge date. Extenuating circumstances must be proven and investment properties are not eligible under this time frame.

        iii. Foreclosure: 7 years from the date of foreclosure.

    b. Freddie Mac guidelines to consider a loan:

        i. Chapter 7, 13 or Foreclosure: Typically 7 years must have passed in order for Freddie to consider approval.

*Note: Participation in credit counseling programs are generally looked upon by credit granting agencies in a similar manner as a Chapter 13 bankruptcy filing

B. Capacity:

1. The qualifying ratios are different.

2. FNMA loans are underwritten using DU which automatically calculates ratios and determines compensating factors that would allow higher ratios.

3. FHLMC loans are underwritten using LP which automatically calculates Both of these programs use a housing expense ratio of 28% and a back-end or debt ratio of 36% for automatic approvals. These ratios can be exceeded only with compensating factors, such as substantial reserves and exceptional credit history.

4. Investment income from rental properties is adjusted by multiplying gross rental income times 75% to estimate net rental income. Actual net income is not used. This estimate of net rental income can then be used as additional income for the borrower in all ratio calculations.

5. Income from an accessory (mother-in-law) apartment may be allowed if:

    a. The appraisal is done as a multi-family residence

    b. The loan to value ("LTV") is calculated as a 2-unit property

    c. The property must be zoned for an accessory apartment

C. Capital:

Minimum borrower down payment of 5% from own funds. Remainder of down payment can come from other sources.

1. 3 months PITI held in reserve is desired.

2. Acceptable sources for down payment and closing costs include:

    a. Savings and checking accounts

    b. Sale of personal property

    c. Gifts may come from relatives with no repayment required, but never from the seller. These gift funds may not be used for payment of the minimum down payment required of the borrower.

3. Unacceptable sources of down payment are:

    a. Unsecured loans

    b. Credit cards

    c. Undocumented cash on hand

    d. Gift or advance from an employer which is not provided through an EAH

4. **Seller contributions** are limited to 3% of sales price, including discount points, buy downs, and prepaid items.

VI. ASSETS AND LIABILITIES (cont'd)			
Name and address of Bank, S&L, or Credit Union	Acct. no.		
Acct. no. $	Name and address of Company	$ Payment/Months	$
Name and address of Bank, S&L, or Credit Union	Acct. no.		
Acct. no. $	Name and address of Company	$ Payment/Months	$
Name and address of Bank, S&L, or Credit Union	Acct. no.		
Acct. no. $	Name and address of Company	$ Payment/Months	$
Stocks & Bonds (Company name/number & description) $	Acct. no.		
Life insurance net cash value $ Face amount: $	Name and address of Company	$ Payment/Months	$
Subtotal Liquid Assets $	Acct. no.		
Real estate owned (enter market value from schedule of real estate owned) $	Alimony/Child Support/Separate Maintenance Payments Owned to:	$	$
Vested interest in retirement fund $			
Net worth of business(es) owned (attach financial statement) $	Job-Related Expense (child care, union dues, etc.)	$	
Automobiles owned (make and year) $			
Other Assets (itemize) $			
	Total Monthly Payments	$	
Total Assets a. $	Net Worth (a minus b) $	Total Liabilities b.	$

Uniform Residential Loan Application
Freddie Mac Form 65   7/05 (rev.6 /09)   Page 4 of 8   Fannie Mae Form 1003   7/05 (rev.6/09)

319

Schedule of Real Estate Owned (If additional properties are owned, use continuation sheet.)

Property Address (enter S if sold, PS if pending sale or R if rental being held for income)		Type of Property	Present Market Value	Amount of Mortgages & Liens	Gross Rental Income	Mortgage Payments	Insurance, Maintenance, Taxes & Misc.	Net Rental Income
			$	$	$	$	$	$
	Totals		$	$	$	$	$	$

List any additional names under which credit has previously been received and indicate appropriate creditor name(s) and account number(s):

Alternate Name	Creditor Name	Account Number

VII. DETAILS OF TRANSACTION		**VIII. DECLARATIONS**				
		If you answer "Yes" to any questions a through i, please use continuation sheet for explanation.	**Borrower**		**Co-Borrower**	
a. Purchase price	$		Yes	No	Yes	No
b. Alterations, improvements, repairs						
c. Land (if acquired separately)		a. Are there any outstanding judgments against you?	☐	☐	☐	☐
d. Refinance (incl. debts to be paid off)		b. Have you been declared bankrupt within the past 7 years?	☐	☐	☐	☐
e. Estimated prepaid items		c. Have you had property foreclosed upon or given title or deed in lieu thereof in the last 7 years?	☐	☐	☐	☐
f. Estimated closing costs		d. Are you a party to a lawsuit?	☐	☐	☐	☐
g. PMI, MIP, Funding Fee		e. Have you directly or indirectly been obligated on any loan of which resulted in foreclosure, transfer of title in lieu of foreclosure, or judgment? (This would include such loans as home mortgage loans, SBA loans, home improvement loans, educational loans, manufactured (mobile) home loans, any mortgage, financial obligation, bond, or loan guarantee. If "Yes," provide details, including date, name, and address of Lender, FHA or VA case number, if any, and reasons for the action.)	☐	☐	☐	☐
h. Discount (if Borrower will pay)		f. Are you presently delinquent or in default on any Federal debt or any other loan, mortgage, financial obligation, bond, or loan guarantee? If "Yes," give details as described in the preceding question.	☐	☐	☐	☐
i. **Total costs** (add items a through h)		g. Are you obligated to pay alimony, child support, or separate maintenance?	☐	☐	☐	☐

j.	Subordinate financing		h.	Is any part of the down payment borrowed?	☐	☐	☐ ☐

VII. DETAILS OF TRANSACTION (cont'd)			VIII. DECLARATIONS (cont'd)				
k.	Borrower's closing costs paid by Seller		i.	Are you a co-maker or endorser on a note?	☐	☐	☐ ☐
l.	Other Credits (explain)		j.	Are you a U.S. citizen?	☐	☐	☐ ☐
			k.	Are you a permanent resident alien?	☐	☐	☐ ☐
m.	Loan amount (exclude PMI, MIP, Funding Fee financed)		l.	**Do you intend to occupy the property as your primary residence?** If "Yes," complete question m below.	☐	☐	☐ ☐
n.	PMI, MIP, Funding Fee financed		m.	Have you had an ownership interest in a property in the last three years?	☐	☐	☐ ☐
o.	Loan amount (add m & n)			(1) What type of property did you own—principal residence (PR), second home (SH), or investment property (IP)?	— —		— —
p.	Cash from/to Borrower (subtract j, k, l & o from i)			(2) How did you hold title to the home— by yourself (S), jointly with your spouse or jointly with another person (O)?	— —		— —

ACKNOWLEDGMENT AND AGREEMENT

Each of the undersigned specifically represents to Lender and to Lender's actual or potential agents, brokers, processors, attorneys, insurers, servicers, successors and assigns and agrees and acknowledges that: (1) the information provided in this application is true and correct as of the date set forth opposite my signature and that any intentional or negligent misrepresentation of this information contained in this application may result in civil liability, including monetary damages, to any person who may suffer any loss due to reliance upon any misrepresentation that I have made on this application, and/or in criminal penalties including, but not limited to, fine or imprisonment or both under the provisions of Title 18, United States Code, Sec. 1001, et seq.; (2) the loan requested pursuant to this application (the "Loan") will be secured by a mortgage or deed of trust on the property described in this application; (3) the property will not be used for any illegal or prohibited purpose or use; (4) all statements made in this application are made for the purpose of obtaining a residential mortgage loan; (5) the property will be occupied as indicated in this application; (6) the Lender, its servicers, successors or assigns may retain the original and/or an electronic record of this application, whether or not the Loan is approved; (7) the Lender and its agents, brokers, insurers, servicers, successors, and assigns may continuously rely on the information contained in the application, and I am obligated to amend and/or supplement the information provided in this application if any of the material facts that I have represented should change prior to closing of the Loan; (8) in the event that my payments on the Loan become delinquent, the Lender, its servicers, successors or assigns may, in addition to any other rights and remedies that it may have relating to such delinquency, report my name and account information to one or more consumer reporting agencies; (9) ownership of the Loan and/or administration of the Loan account may be transferred with such notice as may be required by law; (10) neither Lender nor its agents, brokers, insurers, servicers, successors or assigns has made any representation or warranty, express or implied, to me regarding the property or the condition or value of the property; and (11) my transmission of this application as an "electronic record" containing my "electronic signature," as those terms are defined in applicable federal and/or state laws (excluding audio and video recordings), or my facsimile transmission of this application containing a facsimile of my signature, shall be as effective, enforceable and valid as if a paper version of this application were delivered containing my original written signature.

Acknowledgement. Each of the undersigned hereby acknowledges that any owner of the Loan, its servicers, successors and assigns, may verify or reverify any information contained in this application or obtain any information or data relating to the Loan, for any legitimate business purpose through any source, including a source named in this application or a consumer reporting agency.

Borrower's Signature	Date	Co-Borrower's Signature	Date
X		X	

Uniform Residential Loan Application
Freddie Mac Form 65   7/05 (rev.6 /09)   Page 6 of 8   Fannie Mae Form 1003   7/05 (rev.6/09)

321

© Stringham Schools

X. INFORMATION FOR GOVERNMENT MONITORING PURPOSES

The following information is requested by the Federal Government for certain types of loans related to a dwelling in order to monitor the lender's compliance with equal credit opportunity, fair housing and home mortgage disclosure laws. You are not required to furnish this information, but are encouraged to do so. The law provides that a lender may not discriminate either on the basis of this information, or on whether you choose to furnish it. If you furnish the information, please provide both ethnicity and race. For race, you may check more than one designation. If you do not furnish ethnicity, race, or sex, under Federal regulations, this lender is required to note the information on the basis of visual observation and surname if you have made this application in person. If you do not wish to furnish the information, please check the box below. (Lender must review the above material to assure that the disclosures satisfy all requirements to which the lender is subject under applicable state law for the particular type of loan applied for.)

BORROWER	CO-BORROWER
☐ I do not wish to furnish this information	☐ I do not wish to furnish this information
Ethnicity: ☐ Hispanic or Latino ☐ Not Hispanic or Latino	Ethnicity: ☐ Hispanic or Latino ☐ Not Hispanic or Latino
Race: ☐ American Indian or Alaska Native ☐ Asian ☐ Black or African American ☐ Native Hawaiian or Other Pacific Islander ☐ White	Race: ☐ American Indian or Alaska Native ☐ Asian ☐ Black or African American ☐ Native Hawaiian or Other Pacific Islander ☐ White
Sex: ☐ Female ☐ Male	Sex: ☐ Female ☐ Male

To be Completed by Loan Originator
This information was provided:
☐ In a face-to-face interview
☐ In a telephone interview
☐ By the applicant and submitted by fax or mail
☐ By the applicant and submitted via e-mail or the Internet

Loan Originator's Signature	Date
Loan Originator's Name (print or type)	Loan Originator Identifier	Loan Originator's Phone Number (including area code)
Loan Origination Company's Name	Loan Origination Company Identifier	Loan Origination Company's Address

Uniform Residential Loan Application
Freddie Mac Form 65   7/05 (rev.6 /09)   Page 7 of 8   Fannie Mae Form 1003   7/05 (rev.6/09)

322

CONTINUATION SHEET/RESIDENTIAL LOAN APPLICATION

Use this continuation sheet if you need more space to complete the Residential Loan Application. Mark **B** for Borrower or **C** for Co-Borrower.	Borrower:	Agency Case Number:
	Co-Borrower:	Lender Case Number:

I/We fully understand that it is a Federal crime punishable by fine or imprisonment, or both, to knowingly make any false statements concerning any of the above facts as applicable under the provisions of Title 18, United States Code, Section 1001, et seq.

Borrower's Signature	Date	Co-Borrower's Signature	Date
X		X	

Uniform Residential Loan Application
Freddie Mac Form 65 7/05 (rev.6 /09)

Page 8 of 8

Fannie Mae Form 1003 7/05 (rev.6/09)

323

© Stringham Schools

Application & Underwriting Terms to Know

- ☐ Actual Mortgage Amount
- ☐ Capacity
- ☐ Capital
- ☐ Certificate of Eligibility
- ☐ Certificate of Reasonable Value
- ☐ Chapter 7
- ☐ Chapter 13
- ☐ Collateral
- ☐ Combined Loan to Value Ratio
- ☐ Compensating Factors
- ☐ Debt Ratio
- ☐ Domestic Partner
- ☐ Effective Income
- ☐ Employer Assisted Housing
- ☐ Gross-Up
- ☐ Hazard Insurance
- ☐ Home Owners Protection Act
- ☐ Investment Property
- ☐ Maximum Loan Amount
- ☐ Patriot Act Disclosure
- ☐ Potential Servicing Transfer Statement
- ☐ Prequalification Letter
- ☐ Private Mortgage Insurance
- ☐ Property Flipping
- ☐ Residual Income Analysis
- ☐ Seasoned Funds
- ☐ Seller Contributions
- ☐ Statutory Minimum Down Payment
- ☐ Underwriter
- ☐ Upfront Funding Fee
- ☐ Upfront Mortgage Insurance Premium
- ☐ Zone A

Application & Underwriting-2 Quiz

1. The loan qualifying process involves all of the following EXCEPT:

    A. Credit

    B. Capacity to repay

    C. Commissions

    D. Cash to close

2. The standard application for a mortgage loan is called:

    A. There is no standardized application form

    B. Uniform Residential Loan Application (1003)

    C. Uniform Underwriting and Transmittal Summary (1008)

    D. Good Faith Estimate (GFE)

3. The standard form provided to the underwriter along with the loan application, that provides the underwriter with a snapshot of the borrower is called:

    A. Uniform Underwriting and Transmittal Summary (1008)

    B. Uniform Residential Loan Application (1003)

    C. There is no standardized application form

    D. Truth In Lending (TIL)

4. The underwriting qualifying ratio of 31/43 is applied with what loan program?

    A. FHA

    B. VA

    C. Conventional

    D. Jumbo

5. The underwriting qualifying ratio of 28/36 is applied with what loan program?

    A. Jumbo conventional

    B. VA

    C. FHA

    D. Conforming conventional

6. A borrower can use all of the following for a down payment on an FHA loan EXCEPT:

    A. Unverifiable cash with a proven history of cash only transactions

    B. A gift from a parent that requires repayment

    C. The sale of personal or real property

    D. A gift from an employer that doesn't need to be paid back

7.   An underwriter performs all the following activities EXCEPT:

    A. Setting the interest rate for the loan

    B. Assessing borrowing capacity of borrowers

    C. Verifying that borrowers meet program guidelines

    D. Determining if compliance to federal requirements have been met

8.   All of the following are examined by the underwriter EXCEPT:

    A. Credit

    B. Capital to close and capacity to repay

    C. Blood type

    D. Cash in reserve

9.   Which of the following is NOT an automated underwriting system, but is instead desktop origination software?

    A. Fannie Mae Desktop Underwriter (DU)

    B. Loan pro

    C. Point

    D. Freddie Mac Loan Prospector (LD)

10. Freddie Mac Loan Prospector (LP) What is the function of FHA?

    A. Insure loans to protect lenders from loss due to borrower default

    B. Provide 100% financing to enable more people to buy homes

    C. Be a profitable private company for investors in home mortgages

    D. Provide financing for investment properties, as well as residential

11. The following are advantages of an FHA loan EXCEPT:

    A. Low down payment

    B. Flexible underwriting guidelines

    C. Upfront mortgage insurance

    D. Seller contribution of up to 6% of closing costs

12. FHA loan limits are established based on:

    A. HUD

    B. The legislative body of each state

    C. The U.S. senate, Finance Committee

    D. County

13. The minimum down payment required on an FHA loan is:

    A. 3%

    B. 3.5%

    C. 5%

    D. 20%

14. What are the qualifying ratios on an FHA loan?

    A. 29/41

    B. 31/43

    C. 41/41

    D. Residual income

15. Do FHA loans have an upfront mortgage insurance charge?

    A. Yes, called a funding fee

    B. No, just monthly mortgage insurance

    C. It depends on the loan to value ratio

    D. Yes, both upfront and monthly mortgage insurance

16. What describes the required mortgage insurance on an FHA loan?

    A. UFMIP 2.2%

    B. UFMIP of 1.75% and monthly of .5%

    C. Funding fee of 3.3%

    D. Lender paid .875% added to interest rate

17. Do condominiums using an FHA loan have UFMIP?

    A. No, only monthly mortgage insurance of .5%

    B. Yes, UFMIP

    C. No, it is called a funding fee

    D. There is no mortgage insurance on condominiums

18. What is NOT a purpose of VA loans:

    A. To guarantee loans to lenders in the event of borrower default

    B. To provide affordable housing in low income areas

    C. Providing loans of 100% of the lower of CRV or price

    D. Helping veterans finance homes

19. What is the document provided by the Department of Veteran Affairs showing what a veteran's loan entitlement is?

    A. Entitlement Certificate

    B. Certificate of Eligibility

    C. Proof of Service

    D. Loan commitment

20. The following are all correct regarding a VA loan EXCEPT:

    A. Loans up to 100% loan to value

    B. Flexible underwriting guidelines

    C. Allows seller contribution to closing costs up to 4%

    D. Restricts the price on a home sold to a veteran

21. Instead of the ratio in determining adequate income for loan qualification, the VA uses a formula called:

    A. Ratio qualification formula

    B. Income is not used in qualification for loan

    C. Residual income

    D. Stated income formula

22. In determining if collateral is adequate, the VA utilizes a:

    A. Certificate of Reasonable Value (CRV)

    B. Short form appraisal

    C. Narrative form appraisal

    D. Letter from appraisal

23. In lieu of mortgage insurance, the VA utilizes what?

    A. Loan reduction fee

    B. A standard .5% added to the interest rate

    C. A first time funding fee of 2.15%

    D. A first time funding fee of 3.3%

24. The maximum loan amount for a conventional conforming loan is:

    A. $359,650

    B. $333,700

    C. $417,000

    D. $369,550

25. The qualifying ratios for a conforming conventional loan are:

 A. 28/36

 B. 41/41

 C. 29/41

 D. 29/38

26. When will mortgage insurance be required for a conforming conventional loan?

 A. Anytime the combined loans exceed 80% of the purchase price

 B. Whenever there is more than one loan on the property

 C. When a loan exceeds 80% LTV

 D. Mortgage insurance is only used on FHA loans

27. Conforming conventional guidelines stipulate that borrowers must contribute how much of their own funds to the down payment and closing costs?

 A. 3%

 B. 5%

 C. 20%

 D. No requirement

28. According to federal mandate, at what level must mortgage insurance on conventional loans automatically be removed?

 A. When the LTV reaches 78% of original value

 B. When the buyer requests it and the LTV is 80%

 C. When the lender obtains an appraisal to justify the 78% LTV

 D. Only if loan contains a prepayment penalty

29. Dan purchased a home using a VA 90% LTV loan. Dan's lender is protected against Dan's default by which of the following?

 A. Mortgage Insurance Premium

 B. Veterans Administration guarantee

 C. Private mortgage insurance

 D. Only Dan's good faith promise to pay

30. How much time must have elapsed after a bankruptcy to qualify for an FHA loan?

 A. 1 Year

 B. 2 Years

 C. 5 Years

 D. 3 Years

31. How much time must have elapsed after a bankruptcy to qualify for an FHLMC loan?

    A. 1 Year

    B. 2 Years

    C. 5 Years

    D. 7 Years

32. How much time must have elapsed after a chapter 7 bankruptcy to qualify for an FNMA loan?

    A. 1 Year

    B. 4 Years

    C. 5 Years

    D. 3 Years

Advanced Finance

** It is highly recommended that you take this class AFTER completing Finance Basics, Application and Underwriting 1 & 2**

I. **Finance Contract Clauses:**

Each of these clauses can drastically change the terms, meaning, and character of the loan. The clause may appear on the Trust Deed and/or the note.

  A. Prepayment clauses come in two forms:

    1. **Prepayment penalty clause**, which states that if the principal is paid off faster than has been prescribed in the mortgage or trust deed, a penalty will be applied.

        a. Prepayment penalties are charged against the unpaid balance on the loan.

        b. **"Hard" prepayment penalties** are applied under any condition that pays off the loan balance including sale.

        c. **"Soft" prepayment penalties** are only applied when refinancing.

    2. **Prepayment privilege clause**, allows a borrower to pay off the principal of the loan faster than prescribed without paying a penalty, including paying it all off because of selling the property or refinancing.

        a. FHA, FNMA, FHLMC, and VA loans all provide prepayment privilege.

        b. **Sub-prime loans,** loans to borrowers with poor credit history do not usually include prepayment privilege.

        c. This clause, if it exists, should be carefully studied to determine what limits, if any, are attached to the prepayment privilege (sometimes called an "or more" clause).

  B. **Subordination clauses** are used to alter priority of loans.

    1. Lien priority is set by recording date.

    2. Subordination counteracts the recorded lien date by agreement of the parties.

    3. Example:

The buyer is buying a building lot on contract from the seller that he intends to build on in the near future;

The seller agrees to subordinate his lien in the property to a construction loan when the time comes;

When the buyer applies for construction financing, the construction lender will require a first position lien in order to make the loan;

Because the buyer had the foresight to negotiate subordination with the land purchase the construction loan can go in place without problem;

Because of subordination the buyer is given credit toward the equity requirements of the construction lender for the land.

  C. **Partial release clause** allows individual lots to be excused from the collateral in exchange for an agreed upon balloon payment.

1. This clause is used in a blanket loan to allow for release of lots during subdivision construction to individual buyers.

2. With out this clause the developer would not be able to sell individual lots without first paying off the entire loan balance.

D. **Non-disturbance clause** protects the tenant of a rental property in the event of foreclosure.

1. Owner occupied financing does not include this clause.

2. Non-owner occupied or investor financing does include this clause.

E. **Defeasance clause** creates the responsibility for the lender to re-convey to the borrower all interest in the property (the lien) after the borrower has made the last payment. The instruments to accomplish this are:

1. **Satisfaction of Mortgage**, if the security instrument is a Mortgage; or

2. **Reconveyance of Deed** or **Deed of Reconveyance**, if the security instrument is a Trust Deed and Note.

F. **Escalation clause** provides for a contractual increase in the payments at specified times. It is often used in graduated payment mortgages and growing equity loans.

G. **Acceleration clause** allows the lender to immediately call a loan due requiring payment in full if default occurs.

1. It is this clause that permits the lender to foreclose the entire note.

2. Without this clause the loan would have to be foreclosed one payment at a time making the process very expensive.

3. Typical defaults that trigger acceleration of a loan include:

    a. Non-payment of payments

    b. Non-payment of property taxes

    c. Non-payment of hazard insurance

    d. Permitting waste. If physical condition of the property deteriorates the value of the lender's security declines.

    e. Renting a home with an owner-occupied loan

    f. Sale of the property when there is a due on sale or alienation clause

H. **Alienation clause**, also called due on sale or non-assumption clause.

1. Alienation is the legal separation of title to the property from the owner.

2. It does not refer to physical tenancy.

3. An alienation clause states that alienation that occurs without payment in full of the loan cannot occur without the express written consent of the lender.

4. The clause is not enforceable when the property is being transferred from one joint owner to another (i.e., divorce) or in the case of inheritance.

Notice:
*   The rules regulating FHA, VA, or conventional loans change often.
*   The information provided herein is current as of date of publication.
*   Check with your lender or attend class to obtain current information.

II. **Loan Concepts:**

There are several forms a loan could take each with specific features that favor particular borrower needs.

A. **Open-end mortgage**:

1. The borrower is given a line of credit that allows the borrower to increase the principal at a later time(s).

    a. In real estate, the most frequent uses for open-end loans are construction loans and home equity loans.

B. **Closed–ended mortgage**:

1. The borrower is given one set amount of money at one time and the principal cannot be increased.

    a. Good Examples of closed-ended loans would be a regular 30 year mortgage.

C. **Purchase money mortgage**: A purchase money mortgage is borrowed money for the purpose of purchasing the property the money was borrowed for.

1. Your down payment is considered purchase money.

2. A mortgage used to complete a purchase is considered purchase money. This would include 1st, 2nd, 3rd mortgages, etc.

3. Seller financing is also purchase money. In order to sell the home, the seller agrees to lend all or a portion of the purchase price. The seller will usually "carry back" the borrower's promissory note ("carrying paper"). In this case, the borrower is receiving credit rather than actual cash. The seller can add security to the promissory note with a Trust Deed.

4. Purchase money is not any loan used to refinance or pull equity out of an owned property.

D. **Participation mortgage** is a loan in which the lender, in addition to interest on the loan, is paid a portion of the rental income of the property or an equity percentage.

1. Lenders determine interest rates by market conditions and the risk of the loan.

2. Participation mortgages are just another way for a lender to be compensated for loan risk.

3. This type of loan is most commonly found in financing commercial property.

E. **Wraparound mortgage**: A wraparound mortgage is financing on top of financing.

1. The existing financing is left in place with the original borrower remaining responsible to make loan payments.

2. The wraparound loan is for the full purchase price less the down payment.

3. The wraparound lender collects payments from the home buyer, then uses those payment funds to pay the existing loan payments. The difference provides profit and interest to the lender.

4. Typically a wraparound mortgage is used to create extra income to the lender (who will often be the seller) from the loan(s) in existence prior to the wraparound mortgage.

5. In Utah, the loan can be made with either an All Inclusive Trust Deed or a Uniform Real Estate Contract. In other states the Uniform Real Estate Contract is referred to as a Land Contract, a Contract for Deed, an Installment Contract, or sometimes simply a Real Estate Contract.

6. This type of loan would be a violation of a Due On Sale Clause, if it existed, and could put both the seller/lender and the buyer at risk of the first loan being foreclosed even if payments were made. Utah law could require that licensees make sure that both the buyer and the seller understand the risk they are taking if this type loan is used when a Due On Sale Clause exists. See generally Utah Administrative Code R162-2f-401a(1)(c)(ii).

Example:
- The Seller's are offering their home for $70,000 with an assumable loan for $50,000 at 9% interest;
- The Buyer's offer $70,000 with a $5,000 down payment and will assume the   underlying $50,000 loan. They want the Seller's to carry a second mortgage for the $15,000 balance at 11% interest;
- The Seller's counter offer states that they will carry the whole loan of $65,000 (as   far as the Buyer's are concerned) at 10.5% interest. When the Seller's receive the Buyer's payment each month, they will make the payment on the first, just as when they owned the property;
- The Seller is paying 9% interest on the $50,000 loan and collecting 10.5% rate. The difference of 5% is income to the Sellers. The rest of the payment applies to the Sellers' equity plus 10.5% interest.

F. **Subject to loan**: If an existing loan does not contain a due-on-sale clause, the buyer may purchase the property subject to the existing loan. The buyer takes no direct liability for the loan (it does remain a lien on the property). The lender still looks to the seller for payment of the loan. The buyer and seller decide, as a part of the purchase agreement, how payments will be made:

1. Paid by the seller directly to the lender after receiving payment from the buyer to the seller. The buyer could be at risk that the seller fails to make payments after receiving the payment form the buyer. The loan could go into default harming the buyer's title interest in the property.

2. Paid by the buyer directly to the lender. The seller may not know the loan payments have not been made until notice of default, harming the sellers' credit history.

3. Paid to a trustee who makes the payment to the lender and reports to the seller that the payment has been made.

G. **Non-recourse loan**: A loan in which the borrower is not held personally liable on the note.

1. If the lender foreclosed and did not recover from the foreclosure the entire debt, this type of loan would not allow the lender to obtain a deficiency judgment.

2. Only the foreclosing lender loses recourse. If a second mortgage lender loses as the result of a first mortgage foreclosure, the second mortgage lender may still sue for deficiency unless the lenders loan is non-recourse.

H. **Refinancing** a loan: Obtaining a new loan and paying off the existing loan from the proceeds.

1. Often the new loan is for more than the balance of the old. This is known as a "cash out" refinance

2. Many borrowers think there is no cost to refinancing, since the costs are added into the loan and not paid up front as "closing costs," but this is not true. The new loan includes the costs. The borrower has paid the loan fees using their equity.

3. Some of the reasons for refinancing are:

    a. To lower the interest rate, and therefore the debt service (principal and interest payment).

    b. To generate a non-taxable source of income.

    c. To generate funds for a purchase (such as a car) in such a way that the interest paid for the car purchase will be deductible when computing income tax.

I. **Unsecured loan**: A promissory note does not provide security.

1. The only protection a promissory note provides is the result of the borrower's determination to keep their commitments.

2. If legal action is taken to collect, it would result in a general lien against the individual and the individual's assets.

J. **Chattel mortgage** is a loan secured by personal property. A car loan would be an example of a chattel mortgage. The car is the collateral and the car is personal property or chattel.

K. **Package mortgage** is a loan secured by both real and personal property such as a furnished condominium.

1. The real estate and its furnishings provide the collateral in this case.

2. A package mortgage is a higher risk loan because the furnishings are mobile and easily destructible and might not be available in case of foreclosure.

3. Another example of a package loan might involve the purchase of a business with building and inventory.

L. **Blanket mortgage**: One loan secured by two or more parcels of real property.

  1. An example would be a construction loan on a subdivision. Each of the lots are a separate identity, but the combined subdivision serves as collateral for the loan.

  2. A release clause in the note allows individual lots to be sold and released as collateral in exchange for a predetermined payment against the loan balance.

M. **Compound interest loans** allow interest to be added to the principle balance.

  1. Interest is charged on a schedule of days or months.

  2. Interest that has been added to the loan balance will be included as loan amount when the next interest calculation occurs.

  3. Interest could be charged on interest and is known as compound interest.

  4. Most mortgage loans require that all interest be paid in full with each payment preventing compounding because interest is always paid before it could be added to the loan balance.

N. **Simple interest** is the opposite of compound interest.

  1. Simple interest is only charged on the loan balance, never on interest that has been added to the loan balance.

  2. Most mortgages are simple interest loans.

III. **Additional Loan Concepts**

A. **Interest only loans**: are also known as term or straight loans.

  1. Required payments are of interest only, leaving the principal balance unchange

  2. The final payment of the loan will be for the entire balance plus any interest still owing.

B. **Amortized loans**: have equal, periodic payments of principal and interest.

  1. The payment includes all of the interest accumulated since the last payment so each payment prevents compounding.

  2. The payments are equal, so inside the payment the ratio of interest to principal changes over the life of the loan.

      a. Initial payments include interest on the original loan balance so principal portions are small.

      b. Final payments include interest on a much lower loan balance so most of the payment is principal.

C. **Fully amortized loans**: are repaid by a series of payments made up of principal and interest.

  1. When all of the contracted payments have been made the loan balance is at zero.

  2. All of the contact payments included enough interest to pay the loan interest in full for the period represented by the payment spacing.

D. **Amortization schedule**: A printout showing every payment broken down into principal amount and interest amount, covering the whole life of the loan.

E. **Partially amortized** (also known as a balloon mortgage):

1. The payments include both principal and interest, but the payments do not pay off the loan balance before the loan is due.

2. The final payment pays the balance of the loan in one sum known as a balloon payment.

3. Typical loans of this type are amortized as though the loan was for 30 years. The payments are the same as a 30 year loan would have. But the loan is due much sooner, perhaps 5 years.

4. Seller financing frequently take this form. The note is due in five years but the payments required of the buyer would only pay off the loan over 30 years. The buyer anticipates refinancing the balance in order to pay the balloon payment.

Example:

If the seller carried a second mortgage of $20,000 with an interest rate of 10% and a   term of 30 years, the payment would be $1751;

The seller includes in the loan a provision that it must be paid in full at the end of the   seventh year;

The seller would then receive 84 payments of $1751 or a total of $14,7420 plus   the buyer/borrower would have to pay the remaining balance of the loan at the end of   the seven years, which would be $18,929.87;

This partially amortized loan of $20,000 would then return a total of $33,6708 to the   seller.

F. **Negative amortization** occurs when the required payments are insufficient to cover the interest charge of the loan.

1. The unpaid interest becomes part of the loan balance (compound interest).

2. The interest is compounded with each new interest charge.

3. The loan balance increases with each payment.

G. **Graduated payment mortgage** ("GPM"):

1. The borrowers qualify at a lower than normal interest rate.

2. The expectation is that as their payments increase, so will their incomes.

3. It is not an adjustable rate mortgage.

4. It does have negative amortization.

Example:

A 7% $150,000 FHA 245 loan with a payment increase of 5% per year for five years would start with a PI payment of $710.9 A standard loan would have a level payment of $999

At the end of the five years the payment would be $1080

The loan balance would be $153,520.0

The new fully amortized higher payment would pay off the loan in the remaining 25 years.

The actual payments on this loan would be higher because of the addition of tax and   insurance escrows and MIP

H. **Bridge loan** (swing loan or gap loan): Short term loan with high interest rates used to obtain the equity from a current residence currently for sale, but not yet sold, in order to purchase a new home.

I. **Adjustable rate mortgages** ("ARM's"): With these mortgages the interest rate is flexible and is adjusted to an established index as specified in the mortgage. The interest rate floats up and down with the economy. Terms may include:

1. The **initial interest rate**: The rate at which the borrower qualifies for the loan and the rate that establishes the payment for the first period of time.

2. The **adjusting period**: This period of time determines how often the interest rate will be adjusted. It is usually every six months or every year, although it can be for shorter or longer periods.

3. The **adjusted rate**: The interest rate and payment are adjusted from the rate in the previous period by applying the index and margin to determine the new payment.

   a. The index: The standard by which the interest rate is periodically adjusted. Common indices:

      i. **One-year treasury index** is the most common index used by Fannie Mae and Freddie Mac, and is based on outstanding Federal obligations with a year to maturity.

      ii. **London Interbank Offered Rate** ("LIBOR") reflects the rate on Eurodollars traded between banks in London; quoted in one, three, six-month,and one-year periods. This rate represents the rate international banking institutions with the best credit will pay. It is published in the Wall Street Journal.

      iii. **Eleventh District Cost of Funds Index** ("COFI") reflects a weighted average rate of home loans made by member banks in the Eleventh District of the Federal Home Loan Bank District headquartered in San Francisco.

      iv. **Treasury Bill Index** ("T-Bill") reflects the current market rate of Treasury Bills with a term of mortgage length (10, 15, 20, 25, 30 years). The T-Bill is considered a representation of the risk fee rate of an investment since the T-Bill is guaranteed by the U.S. Treasury for repayment.

   b. The **margin**: The amount over the index to which the interest rate is adjusted. For instance, assume that the index was the six month T-Bill and the margin was 2 points. Also assume the T-Bill at the time of adjustment was 8%, then interest rate would be adjusted to 8 (the rate of the index) + 2 (the margin). The new adjusted interest rate would be 10%.

4. **Caps**: Limits of adjustment – To protect both the lender and the borrower, ARM's have maximum limits established for the interest rate. These limits are called caps. They come in two forms:

    a. Periodic cap: This cap limits the change that can be made in the interest rate regardless of what might have happened to the index. For instance, assume the periodic cap is 1% and the current rate is 9%. When it is time to make the next adjustment, the T-Bill is 9% and the margin is 2% making the adjusted rate 11%, a 2% increase. The cap limits change to a maximum of 1% so regardless of the index change the new rate is only 1 % higher, 10%.

    b. **Lifetime cap**: This cap limits the total change that can be made in the interest rate during the life of the loan. If the beginning rate was 10% and the overall cap was 5%, the interest rate could never go over 15%. The "floor" is the lowest point the interest can reach over the life of the loan.

5. Many, but not all, adjustable rate mortgages allow the borrower to convert to a fixed rate mortgage. In some instances the conversion changes the loan from assumable to non-assumable.

J. **Reverse annuity mortgages** are used most frequently to assist elderly people who own their homes free and clear, but who need to create a cash flow from their equity.

1. The borrowers put up the equity of their home to secure the loan.

2. The mortgagee (the lender) makes monthly payments to the mortgagor (the borrower).

3. Each payment increases the loan balance.

4. The mortgage provides for the lender to be paid from the proceeds of the estate when the mortgagor dies, or when the property is sold.

K. **Option ARM**: Allows the borrower to select a payment option from several choices each month with some restrictions. A full description of this loan product is not included in this course, but two issues of this program are important to discuss:

1. **Inadequate amortization**: The lowest payment option is frequently less than the fully-indexed rate. Choosing this option would not reduce the loan balance enough to keep up with the amortization schedule.

2. **Negative amortization**: The lowest payment option can also be lower than an interest only payment. If all the interest due in one period is not paid, the unpaid amount is added to the loan balance. The payment did not cause the balance to go down or stay the same, but actually caused the loan balance to go up. Either of these choices could have an adverse effect on the borrower.

Option Arm typical payment choices	
i.	Minimum payment (may cause negative amortization)
ii.	Interest only payment (no reduction in principal
iii.	Payment 15 yr amortized (Recalculated schedule base on current rate)
iv.	Payment 30 yr amortized (Recalculated schedule base on current rate)
v.	Fully-indexed payment (Recalculated payment using the remaining term as amortization period)

L.   **Home equity line of credit** ("HELOC"): A revolving line of credit based on a borrower's equity. The borrower can draw money from the line of credit as needed up to the credit limit. Borrowers are required to make at least a minimum payment, normally interest only. The interest rate on a HELOC is always variable using an index as reference. HELOC's are considered short term loans with short term interest rates.

M.   **Jumbo/non-conforming**:

1.   Any loan larger than the conforming loan limit mentioned previously is called a jumbo loan.

2.   Non-conforming loans are loans that do not meet the specific eligibility criteria for Fannie Mae or Freddie Mac, and typically are kept in the originating lenders portfolio of loans held and serviced; however, some secondary market makers do exist to purchase these loan types.

3.   Since loan default risk potentially increases as the loan amounts become larger, the interest rates typically are higher and guidelines more strict.

4.   Because of loan default risk, second homes are customarily not allowed.

N.   **Niche loans**:

1.   Any loan that fits some specialized lending need is referred to as a niche loan. Examples of niche loans could be non-income or asset qualification loans, construction loans, bridge loans, lot loans, etc.

O.   **Subprime loans**: Loans that will not fit into conforming loan guidelines because of issues most commonly associated with the borrower's income, credit, or collateral.

Advanced Finance Terms to Know

- ☐ Adjustable Rate Mortgage (ARM)
- ☐ Amortized Loan
- ☐ Amortization Schedule
- ☐ Balloon Mortgage
- ☐ Balloon Payment
- ☐ Blanket Mortgage
- ☐ Bridge, Gap, or Swing Loan
- ☐ Refinance
- ☐ Chattel Mortgage
- ☐ Compound Interest
- ☐ Fully Amortized Loan
- ☐ Graduated Payment Mortgage (GPM)
- ☐ Index
- ☐ Interest Rate
- ☐ Lifetime Cap
- ☐ London Interbank Offered Rate (LIBOR)
- ☐ Margin
- ☐ Negative or Reverse Amortization
- ☐ Non-Recourse Loan
- ☐ Open-End Mortgage
- ☐ Package Mortgage
- ☐ Partially Amortized Loan
- ☐ Participation Loan
- ☐ Periodic Cap
- ☐ Purchase Money Mortgage
- ☐ Refinancing
- ☐ Reverse Annuity Mortgage
- ☐ Simple Interest
- ☐ Straight Note
- ☐ Subject to Loan
- ☐ Term Loan
- ☐ Take Out Loan
- ☐ Treasury Bill (T-Bill)
- ☐ Unsecured Loan
- ☐ Wraparound Mortgage or All Inclusive Trust Deed (AITD)

Advanced Finance Quiz

1. D secured a loan with a fourplex and a second mortgage on the equity in his home. This would be:

    A. Package mortgage

    B. Wrap Around mortgage

    C. Chattel mortgage

    D. Blanket mortgage

2. When the Beneficiary makes payments to the Trustor, the loan is a:

    A. Wraparound Mortgage

    B. Negatively Amortized Mortgage

    C. Blanket Mortgage

    D. Reverse Annuity Mortgage

3. A partial release clause would most likely be found in which of the following?

    A. Blanket Mortgage

    B. Negatively Amortized Mortgage

    C. Wrap Around Mortgage

    D. Chattel Mortgage

4. If a lender was considering giving a loan for a commercial project, and felt that its possibility for making a profit was so good he wanted some ownership in the project, he would offer the prospective borrower a(n):

    A. Wraparound mortgage or All Inclusive Trust Deed (AITD)

    B. Participation mortgage

    C. Purchase Money mortgage

    D. FHA loan

5. Mr. Alison obtained a loan and gave his home and boat as security for the loan. This would be an example of a(n):

    A. Package mortgage

    B. Blanket mortgage

    C. Chattel mortgage

    D. Wraparound mortgage

6. A loan that requires payments which include both principal and interest, and a final payment that includes a balloon payment would be an example of a(n):

    A. Fully amortized mortgage

    B. Partially Amortized Mortgage

    C. Adjustable rate mortgage

    D. Negatively amortized mortgage

7. M has a loan on which he makes payments of interest only. At the end of the loan M must pay off the entire principal in a single payment. This loan is an example of a:

    A. Reverse annuity mortgage

    B. Package mortgage

    C. Straight loan

    D. Partially amortized mortgage

8. Jim is requesting that the seller carry back a portion of the purchase price. Jim is asking for what type of loan?

    A. Wraparound mortgage

    B. Purchase money mortgage

    C. Straight Mortgage

    D. Contract for deed

9. Jill will be making a single monthly payment to Dan, the seller. Dan will be using that payment to pay Dan's mortgage but Dan will also be keeping a significant amount of Jill's payment. This would probably be an example of which of the following types of loans?

    A. Non-recourse loan

    B. Cash out refinance

    C. Wraparound loan

    D. Partially amortized loan

10. Reginald makes monthly payments that include principal, interest, taxes and insurance. At some future date he will have to make a much larger payment to pay the loan off. Reginald must be making payments on what type of loan?

    A. Straight Loan

    B. Partially amortized Loan

    C. Fully amortized loan

    D. Graduated payment loan

11. Phyllis has been making payments now for over 48 months. Reading her mortgage payment statement she realizes that her balance is larger than the original loan amount, yet her payments have been higher each year. Phyllis must have what type of loan?

    A. Graduated Payment Mortgage

    B. Subject to loan

    C. Balloon mortgage

    D. Chattel Mortgage

12. Sherri has an adjustable rate mortgage. She just received a notice that her payment next month will be higher. On what basis could her lender raise her payment?

    A. The payment cap has changed

    B. The margin has changed

    C. The lifetime cap has changed

    D. The index has changed

13. Nancy's mortgage has scheduled payment increases of 1% per year for the life of the loan. She probably has what type of loan?

    A. Graduated payment loan

    B. Adjustable rate loan

    C. Participation loan

    D. Growing equity mortgage

14. Any one of the following contracts: All inclusive Trust Deed, the Uniform Real Estate contract, the Land Contract or the Contract for Deed could be used to create what type of loan?

    A. Open end loan

    B. Wraparound loan

    C. Take out loan

    D. Shared appreciation loan

15. An open-end loan would best be used for which of the following?

    A. Construction loan

    B. Seller financing

    C. Non-recourse financing

    D. Unsecured financing

Federal Reserve

I. **Federal Reserve, Its Purpose and Functions**

The Federal Reserve System is the central bank of the United States. It was initially founded by Congress to address banking panics. Over the years, its role in banking and the economy has expanded. Now the Fed is charged with a number of broader responsibilities. The Federal Reserve exists to provide the nation with a safer, more flexible, and more stable monetary and financial system. Some of their duties include:

A. Stimulate economic growth

B. Maximize employment

C. Stable interest rates

D. Encourage stable prices

E. Regulate banks

F. Provide financial services to banks, the U.S. gov.

G. Encourage sustainable pattern of international trade

H. Payment processing

Actions by the Federal Reserve impact many aspects of our financial life. Its actions can make borrowing more or less expensive. Their actions can make credit more widely available and can even influence the interest rates on bank savings accounts.

II. **Brief History of the Federal Reserve System**

The Federal Reserve is also known as, "The Fed" or Central Bank.

A. It was created in an effort to moderate boom/bust economic cycles and encourage public confidence in the banking system.

B. On December 23, 1913, the Federal Reserve Act became law, and within a year the 12 Federal Reserve Banks were open for business. The Boston Fed, along with the other11 Federal Reserve Banks nationwide and the Board of Governors in Washington, , make up our nation's central bank.

C. Previous to the enactment of the Federal Reserve Act, the US government was powerless to contain or stimulate the economy and therefore powerless to contain risk.

III. **Federal Reserve Structure**

The Federal Reserve System consists of a Board of Governors and the FOMC with headquarters in Washington, , and twelve Reserve Banks located in major cities throughout the United States

IV. **The Federal Reserve's Role as Bank Regulator**

The Fed has responsibility for examining banks and bank holding companies ("BHCs") in order to protect consumers and, thereby, maintain public confidence. Examinations are risk-focused and each examination is tailored to the institution's risk profile.

345

A. Bank examinations determine the safety and soundness of the institution's financial condition, as well as the integrity of information systems (how well your personal data is safeguarded for example).

B. Examiners evaluate items such as:

1. The quality of the institution's assets

2. Adherence to state and federal banking laws

3. The effectiveness of internal controls

4. Policies and risk management systems

C. Should deficiencies be found, the bank is put on notice, requiring the bank to outline corrective measures. The evaluation factors can be summed up with the acronym CAMELS:

1. Capital

2. Assets

3. Management

4. Earnings

5. Liquidity

6. Sensitivity (to market risks)

V. Federal Open Market Committee

Monetary policy is made by the **Federal Open Market Committee** ("FOMC"), which consists of the members of the Board of Governors of the Federal Reserve System and five Reserve Bank presidents.

A. The FOMC holds eight regularly scheduled meetings during the year. During times of economic unrest they may meet in unscheduled "emergency" meetings.

B. At each meeting the FOMC decides its target for the federal funds rate, or that rate which is charged for bank to bank loans.

C. The FOMC also issues a statement after each meeting explaining its decision to either raise, lower, or hold steady the rate and usually contains information about the FOMC's evaluation of the overall economy.

VI. Monetary Policy

Monetary policy refers to what the Federal Reserve does to influence the amount of money and credit available in the U.S. economy. The objective of monetary policy is to influence the performance of the economy in such factors as inflation, economic output (gross domestic product, GDP), and employment. What happens to money and credit affects interest rates and the performance of the U.S. economy. Monetary policy affects all kinds of financial decisions people make—whether to get a loan, buy a new house or car, to start a company, put savings in a bank or in the stock market. This is done by making the cost of borrowing or saving more or less expensive, relatively speaking. Monetary policy is referred to as either being expansionary or contractionary.

A. **Expansionary policy** – Increases the total supply of money. It is used to combat high unemployment in a recession by lowering interest rates. This makes the cost of credit decrease, which will stimulate investment.

B. **Contractionary policy**: Decreases the total money supply. This is designed to "cool" the economy by increasing interest rates which slows investment in an effort to control inflation.

C. It is important to realize that the Federal Reserve and the FOMC set target rates that are merely meant to INFLUENCE interest rates. It is ultimately the FREE MARKET that sets interest rates that you and I pay, NOT THE GOVERNMENT!

D. There are 3 key instruments that are used by the Fed to influence monetary policy:

1. The discount rate: The interest rate charged by federal reserve banks to depository institutions on short-term loans.

2. Bank reserve requirements: The amount of funds that a depository institution must hold in reserve against specified deposit liabilities or other risks. This can take the form of vault cash or deposits with a federal reserve bank.

3. Open market operation: Purchases and sales of US treasury and federal agency securities.

VII. **Bank Functions**

A. Banks provide financial services to customers while providing investors with a desired return. Banks provide services under three main categories:

1. Credit (lending)

2. Deposit

3. Payment processing

B. Lending is the biggest share of a bank's business, which can account for as much as 70% to nearly 100% in the case of some non-deposit industrial banks. You can see that if a bank is prudent in their lending, business will be good. Like most businesses, the idea is to provide a good or service with the intent of selling it for more than what you pay for it. The same principle is used with banking. If a bank's cost of funds exceeds its ability to make more money by lending to worthy borrowers, banks can and do fail. Customer deposits are held as a liability to the bank because they must be able to return it on demand. In cases where underwriting of credit or lending practices are poor, loan losses will occur. If these losses are severe enough, depositors may panic and demand their money back. When the bank is in danger of running out of cash to meet their financial obligations, the bank is considered a failure and it is taken over by federal regulators.

VIII. **How Banks Make Money**

Banks are in the business of lending out money deposited by their clients and earning interest on money loaned out. An example of a bank's cost of funds and its ability to sell those funds for more is a typical bank customer that holds money in a bank savings account and also has an auto loan. At any given time, the bank must pay less interest on the savings account and turn right around and sell funds back to the same customer for much more as an auto loan. Customer deposits are usually the cheapest form of funds for a bank, which is why banks are eager to have you as a depositor.

A.   Interest is the price that someone pays for the temporary use of someone else's money. The amount of interest can be expressed as APR or APY.

    1.   **Annual Percentage Rate** ("APR"): Includes, as a percent of principal, not only the interest that has to be paid on a loan, but also some other costs associated with creating or originating the loan. Discount points and/or origination fees on a typical mortgage are examples of these other costs.

    2.   **Annual Percentage Yield** ("APY"): The effective interest rate based on the frequency of interest payments paid on deposits. Increasing the frequency will compound your earnings and, therefore, increase the yield.

B.   Interest rates on a loan may differ depending on several factors:

    1.   Availability of funds to the bank

    2.   Loan type risk

    3.   Loan duration/term

    4.   Collateral posted

    5.   Loan purpose

C.   Approximately 2/3 of U.S. households own their own homes and pay a mortgage. The unique characteristics of a mortgage allow rates to generally be lower than other consumer rates. On a 30-year mortgage, interest payments over the life of the loan will add up to more than the amount of the original amount borrowed.

D.   When creating an interest rate, banks must study their risks and be able to cover them and still make a profit acceptable to investors. The process of building a rate involves taking a risk-free rate and adding certain premiums as follows: Interest rate equals:

    1.   Risk free rate (90 day T-Bill)

    2.   Inflation premium

    3.   Borrower default premium

    4.   Liquidity premium

    5.   Maturity premium

    6.   Profit

IX.   **Importance of Federal Reserve Independence**

Concerns over undue influence of the Federal Reserve by politicians include:

A.   Higher inflation

B.   Less stable economy

C.   Monetary policy would be less restrictive, particularly before elections in an effort to "buy" your vote.

1. It is important to understand that the Fed is best known for its role in making and carrying out the nation's monetary policy. That is, for influencing money and credit conditions in the economy in order to promote the goals of high employment, sustainable growth, and stable prices. There is nothing the Fed can do to guarantee that our economy will grow at a healthy pace or that it will provide a job for everyone that wants on The attainment of these goals depends on the decisions that millions of people around the country make regarding such matters as how much to spend and how much to save; how much to invest in acquiring skills and education; and how many hours a week they want to work. What the Fed can do is try to create an environment that is conducive to healthy economic growth.

Federal Reserve Terms to Know

- ☐ Annual Percentage Rate (APR)
- ☐ Annual Percentage Yield (APY)
- ☐ Bank Reserve Requirements
- ☐ Contractionary Policy
- ☐ Discount Rate
- ☐ Expansionary Policy
- ☐ Federal Open Market Committee (FOMC)
- ☐ Federal Reserve System
- ☐ Interest
- ☐ Monetary Policy
- ☐ Open Market Operation

Foreclosure and Credit

I. **Foreclosure Process**

Real estate will always have its boom times. It will also most certainly have its bust times as well. No matter the circumstances surrounding the foreclosure of real property, the emotions of the owner as well as the business-focus of the lender can and will clash. Knowledge of the steps involved in the foreclosure process will be critical in any type of representation when a client faces this situation. In addition, it is important to know what may be in store for a borrower's post-foreclosure credit profile and what that might mean for future real property ownership.

A. **Foreclosure** is the moment that ownership is transferred. Either the bank or a 3rd party will now own the property.

B. It is the note, or **promissory note** (promise to pay), that stipulates the terms of the money lent and when default occurs. When default occurs, the process by which title is transferred from borrower to lien holder is governed and outlined in the mortgage instrument or the Deed of Trust.

   1. The **mortgage instrument** requires a judicial foreclosure process.

   2. A **Deed of Trust** does not require a formal court proceeding to foreclose.

II. **Judicial Foreclosure**

This form of foreclosure is less advantageous for the lender due to the additional time and expense. Therefore it is not used as often as the collateral instrument of choice.

A. If the property is ordered to be sold to satisfy debt, an attorney or actual sheriff will hold the sale at a courthouse. These notices of sale are publicly posted in advance. They can also be found at the Sheriff's office and at the County building. These auctions of real property are typically called "Sheriff Sales."

B. **Redemption period**: The period of time after a foreclosure when the borrower can pay the owed price in full and redeem ownership of the property. Each state governs their redemption periods by statute. Utah does not allow a redemption period for non-judicial foreclosures, but does allow a redemption period for judicial foreclosures under certain circumstances. If the circumstances are met, the redemption period for a judicial foreclosure is 180 days after foreclosure. Utah R. Civ. P. 69C(a)-(e).

III. **Foreclosure Process—Non-Judicial Foreclosure**

Stage 1: Filing of Notice of Default ("NOD")

Legally can file after first missed payment

Standard practice is 3 missed payments or (90) days

Now the bank has retained a local attorney and incurred approximately $1,500 in fees

Stage 2: Reinstatement Period

Borrower has a 90 day window to correct the situation. Typically this is done through a   workout agreement or full payoff

Stage 3:   Posting Period

Standard practice is posting the sale of the property in a circulated newspaper for 3   consecutive weeks, which must be completed at least 10 days prior to the actual sale.

Stage 4: Auction

Must be held at a courthouse in the county the property is located during normal business   hours. This is a public auction and anyone can attend. Once the sale has occurred there is   <u>no</u> redemption period in Utah. The sale will be canceled only if there was a last minute   bankruptcy filing (prior to the time of the sale) or at the lender's request prior to the new   deed being file

IV.   **Title**

Foreclosure attorneys make no representations as to warranties or title, or anything for that matter. Buyer-beware! If you are buying a property in foreclosure as an investor, remember that you may not just be buying the home and property. You are buying whatever the legal description describes, along with any potential hidden defects. There have been cases where no house even exists, or the legal description could be a 10 foot piece of grass behind the house. The property may even have undiscovered liens and encumbrances.

V.   **Deed**

There are several forms of deeds, and it is important to understand each kin Deed types include:

A.   Warranty Deeds

B.   Special Warranty Deeds

C.   Quit Claim Deeds

D.   Trust Deeds

E.   Trustee's Deed

The bank or lending institution is typically foreclosing on a property where a warranty deed was put in place. But the deed that you receive through purchasing a foreclosure is a Trustee's deed. There is no title insurance of any kind when purchasing a foreclosure; however, it can be obtained afterward through a title company.

VI.   **Eviction**

The **eviction process** through foreclosure is slightly different than a rental type eviction. Rental's require a (3) day **Pay or Vacate notice** to start the procedure, while foreclosures require a (5) day Notice to Vacate.

Once the sale has taken place, anyone living in the property is now illegally occupying the home. After the 5 day notice expires, a writ and order of restitution is file The entire process typically takes about 21 to 30 days depending on if there is a hearing or not.

The people occupying the property typically always leave prior to the end of this process.

If not, then a Sheriff will serve them with a 3 day notice. After the 3 days you can call and have a constable or sheriff conduct a lockout on the property. This is extremely rare. It is the new owner's responsibility to call a lock smith and have the property opened. The Sheriff will enter the property and escort the people off the grounds. The Sheriff will then post notices on the property alerting the former owner of the consequences of illegally trespassing or entering their former property.

VII. **Fraud**

Many foreclosures are involved in fraud at some point. This is why title searching prior to the sale is so important. Types of fraud include:

A. Fraudulent deeds

B. Duplication of deeds

C. Multiple closings at different title companies with different lenders on the same day.

D. Straw buyers

E. Money paid outside of closing and not disclosed on the HUD

F. Private lenders selling their position to several different lenders undisclosed to them.

VIII. **Legal Information**

One recent change on a national level is that renters are allowed to stay in the property for the duration of their contract plus 90 days. If no contract exists, or if the renters were on a month-to-month rental contract, then they get 90 days. There are several restrictions, but this new law has not been challenged through the courts very much yet.

IX. **Credit**

As mentioned earlier, foreclosure can be caused by many unfortunate events. No reasonable person purposefully sets out to default on a loan. For those that have been through the foreclosure or bankruptcy process, a natural question is their ability to ever attain homeownership again. Credit bureaus are used to obtain information on an individual's payment behavior. Their report on your credit history can make or break a home purchase. It is important to know how the credit reporting agencies work and how some lenders view negative information they see on these reports for credit decisions.

A. **Credit bureaus** assemble credit data on borrowers creating a risk model, called a credit score.

1. The credit score is a quantitative risk value, with the sum of all values formulated into a single score based on many components about the borrower including:

a. Level of delinquencies

b. Time since last delinquency

c. Proportion of revolving balances to credit limits

d. Bankruptcy:

i. **Chapter 7 bankruptcies** remove all debt from the borrower that is not re-affirmed. A chapter 7 bankruptcy is complete on discharge from the court.

      ii.   **Chapter 13 bankruptcy** always requires monthly payments on at least a portion of the borrower's debt. A Chapter 13 bankruptcy is complete after all the payments have been made. Some lenders may use the court discharge date, which is at the beginning of the payment period, or the final payment date to measure the required time perio

    e.   **Foreclosure** or **deed-in-lieu of foreclosure**.

    f.   **Debt write-offs** need to be explained and may result in minimum waits similar to the above waiting periods depending on the cause of the negative credit event.

    g.   Recent inquires (may need to explain and/or verify that no new unreported debt has been obtained).

2.   **FICO score** is a statistical score used by lenders to gauge the credit risk of borrowers.

3.   There are three credit bureaus:

    a.   Equifax

    b.   Experian

    c.   Trans Union

4.   Each credit bureau issues a unique score using its own model. The three separate scores from the different bureaus will vary.

5.   An underwriter typically uses the middle score from the three bureaus for compliance to underwriting guidelines for the mortgage program requested.

6.   The higher the score, the better the credit, leading to more favorable underwriting and loan pricing guidelines.

7.   FICO scores have a range of 300 to 850:

    720/40-850 excellent

    700-740 very good

    660-700 generally acceptable

    640-660 marginal

    Below-620 caution

B.   **Credit reports** generally have a section detailing a borrower's credit history. This section is divided out into sections.

1.   Creditor Name and Account Number

2.   Date Reported / Last Activity – When the creditor last reported the information and when there was last activity on the account.

3.   Date Opened – When was the account opened?

4. High Credit – What is the highest possible credit limit or loan amount?

5. Current Balance – What was the current loan balance of the debt at the time of the last report date?

6. Past Due Amount – if there is a past due amount, this shows how much at the last reporting.

7. Months Reviewed – How many months has the debt been reported?

8. Times Past Due – How many times has the debt been paid 30, 60, or 90+ days past due.

9. Payment/Term – Shows the minimum payment and how many payments have to be made to pay loan off.

10. Present Status- this will show if the debt is "Paid As Agreed," closed, late, in collection, "charged-off," et

X. **Lending Guidelines for the Credit Challenged**

For those that have negatively reported accounts on their credit report, all hope is not lost. In fact, our lending society does allow borrower "repentance" of sorts. What seems to be the running theme of when and how credit can be given again is based on the following: *When the borrower had their financial mishap, how did they respond?* Being proactive about the credit lines that are still open and showing a consistent payment history after a negative event will be key in an underwriter's decision. Guidelines are different with each lender. FHA, Fannie Mae, and Freddie Mac will lend to borrowers that have been through a previous foreclosure, or even bankruptcy.

A. FHA guidelines to consider a loan for those that have bankruptcies and/or foreclosures can vary greatly depending on the circumstances.

1. **Chapter 7 Bankruptcy**: Generally a minimum of 2 years must have elapsed since the discharge date, but usually takes up to 4 years after discharge date for approval.

2. **Chapter 13 Bankruptcy**: Under extreme circumstances, consideration may be given for those individuals that have 1 year of satisfactorily making payments as stipulated in the chapter 13 discharge. Typically, FHA would prefer 2 years to have elapsed since the discharge date. The bankruptcy court trustee's written approval would be neede A full explanation should accompany the application and the applicants must have re-established good credit.

3. **Foreclosure**: Three years must pass from the date of the foreclosure before FHA will consider granting loan approval. An exception to rule would be if the foreclosure was the borrower's main residence and an extenuating circumstance can be proven. Good credit must have been re-established to be considered.

B. Fannie Mae guidelines to consider a loan:

1. **Chapter 7 Bankruptcy**: A minimum of 4 years must have elapsed since the discharge date.

2. **Chapter 13 Bankruptcy**: As little as 2 years must have passed since the discharge date. Extenuating circumstances must be proven and investment properties are not eligible under this time-frame.

    3.   **Foreclosure**: 7 years from the date of foreclosure.

C.   Freddie Mac guidelines to consider a loan:

Chapter 7, 13, or Foreclosure: Typically 7 years must have passed in order for Freddie to consider approval.

D.   Note: Participation in credit counseling programs are generally looked upon by credit granting agencies in a similar manner as a Chapter 13 bankruptcy filing.

XI.   **Re-Establishing Your Credit**

Once a bankruptcy or foreclosure is reported on credit, it now is up to the individual as to how he/she will handle the situation. Being proactive about the credit profile and future payments will be critical if future credit on good terms is desire Re-establishing credit will take years, but it shouldn't be an intimidating task. Having the determination to rebuild what was destroyed is the mark of great character.

Several means are available to you to immediately begin re-establishing credit.

A.   If accounts remain with balances, continue to pay according to the terms set forth.

B.   Maintain at least 4 credit references or accounts. Make sure that one is housing-related which includes rental payments. If rental payments are made and you would like to apply for a mortgage in the future, be prepared to show proof with:

    1.   Bank statements

    2.   Money orders

    3.   Canceled/cleared checks

C.   Pre-paid credit cards are available. The higher the limit the better.

D.   Maintain a good mix of open account types including:

    1.   Revolving

    2.   Installment

    3.   Mortgage

    4.   Charge/retail

Foreclosure and Credit Terms to Know

- ☐ Deed-in-Lieu
- ☐ Eviction
- ☐ Fair, Isaac and Company (FICO)
- ☐ Foreclosure
- ☐ Judicial Foreclosure
- ☐ Notice of Default (NOD)
- ☐ Promissory Note
- ☐ Quit-Claim Deeds
- ☐ Sheriff Sales
- ☐ Special Warranty Deeds
- ☐ Trust Deeds
- ☐ Trustee's Deed
- ☐ Warranty Deeds or General Warranty Deeds

Mortgage Law

I.   **Definition of Terms**

    A.   **Title**: An abstract term denoting ownership.

    B.   **Deed**: A document that provides evidence of ownership or of holding title.

    C.   **Hypothecation**: Giving something as collateral or security, without giving up possession.

    D.   **Pledge**: Giving something as security and giving up possession.

    E.   **Equitable title**: After a purchase agreement has been signed, the seller holds title in name only, without full ownership rights. However, the buyer now holds equitable title, which gives him the right to transfer his rights as buyer by assignment. Equitable title is negotiable and assignable. It can be sold, given away, or mortgaged; and it passes to the purchaser's heirs and devisees upon the purchaser's death.

II.   **Theories of Mortgage Law**

    A.   **Title theory**: States that follow a title theory approach to mortgages view the mortgage as a conveyance of title to the mortgagee (lender). Only when the mortgagor (borrower) pays off the mortgage will title pass to the mortgagor. Because the mortgagee holds title during the life of the loan, the mortgagee can take possession of the property at any time; however, this usually doesn't happen until the borrower defaults.

    B.   **Lien theory**: A majority of states are lien theory states. This approach views the mortgage as a lien on the property. This means that the mortgagor is the owner of the property, but the mortgagee holds a security interest in it. Only upon foreclosure can the mortgagee claim its security interest and take possession of the property.

    C.   **Intermediate theory**: This theory applies the lien theory until the borrower defaults on the mortgage, whereupon the title theory then applies.

    D.   **Estoppel Certificate**: Current information regarding a loan given by the lender in response to a release signed by the borrower or an order from the court.

    E.   Utah has statutes for both lien and title theory. The Uniform Real Estate contract is written implying title theory (more information on this later in the chapter). However, the courts have held that Utah is a lien theory state. See *Bybee v, Stuart,* 189 P.2d 118, 122-123, (Utah 1948) and *BMBT, LLC v. Miller*, 2014 UT App 64, ¶¶9-10

III.   **How a Mortgage Works**

Though the generic term "mortgage" is used to refer to any debt that is secured by real property, there is a document specifically called a mortgage.

    A.   **Promissory Note**: A contract that documents, and is primary evidence, of the loan. It indicates how much was borrowed, the payment, interest, amortization, term, et The borrower is known as the maker or payor; the lender, the payee.

    B.   **Mortgage**: A document called a mortgage is given as security for a note. Though a note is valid without a mortgage, a mortgage has no purpose or function without a note.

1. A mortgage is a **judicial lien**, and foreclosure must be pursued through the courts.

2. The parties in a mortgage are:

    a. **Mortgagor** = borrower

    b. **Mortgagee** = lender

C. **Mortgage foreclosure process**: This is a <u>judicial</u> process.

1. The mortgagee, seeing the mortgagor is in default, files a "Complaint" with the court.

2. A **Lis Pendens** is filed against the property, giving public notice that there is pending court action. Even though the lis pendens has been filed, the owner/borrower can still sell the property, but the sale would be subject to the court action.

3. **Notice** is posted on the property and in at least three public places. The first mortgagee is notified of the action if the foreclosure is being brought by a junior lien holder. Any others, such as the holder of a mechanic's lien or second mortgage, must file a "Notice of Interest" if they want to be notified of a foreclosure action brought by another party.

4. The mortgagor is notified and given the opportunity to respond to the complaint. If there is no response, the court may give a default judgment which greatly expedites the process.

5. A court date is set, court is held, and a judgment (the decision of the court), is rendered.

6. The right of the defaulting mortgagor to bring the obligation current and avoid the sale before it is held is called the borrower's *equity of redemption*.

7. The **Sheriff's Sale**:

    a. A date is set for the sale to take place.

    b. A three week advertising period is required during which the property must be advertised in the legal section of a local paper at least once a week.

    c. The three weeks is followed by a ten-day moratorium.

    d. The sale must take place within 10 days following the moratorium.

    e. The sale is held, usually at the county courthouse. A buyer bids and buys. He then must pay cash for the property.

    f. The buyer receives a "Certificate of Sale," which is not a deed.

8. **Statutory period of redemption**:

The statutory period is six months.

    a. During this time, the mortgagor retains the right of possession.

    b. The mortgagor must redeem (rather than reinstate) the property to retain ownership. Redeem means to completely pay off all liens against the property.

9. The buyer receives a **Sheriff's Deed** after the statutory period of redemption has passed and the mortgagor must voluntarily give up the property.

10. With the exception of a non-recourse loan, if the mortgagee fails to get the full amount owed through a subsequent sale, they can sue the borrower and obtain a deficiency judgment. This judgment lien is enforceable and collectible in the same manner as any judgment at law. A non-recourse loan means the <u>only</u> means for collecting the amount owed is the foreclosure process itself

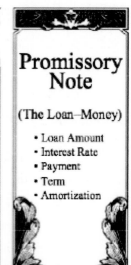

IV. **Trust Deed & Note**

A. This legal process for securing a loan may be used instead of a mortgage.

B. The parties in a Trust Deed and Note include:

1. **Trustor** = borrower

2. **Trustee** = third party

3. **Beneficiary** = lender

C. A Trust Deed and Note is a non-judicial security instrument which avoids the courts and, therefore, hastens the process of foreclosure as well as making it less expensive.

1. The trustor (borrower) conveys the power of sale, sometimes referred to as bare title or naked title, to the trustee. This power of sale can only be exercised if default occurs.

2. The trustor retains title and, thus, will have full right to any increase in value between the date of the purchase and full payment of the loan.

3. The beneficiary has no ownership interest in the property whatsoever.

D. When the loan payments are in arrears, the beneficiary notifies the trustee to proceed with foreclosure.

E. Foreclosure: With a trust deed this is a **non-judicial process**.

1. The trustee, as instructed by the beneficiary, files a "**Notice of Default**," which gives public or constructive notice of the foreclosure action.

2. Notice requirements are the same as for a mortgage foreclosure, see   under *Mortgage foreclosure process* .

3. Depending on state law, an **Equitable Period of Redemption** follows the Notice of Default. This period is determined by statute (e.g., three months).

4. During the redemptive period (if there is one), the trustor has the right to reinstate his loan by paying all back payments and penalties. This stops the foreclosure action.

5. The advertising and moratorium requirements are the same as for mortgage foreclosure, see a, b, c, and d. on the previous page.

361

6. Trustee's Sale:

    a. A buyer bids, pays cash, and receives a Trustee's Deed, sometimes referred to as a Foreclosure Deed. Often the only bidder is the beneficiary or lender.

    b. Depending on state law, the beneficiary could sue and obtain a deficiency judgment. This issue is state specific. In Utah, a lender has three months to sue for a deficiency judgment.

7. Some states allow a statutory redemption period after the sale as mentioned in the discussion on mortgage foreclosure.

8. **Forbearance**: The lender holds off on initiating the foreclosure action to give the borrower a chance to straighten things out. However, they do not forfeit the foreclosure right if they want to proceed with it later.

V. Uniform Real Estate Contract

This document is also known as a **Land Contract**, an Installment Sales Contract, or a Contract for Deed.

A. Special characteristics:

It contains both the note and the security agreement in one document.

1. It is written as though Utah were a title theory state. The lender retains legal title to the property until the debt is paid in full. However, the buyer (borrower) holds equitable title.

B. Remedies for default: The lender can choose one of the following remedies as provided for in the contract. They are:

1. Treat all money received as rent and evict the borrower (buyer) by filing an unlawful detainer action. This process is called forfeiture and is similar to repossession;

2. Bring suit to recover all delinquent payments, penalties, and attorney fees or damages; or

3. Foreclose.

C. It would probably not be wise to use a Uniform Real Estate Contract if a trust deed and note could be used instead.

1. Though the right to repossess the property in case of default may look attractive to the seller, the courts are reluctant to let the lender repossess the home if the buyer has significant equity in the property.

2. A trust deed and note cannot be placed behind an already existing Uniform Real Estate Contract because the lender cannot pass title as required in a trust deed and note.

VI. All Inclusive Trust Deed

This form of security instrument is functionally like a trust deed. The words *All Inclusive* indicate it is used to "wraparound" one or more underlying loans. It is foreclosed in the same manner as a trust deed.

Mortgage Law Terms to Know

- ☐ All Inclusive Trust Deed (AITD)
- ☐ Beneficiary
- ☐ Certificate of Sale
- ☐ Collateral or Security
- ☐ Complaint, Filing a
- ☐ Deed in Lieu of Foreclosure
- ☐ Deficiency Judgment
- ☐ Equitable Period of Redemption
- ☐ Equitable Title
- ☐ Estoppel Certificate
- ☐ Foreclosure
- ☐ Forfeiture
- ☐ Hypothecation
- ☐ Intermediate Theory
- ☐ Land Contract
- ☐ Lien Theory
- ☐ Lis Pendens
- ☐ Mortgage
- ☐ Mortgagee
- ☐ Mortgagor
- ☐ Non-Recourse Loan
- ☐ Notice of Default
- ☐ Notice of Interest
- ☐ Pledge
- ☐ Power of Sale
- ☐ Promissory Note
- ☐ Sheriff's Deed
- ☐ Sheriff's Sale
- ☐ Statutory Period of Redemption
- ☐ Title Theory
- ☐ Trust Deed (Deed of Trust)
- ☐ Trustee
- ☐ Trustee's Deed
- ☐ Trustee's Sale
- ☐ Trustor

Mortgage Law Quiz

1. The process of giving something as collateral for a loan without giving up possession is:

    A. Pledge

    B. Title

    C. Deed

    D. Hypothecation

2. If the borrower is required to sell his property when foreclosure takes place, he lives in what type of state?

    A. Lien theory

    B. Intermediate theory

    C. Title theory

    D. .Deed theory

3. If a Sheriff's Sale is held, the document that dictated the foreclosure process was a:

    A. Uniform Real Estate Contract

    B. Mortgage

    C. Trust Deed and Note

    D. Deed in Lieu of Foreclosure

4. If a trustor wanted to give his property back to the lender in exchange for having the loan forgiven and canceled, and if the lender would agree, this would be accomplished with a:

    A. Uniform Real Estate Contract

    B. Mortgage

    C. Trust Deed and Note

    D. Deed in Lieu of Foreclosure

5. In a Trust Deed and Note, the trustor conveys to the trustee:

    A. Power of Sale

    B. Power of Lien

    C. Power of Attorney

    D. Power of Foreclosure

6. An investor goes to a sheriff's sale, bids and wins the bid. That day when he pays for the property he will receive which of the following as evidence of his purchase?

    A. Certificate of Sale

    B. Trustee's Deed

    C. Sheriff's Deed

    D. Special Warranty Deed

7. When foreclosure proceedings under a mortgage are initiated against a property, which of the following must also be recorded against the property?

    A. Mechanic's lien

    B. Sheriff's lien

    C. Lis pendens

    D. Complaint

8. Utah is which of the following?

    A. Title theory state

    B. Intermediate theory state

    C. Mortgage theory state

    D. Lien theory state

9. The buyer at a Trustee's sale receives which of the following?

    A. Sheriff's Deed

    B. Trustee's Deed

    C. Uniform Real Estate Contract

    D. Certificate of Sale

10. The advantage or the lender when a Uniform Real Estate Contract is used is that in the event of default by the buyer the lender has the possibility of a process called:

    A. Hypothecation

    B. Estoppel

    C. Forfeiture

    D. Cancellation

11. In the Uniform Real Estate Contract, the borrower holds:

    A. Legal title

    B. Equitable Title

    C. No title

    D. Full title

12. MATCH THE FOLLOWING:

___ TRUSTOR   A. Lender

___ TRUSTEE

___ BENEFICIARY   B. Borrower

___ MORTGAGOR

___ MORTGAGEE   C. Third Party

Taxation

I. **Tax Deductions for Homeowners**

A real estate licensee needs to have an understanding about how various tax situations will affect their buyers and sellers.

A. **Tax deductions** are very important in calculating the final income tax owed. Some deductions which are directly associated with the ownership of real estate include:

1. Mortgage interest on up to two homes. The 2nd home could be a boat or an RV if it meets the requirements.

2. Mortgage discount points, if paid in cash at closing. Buyer can deduct them even if they are paid by the seller for the buyer.

3. Mortgage pre-payment penalties. (Note: Items 1,2, and 3 are all forms of interest)

4. Property taxes.

5. Home office.

B. **Allowable deduction**s change as the tax laws change. If there is any question about deductibility, or the issue is material to a decision to buy/rent or not to, advise the person to seek the counsel of their tax accountant.

1. Example of how tax deductions benefit a homeowner. Assume a person is earning $65,000/ year with no deductions, paying $900/month in rent vs. the same person buying a home for $1200/month (Assumes $180,000 loan at 5%, monthly payment includes Principal $197, Interest $825, Taxes $133, Insurance $45) Interest and property taxes are deductible : $825 + $133 = $958 X 12 months = $11,49

Rent		Buy	
Gross Income	$65,000	Gross Income	$65,000
- Deductions	-0	- Deductions	-11,496
Taxable Income	$65,000	Taxable Income	53,504
X Tax Rate	x28%	X Tax Rate	x 28%
Income Tax Due	$18,200	Income Tax Due	$14,981

C. In this example we see that this renter is paying $3219/year more in income tax than if they purchased the house. Their monthly cost of buying the house was $3600/year more than renting. After tax savings they would only pay $381/year more (the difference in monthly payment $3600 and lowered taxes $3219). So for $381/ year extra they receive the principal pay down of their mortgage and all future appreciation. Income is taxable in the year it is realized, or received. For instance, Mr. Meeks rents an apartment to Mr. Blackburn in June with a one year lease. When they sign the lease Mr. Blackburn pays the first month's rent of $800 and last month's rent of $800. Even though $800 for the last month's rent is applied to the following year, all $1600 is taxable in the year it was received.

II. Tax Credits

A. A **tax credit** is different from a tax deduction. A tax deduction is subtracted from the gross income before multiplying the taxable income by the tax rate as in the example above. A tax credit is subtracted from the income tax due after any deductions have been taken.

B. Tax credits are allowed in rare cases and are for specific reasons. For example, there may be a tax credit offered to first time home buyers. Using a tax credit of $8000, the tax benefit for the first full tax year of the home buyer would be calculated as follows:

Income	$65,000
- Deductions	-11,496
Taxable Income	53,504
X Tax Rate	x 28%
Income Tax Due before Tax Credit	$14,981
- Tax Credit	- 8,000
Income tax due after Tax Credit	$6,981

III. Tax on Sale of Primary Residence

A. Capital Gain

A concern that home sellers have is if they will have taxes due on the sale of their home. Several rules apply to calculation if the seller will have to pay tax.

Capital Gain is the amount by which the home's selling price exceeds its initial purchase price. The tax owed on a capital gain is called Capital Gains Tax.

1. Capital gains tax exemption for primary residence is currently $250,000 for individuals and $500,000 for couples. Meaning, the first $250,000 of gain for individuals, and the first $500,000 of gain for couples is exempt from capital gains tax. Any amount above the limit is currently taxed at 15%. Two unmarried people who buy a home together can each exempt $250,000 each, totaling $500,000.

2. To qualify for the exemption, the seller(s) must have owned and occupied their primary residence a total of two of the last five years before selling the home. Occupancy does not have to be continuous. The home does not have to be the seller's primary residence at the time of the sale.

3. This exemption can be used over and over again, but it CANNOT be used more often than every 2 years.

4. For married couples, only one spouse's name needs to be on title as long as both spouses meet the occupancy requirements.

5. If title is held in a living trust, the full tax exemption is still available.

6.   You must prove that this is you primary residence to get the exemption. Proof could include car registration, bank accounts, employment, and tax returns.

Calculating capital gain of a primary residence:

Sales price

-Fix up expenses incurred within 90 days prior to accepting an offer

= Adjusted sales price

- Selling Costs

- Cost Basis (Purchase price + allowable costs)

- Capital Improvements or repairs

= Capital Gain

7.   If the capital gain is greater than the seller's exemption, then capital gains tax is due on the amount of gain above the exemption. Currently the capital gains tax rate is 15%.

Explanation of the above items:

a.   **Sales price**: Contract sale price

b.   Costs of fix up to sell as long as they were incurred within 90 days prior to accepting an offer, not just putting the property up for sale.

c.   **Adjusted selling price**: May be lower than the contract sale price if fix up costs were allowed.

d.   **Selling costs** can include commissions, seller paid concessions, title insurance, recording fees, attorney fees.

e.   **Cost basis**: The original purchase price plus costs paid at the time of purchase for commissions, title insurance, and attorney fees. Cost basis CANNOT include finance costs, insurance, utilities, or moving expenses.

f.   **Capital Improvements or repairs**: Three tests for determining Capital expenses:

i.   Does it add value to the overall property? (E.g., remodeled kitchen.)

ii.   Does it prolong the life of the property? (E.g., new roof.)

iii.   Does it change the use of the property? (E.g., finish the basement.)

B.   The following laws no longer apply to the sale of a primary residence:

1.   The two-year "rollover" rule which required the seller to purchase another home of equal or greater value with two years. Now there is no requirement to buy any other home. The seller can simply keep their tax exempt gain and invest or spend it any way they choose.

2.   The $125,000 "once-in-a-lifetime" exemption for people over 5 Age is no longer a factor in receiving the capital gains tax exemption, and it can be taken every two years.

C. Practice problem: An unmarried couple purchased a home together for $210,000, title insurance and recording fees at time of purchase were $1,750. They lived in the home for 2 ½ years then moved into a new home and rented this home out for 2 years. During the first year they owned the home they installed the landscaping, fencing and RV pad at a total cost of $23,000. The homes in the area we appreciating rapidly so they decided to sell the home when their renters moved out. They spent $6,200 for paint and carpet right before listing the house. The home sold in two months for $390,000. They paid 6% commission, $8,000 for the buyer's closing costs, and $2,850 for title insurance, recording, and closing fees. Using the formula for calculating capital gains on a primary residence, determine how much the capital gain was and the capital gains tax due for this situation.

1. Did the seller own and occupy the property 2 out of the last 5 years?

Sales price	$390,000
–Fix up cost to sell (within 90 of accepting offer	-6,200
=Adjusted sales price	383,800
-Selling costs (commission, closing costs)	-34,250
-Cost basis (purchase price + allowable costs)	-211,750
-Improvements	-23,000
Capital gain	$114,800

2. No capital gains tax is owed since the capital gain is less than the $500,000 exemption. Remember that two individuals who own a home together and both occupy it as their primary residence are eligible for $250,000 exemption each, totaling $500,000.

IV. **Tax on the sale of Investment Property**

A. **Appreciation**: The property value increasing over time. Appreciation has a compounding affect. Calculating the value of a property purchased for $180,000 that appreciated at 5% each year for four years would look like this.

1st year $180,000 + 5% = $189,000

2nd year $189,000 + 5% = $198,450

3rd year $198,450 + 5% = $208,373

4th year $208,373 + 5% = $218,791

B. **Depreciation**: The loss in value of a building over time due to wear and tear, physical deterioration, and age. Depreciation is an important concept for investors. The cost of income producing property is recovered through yearly tax deductions. Depreciation reduces the yearly income tax paid by the investor by reducing the reportable net income. However, depreciation also increases the capital gains tax paid by the investor upon selling the property by reducing the basis for figuring gain or loss on the sale or exchange.

1. There are three basic factors that determine how much depreciation you can deduct:

a. Your basis in the property (how much you paid for it);

      b.   The **recovery period** (27.5 years residential and 39 years commercial (set by statute)); and

      c.   The depreciation method used (straight line – equal amount each year).

2.   Two items that are never depreciated: primary residence and land. Primary residence exemption was discussed in the earlier section, and land is not depreciated because it doesn't wear out over time.

3.   Calculating the depreciation of a residential property:

Purchase price – land = building value / 27.5 years = annual depreciation

      a.   Example: Home purchased for $195,000. Appraiser determined that the land was worth $60,000. $195,000 - $60,000 = $135,000 / 27.5 years = $4,909 annual depreciation.

4.   Calculating the depreciation of a commercial property:

Purchase price – land = building value / 39 years = annual depreciation

      a.   Example: Office building purchased for $5,000,000. Appraiser determined that the land was worth $1,650,000.

$5,000,000 - $1,650,000 = $3,350,000 / 39 years = $85,897 annual depreciation

5.   The depreciation deductions that you take in any year reduce your taxable income thus increasing your profit for that year.

C.   **Cost recovery**: IRS term for depreciation.

The owner has been able to deduct the original cost of the building over time through depreciation expense. Any time that a tax payer pays less tax, the IRS considers it a cost, so when the property is sold, the deductions for depreciation are added back or recovered. That's why the IRS considers it cost recovery.

1.   The property owner is also allowed to depreciate capital improvements, such as a new roof. Example: You have owned a warehouse for 7 years and have been depreciating the original cost of the building (not the land), and now it needs a new roof. You can now start a new depreciation schedule for the roof using the same 39 years to calculate the annual amount. Roof $31,000 / 39 years = $795 annual depreciation for the roof.

2.   All depreciation amounts that you take each year for the building and capital improvements reduce your adjusted cost basis for the property, thus increasing the taxable profit you must declare when you sell.

D.   **Adjusted cost basis**: Formula: Cost + Improvements – Depreciation = Adjusted Cost Basis

E.   **Improvements:** Include additions to the property such as a garage, fence, or new kitchen. Maintenance items or "upkeep" are not considered an improvement. Painting and repairing the building is maintenance not improvements.

1. Practice problem: A carwash was purchased for $900,000. The appraiser determined that the land value was $350,000. The new owner bought new equipment totaling $45,000 and kept the property for 6 years. Using the formula above, what is the Adjusted Cost Basis?

    a. Cost   + Improvements   - Depreciation   = Adjusted Cost Basis

$900,000 + $45,000   - $84,615   = $860,385

(Depreciation was calculated by purchase price $900,000 – land $350,000 = $550,000 / 39 years = $14,102 x 6 years = $84,615)

V. 1031 Tax Deferred Exchange

A. The tax on the gain from the sale of an investment property is deferred until some future date. There is no such thing as a "tax free" exchange.

B. The property owner can exchange one or more properties for one or more replacement properties. The idea behind Section 1031 of the IRS tax code is that when a property owner reinvests the sale proceeds into another property, the economic gain has not been realized in a way that generates funds to pay any tax. The taxpayers investment is still the same, only the form has changed, for example vacant land exchanged for an apartment building.

   1. Must exchange "Like for Like" which means any real estate for any other real estate. Does not mean you have to exchange the same type of real estate.

   2. All of the net proceeds from the sale of the relinquished (sold) property must be used to acquire the replacement property in order to be tax deferred.

   3. **Exchange** does not mean trading properties with someone. It means exchanging the equity into other properties. The relinquished property is sold, and the proceeds are used to purchase the replacement property.

C. Types of "**boots**":

   1. **Boot**: Any property received by the taxpayer in the exchange which is not "like-kind" or real estate. Boot is characterized as either cash boot or mortgage boot.

   2. **Cash boot**: Any cash or property received in the exchange that is not mortgage boot.

   3. **Mortgage boot:** Debt relief. If the taxpayer does not acquire debt that is equal to or greater than the debt that was paid off, they are considered to be relieved of debt.

   4. **Qualified intermediary**: Independent party who facilitates the tax-deferred exchange. Cannot be the taxpayer who is doing the exchange and must meet the qualifications of the IRS.

     a. Duties of the **Intermediary**:

       i. Acquire the relinquished property and transfer it to the new buyer

       ii. Holds the sales proceeds to prevent the taxpayer from having actual or constructive receipt of the fund. The taxpayer cannot have access to the proceeds.

        iii.   Acquires the replacement property and transfers it to the taxpayer to complete the exchange.

    b.   The taxpayer may not receive the proceeds or have access to them in any way without disqualifying the exchange.

    c.   The intermediary does not actually take title to the properties. The properties are deeded directly between the parties, just as in a normal sale transaction. The taxpayer's interests in the contracts of the properties being purchased and sold are assigned to the intermediary.

D.   Time lines:

    1.   The taxpayer has 45 days after the date that the relinquished property is transferred to identify potential replacement properties.

    2.   The exchange must be completed within 180 days after the transfer of the relinquished property.

Taxation Terms to Know

- ☐ Adjusted Cost Basis
- ☐ Appreciation
- ☐ Boot
- ☐ Capital Gain
- ☐ Cost Basis
- ☐ Cost Recovery (Depreciation)
- ☐ Deductions
- ☐ Exchange, Tax Deferred
- ☐ Tax Credit
- ☐ Tax Deferred Exchange

Taxation Quiz

1. Which of the following would NOT get $500,000 exempt from income taxes upon selling a primary residence?

    A. A man and woman owning and living together in the home for four years.

    B. A married couple filing jointly who lived there 20 years and then rented it out for four years.

    C. A married couple, both over 55, who owned and lived in it the last 3 years.

    D. Two spinster sisters who owned and lived in the home for many years after inheriting it from their parents.

2. The taxable difference in the exchange of property is known as:

    A. Depreciation

    B. Boot

    C. Cost recovery

    D. Capital gain

3. The purchase price that is paid for a property is referred to as its:

    A. Cost Basis

    B. Adjusted Cost Basis

    C. Capital Improvement

    D. Cost Recovery

4. The least number of years that can be used for computing cost recovery for residential investment property is:

    A. 35

    B. 19

    C. 27.5

    D. 15

5. Gain or loss is recognized as income:

    A. The year after it is realized

    B. The year after it is realized, except in the case of investment situations

    C. In the year it is realized

    D. In the year it is realized, except in the case of commercial properties.

6. Depreciation, as viewed by the IRS is known as:

    A. Appreciation

    B. Cost Recovery

    C. Adjusted Cost Basis

    D. Boot

7. Which of the following cannot be depreciated, regardless of the circumstance?

    A. Personal property

    B. Investment property

    C. Commercial property

    D. Personal residence and land

8. If the cost of an income property was $150,000, the depreciation that had been taken during the period the property was owned was $21,800, and $6,300 worth of improvements had been made just prior to the sale, the adjusted cost basis would be:

    A. $150,000

    B. $171,800

    C. $165,500

    D. $134,500

9. For the ordinary taxpayer, which of the following would be most beneficial to him/her when computing taxes?

    A. Capital gain

    B. Deduction

    C. Depreciation

    D. Tax credit

VALUATION AND APPRAISAL

APPRAISAL & VALUATION

ADVANCED APPRAISAL

MARKET EVALUATION

Appraisal and Valuation

I. **Appraiser Qualifications and Classifications**

An **appraiser** provides an independent, educated and experienced estimate of a specific property's value at a particular point in time. There are different appraiser classifications and they each have specific qualifications.

A. A **state licensed appraiser** may appraise residential real estate up to four units and up to $1,000,000 in value if the property is non-complex. If the property is complex the max value is $250,000.

B. A **Certified Residential Appraiser** may appraise all residential real estate not requiring a development analysis appraisal regardless of value or complexity.

C. A **Certified General Appraiser** may appraise all types of real estate.

D. Real estate licensees, though not licensed as appraisers, may give an opinion as to value so long as they do not call it an appraisal. They may give these opinions in the normal course of their business, such as assisting a seller to set a price when listing a home or a buyer deciding upon a purchase price when making an offer. See Utah Code Annotated § 61-2g-301(1) & (2).

Section 62-2g-301(2) carves out the rule regarding real estate agents valuing property:
"(a) A principal broker, associate broker, or sales agent as defined by Section 61-2f-102 licensed by this state who, in the ordinary course of the broker's or sales agent's business gives an opinion:
(i)regarding the value of real estate;
(ii)to a potential seller or third party recommending a list price of real estate; or
(iii)to a potential buyer or third party recommending a purchase price of real estate."

E. A fee appraiser is hired for a fee, usually by financial institutions.

F. The FHA & VA "approve" appraisers. Lenders who give FHA or VA loans select appraisers from the approved list, and these appraisers must be Certified Residential or Certified General Appraisers.

II. **Essential Parts of an Appraisal**

A. **Date**: The appraiser only takes responsibility for the value of the property he appraises for the day he dates the report. The lender will usually accept the appraised value for the following six months in order to process loans.

B. **Property description**: It is important that everyone agrees that the property description identifies the exact property involved in the appraisal.

C. **Estimate of value**: The appraiser is responsible to give a professional estimate of value, not a guess. Decisions will be made on the basis of the appraiser's valuation; and, therefore, if he is not reasonably accurate he could be liable and be sued.

D. **Signature of the appraiser**: His signature verifies that he accepts the liability and that the estimate is a "professional estimate of market value that can be relied on for decision making."

III.   **The Appraisal Process**

   A.

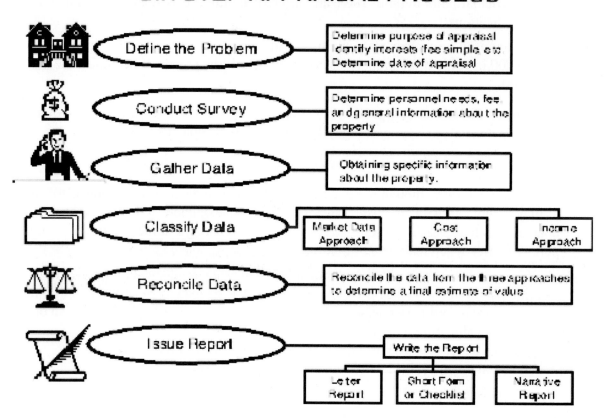

SIX STEP APPRAISAL PROCESS

Define the Problem	Determine purpose of appraisal / Identify interests (fee simple, etc.) / Determine date of appraisal
Conduct Survey	Determine personnel needs, fee and general information about the property
Gather Data	Obtaining specific information about the property.
Classify Data	Market Data Approach / Cost Approach / Income Approach
Reconcile Data	Reconcile the data from the three approaches to determine a final estimate of value
Issue Report	Write the Report / Letter Report / Short Form or Checklist / Narrative Report

IV.   **Reports**

   A.   The loan application process and decision to lend money is heavily dependent on the appraisal report. Lenders have strict guidelines on how much to lend and it's generally based on a maximum percentage of the market value of the property. The Appraisal Report has no margin for error.

   B.   The **Letter Form** is a quick, easy way to report the estimate of value. It is simply a letter that contains the four parts of the appraisal and often is less than a full page. It is used by a buyer or seller who doesn't want to pay much for the report and is only looking for a simple statement of value. Though the report is relatively simple, the gathering of the information and the accuracy of the conclusion should be the same as it would be for any other report form.

   C.   The **Short Form or Check List** is used primarily by institutional lenders since they standardize the effort of many appraisers who may work for the same institution.

   D.   The **Narrative Report** provides an estimate of value and then gives everything reasonable to justify that declaration of value. It includes photographs, maps, inventories, personnel records,

382

as well as comparables and income information and computations. It is used most often for commercial/industrial appraisals, court cases, and by out-of-town buyers. This is the most comprehensive form of appraisal.

V.   **The Nature of Value**

Four Essential Elements of Value

A.   Mnemonic = **DUST**

1.   **Demand** - must be effective demand, meaning it is backed by financial capacity.

2.   **Utility** or usefulness

3.   **Scarcity** - this involves the economic principle of supply and demand.

4.   **Transferability** - you must be able to exchange ownership legally.

B.   All four elements must be present or there is no value.

C.   **Value** is said to be in the eye of the beholder. The "beholder" can be either the buyer or the seller.

D.   Value is sometimes defined as the present worth of future benefits. In other words, how much a person thinks he will enjoy an item tomorrow determines what he will pay for it today.

E.   Value is also referred to as the ability of a thing to command other things in exchange.

VI.   **Types of Value**

A.   **Value in exchange**:

1.   It is an objective approach to value.

2.   It takes the point of view of the purchaser.

3.   It most nearly reflects market value.

4.   Example: The price paid recently for a similar type property.

5.   It answers the question, "What would a buyer who understands value pay to a seller who also knows value?"

B.   **Value in Use**:

1.   It is subjective.

2.   It is determined by the seller (owner).

3.   It often involves emotions which sometimes distort the value.

4.   Example: The value of a home the owner built himself.

C.   **Fair Market Value**: There are four necessary dimensions of fair market value:

1.   Willing buyer.

2.   Willing seller.

3.   Neither the buyer or seller are under duress.

4. The property has been on the market sufficient time for the seller to discover its approximate value.

D. **Market price**: What the property actually sold for in the market place.

E. **Cost vs. Price**: Cost is what was originally paid for something. Price is what it is worth today. In other words, cost is value of the past, price is value in the present.

VII. **Principles of Appraisal**

A. **Highest and best use**: This principle will define what will give the property the highest value for the owner.

 1. Three questions that determine highest and best use.

 a. Is it legal? (E.g., zoning.)

 b. Is it possible? (E.g., considers the physical limitations.)

 c. Of the possibilities that still exist, which use would bring the highest return now and in the future?

 2. Highest and best use is the first principle of appraisal an appraiser must consider. This is especially true when appraising raw land.

B. **Substitution**: The principle of substitution states that no prudent person will pay more for something than he/she has to. It is the basic principle of the comparison approach. If two homes which are very much alike are available, the prudent buyer will purchase the one with the lower price. This is perhaps the most important principal when it comes to the market data approach in appraising.

C. **Conformity**: This principle operates on the idea that value is created and maintained when a reasonable amount of similarity is maintained on properties in a given are Two sub-principles are illustrated below:

 1. **Progression**: A smaller home next to a large one increases the value of the small home.

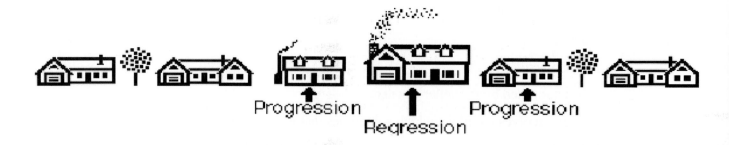

 2. **Regression**: A larger home in a small home neighborhood decreases in value. Regression is sometimes referred to as economic obsolescence.

 3. The most common and obvious application of the principle of conformity is in subdivisions.

D. **Contribution**: This principle says that an improvement must contribute its cost to the value of the property.

   1. The principle of increasing and decreasing returns reveals that adding improvements to property can reach a point where the improvements can no longer contribute to the value.

   2. Example: Building a $15,000 swimming pool on a $70,000 property will probably not add $15,000 to the value. Adding a $4,000 garage might add $4,000 to the value.

   3. Very few items add their full value, and many add little or nothing.

E. **Change or Neighborhood cycle:** This principle is represented by a cycle beginning with growth (integration), progressing to equilibrium, going to disintegration, and perhaps starting over with growth. When appraising, the appraiser must determine where the property is in the cycle. If it is in growth it will be worth more, whereas if it is in disintegration, even though it is in exactly the same condition, it will be worth less.

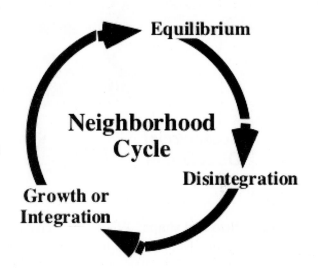

When a developer is building and selling homes in a subdivision, the development is in the growth or integration stage. When the last home is built and sold, equilibrium is achieved. When, and if the owners begin to let their homes run down, deterioration begins.

F. **Anticipation**: This principle takes into consideration benefits that can be derived from future enjoyment or income from the property. For instance, if the appraiser knows there is going to be a commercial development, a school built, or perhaps a freeway constructed nearby, he should reflect these benefits in the statement of value.

G. **Competition**: Competition suggests that when an excess of demand and profits exist, there will be an influx of new producers seeking to increase the quantity of goods supplied. As that trend changes and there is an oversupply, the demand will go down. For instance, split level homes become popular, so contractors and developers build large numbers of them. As they become too common, the demand goes down and it is difficult to maintain their value.

H. **Balance**: Balance is based on an interrelationship between four dimensions of production, labor, capital, management, and land. The idea is to keep a reasonable balance between them so that value is maintained.

VIII. **Some Additional Considerations**

A. **Assemblage/Plottage**:

   1. Assemblage is the process of joining two or more contiguous parcels of property.

   2. Plottage is joining two or more parcels of property to increase value.

385

3.   Plottage is the opposite of subdividing, where property is broken into smaller parcels to increase value.

B.   **Direction of growth**: The value of a property will be higher if it is in the direction of growth, as illustrated below.

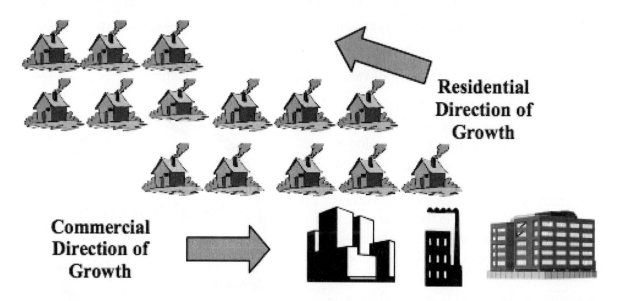

C.   **Size and shape**: When a property is too small to be utilized at its highest and best use, it loses value. Depth is also important. Property close to a street is considered far more valuable than the land at the back of the lot. This is illustrated below. The boundary along the street is called front feet. In a property described as 128' x 119', 128' are the front feet. (See the diagram that follows.)

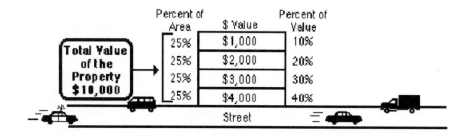

D.   **Situs**: This is a term that captures the essence of the importance of location. It refers to personal preference for a particular location and how that preference or lack of preference, when it is shared by many, affects the value of property.

Appraisal and Valuation Terms to Know

- ☐ Anticipation
- ☐ Appraisal
- ☐ Assemblage
- ☐ Change (Cycle of Change)
- ☐ Competition
- ☐ Conformity
- ☐ Contribution
- ☐ Cost
- ☐ Fair Market Value
- ☐ Highest and Best Use
- ☐ Letter Form Report
- ☐ Narrative Report
- ☐ Plottage
- ☐ Price
- ☐ Short Form (Checklist) Report
- ☐ Substitution
- ☐ Supply and Demand
- ☐ Value

Appraisal and Valuation Quiz

1. Which of the following is NOT a requirement for a valid appraisal?

   A. A designation from an appraisal professional organization such as MAI

   B. The signature of the appraiser.

   C. An estimate of value

   D. A description of the property

2. Which of the following is NOT an essential element of value?

   A. Scarcity

   B. Utility

   C. Cost

   D. Transferability

3. For a commercial project, which of the following appraisal reports would most often be appropriate?

   A. Narrative

   B. Short Form

   C. Letter

   D. Comprehensive

4. Mr. Kelly is trying to decide if he should put in a $15,000 swimming pool to increase the value of his property. He should give consideration to which of the following principles of appraisal?

   A. Substitution

   B. Conformity

   C. Anticipation

   D. Contribution

5. The first step of preparing an appraisal is:

   A. Reconciliation

   B. Gather the data

   C. Determine the purpose or define the problem

   D. Apply as many of the three approaches to appraisal as possible

6. When appraising a vacant lot, the first principle an appraiser should consider is:

   A. Highest and best use

   B. Substitution

   C. Conformity

   D. Define the purpose

7. When all of the homes in a defined area are similar in design and value, it is an example of the appraisal principle of:

    A. Highest and best use

    B. Substitution

    C. Conformity

    D. Change or neighborhood cycle

8. A property which is overpriced due to an emotional attachment created when the owner built the house himself becomes an example of:

    A. Fair market value

    B. Value in exchange

    C. Value in use

    D. Value in distortion

9. When an appraiser is trying to estimate value by finding the best comparables he can, he is applying the principle of:

    A. Highest and best use

    B. Substitution

    C. Conformity

    D. Contribution

Advanced Appraisal

I. **Types of Property**

Appraisers classify all property into one of three categories. They are:

A. **Service properties**: Includes properties used by the public. Also, they are non-profit such as a schools, churches, or government buildings.

B. **Investment properties**: Have a cash flow, such as apartment buildings. Debt service (mortgage payments) is not considered part of cash flow by an appraiser.

C. **Non-investment properties:** No cash flow, such as a homes or vacant lots.

II. **Three Approaches to Appraisal**

There are three approaches to appraisal. They are the market data, cost, and income approaches. When doing an appraisal, the appraiser should use as many of these approaches as are appropriate for the particular property.

THREE APPROACHES TO APPRAISAL
Market Data or Comparison Approach
Cost Reproduction or Cost Replacement Approach
Income or Capitalization Approach

III. **Comparison Approach or Market Data Approach**

The comparison approach is the most commonly used of the three methods because it is a direct reflection of the market place. The basic principle of this approach is substitution. It functions independent of cost. The following are some things to remember about the market data approach.

A. Formula: Comparables + or − Adjustments = Appraised Value

B. The property being appraised is called the subject property.

C. **Amenities**:

1. Amenities are personal pleasure items.

2. Characteristics:

a. They can be tangible or intangible.

b. They can be internal or external to the property.

3. An amenity to one person may not be an amenity to another.

4. Amenities are one of the major items that require adjustment in price when comparing properties.

D. There are three criteria upon which comparable properties are selected by the appraiser:

1. **Date** of the sale of the comparable;

2. **Proximity of comparable** to the subject property; and

391

3. **Similarity** of the comparable to the subject property.

E. Other factors the appraiser would take into consideration are:

1. Terms and conditions of the sale: for example, a foreclosure sale; and

2. If the appraiser has difficulty finding comparable properties which have recently sold, current listings may be considered to give a rough indication of area values. However, the listed price represents the ceiling value or highest price the property would probably sell for. Therefore, the subject property would probably sell for less. Listings or properties currently under contract would not be acceptable as comparables in an appraisal report for most loans.

F. The appraiser should try to avoid making **adjustments** for basic items that can usually be found in the comparables, such as number of bedrooms, number of bathrooms, style (rambler, split entry, two story, etc.), exterior (brick, stucco, etc.), basement, garage, etc. However, sometimes the property is unusual and comparisons cannot be found for any of these and adjustments must be made. The more adjustments that must be made, the greater the opportunity for error.

G. Look at the illustration below. Notice the differences between the subject property and the comparable. The subject property has a fireplace and the comparable does not. The comparable property has a carport and the subject property does not. If the fireplace is worth $1,600 and the carport is valued at $2,750, since the comparable property recently sold for $56,000, what would be the value of the subject property? Assume that all else is comparable.

Subject Property   Comparable Property

The idea is to make the comparable property like the subject property. To do this you would have to eliminate the carport and add a fireplace to the comparable property. The arithmetic would look like this:

$56,000 -- $2,750 + $1,600 = $54,850

After using this method with several properties, the appraiser continues to make adjustments. The appraiser always compares the comparable properties with the subject property; never with each other. He or she does not compute an average because each property is unique and must be matched on its individual merits.

IV. Cost Approach

Sometimes it is difficult to locate comparable properties. Therefore, there has to be another approach that will allow one to arrive at a professional estimate of value. The cost approach is essentially asking what it would cost if the building being appraised were to be built today.

A. **Cost reproduction**: How much would it cost to build an exact replica the building? This approach to appraisal can be difficult and costly since accuracy is important.

B. **Cost replacement**: What does it cost to construct a building having the same utility as the subject property? Since the utility is the key factor, the building may vary in non-essential ways.

C. Formula: Land + Improvements - Depreciation = Value

D. NOTE: The structural improvements (buildings) are depreciated, but land is not depreciated.

E. The cost approach is the only one of the three appraisal approaches which gives a separate, specified value to the land. The comparison, or market data approach, is used to find the value of the land.

F. Methods to determine cost of **improvements** include:

1. **Quantity survey**: The formula is:

2. Materials + Labor + Management Fees + Profit = Value

3. **Unit-in-place**: With this method, the appraiser determines the cost of components or estimates of subcontractors. For instance, what would it cost to have an arched entrance built between the living room and the dining room (component) or what would an electrician charge to do the electrical work (subcontractors).

4. **Cubic foot method**: A value is assigned to each cubic foot in the building. The total value is determined by multiplying the total number of cubic feet times the cost per cubic foot. This method is used when vertical space is considered as valuable as horizontal space, such as in a warehouse.

5. **Square foot method**: This method is the most common method used in the cost approach.

   a. A price per square foot is determined based on features and quality of the improvement and multiplied by the total number of square feet in the property.

   b. The Marshall & Swift Subscription Service is the most commonly used service in Utah to determine the cost per square foot.

   c. When measuring, the appraiser uses outside, not inside, dimensions of the structure.

G. **Depreciation** refers to any problem that causes an actual or accrued loss of value.

1. Three causes of depreciation:

   a. **Physical deterioration**: Something is not working properly, such as a leaky roof or a faulty foundation.

b. **Functional obsolescence**: Everything works fine, but nobody wants it. It is internal to the property such as a poor floor plan, not enough electrical outlets, outdated appliances and fixtures etc.

c. **Economic, or external, obsolescence** (also called locational, political, or social obsolescence): Things that cause economic obsolescence originate outside the boundaries of the property, and are usually considered incurable. Examples would include a run-down neighborhood, high property taxes, depression of the economy, etc. Regression can also equal economic obsolescence.

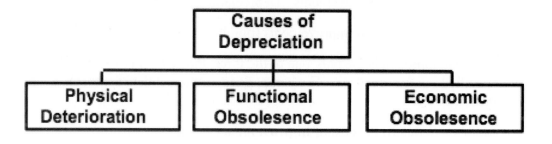

2. **Curable depreciation** occurs when it is cost effective to repair a problem that is causing loss of value.

3. **Incurable depreciation** occurs when it isn't cost effective to make needed repairs.

4. **Deferred maintenance** develops when repairs have been delayed.

V. **Income Approach or Capitalization Approach**

This is a totally different approach from the first two. The appraiser is no longer concerned with what the property is worth, but with how much money it can make. Its value is based on a determination of the present worth of future income.

A. The appraiser is trying to answer the question, "How much will a potential investor pay for the anticipated cash flow?" To determine this, the appraiser is interested in two numbers, the Rate of Capitalization and the Net Operating Income ("NOI").

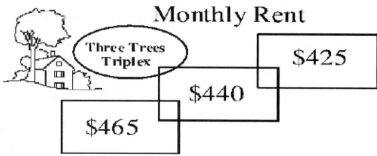

1. The rate of capitalization, sometimes called the cap rate, or rate of return, is a ratio (%) between the value and the net operating income. Value and net operating income can be

obtained from similar, recently sold property giving the appraiser justifiable numbers from which to determine the value of the property.

2. Where does the cap rate come from? The appraiser usually obtains it from comparable sales using the formula. The appraiser finds similar properties which recently sold and using the sales price (value) and the NOI for each property, he determines a cap rate for each.

3. To determine the property's **cash flow**, the following simplified cash flow analysis can be used. The Three Trees Triplex rents three units as indicated in the illustration. It has 12% vacancy and lost rents, 17% operating expenses and has a mortgage payment of $81 From this information, the following cash flow analysis can be developed. All computations are annual.

GSI - Gross Scheduled Income Formula = Gross Total Rents x 12 **$465 + $440 + $425 x 12**	**$15,960.00**
GOI - Gross Operating Income Formula = GSI - Vacancies and Lost Rents Assuming vacancies and lost rents total 12% **$15,960 x 88% (100% - 12%)**	**$14,0400**
NOI - NET OPERATING INCOME Formula = GOI - Operating Expenses Assuming Operating expenses total 17% **$14,0400 x 83% (100% - 17%)**	**$11,657.00**
Cash Flow: CFBT = before taxes, CFAT = after taxes Formula = NOI - Debt Service or Mortgage payments Assuming mortgages total $812 **$812 x 12 = $9,744 subtracted from the NOI**	**$1,9100**

B. Since the appraiser normally treats all purchases as though they were cash, he is most interested in the NOI.

1. To determine the value, the appraiser applies the rate of capitalization, also called the cap rate to the NOI this way: NOI ÷ Cap Rate = Value.

2. If the cap rate was determined to be 11%, the calculation would be:

$11,657 (NOI) ÷ 11% (Cap Rate) = $105,973 (Value)

C.   Characteristics of the **cap rate**:

1.   It is always stated as an annual rate and is sometimes called a rate of return. Thus, some think of it as an indicator of how quickly the investor will recover his investment.

2.   It usually represents the most recent year's performance.

3.   When the cap rate increases, and the NOI remains the same, the value decreases.

4.   When the cap rate decreases, and the NOI remains the same, the value increases.

5.   For instance, in the sample problem, if the cap rate were reduced to 9%, what would be the value of the property?

F $?

R   9%

L $11,657   Solution: $11,657 ÷ 9% = $129,522

6.   When the cap rate increases, the risk increases.

D.   A formula for solving cap rate problems is (see formula in Math A&B):

First=Value

Rate=Cap Rate

Last=NOI

Value x Cap Rate = NOI

NOI ÷ Cap Rate = Value

NOI ÷ Value = Cap Rate

E.   Example: If the value of a property was $200,000 and the NOI was $25,000, the cap rate, or rate of return, could be expressed as:

1.   Dollars -- The property has a net operating income of $25,000.

2.   Time --   If the property continues to perform the same each year it will take eight years to recapture the value, or purchase price.

3.   The net operating income represents 15% return of the value, or a cap rate of 15%. Value = $200,000; NOI = $25,000; thus, the rate of capitalization (or cap rate) would be 15%. ($25,000 ÷ $200,000).

4.   Sample problem: A property with a value of $60,000 had a net operating income of $7,200. What is the rate of capitalization?

F $60,000(Purchase or Sold price)

R   ?%(Capitalization Rate)

L $7,200(Net Operating Income - NOI)

(Answer: A cap rate of 12%. The computation is $7,200 ÷ $60,000 = .12 or 12%)

396

VI.   Age

There are various ways to view the age of a building. Included in them are:

A.   **Physical life or age**: How many years since the building was actually built?

B.   **Economic life or age**: How much longer is it estimated that the building can be productively used?

C.   **Effective life or age:** How many years old is the building when compared to other buildings in its condition? The effective age can be several years more or less than its physical age due to the care it has received.

D.   A building's physical life is generally considered to be longer than its economic life.

VII.   Reconciliation or Correlation

It is the obligation of the appraiser to apply as many of the three approaches as possible. On income property he may be able to use all three. However, once he has completed this task, he must determine the final number he is going to use as the value of the property.

A.   The first step of an appraisal is to state the problem.

B.   The final step before writing the report is to reconcile the results of each of the approaches which have been used.

C.   Each of the approaches may indicate a different value.

D.   One approach may be a more accurate reflection of fair market value than another (it will almost always be the market data approach).

E.   The appraiser never averages, he reconciles.

VIII. Gross Rent Multiplier

Appraisers and investors often use this simple shortcut method to determine a rough estimate of the value of an income property.

A.   It is not an appraisal approach.

B.   It is a "seat of the pants" method ("quick and dirty").

C.   It shows a relationship between the value and the gross rents, but tells nothing else about the property. You don't know what the lot looks like, what the condition of the building is, the floor plan, or anything else.

D.   It is an index number to be used for comparing, not a percentage.

E.   Formula: Selling Price ÷ Gross Rents = GRM (Gross Rent Multiplier)

F.   The **gross rent multiplier** (GRM) can be multiplied by the gross rents of any rental property to determine a rough estimate of value.

G.   Sample problem: A property is being offered at the price of $120,000. Its gross monthly rent is $1,600. Using the information below determine the average monthly GRM and apply it to this property to see if $120,000 is a reasonable price.

GRM   **MO.**

Property A Recently sold for $128,000	Gross rents were $1,500	85.3
Property B Recently sold for $117,000	Gross rents were $1,400	83.6
Property C Recently sold for $134,500	Gross rents were $1,760	76.4

AVG. MONTHLY GROSS RENT MULTIPLIER $85.3 + 83.6 + 76.4 = 245.3 \div 3 = 81.8$

$1,600 \times 81.8 = $130,880$

GRM   **Annual**

Property A Recently sold for $128,000	Gross rents were $18,000	7.11
Property B Recently sold for $117,000	Gross rents were $16,800	6.97
Property C Recently sold for $134,500	Gross rents were $21,120	6.37

AVERAGE GROSS RENT MULTIPLIER $7.11 + 6.97 + 6.37 = 20.45 \div 3 = 6.82$

$1,600 \times 12 \times 6.82 = $130,944$ This property might be worth looking at!

Cap Rate Problems

The property of S. O. Smart was sold at a price based on a net operating income of $13,575 and a capitalization rate of 7%. What was the selling price?

F $

R   %

L $

The Easy Seller property earned a net income of $150 per month. What is the value of the property if the cap rate is 5%?

F $

R   %

L $

An income property improved with a building worth $80,000 showed a net operating income of $8,700. This represented a cap rate of 8%. What was the amount invested in the land?

F $

R   %

L $

O. R. Nottobee owns a property worth $320,000 that nets income equivalent to a 9% cap rate. What would investors pay if they capitalized the property at 11%?

F $

R _____ %

L $

F $

R _____ %

L $

If property taxes increase $700, and the other expenses remain the same, how much value would the property lose with a cap rate of 9%?

F $

R _____ %

L $

Advanced Appraisal Terms to Know

- ☐ Amenity
- ☐ Capitalization Rate or Cap Rate
- ☐ Cost Approach
- ☐ Cubic Foot Method
- ☐ Deferred Maintenance
- ☐ Depreciation
- ☐ Economic Life
- ☐ Economic Obsolescence
- ☐ Effective Age
- ☐ Functional Obsolescence
- ☐ Gross Operating Income (GOI)
- ☐ Gross Rent Multiplier (GRM)
- ☐ Gross Scheduled Income (GSI)
- ☐ Income (Capitalization) Approach
- ☐ Incurable Depreciation
- ☐ Investment Property
- ☐ Market Data (Comparison) Approach
- ☐ Net Operating Income (NOI)
- ☐ Non-Investment Property
- ☐ Physical Deterioration
- ☐ Physical Life
- ☐ Quantity Survey Method
- ☐ Rate of Return
- ☐ Reconciliation or Correlation
- ☐ Service Property
- ☐ Square Foot Method
- ☐ Unit-in-Place Method

Advanced Appraisal Quiz

1. According to appraisers, a public school would be considered which of the following types of property?

    A. Investment property

    B. Non-investment property

    C. Economic Property

    D. Service Property

2. Which of the following is NOT true of an amenity?

    A. It may be internal to the property.

    B. What is an amenity to one person may not be an amenity to another person.

    C. It may be located outside the property boundaries.

    D. They are found only on residential properties.

3. When the cap rate goes up and the net operating income remains the same, the value will:

    A. Remain the same.

    B. Increase.

    C. Decrease.

    D. It depends upon the economy.

4. Which of the following is NOT an example of obsolescence?

    A. Poor floor plan.

    B. Insufficient insulation in the exterior walls.

    C. Increase of property taxes.

    D. Paint coming off the exterior of the building.

5. Land is given as a separate value in which of the following appraisal methods?

    A. Market data

    B. Cost replacement

    C. Income or capitalization

    D. Land is never given a separate value in any of the approaches.

6. When using the comparison approach, the appraiser is attempting to:

    A. Adjust the subject property to the comparables.

    B. Adjust the comparables to the subject property.

    C. Find a property that is exactly identical to the subject property.

    D. Adjust himself so he can divine the value of the property.

7.   In determining the value of an income property, the appraiser is most interested in:

    A. Location

    B. Interest rates

    C. Projections of future expenses and rents

    D. Cash flow

Market Evaluation

I. **Analyzing Property Value**

Whether you are working with a buyer or a seller, it is important to be able to accurately evaluate property. Buyers and sellers were surveyed and said, pricing property is one of the most important services real estate agents and brokers offer. Therefore, the process of researching, gathering data, compiling and presenting should be a process the real estate agent knows well.

A. **Comparative Market Analysis ("CMA")**

A CMA is a report that a real estate agent or broker compiles to assist the buyer or seller in determining either the proper list price, or for a buyer, a proper offer price. The agent should be careful in compiling comparables and suggesting a property value. It is ok to provide opinions of value as long as it is not used for lending purposes. A CMA is usually composed in a format the agent chooses.

B. **Appraisal**

An appraisal is a valuation of property by the estimate of an authorized person. Appraisals are typically used to establish market value for lenders to base the loan amount. Appraisals are also used for either taxation purposes or to discover a possible selling price for the property in question. Appraisals must be completed by a licensed Appraiser. Though a CMA and an appraisal both use comparables, only an appraisal can be used for lending purposes. The seller may choose to pay to have an appraisal completed before establishing a list price.

C. **Broker Price Opinion ("BPO")**

A BPO is used to evaluate property value, but is not used for lending purposes. This type of report is often requested by lenders who have either already foreclosed or are considering it. A BPO is useful to lenders and Relocation companies to analyze data in a format they choose. Each company has their own BPO format. The difference between a CMA and a BPO is that a CMA is done in a format the agent chooses, and a BPO is done in the requesting company's format.

II. **Comparison Approach**

To accurately evaluate a property, we must first have a detailed understanding about the subject property in order to find good comparables. As with all forms of opinions of value, they are only as good as the data is accurate.

A. **Subject Property**

Agents and appraisers begin by gathering all of the specifications of the subject property. For example, the lot size, square footage, number of bedrooms and bathrooms, age, style, garage, and any other amenities such as out buildings, pool, or view.

B. **Comparable Properties**

A good comparable is one that is most like the subject property. Meaning; close in proximity, same style, age, and size. For example, a condo is the easiest to find comparables for, while a unique property is more difficult. The best thing about a comparison approach is that it makes the assumption that if one buyer is willing to pay a certain amount for a particular property, then another buyer must be willing to do the same. As long as the comparables are a good match to the subject property, this usually holds true.

403

C.   **Comparables** in a Changing Market

Because comparables are always sales in the past, they may not always be the best indicator of value just by themselves. In a declining market for example, it may be necessary to adjust comparables by the projected percentage of decline. The opposite is true for markets that are in an appreciation cycle.

D.   **Adjustments** to Comparables

Using comparables in contrast to the subject property requires that opinions of adjustments are made for amenities, size, age, et The adjustments may not always be a true indication of the buyer's opinion. One buyer may see value in a garage, pool, vaulted ceilings, et while another might see little or no value in such amenities.

III.   **Real Estate Factors**

A.   **Price**

Price is the one factor that can make up for all of the other factors and is one that the seller has control over. Though an agent makes recommendations regarding price, the seller is the only one who can put a price on their property.

B.   **Location**

While no one has control over this, it certainly has a lot to do with the value and time on the market. Because property by nature is scarce, the most sought after property holds the highest value and demand, and historically sells for the highest price in the shortest amount of time.

C.   **Condition**

If a property is well maintained and has the amenities that buyers are looking for, then buyers are more drawn to it. The opposite is also true. If a buyer must invest additional money into the property, it will affect its value and could also lower the number of buyers that can financially afford the property. The seller does have control over this factor. The seller could choose to invest monies into improving the condition or leave it the way it is.

D.   **Financing**

The more financing options available, the larger the buyer pool is. The larger the buyer pool, the higher the demand will be. Some properties are difficult to finance. These usually take a unique buyer and much longer to sell.

1.   For example, an estate property that is selling for $10 million, has many great amenities and is in incredible condition, may still take a considerable amount of time to sell because the buyer pool is small.

2.   The seller may consider assisting with the financing options, by either financing the

E.   **Market Conditions**

When the inventory of homes increases, it usually drags down values and increases the days on market. Of course the opposite is also true: a small inventory means less to choose from and decreases the days on market. Neither the seller nor the agents have any control over this factor. Market conditions can vary from one area to another.

F. **Marketing**

Getting the word out about the availability of real estate or any product is essential to whether or not it sells and how long it takes. Reaching the widest audience of buyers will insure the best buyer is found. The real estate agent and his/her company certainly have control over this factor. It is important to accurately explain to the seller what kinds of marketing efforts will be done.

IV. **Other Concepts**

A. **Property Tax Assessments**

In most areas of the country, property is assessed as a way to tax property owners relative to the value of the property. It is always a good idea to review the assessor's evaluation. However, there are many times these values are off from actual market value. Most of the time it's a good way to know your price evaluation is in the "ball park." Never solely rely on the assessor's opinion. Often the assessments are many years old.

B. **Bank Owned Property**

Typically, bank owned properties sell for less than the traditional seller owned properties. If a comparable is bank owned, this may need to be considered and adjusted for.

C. **Buyer Pool**

The amount of buyers that are currently willing and able or qualified that are looking for a type of property similar to the subject property. If the buyer pool is large, then the days on market will be less.

D. **Days On Market**

The amount of time it takes to find and contract with a buyer. Usually this refers to the time between active status on the MLS and to the time the property goes under contract or the seller accepts the date of the offer.

E. **Percentage of List Price**

This statistic illustrates the average percentage amount that sellers actually get for their property. This percentage is also affected by any adjustments to the price and any concessions that are paid.

F. **Price Per Square Foot**

Calculating price per square foot can be a short cut to the approximate property value. The upside to price per square foot is that it simply makes the adjustments by the size of the property. However, this doesn't take into consideration the quality or effective age. Price per square foot is higher in areas that are most sought after and lower in the least desirable areas.

1. With new construction properties, it can be a more effective way of comparing. Just like in existing property, just because the price per square foot is higher does not mean it's "overpriced." The builder may have included more expensive materials or more labor in the finishing of the property.

V. **Buyer's Perspective**

Buyers don't typically compare property the way an agent or appraiser would. Often buyers simply go out shopping in an area they like and look at houses, all styles, ages, and sizes. The properties they chose to see have often been selected from real estate internet sites ahead of time.

A.   It is important to compare the subject property to others in the are Pay attention to where you are priced, and how that relates to how buyers and agents do property searches. When considering price adjustments, ask yourself if it would be helpful to be in a different search bracket, such as below $300,000, or below $250,000. A search bracket is defined as a commonly used range used to search for properties.

B.   Comparing is part of the buying process. Buyers typically shop all of the properties that fit their criteri While doing this, buyers will typically select the house that is the best deal. They consider all of the properties. If some of those properties looked at are over-priced, these over-priced properties help sell the property that is priced right.

C.   Compare a wider are When considering a value, look at a wider area like a buyer would. Consider the following factors:

      1.   How many properties are listed in the area that are similar to the subject?

      2.   .How many of them went under contract?

      3.   What percentage of the active properties go under contract each month?

      4.   This information can be helpful when trying to set realistic expectations like how long it might take to sell.

VI.   **Study the Market Response**

It has been said of many products that the only true way to know of a product's value, is to place it on the market. This is very true for real estate. A professional agent will go to great length to study and account for the response to the market.

A.   As good as the research may be, nothing can be better than evaluating how the real buyers respond. The agent should gather data about how the market is responding to the product being offered for sale. This can be very helpful when it comes time to make decisions about price adjustments.

B.   Feedback from a listing can give a lot of information. For example, how many inquires have there been? How many initial showings have there been? How many of these buyers came back for a second look. This information becomes very valuable to sellers who are trying to make good decisions about their price.

Market Evaluation Terms to Know

- ☐ Appraisal
- ☐ Broker Price Opinion (BPO)
- ☐ Comparative Market Analysis (CMA)

Market Evaluation Quiz

1. ABC Lenders is considering foreclosing a property. To help determine a market value, they may ask an agent for a(n):

    A. Appraisal

    B. BPO

    C. CMA

    D. List of Current Comparables

2. The amount of buyers that can be considered as potential buyers is called what?

    A. Potential buyers

    B. Buyer demographic

    C. Buyer pool

    D. Scarious

3. List the six factors that determine the time it takes a property to sell.

    _____

    _____

    _____

    _____

    _____

    _____

4. Which factor can make up for all of the other factors?

    A. Location

    B. Price

    C. Square footage

    D. Days on Market

5. Which of the factors has the most influence on the amount of buyers in the market?

    A. Financing

    B. Inventory

    C. Overall market conditions

    D. Property prices

6. The same floor plan is built by the same contractor at the same time, with the same materials. Why would one property be valued higher than the other?

   A. Financing

   B. Location

   C. Color choices

   D. The inherent nature of real property

7. What is the only true way to know if the property is priced right?

   A. Obtain a Certified Appraisal

   B. Check the Assessors evaluation

   C. Do a comprehensive CMA

   D. Place the property on the market and see how buyers respond

8. If an agent wanted to visually illustrate comparables to a seller, what format might they use?

   A. BPO

   B. CMA

   C. Stepping Stone Concept

   D. Pricing grid

9. What kind of property is the easiest to find comparables for?

   A. New Construction

   B. Condo

   C. Vacant Land

   D. Bank Owned

10. What statistic is kept to illustrate the amount sellers typically get for their property?

    A. Selling percentage

    B. Percent of List Price

    C. Offer Percentage

    D. Sold Price Percentage

FEDERAL LAWS

FEDERAL LAWS A

FEDERAL LAWS B

FEDERAL LAWS C

TRUTH IN LENDING ACT (TILA)

Federal Laws A

I. **Federal Fair Housing Laws**

A. The first federal housing law of significance in the United States was passed in 186 The law stated that "All citizens of the United States . . . shall have the same right, in every state and territory in the United States, . . . to inherit, purchase, lease, sell, hold, and convey real and personal property . . ." **Civil Rights Act of 1866**, 14 Stat. 27 186

1. The act prohibited race discrimination only, and there were no exceptions.

2. The act was vague and difficult to enforce in many situations.

B. **Fair Housing Act of 1968**, Title VIII (42 U.S. §§ 3601 et. seq.):

1. The act is administered by the **Office of Equal Opportunity** ("OEO") under the direction of the Department of Housing and Urban Development ("HUD").

2. It made it unlawful to discriminate based on any of the following:

    a. Race

    b. Color

    c. Religion

    d. Sex

    e. National Origin

3. The **Fair Housing Act** provides protection against the following acts of discrimination:

    a. Refusing to sell, rent, or negotiate.

    b. Altering terms of the sale or rental agreement.

    c. Advertising that excludes certain groups.

    d. Denying the right to inspect.

4. Exceptions to the 1968 law include:

    a. The owner of three or fewer units who is not using a brokerage service and does not discriminate in advertising.

    b. The sale, rental, or occupancy of dwellings owned and operated by a religious organization for other than commercial purposes to persons of the same religion, if membership in that religion is not restricted on account of race, color, or national origin.

    c. A private club, not open to the public, restricting its lodgings in accordance with its primary purpose may rent to only its own members.

5. Jones v. Mayer, 392 U.S. 409 (1968): A supreme court ruling that held that the private individual could not discriminate in selling or renting real property because of race.

413

      a.   The statute at issue was <u>42 U.S. § 1982</u> (the 1866 civil rights act; see section I. of this chapter above), and whether that statute could apply to private parties or only state action.

      b.   The Court ruled that Congress had the power under the 13th Amendment to enact § 1982 as 'necessary and proper for abolishing the badges and incedents of slavery in the United States.'

      c.   This case made a sharp distinction between § 1982 and the Fair Housing Acts, which apply to more than just racial discrimination.

6.   Certain acts, defined by the following terms, are specifically prohibited:

      a.   **Steering**: Directing customers or clients to or away from certain areas for discrimination purposes.

      b.   **Block busting**: Sometimes called "panic peddling." A broker or developer sometimes tries to persuade home owners that the value of their home is less and they should sell immediately because members of a minority or ethnic group are moving into the neighborhood.

      c.   **Redlining**: Lenders refuse to give loans in specified geographic areas because they are populated by certain groups. In addition to race, lenders cannot discriminate based on marital status, age. or handicap.

      d.   In 2015, the United States Supreme Court ruled that housing providers violate the Fair Housing Act when they institute rules or policies over their units that appear neutral and nondiscriminatory on their face, but, in fact, create a disparate impact (discriminatory effect) on the residents. The intent of the housing provider in instituting these rules is irrelevant. <u>Texas Dept. of Housing and Community Affairs v. The Inclusive Communities Project, In, 135 S.Ct. 2507 (2015).</u>

          i.   An example of a rule creating a disparate impact would be one that requires all doorways to be free of clutter, debris, and décor. While appearing neutral on its face, the rule actually discriminates against those of the Jewish religion because that religion calls for prayer scrolls to be attached to the residence door frame.

7.   Licensees should keep detailed records of all transactions and rentals in order to defend themselves against complaints. Violations are frequently proven through the use of "testers" and the courts have ruled that there is no requirement that the testers be actual bona fide purchasers or renters.

C.   The **1988 Amendment to the Fair Housing Act** added two new protected classes. It became effective March 12, 1989. You cannot discriminate on the basis of familial status (children under 18) or handicap. A **handicapped** individual is defined as:

1. Anyone having a physical or mental impairment which substantially limits one or more major life activities.

2. Anyone having a record of having such impairment.

3. Anyone regarded as having such impairment.

4. Persons who may not be handicapped in fact, but who are incorrectly believed to be handicapped.

5. "Handicapped" does NOT include someone who currently abuses controlled substances. However, if that person has completed rehabilitation treatment, the housing provider may not discriminate against them.

D. Discrimination against the handicapped would include:

1. Refusing to permit reasonable modifications to the property, if the changes are necessary to provide for full enjoyment of the property.

    a. The lessor can require that the changes be made at the expense of the handicapped person.

    b. The lessor can require that s/he approve plans for such changes.

    c. The handicapped person may be required to reasonably restore the premises at his/her expense at the termination of the lease.

2. Refusing to make reasonable accommodations in rules, policies, or practices in order to allow the handicapped person full enjoyment of the premises. For example, a prohibition of pets does not apply to handicapped persons requiring the animals, such as a guide dog for a blind person.

E. Requirements regarding accessibility and adaptability only relate to multi-family dwellings (more than four units) where construction was completed after March of 1991 (two years after the amendment took effect).

1. **Accessibility**: Ground floor units of all buildings must be accessible. If the building has an elevator, all units must be accessible. Accessible means someone in a wheel-chair could get to and into the front door.

2. **Adaptability**: All units which are required to be accessible must also be adapted for the handicapped.

    a. Environmental and electrical controls and outlets are reachable from a wheelchair.

    b. A wheelchair can get through all doorways.

    c. Reinforced bathroom walls to allow installation of grab bars.

    d. Kitchen and bathrooms with space to allow a wheelchair to maneuver.

F.   Discrimination on the basis of **Familial Status:** A building can qualify as an exempted project for the elderly in three ways:

    1.   HUD approved housing specifically designed and operated to assist elderly persons.

    2.   Housing intended for, and solely occupied by persons 62 years of age or older (the elderly).

    3.   A unit that provides housing generally intended and operated for persons 55 years of age or older (the near elderly) that meets certain regulations, including:

        a.   Eighty percent (80%) of the units in the housing project are occupied by at least one person 55 years of age or older.

        b.   Advertise and adhere to written policies and procedures, which demonstrate intent by the owner or manager to provide housing for persons 55 years of age or older.

G.   Penalties and risk reduction: The penalties for violation of fair housing laws can range anywhere from $16,000 to $150,000, as well as putting your license at risk. The following procedures can help alleviate that risk.

    1.   Keep accurate and thorough records.

    2.   Establish systematic procedures for the office and as an individual.

    3.   Use objective criteria in selecting the properties to show buyers or renters.

    4.   Let the customer set the limits.

    5.   Provide a variety of choice.

II.   **Equal Credit Opportunity Act of 1974 ("ECOA") [**15 U.S. §§ 1691et. seq. (1974)**]**

This act focused on discrimination being practiced by lenders. This would include property managers checking the credit of prospective tenants.

A.   It made it illegal to discriminate (in granting credit) on the basis of age or marital status.

B.   The lender cannot make oral or written statements which would discourage a reasonable person from making an application for a loan.

C.   Other things that the lender cannot inquire about include, child care problems and receipt of alimony or child support payments (unless voluntarily disclosed).

D.   Utah note: Utah fair housing laws prohibit discrimination in lending based on the source of funds (such as public assistance).

III.   **Americans with Disabilities Act ("ADA") [**42 U.S. §§ et. seq. (1990)**]**

A.   The purpose of this act is to eliminate discrimination against those with disabilities and allow them to enter the economic and social mainstream. This is done by providing equal opportunities in employment, transportation, communications, and access to goods and services offered by both public and private providers.

B.   Title I of this act covers employment discrimination for employers with 15 or more employees.

C.   Title II covers all levels of government employment, programs, activities, and services, including transportation.

D.   Title III calls for full and equal enjoyment of goods, services, facilities, and privileges of private entities serving the public. These organizations must remove architectural and communication barriers, modify policies, practices and procedures, and provide auxiliary aids or services to remove the discrimination. They may be exempt if to do so would fundamentally alter the nature of the goods or services, would result in an undue hardship, or would pose a direct threat to the health or safety of others. Title III covers owners, lessors, lessees, and operators of places of public accommodation.

It is critical to remember that the ADA has nothing to do with housing. All handicap discrimination issues pertaining to housing fall under the purview of the 1988 FHA Amendment.

Federal Laws A Terms to Know

☐ Americans with Disabilities Act (ADA)

☐ Blockbusting

☐ Equal Credit Opportunity Act (ECOA)

☐ Disparate Impact

☐ Familial Status

☐ Federal Fair Housing Act of 1866

☐ Federal Fair Housing Act of 1968

☐ Federal Fair Housing Amendment of 1988

☐ Redlining

☐ Steering

Federal Laws A Quiz

1. Under the 1866 laws regarding unfair discrimination, which of the following was true:

    A. You could not discriminate because of a person's nationality.

    B. All women had the same rights as men had.

    C. American Indians rights to own property were protected.

    D. All people were to be treated like white people.

2. Under the 1968 fair housing laws, which of the following is not one of the protected classes?

    A. Race

    B. Sex

    C. Age

    D. Color

3. Which of the following persons would be most likely to be found guilty of redlining?

    A. Real estate broker

    B. Title officer

    C. Lending officer

    D. Sales agent

4. Which of the following fits one of the added classes from the 1988 Fair Housing Amendments Act?

    A. A black person.

    B. A paraplegic

    C. A person 50 years old.

    D. A catholic

5. The Americans with Disabilities Act covers all the following situations except:

    A. A mobility impaired person seeking employment.

    B. A blind person who would need to have their Seeing Eye dog at work.

    C. A person who is addicted to illegal drugs.

    D. A wheelchair bound person desiring to attend the theatre.

6. Under the Fair Housing Act, a housing provider's intent to discriminate is irrelevant when it comes to which act?

    A. Rules and policies

    B. Blockbusting

    C. Redlining

    D. Refusing housing

7. When housing rules or policies are instituted that create a discriminatory effect, it is known as:

    A. Discrimination

    B. Disparate impact

    C. Unfair practices

    D. Disparate treatment

Federal Laws B

I. **The-Do-Not Call Registry Act of 2003** [15 U.S. § 6151]

If you call the wrong person, it could cost you $16,000!

A. All real estate licensees must comply with the National Do Not Call rules.

B. Anyone who has placed their number on the Do Not Call list, or registry, must not be called.

C. All businesses must "scrub" their potential contacts' phone numbers against the national registry at least once a month. There are several software products available to assist in that process.

D. A business must also maintain a company **do not call list**.

   1. If you call someone who is not on the national do not call list, but they ask to be put on your do not call list, you must comply within 30 days.

   2. Subsequently, no one in your company should call that phone number.

E. When placing calls, you must let the phone ring for four rings, or 15 seconds before hanging up.

F. You must transmit your caller ID information.

G. If using predictive dialers, check with an attorney as there are many other rules which apply.

H. Allowed phone calls are those exemptions listed below, and the calls must be made between 8 m. and 9 p.m.

   1. Someone with whom there is an **established business relationship**.

      a. It exists for 18 months past the consummation of your last transaction.

      b. It goes forward for three months from the person's initial inquiry.

   2. You or an affiliated company can call, if the service you're calling about relates to the service that was originally provided.

   3. You have express written permission to call.

      a. The Utah Association of Realtors recommended agency contracts have that language preprinted.

      b. It would be a good idea to add language to cover this to any agreements you enter into.

   4. You have a personal relationship with the person. This does not extend to referrals from the person you have the personal relationship with.

   5. If you call any of the exceptions above, they could still request that you put them on your company do not call list. If so, don't call again.

I. Create **"Safe Harbor" procedures** to avoid liability regarding do not call rules:

   1. Have written procedures that comply with the rules.

2. Train all personnel on what those procedures are and document the training.

3. No calls are made without referencing the national do not call registry and the company do not call list. Those lists are updated regularly.

4. Create a process for avoiding calling phone numbers on either list.

J. Do not fax rules and anti-spam rules:

1. Stay up to date on the requirements of these rules.

2. Have procedures and training so licensees in your office stay in compliance as they market properties with fax's or email.

3. Comply with opt-out provisions requirements.

II. Privacy Issues

As a brokerage maintains paper files, electronic files, et all kinds of information is collected about buyers, sellers, lessors and lessees. It is important to protect the privacy of those individuals.

A. Create procedures to protect clients, customers, and anyone else whose personal information is collected. The procedures would cover:

1. Access to file cabinets.

2. Access to electronic files.

3. Information in an agent's PDA or cell phone – what if it's lost, or stolen? What procedures should be followed?

4. What about handwritten notes, later thrown in the trash?

5. Shred, shred, shred!

B. The procedures should be documented in the policies and procedures manual and all agents trained to follow them.

III. Sherman Antitrust Act [15 U.S. § 1-7 (1890)]

The purpose of this act is to promote competition in the open market place. The real estate industry comes under fire from time to time from those asserting the commission rate in a given area comes from "price fixing." A brokerage can establish whatever compensation fee and structure it wishes to. It may be a percentage amount, a flat fee, or a combination of the two. The amount of the compensation is negotiable between the broker (principal) and the buyer or seller (client).

A. Some ways anti-trust laws affect the real estate industry are as follows:

1. **Price fixing** (by colluding with competitors and setting commission rates);

2. Territory agreements among competitors (market allocation);

3. Bid rigging;

4. Group boycotts (boycotting competitors); and

5. Industry discrimination within associations and groups.

If one were convicted of price fixing, the penalty could include time in a federal penitentiary in addition to a substantial fine. Therefore, it is best to *never, under any circumstances,* discuss fees with anyone outside your office except the owner of the property. *See* 15 U.S. § 1.

IV. **Uniform Commercial Code ("UCC")**

    A. The **UCC** is the product of the National Conference of Commissioners on Uniform State Laws and the American Law Institute. The UCC's first drafting began in 1942 and was completed and published in 1952. Since then, the UCC has had several revisions.

    B. The UCC is not federal law but, in basic terms, a suggestion for all the states to adopt to ensure that the law is "uniform" among the states. Each state has its own adoption or adaptation of the UCC, but are all relatively similar to keep uniformity. The UCC governs personal property, sales agreements, banking and commercial paper, and security interests among topics.

    C. The UCC governs many different issues with commerce. For your purposes, know that the UCC governs sales of goods from merchants.

V. **Interstate Land Sales Full Disclosure Act** [15 U.S. §§ 1701 et. seq.]

A law designed to protect the public from unscrupulous developers marketing ownership interests across state lines for properties which are not yet built. Full disclosure is to be made to prospective buyers before they decide to buy. The developer must:

    A. Prepare a statement and register with the Director of the Consumer Financial Protection Bureau.

    B. Deliver a property report to the prospect and obtain a receipt for it.

    C. Give the buyer a seven-day cooling off period.

    D. Some exemptions are allowed, but they fit very narrowly defined specifications.

VI. **Wetlands and Floodplains**

    A. If **groundwater** is at or near the surface enough of the year to produce a wetland plant community, that area is regarded as wetlands.

        1. Examples would be swamps, marshes and floodplains.

        2. These areas are very susceptible to flooding.

        3. They are subject to many federal, state, and local controls.

        4. Often environmental protections apply for preservation and conservation.

    B. **Floodplains** are flat areas of land near waterways that are subject to overflowing.

    Building in these areas is often restricted by government controls.

        a. Wetlands and floodplans are typically regulated and controlled by the U.S. Army Corps of Engineers.

        1. Properties in floodplains identified by FEMA will require flood insurance

Federal Laws B Terms to Know

- ☐ Bid Rigging
- ☐ Do Not Call Registry
- ☐ Established Business Relationship
- ☐ Group Boycott
- ☐ Industry Discrimination
- ☐ Interstate Land Sales Full Disclosure Act
- ☐ Market Allocation
- ☐ Price Fixing
- ☐ Sherman Anti-Trust Act
- ☐ Uniform Commercial Code
- ☐ Steering

Federal Laws B Quiz

1. The Uniform Commercial Code is:

    A. The code with the little bars for scanning at the supermarket

    B. The code that ties the product to a specific commercial on TV

    C. The code that indicates whether a business can be sold.

    D. The code that applies when selling personal property, such as merchant goods

2. According to the Do Not Call law, it is okay to hang up after:

    A. 4 rings or 15 seconds

    B. 3 rings

    C. Anytime

    D. At least 30 seconds, no matter how many rings

3. The best way to get rid of private information is:

    A. Throw it away

    B. Send it back

    C. Put it in the recycling bin

    D. Destroy it

4. The Do Not Call law allows phone solicitations between what times?

    A. 7:00am - 5:00pm

    B. 8:00am - 5:00pm

    C. 9:00am - 9:00pm

    D. 8:00am - 9:00pm

5. If two agents collude to charge the same commission rate, which law is at play?

    A. Uniform Commercial Code

    B. Interstate Land Sales Full Disclosure

    C. Sherman Antitrust

    D. Contract law

6. Real estate agents are governed by the Do Not Call law:

    A. True

    B. False

Federal Laws C

I. **Comprehensive Environmental Response Compensation & Liability Act** ("CERCLA") [42 U.S. §§ 9601 et. seq.]

   A. **CERCLA** is also known as the Superfund Act.

   B. This act contains prohibitions and requirements relating to hazardous waste sites that are closed and abandoned.

   C. It provides for liability of those who were responsible for the release of hazardous waste at those sites.

   D. It establishes a trust fund to provide for cleanup when it is not possible to identify and find a responsible party.

   E. In the chain of ownership beginning when the pollution started up to the cleanup process, all owners could be held responsible.

      1. If there is the least suspicion of pollution on a property a client is considering buying, they might want to get an environmental impact study done.

      2. Even though the buyers, themselves, did not contribute to the pollution or toxic waste, they could still be held responsible for costs of cleanup.

II. **The Superfund Amendments and Reauthorization Act (SARA)**

The Superfund Amendments and Reauthorization Act (SARA) amended the Comprehensive Environmental Response, Compensation, and Liability Act (CERCLA) on October 17, 1986. The SARA amendments included the following:

   A. Stressed the importance of permanent remedies and innovative treatment;

   B. Required Superfund actions to consider the standards and requirements found in other State and Federal environmental laws and regulations;

   C. Provided new enforcement authorities and settlement tools;

   D. Increased State involvement in every phase of the Superfund program;

   E. Increased the focus on human health problems posed by hazardous waste sites;

   F. Encouraged greater citizen participation in making decisions on how sites should be cleaned up; and

   G. Increased the size of the trust fund to $8.5 billion.

SARA also required EPA to revise the Hazard Ranking System to ensure that it accurately assessed the relative degree of risk to human health and the environment posed by uncontrolled hazardous waste sites that may be placed on the National Priorities List.
- Superfund, https://www.epgov/superfund/superfund-amendmentes-and-reauthorizations-act-sara (last visited Dec, 29, 2016).

III. **Environmental Disclosure**

A. Real estate licensees are expected to obey all lawful instructions of the principal and fulfill all other fiduciary duties of an agency relationship. Although there is no specific disclosure form at this time for mold, radon, et, real estate professionals should make their principals aware of the ramifications of non-disclosure.

B. If you, as an agent, suspect a home of having any type of environmental issue and your principal is not forthcoming with details, you should consult with your broker and discuss the right course of action. Never put yourself in a position that could jeopardize a wonderful and fulfilling career!

IV. **Environmental Protection Agency ("EPA")**

A. The purpose of an **environmental impact statement** ("EIS"), also called an environmental impact report, is to show in one document the environmental effects of a project. This is part of the process of obtaining approval to proceed with a development. It could deal with many environmental issues, some of which are: noise, air quality, water and sewage, drainage, wildlife and vegetation, radon gas, lead-based paint, asbestos, mold, and toxic waste.

B. **Lead-based paint disclosure**

1. 24 F.R. 35.88(a) (1999) Requires:

a. Disclosure of known lead-based paint or hazards in residential dwellings built prior to 1978;.

b. Pamphlet "Protect Your Family From Lead in Your Home" is given to buyers and renters;

c. Buyers get a 10-day period to conduct an inspection or assessment at their own expense, if desired; and

d. Language in contracts assuring the disclosure took place.

2. Not required: Any testing, removal, or abatement. The lead-based paint requirement does not invalidate leasing or sales contracts.

3. Housing exempt from the disclosure requirement includes See 24 F.R. 35.82 (2014):

a. Housing sold at foreclosure;

b. Housing being leased that have been found to be free of lead-based paint by an inspector certified under the Federal certification program or under a federally accredited State or tribal certification program;

c. Short-term leases of 100 days or less, where no renewal or extension can occur; and

d. Renewals of existing leases in housing in which the lessor has previously disclosed all information required under the law and where no new information has come into the lessor's possession.

4. The parties and the agent must keep records of the lead-based paint disclosure for 3 years after the transaction. 24 F.R. 35.92(c)(1).

C. **Ground contamination**.

1. Ground contamination is typically noticed by discolored soil.

The EPA's official classification for a hazardous site or piece of land is "brownfield." 42 U.S.C § 9601(39)(A).

V. **Radon**

A. Radon is an odorless, tasteless, invisible cancer-causing radioactive gas that is found in nearly every part of the world. Although research is ongoing, the EPA estimates 20,000 annual deaths are attributable to radon exposure that leads to lung cancer. If this estimate holds true, then radon would be second only to smoking as the primary cause of lung cancer deaths.

B. Radon is caused by a natural break down of uranium. As this radioactive material, contained in soil, rocks, and water naturally breaks down, radon can be released into the air that you breathe. Because of its gaseous state, radon will enter buildings typically through cracks and other holes in the foundation and building structure.

C. RADON GETS IN THROUGH:

1. Cracks in solid floors

2. Construction joints

3. Cracks in walls

4. Gaps in suspended floors

5. Gaps around service pipes

6. Cavities inside walls

7. The water supply

D. Once inside, radon can collect and settle at the lower levels of a building structure. basement would be the presumed location of the greatest amounts of radon.

A

E. The presence of radon can be quickly and inexpensively tested in any home or building. If detected, don't throw in the towel altogether. There are methods to reduce radon transfer. For more information on reducing radon transfer, refer to the EPA's "Consumer's Guide to Radon Reduction."

VI. **Mold**

Moldy bread can make a real mess of a good sandwich. When it comes to mold in the home, it can be destructive, unhealthy, and even deadly.

A. Mold spores are present everywhere and even the best of air purifiers cannot eliminate 100% of them.

1. The key to mold control is to control moisture levels and water leaks.

429

2.   Homes that are prone to flood or have had flooding should be inspected further for possible mold issues.

3.   Mold can cause allergic reactions, asthma and lung infections by either inhaling the mold spores themselves or by inhaling the toxins that are released by the mold as it grows.

B.   Common places include between wall studs, kitchen sink cabinets, and shower pans.

1.   You may suspect mold issues even if there are no visual signs of it. Mold growth can be found where moisture, oxygen, and organic matter are available.

2.   If the space smells musty, it is well worth further investigation.

VII.   **Asbestos**

Asbestos is best described as a mineral fiber.

A.   Left undisturbed, asbestos is not harmful, but when materials containing this fiber are agitated, the asbestos fibers become airborne and can become lodged in the lungs.

B.   Inhalation of high levels of asbestos fibers can lead to an increased risk of lung cancer, mesothelioma and asbestosis.

C.   Prior to the 1970's, asbestos was used to enhance the effectiveness of certain insulations and fire retardant materials. Even today asbestos can be used, but inhalation warning labels are required on such products. Places where asbestos can be commonly found include:

1.   Homes built between 1930 and 1950

2.   Furnace, boiler, and steam pipe ducting tape.

3.   Soundproofing or decorative material on walls and ceilings.

4.   Automobile brake pads and linings, clutch facings, and gaskets.

D.   If you find asbestos in your home, the best course of action is to leave it alone if it is in good condition. If you plan to remodel your home, it may be wise to inspect the materials to be removed (if any) and have them analyzed by a professional before demolition is starte

E.   A professional is not necessary to remove asbestos. Although some homeowners may desire a professional to ensure safety, as long as the asbestos is carefully removed without disturbing or breaking up the substance, and then properly bagged and sealed, the material can be removed and disposed of without harm.

Federal Laws C Terms to Know

- ☐ Asbestos
- ☐ CERCLA
- ☐ Environmental Protection Agency (EPA)
- ☐ Lead-Based Paint Disclosure
- ☐ Radon
- ☐ Superfund Amendments and Reauthorization Act (SARA)

Federal Laws C Quiz

1. The most common health effect of radon is:

    A. Respiratory failure

    B. Heart failure

    C. Lung cancer

    D. Mesothelioma

2. CERCLA provides a remedy for liability by establishing which of the following?

    A. A trust fund

    B. The definition of guilt

    C. A State action

    D. Guidelines for hazardous material clean up

3. Asbestos is best described as:

    A. A benign manufacturing material

    B. A noxious odor

    C. A microscopic dust

    D. A mineral fiber

4. According to the EPA, what is the maximum level of radon a home should not exceed?

    A. 2 PiC/L

    B. 4 PiC/L

    C. 6 PiC/L

    D. 8 PiC/L

5. A common sign of mold growth is:

    A. A musty smell

    B. A dark space

    C. A cool space

    D. A wet surface

6. CERCLA provides prohibitions and requirements relating to which of the following?

    A. Natural environmental hazards

    B. Hazardous waste sites now abandoned

    C. Hazardous material clean up

    D. Environmental business issues

7.   The best way to control mold is to control:

   A. Bacteria growth

   B. Light and ventilation

   C. Moisture and water leaks

   D. Outside water entrances

8.   Asbestos can commonly be found in homes built when?

   A. Between 1930 - 1950

   B. Between 1950 - 1970

   C. Between 1980 - 2000

   D. Asbestos wasn't used in homes

Truth In Lending Act

I. **Federal Consumer Credit Protection Act** [15 U.S.C. §§ 1601 et. seq.]

The practices of mortgage lending today are controlled to a significant extent by a series of federal laws and regulations. The Consumer Credit Protection Act of 1968 was the first to shape the concept of consumer protection regarding mortgage lending. Title I of this Act, better known as Truth In Lending Act ("TILA"), laid the foundation for consumer protection with its focus on requirements for advance disclosure to consumers of the costs of obtaining credit. Since 1968, additions to this Act and other consumer protection statutes have focused on removing inequalities in residential lending. This Act is administered and regulated by the Consumer Finance Protection Bureau ("CFPB").

II. **Truth In Lending**

A. **TILA**, also known as **Regulation Z** (which is codified as 12 C.F.R. § 1026 (2014)), requires specific disclosures to consumers in certain credit transactions.

B. Regulation Z applies to businesses or individuals who make a regular business of lending to consumers, and who collect a finance charge paid on more than four installments for personal, family, or household purposes. Consumers must be given detailed information about financing terms in advertising and at the time of the loan.

III. **The Annual Percentage Rate**

A. The purpose of the annual percentage rate ("APR") is to allow borrowers to easily and fairly compare rates and fees offered by different lenders.

B. The APR is a measure of the total cost of credit expressed as an annual rate. 12 C.F.R. § 1026.14(a) (2014); and 12 C.F.R. § 1026.22(a)(2014).

C. The following fees are generally included in the APR calculation:

1. Interest

2. Origination fee

3. Discount points

4. Processing fee

5. Underwriting fee

6. Document preparation fee

7. Private mortgage insurance

8. FHA Up Front Mortgage Insurance Premiums (UFMIP)

9. VA funding fee

10. Warehousing fees

11. Loan application fee

12. Credit life insurance on the mortgage

435

D.   APR calculations do not include fees such as:

1.   Fees paid to third-party vendors such as: appraisal, credit check, tax service, attorneys, recording fees, home inspection, and document preparation fees charged by the closing agent.

2.   Escrow company fees

3.   Title insurance premiums

4.   Reserves collected for taxes and insurance

5.   Property purchase costs

E.   If the APR changes by more than 1/8 of one percentage point, above or below the initially stated APR, it must be re-disclosed before closing. 12 C.F.R. § 1026.17(f)(2) (2014).

IV.   Disclosures for an Adjustable Rate Mortgage

A.   Any loan that includes a change in the interest rate during the life of the loan is considered an **Adjustable Rate Mortgage** ("ARM"). The following disclosures are some of many required by mail or directly no later than three business days following receipt of the application: See 12 C.F.R. § 1026.19(a) (2014).

1.   An educational brochure about ARMs: Either the "Consumer Handbook on Adjustable Rate Mortgages," published jointly by the Federal Reserve Bank and the Federal Home Loan Bank, or a suitable substitute. 12 C.F.R. § 1026.19(b)(1) (2014).

2.   An ARM disclosure that details the specifics of any ARM program the borrowers may have an interest in. 12 C.F.R. § 1026.19(b)(2) (2014).

3.   An historical perspective of the index's fluctuations, based on a $10,000 loan history as it would have been in the preceding ten years. 12 C.F.R. § 1026.19(b)(viii)(A) (2014).

4.   Disclosure of the initial and maximum interest rate. 12 C.F.R. § 1026.19(b)(viii)(B) (2014).

V.   72-Hour Right of Rescission

The **right of rescission** gives the borrowers a three-day (72-hour) right to rescind their agreement to borrow following delivery of the "Notice of Right to Cancel" (Rescind). See 12 C.F.R. § 1026.23(a)(3)(i) and (b)(1) (2014).

A.   This **cooling off period** allows the borrowers to more closely examine the documents signed at settlement, to seek advice of others and to reconsider their decision to borrow, including their decision to place a lien on their property.

B.   The rescission right applies only to real estate financing transactions, such as refinancing an existing loan or borrowing on equity, and not to a purchase money transaction. 12 C.F.R. § 1026.23(f) (2014).

C.   Each borrower whose ownership interest is or will be subject to the new mortgage security interest shall have the right to rescind the transaction. Co-borrowers (co-signers) have the same rights as primary borrowers.

D. All borrowers in a real estate refinance transaction must receive and sign two copies of the required "Notice of Right to Cancel." 12 C.F.R. § 1026.23(b)(1) (2014).

E. The rescission period starts when all borrowers have signed the receipt of notice at settlement. 12 C.F.R. § 1026.23(a)(3)(i) (2014).

F. If the borrowers rescind, the lender must, within 20 days, refund all fees paid to the mortgage originator, including any money or property that has been given to anyone in connection with the transaction, 12 C.F.R. § 1026.23(d)(2) (2014).

G. Failure to disclose rights of rescission, or failure to execute the right of rescission properly, entitles the borrowers to rescind the mortgage for an extended period of three years from consummation of the transaction. 12 C.F.R. § 1026.23(a)(3)(i) (2014).

VI. **Consumer Advertising**

Advertising must include disclosures to promote the informed use of consumer credit.

A. If the annual percentage rate may be increased after consummation, the advertisement shall state that fact. 12 C.F.R. § 1026.24(c) (2014).

B. The APR must be included any time an interest rate is advertised. Id.

C. If an advertisement states a rate of finance charge, it shall state the rate as an "annual percentage rate," using that term. Id.

D. **Trigger terms** are terms of the loan agreement that, when included in advertising, trigger full disclosure of all terms of the loan agreement. Under 12 C.F.R. § 1026.24(d) (2014), four specific disclosures must appear in any ad that contains even one of the following trigger terms:

1. The amount or percentage of any down payment;

2. The number of payments or period of repayment;

3. The amount of any payment; or

4. The amount of any finance charge.

E. The five required disclosures when a trigger term has forced full disclosure in the advertisement are:

1. The amount or percentage of the down payment;

2. The terms of repayment, which reflect the repayment obligations over the full term of the loan;

3. Any balloon payment;

4. The "annual percentage rate," using that term; and,

5. If the rate may be increased after consummation, that fact. 12 C.F.R. § 1026.24(d)(2)(i)-(iii) (2014).

VII. **The Home Ownership and Equity Protection Act of 1994** [15 U.S.C. § 1639]

This Act identifies and clarifies disclosure requirements regarding high-rate, high-fee loans.

A. This Act addresses certain deceptive and unfair practices in home equity lending. It amends TILA and establishes requirements for certain loans with high rates and/or high fees. Because the rules for these loans are contained in 12 C.F.R. § 1026.32 (2014), the loans are occasionally called "Section 32 Mortgages."

B. The rules primarily affect refinancing and home equity installment loans that also meet the definition of high-rate or high-fee loans. These rules do not cover loans to buy or build a home, reverse mortgages or home equity lines of credit. 12 C.F.R. § 1026.32 (a)(2) (2014).

C. Loans that meet the following tests are covered under this Act:

1. A first-lien loan where the APR exceeds, by more than 8%, the rates on Treasury securities of a comparable term of maturity. 12 C.F.R. § 1026.32(a)(i) (2014).

2. A second mortgage where the APR exceeds, by more than 10%, the rates on Treasury securities of a comparable term of maturity. Id.

3. Total fees and points payable by the consumer exceed 8% of the total loan amount. 12 C.F.R. § 1026.32(a)(ii) (2014).

D. Borrowers must receive the following set of high-cost loan disclosures (Section 32 disclosures) three business days prior to closing (See 15 U.S.C. § 1639(b)(1) (2014)):

1. A written statement that the loan need not be completed, even though there is a signed loan application and required disclosures have been issued. The borrowers have three business days to decide whether to sign the loan agreement after the special Section 32 disclosures are received. 15 U.S.C. § 1639(a)(1)(A) (2014).

2. A written notice warning the borrowers that, because the lender will have a mortgage on the property as collateral, the borrowers could lose the property and any money put into it if payments are not made. 15 U.S.C. § 1639(a)(1)(B) (2014).

3. The lender must disclose the APR, the regular payment amount, and the loan amount. 15 U.S.C. § 1639(a)(2)(A)-(B) (2014).

E. This Act was amended in 2008 to define and regulate a newly defined loan category called "higher-priced mortgage loans." To provide a reference, the Federal Reserve Board will publish the "average prime offer rate," which will be based on a survey currently being conducted by Freddie Mac. A higher-priced mortgage loan is defined as a loan on a consumer's principal residence where, in the case of a credit transaction secured—

1. By a first mortgage on the consumer's principal dwelling, the annual percentage rate at consummation of the transaction will exceed by more than 6.5 percentage points (8.5 percentage points, if the dwelling is personal property and the transaction is for less than $50,000) the average prime offer rate; or

2. By a subordinate or junior mortgage on the consumer's principal dwelling, the annual percentage rate at consummation of the transaction will exceed by more than 8.5 percentage points the average prime offer rate. 15 U.S.C. § 1602(bb)(1)(a)(i)(I)-(II) (2014).

F. Lenders who provide higher-cost mortgages are (mortgages described in section C above):

1. Prohibited from making a loan without regard to the borrower's ability to repay the loan from income and assets. 12 C.F.R. § 1026.34(a)(4) (2014).

2. Required to verify the income and assets from a reliable third-party documents to determine repayment ability (e.g., IRS Form W-2, tax returns, payroll receipts, financial institution records, etc.). 12 C.F.R. § 1026.34(a)(4)(ii)(A) (2014).

G. Lenders who provide higher-priced mortgage loans:

Higher priced mortgage loans are defined as:

1. A closed-end consumer credit transaction secured by the consumer's principal dwelling with an annual percentage rate that exceeds the average prime offer rate for a comparable transaction as of the date the interest rate is set:

   a. By 5 or more percentage points for loans secured by a first lien with a principal obligation at consummation that does not exceed the limit in effect as of the date the transaction's interest rate is set for the maximum principal obligation eligible for purchase by Freddie Mac;

   b. By 5 or more percentage points for loans secured by a first lien with a principal obligation at consummation that exceeds the limit in effect as of the date the transaction's interest rate is set for the maximum principal obligation eligible for purchase by Freddie Mac; or

   c. By 5 or more percentage points for loans secured by a subordinate lien. 12 C.F.R. § 1026.35(a)(1)(i)-(iii) (2014).

2. Prohibited from assessing a prepayment penalty if the rate can change in the initial four years. All other loans are limited to a maximum of a two year prepayment penalty. 12 C.F.R. § 1026.35(e)(2) (2014).

3. Required to establish escrow accounts for the payment of taxes and homeowner's insurance for all first-lien mortgages. 12 C.F.R. § 1026.35(b) (2014).

Truth Lending Act Terms to Know

- ☐ 72-Hour Right of Rescission
- ☐ Annual Percentage Rate (APR)
- ☐ Co-borrowers (Co-signers)
- ☐ Federal Consumer Credit Protection Act
- ☐ Federal Trade Commission (FTC)
- ☐ Home Ownership and Equity Protection Act of 1994 (HOEPA)
- ☐ Regulation Z
- ☐ Trigger Term

Truth In Lending Act Quiz

True or False

1. ___ Discount points are included in the APR.

2. ___ Title insurance is included in the APR.

3. ___ Document Preparation fees are included in the APR.

4. ___ Reserve account payments are included in the APR.

5. ___ If the APR changes by 0.0120 the TIL must be given again.

6. ___ 6. The VA funding fee is included in the APR.

7. ___ 7. The credit report fee is included in the APR.

8. ___ 8. The tax service fee is included in the APR.

9. ___ 9. The home inspection fee is included in the APR.

10. ___ 10. Only one borrower must rescind to cancel a loan.

11. ___ 1 If a trigger term is used then loan amount is a required disclosure.

12. ___ 1 If a trigger term is used than APR is a required disclosure.

13. ___ 1 If a trigger term is used then the number of payments is a required disclosure.

Multiple Choice

14. What law was enacted in 1968 as part of the Consumer Credit Protection Act?

    A. RESPA

    B. FCRA

    C. HMDA

    D. TILA

15. Truth In Lending is administered by?

    A. Consumer Financial Protection Bureau

    B. Housing and Urban Development

    C. Federal Reserve

    D. Department of Veteran Affairs

16. What required disclosure under the Truth In Lending Act, is intended to provide meaningful information regarding the cost of credit and terms of a prospective loan?

    A. Loan Estimate

    B. Rate cap

    C. Annual Percentage Rate (APR)

    D. Settlement Costs & You

17. When must the written APR disclosure be delivered to the borrowers?

    A. 3 business days following receipt of loan application.

    B. It is not required until the loan closes.

    C. No later than 3 business days following loan approval.

    D. Verbal notification is all that is necessary.

18. The fees used in calculating the APR include all of the following EXCEPT:

    A. Interest charged

    B. Lender fees

    C. Mortgage insurance

    D. Title insurance premium

19. The requirements of Truth In Lending include all of the following EXCEPT:

    A. Consumer Handbook on Adjustable Rate Mortgages

    B. The right of rescission

    C. Fair advertising disclosures

    D. Good Faith Estimate

20. According to Truth In Lending, what is NOT correct regarding the right of rescission?

    A. There is a 3 days or 72-hour right of rescission.

    B. All parties must acknowledge the right of rescission.

    C. It includes not only the loan, but also the purchase.

    D. If not applied correctly, the borrower has 3 years to rescind the loan.

21. To identify and clarify disclosures regarding high interest rates, and/or high-fee loans, what Federal law was enacted?

    A. Fair Housing Act

    B. Fair Credit Reporting Act

    C. Home Mortgage Disclosure Act

    D. Home Ownership and Equity Protection Act (HOEPA)

22. A loan that stipulates a charge for early payoff, before a specified period of time, is likely to include a(n):

    A. Due-on-sale clause

    B. Lock or float agreement

    C. Prepayment penalty

    D. Alienation clause

23. When can a loan officer fill out, alter, or interpret a Real Estate Purchase Contract (REPC) for the borrowers?

   A. If the seller asks for help

   B. When a real estate agent seeks help structuring the transaction

   C. If the loan officer is qualified to do so

   D. Never

REVIEW TESTS

Review Test 1

1. Which of the following is a complete definition of real property?

    A. Land and the air above it

    B. Land, the buildings thereon, and anything permanently affixed to the land and/or the buildings

    C. Land and its appurtenances, all the air space to infinity and everything below the surface to the earth's center

    D. Land and the mineral rights

2. Which of the following is an economic rather than a physical characteristic of real property?

    A. Indestructibility

    B. Area preferences – situs

    C. Immobility

    D. Non-homogeneity

3. The definition of the term "real property" includes:

    A. Items of personal property included in the Real Estate Purchase Contract

    B. Emblements

    C. Air space and subsurface rights

    D. Chattels

4. Which of the following would be an example of chattel?

    A. Cattle

    B. Fence

    C. Fixtures

    D. River

5. The definition of an emblement includes which of the following?

    A. Mineral rights if mined in the year of the transfer of the property

    B. The air above the ground sold separately from the land

    C. Swimming pools, tennis courts and other amenities

    D. Crops nurtured in the year of the sale of the property

447

6.   Real property includes all of the following EXCEPT:

   A. Buildings affixed to the land

   B. Water courses appurtenant to the land

   C. Minerals, oil and gas

   D. Trade fixtures

7.   An important characteristic of land is that it can be improve These modifications become a part of and tend to increase the value of the real property. Which of the following is such a modification?

   A. Crops

   B. Chattels

   C. Trade fixtures

   D. Access roads

8.   A fixture is:

   A. Considered real estate

   B. Considered personal property

   C. Attached to a business

   D. Sometimes real property and sometimes personal property, depending upon how it is attached

9.   Which of the following best explains the difference between trade fixtures and fixtures?

   A. Trade fixtures require installation, and fixtures do not.

   B. Trade fixtures are transferred by bill of sale, fixtures transfer with the deed.

   C. Trade fixtures always belong to the owner of the property, and fixtures do not.

   D. Trade fixtures are considered amenities, and fixtures are not.

10. If a cabinet in a house is a fixture, which of the following is true?

   A. Title to it passes to the buyer upon the sale of the house.

   B. It is not pledged as security for any mortgage loan.

   C. It is NOT part of the assessed value of the property for tax purposes.

   D. It will pass to the new owner only if the Real Estate Purchase Contract says it will.

11. For a deed to be valid, it must be:

    A. Dated

    B. Acknowledged

    C. Signed by the grantor

    D. Recorded

12. In a deed, the habendum clause is a(n):

    A. To have and to hold clause

    B. Exclusive right of possession clause

    C. Personal property inclusion clause

    D. Corporate ownership clause

13. Lester makes out a deed to Charlie, his partner. Lester signs the deed and has it acknowledged, after which he places it in a safe deposit box. Shortly thereafter, he is killed in an accident. Will Charlie get the property?

    A. Yes, the deed is valid.

    B. Yes, but it will first have to go through probate.

    C. No, Lester obviously left out an important step.

    D. No, since Lester cannot pass property to anyone in the event of accidental death.

14. Which of the following best describes the covenant of Quiet Enjoyment?

    A. The grantor is the owner and has the right to convey title.

    B. The grantee will not be disturbed by someone else claiming an interest in the property.

    C. The grantor guarantees the title has no easements, restrictions or liens other than those specified before the sale.

    D. The grantor will bear the expense of defending the grantee's title if other person or persons make a claim against the property.

15. Ellis bought a service station from Grant and received a Quit Claim Deed for it. A court ruling later decreed that Grant never had a valid interest in the property. What interest does Ellis now have?

    A. Since he paid for it, Ellis now has a fee simple estate.

    B. It's not what he wanted, but Ellis now has a fee defeasible estate.

    C. He can't own it, but the court will likely grant Mr. Ellis a life estate.

    D. Mr. Ellis has no interest in the property.

16. Moss leased a lakeside lot from Mayes. Upon arriving at the lot to begin sunbathing, Moss found the home infested with rodents. Under which of the following justifications could Moss move and refuse to pay rent on this lot?

    A. Constructive eviction

    B. Unlawful Detainer

    C. Tenancy in sufferance

    D. Fair Housing violations

17. A purchaser of real estate learned that his ownership rights would continue forever and that no other person had any ownership or control over the property. Therefore, this person owns a:

    A. Fee simple interest

    B. Life estate

    C. Determinable fee estate

    D. Fee simple estate subject to a condition subsequent

18. Alison Gray held fee simple title to a vacant lot adjacent to a hospital. She was persuaded to make a gift of the lot to the hospital. She wanted to have some control over its use, so her attorney prepared her deed to convey ownership of the lot "as long as it is used for hospital purposes." After conveyance of the gift, the hospital would own:

    A. A fee simple estate

    B. A license

    C. A determinable fee estate

    D. A leasehold estate

19. Which of the following best describes a life estate?

    A. An estate conveyed to Abel for the life of Abel and upon Abel's death to Baker.

    B. An estate held by Abel and Baker in joint tenancy with full rights of survivorship.

    C. An estate that reverts to the grantor if a certain covenant is disregarded

    D. An estate given by law to a wife under the Uniform Probate Code.

20. Mr. and Mrs. Nichols own their property as joint tenants. Mr. Nichols wills all of his real and personal property to a son from a previous marriage. When Mr. Nichols dies, who will own the property and how?

    A. Mrs. Nichols will own the property in severalty.

    B. Mrs. Nichols and the son will be joint tenants.

    C. Mr. Nichols' son will hold a life estate in his father's half.

    D. Mrs. Nichols' and the son will own as tenants in common.

21. The holder of a life estate can do all of the following EXCEPT:

    A. Lease the life estate

    B. Borrow against the life estate

    C. Sell the life estate

    D. Will the life estate

22. When a life estate is based on the life of someone other than the holder of the life estate, it is said to be:

    A. A life estate in remainder

    B. A life estate in reversion

    C. A life estate caveat emptor

    D. A life estate pur autre vie

23. A person voluntarily gives up private property for public use by:

    A. Dedication

    B. Accession

    C. Adverse possession

    D. Escheat

24. Which of the following persons would file a Quiet Title Action in order to obtain official recorded title to a property?

    A. A subdivider

    B. A developer

    C. An adverse possessor

    D. A buyer in a transaction involving a life estate

25. Which of the following is NOT part of the Bundle of Rights?

    A. Use or control

    B. Quiet enjoyment

    C. Interest

    D. Disposition

26. A lessee signs a leasehold agreement for six months from February 1 to July 31. This would be an example of:

    A. Periodic tenancy

    B. Tenancy at sufferance

    C. Tenancy at will

    D. Tenancy for years

27. Which of the following describes tenancy at will?

    A. It automatically renews itself.

    B. Possession is given for a stated period of time.

    C. An unwanted lessee is in illegal possession.

    D. The lease is of uncertain duration.

28. Harlow signed a three-year lease to occupy a house. When the lease expired, Harlow continued to live in the house without the owner's consent. Harlow now holds:

    A. Tenancy at sufferance

    B. Tenancy at will

    C. Tenancy in common

    D. An estate in remainder

29. The lessor collects rent and pays all the operating expenses. This would be an example of:

    A. Net lease

    B. Percentage lease

    C. Gross lease

    D. Proprietary lease

30. When a lessee assigns his lease, he:

    A. Gives up the remaining rights of the lease, but retains liability if the assignee defaults,

    B. Gives up the remaining rights of the lease, and is released from all liability,

    C. Gives up the remaining rights of the lease, but the assignee is responsible to the lessee,

    D. A lease cannot be assigned.

31. When a lessor doesn't make the premises habitable, the lessee's legal right to vacate is called:

    A. Constructive eviction

    B. Unlawful Detainer action

    C. Defeasance

    D. Injunctive Action

32. When one person owns a property as sole owner, it is legally known as:

    A. An Estate in Trust

    B. An Estate in Severalty

    C. A Life Estate

    D. Tenancy by Entirety

33. Dick Richardson, a private individual, wants to enter into co-ownership with the UGO Corporation. By law, this arrangement would have to be:

    A. Joint Tenancy

    B. Severalty

    C. Tenancy in Common

    D. Tenancy by the Entirety

34. The fewest number of General Partners that could exist in a Limited Partnership would be:

    A. Zero

    B. One

    C. Two

    D. Unlimited

35. Which one of these is largest in area?

    A. The NE 1/4 of the SW 1/4 of a section

    B. The SE 1/4 of the SW 1/4 of a section

    C. The NE 1/4 of a section

    D. The NE 1/4 of the SW 1/4 of the NW 1/4 of a section

36. When a garage is built a few inches onto a neighbor's property, it is:

    A. An easement

    B. An encroachment

    C. A violation of deed restriction

    D. Granted to the neighbor through adverse possession

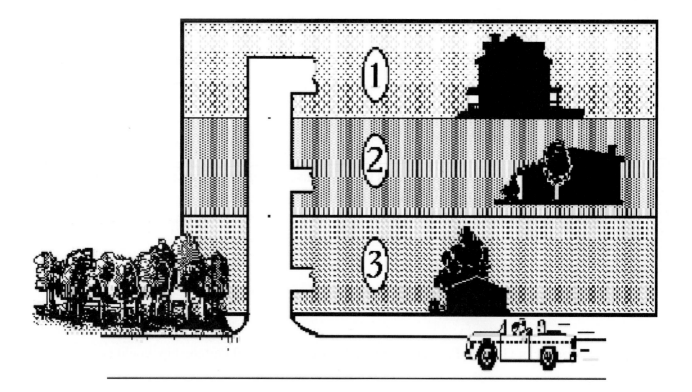

37. In the illustration above, the dominant tenement(s) would be:

    A. 1 only

    B. 1 and 2

    C. 3 only

    D. 2 and 3

38. The right to use another person's land without the existence of an adjacent or dominant estate, and which will exist during the life of the grantee, or the need for which it was created is called an:

    A. Easement in gross

    B. Easement appurtenant

    C. Easement by prescription

    D. Encroachment

39. Mr. Moore's property was not condemned when a freeway was built near his home. However, he feels that because of the freeway, his property has been damaged. Perhaps Mr. Moore should:

    A. Sue for inverse condemnation.

    B. Just forget it because he has no chance to win.

    C. Initiate a condemnation action.

    D. Realize a private individual cannot sue the government.

40. The major difference between eminent domain and police power is:

    A. Right of legal encroachments

    B. Compensation

    C. Level of government authority involved

    D. Eminent Domain is only exercised at the state level of government

41. If a person wanted to build a small convenience store in a residentially zoned area and was granted a change in zoning classification for that specific property, it is likely an example of:

    A. A variance

    B. An illegal non-conforming use

    C. Spot zoning

    D. Legal non-conforming use

42. A variance is:

    A. A form of spot zoning

    B. An unusual change in zoning

    C. A legal non-conforming use created prior to a change in zoning classification

    D. A legal non-conforming use granted after a zoning classification has been established

43. The land description method of using monuments and measurements to establish boundaries is called:

    A.   Townships and sections

    B. Metes and bounds

    C. Rectangular survey

    D. Meridian measurement

44. How many feet of wire would be required to build a three-strand fence around the NW 1/4 of any section?

    A. 7,921

    B. 15,840

    C. 3,840

    D. 31,680

45. How many acres are there in the SW 1/4 of the S 1/2 of any section?

    A. 10,800

    B. 5,760

    C. 10

    D. 80

46. A lot 1780 feet square is how many acres?

    A. 78

    B. 25

    C. 4,950.6

    D. 72.74

Review Test 2

1. Shaw offers to purchase Anderson's lot, but before Anderson responds, Shaw cancels his offer. Shaw's action constitutes a:

   A. Rejection

   B. Lapsed offer

   A. Counteroffer

   C. Withdrawal of the offer

2. According to the Statute of Frauds, a contract for the sale and purchase of real estate:

   A. Must be free of the elements of fraud and misrepresentation

   B. Must not be induced through duress

   C. Must be in writing to be enforceable

   D. Must be acknowledged and recorded

3. Constructive fraud is:

   A. Sometimes known as puffing

   B. Fraud that had no evil intention but, with reasonable care, could have been avoided

   C. A purposeful omission or concealment of information

   D. Deliberate false representation of facts

4. The Statute of Limitations refers to:

   A. Accord and satisfaction

   B. Time periods for bringing legal action as specified by law

   C. The requirement that certain contracts must be in writing

   D. The upper limit of interest a lender can

5. Seller Biggs sells a property to sixteen-year-old Buyer Kid When Seller Biggs learns that Buyer Kidd is not of legal age, Biggs wishes to void the contract. Can Biggs do this legally?

   A. Yes, because buyer Kidd is not of legal age.

   B. Yes, because contracts with legally incompetent persons are automatically voi

   C. No, because Buyer Kidd, but not Seller Biggs, may disaffirm the contract.

   D. No, because discrimination on the basis of age is illegal.

6. A contract where the intentions of the parties are shown by conduct is a(n):

    A. Express contract

    B. Implied contract

    C. Bilateral contract

    D. Executory contract

7. A voidable contract:

    A. Is created due to negative circumstances surrounding the contract's formation

    B. Is absolutely unenforceable and may, therefore, be disregarded

    C. Requires only mutual agreement to rescind

    D. May be enforceable

8. Rescission is:

    A. A contract to end a contract

    B. Altering the terms of a legal contract by one party

    C. Suing for damages

    D. When the buyer defaults on a contract

9. Charles Post and Peter Hollub enter into a contract wherein Post agrees to sell his house to Hollub. Post thereafter changes his mind and defaults. Hollub then sues Post to force him to go through with the contract. This is a suit for:

    A. Specific performance

    B. Damages

    C. Liquidated damages

    D. Forfeiture

10. A tenant farmer pays his landlord rent in the form of a share of the crops. This is an example of:

    A. Good consideration

    B. Valuable consideration

    C. Crops are not considered consideration

    D. Good and valuable consideration

11. Buyer Stamp submits an offer to buy the home of Seller Stanford. The earnest money deposit is $8,000. Should Buyer Stamp discover the need to recover the $8,000 an hour later, and before Stanford has accepted the offer, which of the following would be true about the situation?

    A. Stamp would be unable to obtain this money until closing.

    B. Stamp must obtain an injunction to prevent Seller Stanford from spending the money.

    C. Stamp may obtain the money without revocation of the offer.

    D. Stamp must withdraw the offer before Seller Stanford accepts it.

12. Mr. Jackson, a buyer, enters into a contract to buy a home from Mr. Mills. Before the closing, Jackson assigns Harris into his contractual position without the approval of Mr. Mills. In this case:

    A. The contract is void.

    B. The contract is valid.

    C. The contract is voidable by Mr. Mills.

    D. The contract is voidable by Mr. Harris.

13. Which of the following involves a release of liability?

    A. Time is of the Essence clause

    B. Novation clause

    C. Acceleration clause

    D. Assignment of contract

14. In a listing agreement, the relationship of the seller to the principal broker could best be described as:

    A. Customer and Principal

    B. Third Party and Trustee

    C. Agent and Customer

    D. Principal and Agent

15. In an option negotiated through a real estate broker to purchase real property, the optionor is the:

    A. Buyer

    B. Seller

    C. Broker

    D. Seller or Buyer

16. Green has offered to sell her house for $100,000 with a $50,000 down payment. Berry wants to consider the purchase of that house on those terms, and asked Green for a week-long option. Which of the following is NOT necessary to make the option valid?

    A. Consideration for the option

    B. A date of expiration

    C. A proposed purchase price

    D. Closing date and date of possession

17. The sellers told the listing agent they were offering the property at a reduced price because the roof leaked, but they weren't going to fix it. It was listed with that problem. What should the agent writing the offer do?

    A. Write an addendum stating the property is being sold as is

    B. On the addendum, note the roof leaks and the property is sold "as is"

    C. Nothing, if the buyers agree to the "as is" clause

    D. On an addendum, state that the "as is" provision does not apply

18. Which of the following is NOT true of a listing contract?

    A. A corporation may be a principal.

    B. A natural person may be an agent.

    C. A sales associate may be an agent.

    D. Purchasers are not involved in the contract.

19. According to agency law, a real estate broker does NOT owe the principal the duty of:

    A. Exercising reasonable care

    B. Disclosing information about the other side

    C. Conforming with the principal's instructions

    D. Giving legal advice

20. A real estate sales agent may act as the direct agent of:

    A. His/her principal broker

    B. Several licensed brokers at any one time through a co-brokering arrangement

    C. Sellers who listed their property

    D. Buyers who make an offer which is accepted by the sellers

21. When the principal takes the role of being partially disclosed:

    A. The buyer knows who the agent and the principal are.

    B. The buyer knows who the agent is, but thinks he/she is the principal.

    C. The third party (or other party) knows who the agent is, knows there is a principal, but doesn't know the principal's name.

    D. The buyer doesn't know who the agent or the principal are.

22. Which of the following would be considered creation of agency by the operation of law?

    A. Express

    B. Estoppel

    C. Ratification

    D. Implication

23. Which of the following will NOT terminate an agency contract?

    A. Death of either party

    B. Destruction of the property

    C. Performance of the terms of the contract

    D. The principal moves to another city

24. Under which of the following circumstances can a listing contract be assigned with the broker's permission?

    A. If another broker can better handle the principal's listing

    B. If the listing sales agent has moved to a new brokerage

    C. If the principal wants the benefits of a multiple listing service

    D. Agency contracts cannot be assigned

25. Nonfactual or extravagant statements which would be recognized by a reasonable person as exaggeration or salesmanship:

    A. Intentional fraud

    B. Puffing or puffery

    C. Constructive fraud

    D. Indemnification

26. When Agent Wilson of Happy Realty discovers that one of her listings consisting of a house and lot has been rezoned to industrial, which of the following statements would NOT be true?

   A. She must disclose the zoning change to the owner of the affected house and lot.

   B. She must disclose the zoning change to a buyer who is submitting an offer.

   C. She must disclose the zoning change only to those prospects preparing to sign written offers for the property.

   D. She must note that change in the listing given to the Multiple Listing Service.

27. Jan Green lists her property for sale with Dale Rowan, a broker. In the listing contract it is stipulated that Green will receive $62,000. All proceeds over $62,000 will be the broker's commission. This type of listing would be a(n):

   A. Open listing

   B. Exclusive Agency listing

   C. Exclusive Right to Sell listing

   D. Net listing

28. Broker Morse has fifteen days left to sell Owner McCloud's house under an exclusive right to sell listing. Which of the following events would automatically terminate the agency before the contract expires?

   A. Owner McCloud tries to sell the house herself and Broker Morse finds out about it.

   B. Owner McCloud discovers that Broker Morse has a family history of mental illness.

   C. Broker Morse's office records are destroyed by fire.

   D. Owner McCloud and Broker Morse agree to end the listing arrangement prematurely.

29. The seller is willing to enter into an exclusive listing with a principal broker. However, the seller insists on retaining the right to find a buyer himself without paying the broker a commission. Therefore they would enter into a(n):

   A. Exclusive agency listing

   B. Exclusive right to sell

   C. Exclusive right to sell with exclusions

   D. Single party exclusive right to sell

30. In which of the following situations has the broker placed the sellers' interest in extreme jeopardy?

    A. The broker delegates certain responsibilities.

    B. The broker will not give opinions on legal matters when asked.

    C. The broker acts as an undisclosed dual agent.

    D. The broker reveals to the buyer defects in the property.

31. Broker Albertson is hired to sell Harmon's house. Harmon admits to being anxious to sell because of a job transfer to another city. Seller Harmon also tells Broker Albertson that the listed house is connected to the city's natural gas line. Broker Albertson knows that city gas lines have not yet been extended to the subdivision where the listed house is located. Which of the following should Broker Albertson tell all prospective buyers?

    A. The listed house is not connected to city gas lines; and, therefore, Seller Harmon may sell for less than the listed price.

    B. The house has possibly been connected to city gas lines, and Seller Harmon may sell for less than the listed price.

    C. The listed house is not connected to city gas lines.

    D. Seller Harmon may sell for less than the listed price.

32. Which of the following is NOT required for an appraisal?

    A. Property description

    B. A Real Estate Purchase Contract

    C. A specified date

    D. The estimated value

33. The economic value of situs is directly related to:

    A. The cost of land and improvements

    B. A personal preference for a certain location

    C. A method of calculating depreciation

    D. Reproduction cost new

34. Which of the following reports is most frequently used by lending institutions for an appraisal of a personal residence?

    A. Letter form report

    B. Narrative form report

    C. Short form report

    D. CRV form

35. The ultimate determiner of value is:

    A. What the buyer is willing to pay

    B. What the seller is willing to accept

    C. An official appraisal by a certified appraiser

    D. A willing buyer and willing seller, neither under duress

36. Which of the following is NOT one of the four essential elements of value?

    A. Transferability

    B. Scarcity

    C. Utility

    D. Price

37. When two or more contiguous properties are purchased by one owner to increase the value of their combined areas, the process is called:

    A. Contribution

    B. Plottage

    C. Anticipation

    D. Subdivision

38. Substitution is a principle which states that:

    A. When demand increases, value increases.

    B. A change in the highest and best use increases the value.

    C. Homes are somewhat uniform and harmonious in design and value.

    D. No prudent person pays more than she has to, to get what she wants.

48. In appraising a property using the income or capitalization approach, one of the most important steps is the selection of an appropriate capitalization rate. In this selection process, you will find that, as the capitalization rate increases the:

    A. Value goes up

    B. Risk goes up

    C. Value is unaffected

    D. Risk goes down

49. Analyzing results obtained by the three appraisal approaches in order to determine the final estimate of value of a property is known as:

    A. Ad valorem

    B. Capitalization

    C. Averaging

    D. Reconciliation

50. Determine the annual GRM of an income property that recently sold for $132,480 and has monthly gross rents of $960.

    A. 138

    B. 114.6

    C. 73

    D. 11.5

51. The first principle an appraiser should apply when appraising a property is:

    A. Determine level of contribution

    B. Obtain a list of comparables

    C. Determine highest and best use

    D. Define the problem

52. The primary money market does NOT include:

    A. First mortgages

    B. Second mortgage loans

    C. The purchase of existing loans

    D. Loans made directly to a home purchaser

53. The difference between the price of a property and the balance owed on existing mortgages and liens is called:

   A. Profit

   B. Equity

   C. Discount rate

   D. Loan to value ratio

54. As used in real estate financing, the term "impounds" most nearly means:

   A. Moratorium

   B. Escalation

   C. Reserves

   D. Penalties

55. Lenders of conventional loans with an LTVR in excess of 80% usually require the borrower to obtain:

   A. Mortgage Insurance Premium (MIP)

   B. Private Mortgage insurance (PMI)

   C. Federal Mortgage insurance (FMI)

   D. Conventional Mortgage insurance (CMI)

56. A loan that requires payments of interest only during the full term of the loan and the entire principal paid in a balloon payment at the end is called a(n):

   A. Straight note

   B. Partially amortized loan

   C. Fully amortized loan

   D. Open end loan

57. Elsie Litner obtained a loan for a new fully furnished home and used both the home, and the furnishings as collateral for the loan. This loan would be a:

   A. Purchase mortgage

   B. Package mortgage

   C. Blanket mortgage

   D. Wraparound mortgage

58. In order to complete the sale of his property, Ernie Easterbrook carried back a third mortgage. This mortgage would be called a:

    A. Blanket mortgage

    B. Package mortgage

    C. Purchase money mortgage

    D. Wraparound mortgage

59. A seller lends the entire amount required to purchase his home without disturbing the existing first mortgage. This loan is an example of a(n)?

    A. Wraparound mortgage

    B. Blanket mortgage

    C. Package mortgage

    D. Illegal form of financing

60. The process of a buyer using a small amount of his own money and a large amount of a lender's money is called:

    A. Leverage

    B. Compounding

    C. Amortization

    D. Defeasance

61. A certain property was purchased for $84,000. The first mortgage was $68,000, and the second mortgage was $2,560. What is the loan to value ratio (LTVR)?

    A. 81%

    B. 84%

    C. 30%

    D. 119%

62. What effect does discounting a loan have?

    A. It increases the secondary lender's effective yield.

    B. It reduces the amount of the prepayment penalty that can be charged.

    C. It increases the cost of the loan to the secondary mortgage market.

    D. It decreases the secondary lender's effective yield.

63. John Barnes obtained a loan which was guaranteed by the government against loss. The loan was a(an):

    A. FHA loan

    B. Conventional loan

    C. VA loan

    D. Privately insured loan

64. Charles is purchasing a home with a VA loan. With a VA loan, the payment of $1,200 in discount points could appear on the closing statement as all EXCEPT:

    A. A reduction in buyer's down payment

    B. A reduction in proceeds due the seller

    C. An addition to funds due from buyer

    D. Half paid by buyer, half by seller

65. An FHA loan requires which of the following?

    A. Mortgage insurance to protect the lender

    B. Federal tax monies to guarantee the loan

    C. A prepayment penalty clause to protect the lender

    D. Federal tax money to insure the loan

66. Which best describes the function and purpose for the required mortgage insurance on an FHA or a conventional loan?

    A. It gives protection in case of fire.

    B. The loan will be paid off if the borrower dies.

    C. It ensures there are no hidden claims on the title.

    D. It protects the lender in case of default.

67. The clause in a mortgage which states that if the borrower defaults, the lender has the right to declare the entire debt due and payable is called the:

    A. Defeasance clause

    B. Subordination clause

    C. Escalation clause

    D. Acceleration clause

68. A subordination clause is the agreement in a junior lien which:

   A. Provides for a balloon payment.

   B. Eliminates any previously allowed acceleration clauses.

   C. Permits a first lien to be refinanced without a loss of priority.

   D. Guarantees the allowance of funds for property maintenance even if mortgage payments need to be interrupted.

69. Jones is a mortgagor. The defeasance clause included in his mortgage will take effect when and if Jones:

   A. Repays the entire debt

   B. Should miss a single payment on the debt

   C. Defaults on the entire remaining debt

   D. Sells the property and allows the buyer to assume the loan

70. Last Security Bank is making a loan which they do not want anyone to be able to assume without their approval or their right to increase the interest rates. Therefore, they insert what clause?

   A. Release

   B. Defeasance

   C. Alienation

   D. Prepayment Penalty

71. Utah is a(n):

   A. Lien theory state

   B. Title theory state

   C. Intermediate theory state

   D. Foreclosure theory state

72. A trust deed involves:

   A. Money

   B. Hypothecation

   C. Amortization

   D. Payments

73. In case of default, a Trust Deed conveys to the Trustee the:

A. Right to repossess the secured property.

B. Authority to call upon the courts to order the sale of the property.

C. Power of sale.

D. Exercise of each of these alternatives, as directed by the beneficiary.

74. In a Uniform Real Estate Contract or Land Contract, which of the following is NOT a possibility in the event of default?

A. Past payments can be considered as rent and an unlawful detainer suit can be initiate

B. The seller may hire an attorney to bring suit for delinquent payments and other incurred damages.

C. The seller can foreclose

D. The seller can physically evict the owner and return the money he paid

75. The right of a title insurance company to step into the shoes of an indemnified policy holder and assert all of the insured's legal rights against a claimant is called:

A. Subordination

B. Subrogation

C. Special Endorsement

D. Satisfaction of Title

76. Which of the following is considered a correct match?

A. Mortgage – Non judicial foreclosure

B. Trust Deed – Forfeiture

C. Uniform Real Estate Contract – Forfeiture

D. Trust Deed and Note – Judicial foreclosure

77. A property valued at $94,000 is taxed based on an assessed rate of 20% and a mill levy of 108 mills. What is the amount of taxes due?

A. $10,152

B. $18,800

C. $2,030.40

D. $203.04

472

78. The minimum time allowed for depreciation on a personal residence is:

    A. 20-25 years

    B. 26-30 years

    C. 10-19 years

    D. 0 years

79. The cost basis is:

    A. What you paid for the property

    B. What you pay to replicate the property, minus depreciation

    C. What you pay, plus improvements, minus depreciation

    D. Improvements minus depreciation

80. The technical term for depreciation is:

    A. Appreciation

    B. Cost Basis

    C. Cost Recovery

    D. Price Adjustment

Math Et

Math Et Practice Problems (Optional)

These are optional practice questions and are discussed online in the Math Review class.

1. The purchase price of Penny Piccalo's property was $98,000. If Big Bonker's Bank gave Penny an 84% LTVR, how much did Penny Piccalo borrow from Big Bonker's Bank?

2. If agent Sam Signleton sold Penny Piccalo her property for $98,000 and charged the seller a 6% commission, how much did Sam Singleton earn?

3. Penny Piccalo borrowed the money for her property from Big Bonker's Bank on a straight note for 14% (see 1a for loan amount). How much interest did Penny Piccalo pay the first year?

4. If agent Tree was paid a commission of 6% and it amounted to a total of $5,076.00, what was the selling price of the property he sold?

5. If agent Mathews was paid $6,720.00 for selling a home for $96,000, what was the percent of his commission?

6. If Agent Dollarson was paid a 9% commission and he earned $19,080, what was the purchase price of the home that he sold?

7.   Karen Kwick sold her property for $120,000. If she lost 20%, how much had she originallypaid for the property?

8.   Mason Dix realized a loss of 8% when he sold his property for $73,600. How much did he pay when he bought the property?

9.   Mason Dix realized a loss of 8% when he sold his property. Since he bought it for $80,000, how much money did he lose on the sale?

10. Marilyn Michals sold her home for $118,000 which was 28% more than she paid for it. How much had she originally paid for it?

11. Pete Carnation sold his home for $360,000 to pay some gambling debts. If he sold it for 3% more than he paid for it, how much had he paid for it?

12. George Dubkakis bought his home for $125,000. He made a 13% profit on the sale. How much was his profit?

13. If seller Staton wanted to receive a net of $95,000 for his home, and he had to pay a commission of 5%, what should be the selling price of the home?

14. Agent MacKee knew seller MacKoo wanted to take home $47,000.00 after paying a 6% commission. What should agent MacKee establish as the selling price of the home?

15. The seller insisted that he clear $58,590.00 from the sale of his home to pay off the mortgage. If he paid a 7% commission, what would the selling price of his home have to be?

16. When Zeb sold his home he had to pay closing costs of $400 and a commission of 6%. At the closing he received a check for $63,520. What was the selling price?

17. After paying the attorney $1,200, the agent a 7% commission, and the title company $480 for their services; Mae East received a check of $175,020. How much did she sell her home for?

18. Zebedee received a check for $113,785.50 after paying the title company $1,866.90, the real estate agent 6%, and other closing costs of $1,340. What was the selling price of his home?

Sales agent Quickstart was paid a commission of 60% of the gross commission. If his commission was $2,952 and the broker was paid 6%, what was the selling price of the home?

19. A broker was paid 7% and he split that commission by paying 70% to the sales agent. What was the selling price of the home if the sales agent received a commission check for $6,076.00?

20. Agent Nickel earned a 65% split of the broker's 5.5% commission. If the amount paid to sales agent Nickel was $3,467.75, what was the selling price of the property?

21. Bill Bates borrowed $52,000 dollars on a straight note. He ended up paying $3,069.44 in interest at the end of 170 days. What was his interest rate?

22. Bic Barrows borrowed some money at an interest rate of 13%. If he paid a total of $2,405 at the end of six months, how much had he borrowed?

23. Lanny Lendl lent Louie Little lots of loot as a loan. If the interest on the loot was 9.5% and Louie paid $6,115.28 for the first 140 days, exactly how much loot did Lanny Lendl lend Louie Little?

24. If 15% of Bennie the Broker's agents were on a 50/50% commission split, 35% were on a 60/40% commission, and the other 24 agents were on a 70/30% commission split, how many agents did Bennie have in his office?

25. Freddie Farmer planted 42 apple trees in his orchard. If 25% of his orchard consisted of cherry trees and 45% were peach trees, how many trees did Freddie have in his orchard?

26. Charlie Connors, the contractor found that 19% of his income from developing his subdivision was management fees, 41% was material, and 32% was labor. If he made a profit of $210,000, what was the sales price of the development?

27. A sporting goods store has a lease for $3,000 per month base rent, plus the owner pays 3% of any gross income over $200,000. They paid $40,200 in rent last year. How much was their gross income?

28. I.M. Seller In, paid base rent of $1,500 based on $90,000 in gross sales. They paid 4% of everything over the $90,000. If their total rent for October was $2,150, how much was their total gross sales?

29. During April, Top Sales Limited paid a total of $6,400 rent. If they paid 5.2% for all gross sales in excess of $300,000 and a base rent of $2,500, how much was their gross sales for April?

30. Amy Andrews decided to develop a 6.4 acre parcel of land she had inherite She cleared zoning for lots 94 feet by 130 feet. The city also required that she dedicate 21% of the project for streets, curbs and gutters. How many full sized lots will she be able to build?

31. Donnie Dunkle owns a dinky lot 84 feet by 96 feet. How many acres are in his tiny parcel?

32. Douglas Doogan dug a deep dungeon. It was 7 feet deep, 14 feet long, and 9 feet wide. How many cubic yards of dirt did Doug Doogan displace to dig his deep dungeon?

Math Review

INSTRUCTIONS: Following are some additional math questions. Work these on your own (do not do them as a group effort -- you want to see if you could handle them on the test). We do not go over these in a class setting.

1. The taxes due amount to $540, the assessed rate is 20% and the tax rate is 20 mills. What is the appraised value of the property?

2. A property valued at $120,000 had a gross income of $25,000. If their operating expenses were 52%, what was the rate of return?

3. A sales agent received a monthly salary of $200 and a 3% commission on all his sales. He was paid $750 for the month. What was the value of the property he sold that month?

4. S paid $28,000 for the vacant land and $250,000 for the home he built. He wants to sell for a profit of 5% on the land and 30% on the home. What does he have to sell for in order to meet his objectives?

5. T wants to clear $79,000 when he sells his property. He needs to pay a 6% commission, $550 in closing costs, and $350 to the attorney who assisted in the transaction. What should he sell the property for?

6. K purchased a home for $55,000 and obtained an 80% loan. He paid three discount points and had additional closing costs of $2,000. How much cash must he bring to the closing?

7. A lot was purchased as an investment for $10,500. It was sold a year later at a loss of 20%. The owner paid a 10% commission to the agent. What was the net loss on the sale?

8. G borrowed $15,000 to buy a business. The interest was 11%. All interest and the borrowed amount was paid in a single payment at the end of 16 months. How much was the payment?

9. J. got a loan for $84,000 from a mortgage company at 11% interest with a 30 year term. The monthly payment of principal and interest was $799.95. How much of the first payment was principal?

10. K obtained a 20 year loan at 9.5% interest. The next payment will have $427.50 in interest. Before the next payment, how much was the remaining principal balance.

ANSWERS

490

Answers for Chapter Quizzes

DEEDS AND TRANSFER

1. B
2. C
3. C
4. B
5. C
6. A
7. C
8. B
9. A
10. B
11. B
12. C
13. D

OWNERSHIP BASICS

1. D
2. B
3. A

OWNERSHIP PRINCIPLES

1. A
2. A
3. A
4. C
5. B
6. B

PROPERTY

1. B
2. A
3. B
4. C
5. A
6. B
7. D
8. B
9. A
10. C

11. D
12. C
13. B
14. B
15. B

PUBLIC AND PRIVATE CONTROL

1. D
2. C
3. B
4. C
5. A
6. D
7. B
8. A
9. A
10. D

SURVEY & DESCRIPTION

1. C
2. A
3. C
4. B
5. A
6. B
7. C
8.
9. SW 1/4, NE 1/4, SE 1/4
10. A: NORTH 5° EAST
    B: NORTH 50° WEST
    C: NORTH 65° EAST
    D: SOUTH 20° WEST

AGENCY A

1. B
2. C
3. D
4. C
5. D
6. C
7. D

8. A
9. B
10. A
11. B
12. B
13. D

AGENCY B

1. C
2. A
3. B
4. D
5. A
6. B
7. C
8. A

BROKERAGE TYPES AND AFFILIATIONS

1. True
2. D
3. True
4. False

MINIMUM SERVICE REQUIREMENTS

1. D
2. A
3. D
4. D
5. B

CONTRACT LAW 1

1. C
2. D
3. A
4. A
5. C
6. B
7. B

CONTRACT LAW 2

1. B
2. D
3. B
4. B
5. A

ADVANCED CONTRACT LAW

1. D
2. D
3. C
4. A

LISTINGS & OPTIONS

1. D
2. C
3. A
4. B
5. D
6. B
7. C
8. C
9. A
10. D

NEW CONSTRUCTION CONTRACT

1. A
2. D
3. B
4. B
5. C

Answers

6. A
7. C
8. D

LEASES
1. D
2. A
3. B
4. A
5. C
6. A
7. C
8. B
9. C
10. B
11. A

PROPERTY MANAGEMENT
1. B
2. D
3. A
4. D
5. D
6. C
7. B
8. C
9. C
10. D

MATH A & B
1. B
2. D
3. C
4. C
5. A
6. A
7. D
8. C
9. A
10. B

PROPERTY TAX & TITLE INSURANCE
1. C
2. D
3. B
4. A
5. C
6. B
7. $68,000 x 34% ÷ 100 x $8.76 = $2,025 (ROUNDED)
8. $105,000 x 68% x .019468 = $1,390.02
9. ($314,000 x 28%) ÷ 1,000 x $64.72 = $5,690
10. ($1,200,000 x 24%) x .098674 = $28,418
11. ($1,789 ÷ .0784) ÷ 32% = $71,309

RESPA
1. T
2. F
3. F
4. T
5. F
6. T
7. T
8. F
9. T
10. T
11. MONEY
12. 1-4 RESIDENTIAL
13. B
14. C
15. C
16. C
17. A
18. D
19. A
20. C
21. C
22. B
23. A

24.	D		13.	C
25.	A		14.	A
26.	D		15.	A
27.	A		16.	C
28.	C		17.	D
			18.	A
			19.	C
			20.	B
			21.	B
			22.	D
			23.	C
			24.	A

SETTLEMENT PROCEDURES

Proration Problems

1. D
2. A
3. B

Quiz
1. B
2. D
3. C
4. A
5. B
6. D
7. C
8. B
9. A
10. B
11. C
12. B
13. D
14. B

APPLICATION & UNDERWRITING 1

1. A
2. C
3. A
4. B
5. A
6. C
7. A
8. B
9. A
10. C
11. B
12. D

APPLICATION & UNDERWRITING 2

1. C
2. B
3. A
4. A
5. D
6. B
7. A
8. C
9. C
10. A
11. C
12. D
13. B
14. B
15. D
16. B
17. B
18. B
19. B
20. D
21. C
22. A
23. C
24. C
25. A
26. C
27. B

494

28.	A
29.	B
30.	B
31.	D
32.	B

FINANCE BASICS

1.	C
2.	B
3.	B
4.	A
5.	D
6.	B
7.	B
8.	A
9.	C
10.	D
11.	C
12.	B
13.	A
14.	D
15.	C

ADVANCED FINANCE

1.	D
2.	D
3.	A
4.	B
5.	A
6.	B
7.	C
8.	B
9.	C
10.	B
11.	A
12.	D
13.	D
14.	B
15.	A

MORTGAGE LAW

1.	D
2.	A
3.	B
4.	D
5.	A
6.	A
7.	C
8.	D
9.	B
10.	C
11.	B
12.	↓
	B TRUSTOR
	C TRUSTEE
	A BENEFICIARY
	B MORTGAGOR
	A MORTGAGEE

TAXATION

1.	B
2.	B
3.	A
4.	C
5.	C
6.	B
7.	D
8.	D
9.	D

APPRAISAL & VALUATION

1.	A
2.	C
3.	A
4.	D
5.	C
6.	A
7.	C
8.	C
9.	B

Answers

ADVANCED APPRAISAL
1. D
2. D
3. C
4. D
5. B
6. B
7. D

CAP RATE PROBLEMS
1. F $ **193,929**
   R 7%
   L $ 13,575
2. F $ **36,000**
   R 5%
   L $ 1,800
   (150 x 12 MO. = 1,800)
3. F $ **108,750**
   R 8%
   L $ 8,700
   $108,750
   - 80,000
   $ 28,750 LAND VALUE
4. F $ 320,000
   R 9%
   L $ 28,800
   F $ **261,818**
   R 11%
   L $ 28,800
5. F $ **7,778**
   R 9%
   L $ 700

MARKET EVALUATION
1. B
2. C

3. Price, Location, Condition of Property, Market Conditions, Marketing, Financing
4. B
5. A
6. B

7. D
8. D
9. B
10. B

FEDERAL LAWS A
1. D
2. C
3. C
4. B
5. C
6. A
7. B

FEDERAL LAWS B
1. D
2. A
3. D
4. D
5. C
6. A

FEDERAL LAWS C
1. C
2. A
3. D
4. B
5. A
6. B
7. C
8. A

TRUTH IN LENDING
1. T
2. F
3. T
4. F
5. F
6. T
7. F
8. F

9.   F
10. T
11. T
12. T
13. T
14. D
15. A
16. A
17. A
18. D
19. D
20. C
21. D
22. C
23. D

Answers to Review Test 1

1.	C
2.	B
3.	C
4.	A
5.	D
6.	D
7.	D
8.	A
9.	B
10.	A
11.	C
12.	A
13.	C
14.	B
15.	D
16.	A
17.	A
18.	C
19.	A
20.	A
21.	D
22.	D
23.	A
24.	C
25.	C
26.	D
27.	D
28.	A
29.	C
30.	A

31.	A
32.	B
33.	C
34.	B
35.	C
36.	B
37.	B
38.	A
39.	A
40.	B
41.	C
42.	D
43.	B
44.	D
45.	D
46.	D

Answers to Review Test 2

1. D
2. C
3. B
4. B
5. C
6. B
7. A
8. A
9. A
10. B
11. D
12. B
13. B
14. D
15. B
16. D
17. C
18. C
19. D
20. A
21. C
22. B
23. D
24. D
25. B
26. C
27. D
28. D
29. A
30. C
31. C
32. B
33. B
34. C
35. D
36. D
37. B
38. D
39. B
40. C
41. A

42. A
43. B
44. B
45. C
46. B
47. C
48. B
49. D
50. A
51. C
52. C
53. B
54. C
55. B
56. A
57. B
58. C
59. A
60. A
61. B
62. A
63. C
64. A
65. A
66. D
67. D
68. C
69. A
70. C
71. A
72. B
73. C
74. D
75. B
76. C
77. C
78. D
79. A
80. C

Answers

Math A & B Answers

1.   F $ 120,000
     R   5.5%
     L $ $6,600

2.   F $ 14,000
     R   14%
     L $ 1,960

3.   F $ 2,700
     R   35%
     L $ 945

4.   F $ 350,000
     R   12%
     L $ 42,000

5.   F $ 350,000
     R   112%
     L $ 392,000

6.   F $ 560,000
     R   71%
     L $ 397,600

7.   F $ 135,000
     R   93%
     L $ 125,550

8.   F $ 86,000
     R   20%
     L $ 17,200 down

$17,200 down
  $ 1,032 origination fee
  $ 825 closing
  $ 19,057

9.   F $ 12,000
     R   15%
     L $ 1,800
  625 ÷ 125 days = $5.00 /day x 360 = 1,800

10.   F $ 69,000
     R   9%
     L $ 6,210

$6,210 ÷ 12 = $517.50 /mo.
$13,972.50 ÷ 517.50 = 27 Months

11.   F $ 70,000
     R   95%
     L $ 66,500

12.   F $ 150
     R   52%
     L $ 78

© Stringham Schools

13.   F $ 326,700 sq. feet

      R _____ 65%

      L $ 212,355 sq. feet

      211,355 ÷ 18,000 = 11.7 lots

14.   F $ 62,500

      R _____ 4%

      L $ 2,500

15.   F $ 250,000

      R _____ 9%

      L $ 22,500

16.   A $ 161,250

      A   x   .80

      A $ 129,000

      T   x   .008

      T $ 1,032

17.   F $ 4,800

      R _____ 70%

      L $ 3,360

      F $80,000

      R _____ 6%

      L $ 4,800

Math Etc. Answers (Optional Class)

1a. $82,320

1b. $5,880

1c. $11,524.80

2a. $84,600

2b. 7%

2c. $212,000

3a. $150,000

3b. $80,000

3c. $6,400

4a. $92,187.50

4b. $349,514.56

4c. $16,250

5a. $100,000

5b. $50,000

5c. $63,000

6a. $68,000

6b. $190,000

6c. $124,460

7a. $82,000

7b. $124,000

7c. $97,000

8a. 12.5%

8b. $37,000

8c. $165,526.27

9a. 48 agents

9b. 140 trees

9c. $2,625,000

10a. $340,000

10b. $106,250

10c. $375,000

11a. 18 lots

11b. 0.19 acres

11c. 32.67 cu. yards

Math Review Answers Explained:

1. This question requires you to take information and solve the equation "backwards"; where information is given at the bottom of a traditional equation that is used to solve the items at the top. First compute the assessed value, then the appraised value.

Appraised Value   **?**

  * Assessed Rate   * 20%
   Assessed Value   **?**
  * Tax Rate   * 0.020 (20 mills)
   Taxes Due $540
  Appraised Value   **$135,000 ← ANSWER**
  * Assessed Rate   * 20%
   Assessed Value   **$27,000**
  * Tax Rate   * 0.020 (20 mills)
   Taxes Due $540

2. We need to know the NOI and then use the cap rate formula to answer this problem:

   Gross Income $25,000
  * Expense Rate   * 52%
   Expenses   **?**
   Gross Income $25,000
  - Expenses   - **?**
   NOI   **?**
   Appraised Value $120,000
  * Cap Rate   * **?%**
   NOI   **?**
   Gross Income $25,000
  * Expense Rate   * 52%
   Expenses   **13,000**
   Gross Income $25,000
  - Expenses   **-13,000**
   NOI   **12,000**
   Appraised Value $120,000
  * Cap Rate   * **10% ← ANSWER**
   NOI   **$12,000**

3. We need to compute the commission portion of the agent's payment, and then use that information to compute the property value.

Gross Pay	$750
- Fixed Salary	- $200
Commission	?
Property Value	?
* Commission Rate	* 3%
Commission	?
Gross Pay	$750
- Fixed Salary	- $200
Commission	**$550**
Property Value	**$18,333** ← ANSWER
* Commission Rate	* 3%
Commission	**$550**

4. We need to multiply each piece by its respective profit rate and then add them together:

Land	$28,000
* Land & Profit Margin	* 105%
Land Sales Price	?
Home	$250,000
* Home & Profit Margin	* 130%
Home Sales Price	?
Home Sales Price	?
+ Land Sales Price	+ ?
Total Sales Price	?
Land	$28,000
* Land & Profit Margin	* 105%
Land Sales Price	**$29,400**
Home	$250,000
* Home & Profit Margin	* 130%
Home Sales Price	**$325,000**
Home Sales Price	**$325,000**
+ Land Sales Price	+ $29,400
Total Sales Price	**$354,400** ← ANSWER

5. This is a seller's net question (Don't you just love these!). Here is the formula you'll need:

Minimum Selling Price		?
* Seller's Rate	*	94% (100%-6%)
Gross to Seller		?
- Expenses	-	$900 (550+350)
Net to Seller		$79,000
Minimum Selling Price		**$85,000 ← ANSWER**
* Seller's Rate	*	94% (100%-6%)
Gross to Seller		**$79,900**
- Expenses	-	$900 (550+350)
Net to Seller		$79,000

6. You'll need to use the LTV equation to find the loan amount, and then use the discount point equation. Add the costs that will not be loaned:

Purchase Price		$55,000
* Loan Ratio	*	80%
Loan Amount		?
* Discount %	*	3%
Discount Fee		?
Purchase Price		$55,000
* Down Payment Ratio	*	20%
Down Payment		?
Discount Fee		?
Down Payment		?
+ Closing Costs		+ $2,000
Total to Closing		$?
Purchase Price		$55,000
* Loan Ratio	*	80%
Loan Amount		**$44,000**
* Discount %	*	3%
Discount Fee		**$1,320**
Purchase Price		$55,000
* Down Payment Ratio	*	20%
Down Payment		**$11,000**
Discount Fee		**$1,320**
Down Payment		**$11,000**
+ Closing Costs		+ $2,000
Total to Closing		**$14,320 ← ANSWER**

7. We need to figure the sale price when it sold a year later and also figure the agent's commission on that sale. We'll use those figures to calculate the net dollar loss.

```
 Original Sales Price   ?
* Sales Ratio          *    80% (100%-20%)
  Current Sales Price  ?
  Original Sales Price           ?
* Loss Ratio           *     20%
  Loss Amount          ?
      Current Sales Price     ?
      * Commission Rate        *      10%
        Commission                    ?
      Loss Amount             $?
 + Commission            + $?
   Net Loss              $?


  Original Sales Price         $10,500
* Sales Ratio          *    80% (100%-20%)
  Current Sales Price  $8,400
  Original Sales Price         $10,500
* Loss Ratio           *     20%
  Loss Amount          $2,100
  Current Sales Price  $8,400
      * Commission Rate        *      10%
        Commission                    $840
  Loss Amount          $2,100
+ Commission           +   $840
      Net Loss                 $2,940 ← ANSWER
```

8. We need to calculate interest per month to find the total interest due over 16 months and then add that to the original loan amount to answer this:

```
  Annual Interest            11%
    ÷ Months in a year     ÷  12
      Monthly Interest Rate      ?
  Loan Amount              $15,000
      * Monthly Interest Rate  *   ?
        Monthly Interest       $?
      * Loan Term              *  16
  Interest Due             $?
  Loan Amount              $15,000
+ Interest Due           +  $?
      Total Due             $?
  Annual Interest          11%
    ÷Months in a year      ÷  12
    Monthly Interest Rate    0.917%
  Loan Amount              $15,000
    *Monthly Interest Rate   *   0.917%
```

Monthly Interest	**$137.50**
* Loan Term	* 16
Interest Due	**$2,200**
Loan Amount	$15,000
+ Interest Due	+ **$2,200**
Total Due	**$17,200 ← ANSWER**

9. Here, we figure how much interest is due in the first month, and then we simply subtract the interest from the principal and interest payment:

Annual Interest	11%
÷ Months in a year	÷ 12
Monthly Interest Rate	**?**
Loan Amount	$84,000
* Monthly Interest Rate	* **?**
Monthly Interest	**$?**
P&I Payment	$799.95
- Interest Due	- **$?**
Principal Due	**$?**
Annual Interest	11%
÷ Months in a year	÷ 12
Monthly Interest Rate	**0.917%**
Loan Amount	$84,000
* Monthly Interest Rate	* **0.917%**
Monthly Interest	**$770**
P&I Payment	$799.95
- Interest Due	- **$770.00**
Principal Due	**$29.95 ← ANSWER**

10. This one is similar to previous math problems, only you need to work "backwards" on this one:

Loan Amount	**?**
* Annual Interest Rate	* 9.5%
Annual Interest Due	**?**
÷ Months in a year	÷ 12
Monthly Interest	$427.50
Loan Amount	**$54,000 ← ANSWER**
* Annual Interest Rate	* 9.5%
Annual Interest Due	**$5,130**
÷ Months in a year	÷ 12
Monthly Interest	$427.50

NOTE

IF YOU DIVIDE THE INTEREST BY TWELVE, REMEMBER **NOT** TO CLEAR THE INFORMATION FROM YOU CALCULATOR. There are lots of extra numbers after the decimal that will cause your answer to be about $23 off when calculating the balance.

THE ESSENTIALS

510

The Essentials

Essential Elements of a Deed
Intent of the Grantor
Names of the Parties
Description of the Property
Granting Clause
Consideration
In Writing
Signature of the Grantor
DELIVERY

Covenants of a Warranty Deed
Seizin
Against Encumbrances
Quiet Enjoyment
Further Assurance
Warranty Forever

Essential Elements of a Contract
Mutual Agreement
Consideration
Capacity/Competency
Legal Purpose
In Writing (if for sale or purchase of real estate)

Essential Elements of Value
Demand
Utility or usefulness
Scarcity
Transferability

Four Unities of Joint Tenancy
Possession
Interest
Time
Title

Joint Tenancy & Tenancy by the Entirety conveys full rights of survivorship

511

Bundle of Rights

Possession

Use/Control

Quiet Enjoyment

Disposition

Four C's

Credit

Capacity

Capital

Collateral

Three Credit Bureaus

Experian

Equifax

Trans Union

CAMEL

Capital

Assets

Management

Earnings

Liquidity

Sensitivity (to market risks)

MEASUREMENTS

1 square yard = 9 square feet

1 cubic yard = 27 cubic feet

1 mile = 5,280 linear feet

1 section = 640 acres

1 section = 1 mile square

1 township = 36 square miles

1 acre = 43,560 square feet

1 rod = 16.5 feet

1 chain = 66 feet or 100 links

1 link = .66 feet

Real Estate Glossary

3/1 ARM	A loan with three years of the same rate then rate adjustments every year thereafter.
72-HOUR RIGHT OF RESCISSION	All borrowers must receive this notice if the loan is a refinance loan.
ABANDONMENT	When a tenant leaves a property before the expiration of the lease agreement.
ABOVE PAR	An interest rate quoted that would give a credit to the borrower.
ABROGATION	To nullify or replace. Signing of the closing documents nullifies the Real Estate Purchase Contract except for warranties which extend beyond the closing date.
ACCELERATION CLAUSE	Allows a loan to become due and payable immediately if certain requirements are not met, such as making payments, maintaining the physical condition of the property or paying property taxes and hazard insurance.
ACCESSION	The process of adding to real property.
ACKNOWLEDGE	The legal process of having the signature on a contract or other legal document verified by a notary public.
ACRE	43,560 square feet.
ACRE FEET	Consists of 43,560 cubic feet of water, or an acre of land covered by 12 inches of water.
ACTUAL DELIVERY	Transferring a deed from the grantor to the grantee by handing the deed to the grantee or sending it by certified mail.
ACTUAL EVICTION	The legal process by which a lessor evicts the lessee and regains possession of the property.
ACTUAL MORTGAGE AMOUNT	The loan amount including upfront funding fee.

AD VALOREM TAX	A tax levied according to the value of the property.
ADDENDUM	Additions or changes incorporated into the REPC by reference.
ADDENDUM TO LEASE AGREEMENT WITH OPTION FOR PURCHASE	This form is used for any additional terms the buyer or seller wish to include in the agreement.
ADJUSTABLE RATE MORTGAGE (ARM)	A loan where the interest rate is periodically adjusted based on a specific economic indicator (or financial index).
ADJUSTED COST BASIS	Cost basis plus improvements, minus depreciation claimed during the years the property was owned.
ADJUSTMENT PERIOD	Lengthen of time between interest rate adjustments on an adjustable rate loan.
ADMINISTRATOR	A person appointed by the court to carry out the terms of a will.
ADVERSE POSSESSION	The process whereby a non-owner can gain ownership of property by occupying it in hostile, continuous, open, and notorious possession, and in Utah, paying the property taxes for the statutory period of time (7 years in Utah).
AFFILIATED BUSINESS ARRANGEMENT (AfBA)	A financial interest in a business that could provide services to a borrower in a loan transaction. The lender is required to disclose such affiliations to the borrower and may not require that the borrower use the affiliate. Disclosure is also required when it is the policy of the lender to share private information of borrowers with its affiliates. The borrower may refuse permission to share information by returning the notice indicating that they Opt Out of the companies sharing policy.
AGENCY	A relationship between two parties wherein the principal hires another person to represent him or her.
AGENCY BY ESTOPPEL	The principal seeks to deny an agency relationship, but the court stops him from denying the agency, and thereby confirms it.
AGENCY BY RATIFICATION	The agency is created by implication, or actions, and the principal approves it by agreeing after the agency service has been performed to compensate the agent.

AGENCY BY STATUTE	The law has given rise to the agency, such as a Sheriff appointed by the court to be the agent of the owner in a foreclosure sale.
AGENT	The person hired by a principal to act for and in behalf of, or to represent the principal, always acting in the principal's best interest.
AGGREGATE ESCROW ANALYSIS	A formula for determining that no more than the RESPA allowed amount is being held in the borrower's reserve account.
AIR SPACE	In condominium ownership, what is actually owned by the unit owner (in addition to tenancy in common for common areas).
ALIENATION OF TITLE	A change of ownership. May be voluntary (sold the property) or involuntary (foreclosure sale).
ALIENATION, DUE ON SALE, NON-ASSUMPTION CLAUSE	A clause which allows the lender to call the loan due and payable immediately if the property is sold or the loan is assumed.
ALL-INCLUSIVE TRUST DEED (AITD)	A State-approved document used for security, usually in seller financing, where the financing is structured as a wraparound.
ALLODIAL	A socio-economic system that allows for private ownership of real property.
ALTA POLICY	The lender's title insurance policy which offers coverage in the amount of the loan which includes a site visit to discover unrecorded encumbrances.
AMENITY	A "nice, but not necessary" feature which provides personal pleasure to the owner of real property. It can be tangible or intangible.
AMERICANS WITH DISABILITIES ACT (ADA)	An act designed to eliminate discrimination against handicapped persons in employment, government services, and all facilities and services offered to the public.
AMORTIZED LOAN	A loan which has regular monthly payments of principal and interest that if paid would reduce the balance of the loan with each payment until the balance is zero at the end of the amortization period.

AMORTIZATION SCHEDULE	A schedule of payments toward principal and interest and loan balance after each payment through the life of a loan.
ANNUAL PERCENTAGE RATE (APR)	The interest rate plus any other charges for the loan, including such things as discount points and origination fees; computed as a yearly percentage rate. It is used for comparing loans.
ANNUAL PERCENTAGE YIELD (APY)	The effective interest rate based on the frequency of interest payments paid on deposits.
ANTICIPATION	The appraisal principle that weighs the value of the future benefits a product or property will bring.
APPLICATION FRAUD	Materially representing or even omitting any item on the 1003 or other loan application with the intent of misleading a lender.
APPRAISAL	A professional process for estimating the value of real property.
APPRAISAL FRAUD	Inflation or materially overstating the value of a property with the intention of obtaining a higher loan or even cash-out.
APPRECIATION	A percentage of increase in the value of the property over its value when it was originally purchased.
APPURTENANT	Attached to the land (such as a house) or the deed (such as a recorded easement).
ARBITRATION	The two parties in disagreement agree to accept the decision of a third party who acts both as a mediator and a judge. It avoids the excessive time and high costs of a court action.
"AS IS" CLAUSE	The clause in the Real Estate Purchase Contract that stipulates the buyer is buying the property in its current condition and with the faults that have been disclosed.
ASSEMBLAGE	Combining two or more parcels of land into one.
ASSESSED VALUE	A percentage of the appraised value, as determined by law, upon which the tax rate will be levied to determine the property tax.

ASSIGNMENT OF CONTRACT	One party in a contract substitutes another party in his place. The original party retains secondary liability for the performance of the contract. It does not require the agreement of the other original party in the contract.
ASSIGNMENT OF INTEREST ADDENDUM	Should be used when a contract was entered into between Seller and Buyer #1. Before closing, Buyer #1 wishes to assign his/her position in the contract to Buyer #2.
ASSIGNMENT OF LEASE	A contract that substitutes a new tenant in the lease. The assignee becomes liable for the remaining term of the lease. Unless prohibited by the lease contract, this can be done without the approval of the lessor, but the original lessee retains secondary liability.
ATTACHMENT	The legal process when real or personal property is seized by the court and held as security for satisfaction of a judgment.
ATTORNEY IN FACT	A person who has been given power to sign in behalf of another.
ATTORNEY'S OPINION	A lawyer's examination and evaluation of the history of title. It includes a brief summary of all recorded instruments which affect the title, including records of taxes, special assessments, judgments, mortgages and trust deeds.
AUTHORITY TO SIGN LEASE	Authority for the property manager to sign leases effectively binding the owner to the lease agreement must be specifically stated in the agency agreement.
BALLOON MORTGAGE	A loan with a balloon payment at the end of its term. It could be a partially amortized or a straight loan or note.
BALLOON PAYMENTS	Required payments larger than the regular payment. These payments are often made at the end of the loan, retiring the loan early; but can be made at other times during the term of the loan.
BANK RESERVE REQUIREMENTS	The amount of funds that a depository institution must hold in reserve against specified deposit liabilities or other risks.
BARGAIN AND SALE DEED	This deed makes no guarantees as to the condition of the title, but unlike the Quit Claim Deed, the grantor implies some actual interest in the property.

BASE LOAN AMOUNT	This loan amount is set based on the median home price in a county.
BASELINE	An east-west line which intersects the meridian and creates a point from which land can be measured under the Government or rectangular survey method.
BASIS POINT	A finance term meaning a yield of 1/100th of 1% annually. 100 basis points = One percent.
BELOW PAR	An interest rate quoted that would require a charge to the borrower.
BENEFICIARY	The lender under a Trust Deed & Note.
BEQUEST OR LEGACY	A gift of personal property given in a will.
BILATERAL CONTRACT	A contract wherein a promise is exchanged for a promise, thus making the contract binding on both parties.
BILL OF SALE	Evidence of transfer of ownership of personal property.
BUSINESS DAY	Monday through Saturday except holidays.
BLANKET MORTGAGE	A loan that uses two or more parcels of real property as security.
BLIND AD	An advertisement which fails to indicate that the advertiser is a real estate brokerage or that sales agents or brokers are selling their own property.
BLOCKBUSTING	The illegal practice of inducing panic selling in a neighborhood by starting rumors involving minorities moving in.
BOARD OF ADJUSTMENT	The body to which one would appeal in order to obtain a variance to do something contrary to the current zoning law.
BOARD OF EQUALIZATION	The body of appeal if you think your property tax appraisal is too high.

BOOT	Personal property or money needed to make up a difference in value when exchanging real property.
BRANCH OFFICE	Any remote operation of the main real estate office which will be in operation more than 12 months and must be registered with the Real Estate Division.
BRIDGE, SWING OR GAP LOAN	A short term loan to help the buyers have up-front funds to get into their new home, when the sale on the old one is going to close later than the closing to purchase the new one.
BROKER PRICE OPINION (BPO)	A broker's written opinion of the value of a particular property that may not be used in connection with the originating a federally related loan; not an appraisal.
BUFFER ZONE	An area established by the zoning and planning commission to separate commercial and industrial areas from residential. Its purpose may be safety or economics.
BUILDING CODES	Rules set by government to establish minimum standards of construction.
BUNDLE OF RIGHTS	All rights and interests that can be legally held in real property. They are separated into Possession, Use & Control, Quiet Enjoyment and Disposition.
BUSINESS PLAN	A written overview that reveals the basic philosophy and strategy for an investment property.
BUYDOWN	A financing technique in which a borrower is able to obtain a lower interest rate by paying discount points at the time the loan is originated. (1 point = 1% of the loan amount).
BUYER'S BROKER	A broker who represents the buyer in a fiduciary capacity.
CC&R'S	The abbreviation given to restrictions and requirements created in the Uniform Declaration of Restrictions for condominiums.
CAPACITY	The borrower/co-borrowers' ability to repay the loan.

CAPITAL	Total value of assets. This term is sometimes used to refer to the amount actually paid as down payment and closing costs, as in "the borrower's capital in the transaction". Also used to refer to the total value of an investment as in "CAP Rate (Rate of return on capital invested or purchase price)."
CAPITAL GAIN	The taxable profit derived from the sale of a capital asset, such as real property.
CAPITAL MORTGAGE MARKET	Markets (including informal markets as well as organized markets and exchanges) in which mortgage backed securities are bought and sold.
CAPITALIZATION RATE OR CAP RATE	The ratio created when the net operating income is divided by the value of the property. It is also called the rate of return.
CAVEAT EMPTOR	The philosophy that says "Let the buyer beware."
CERCLA	Comprehensive Environmental Response, Compensation & Liability Act, which is also known as the Superfund Act.
CERTIFICATE OF ELIGIBILITY	Endorsement from the Veterans Administration indicating the right of a veteran to obtain a VA loan and the amount of his eligibility.
CERTIFICATE OF REASONABLE VALUE	The document required for a VA loan that verifies the value of property being used as security for the VA loan (VA appraisal).
CERTIFICATE OF SALE	The document given to the individual who successfully bids and purchases a property at a Sheriff's Sale. It does not convey title to the property.
CHAIN OF TITLE OR ABSTRACT OF TITLE	A historical record of land ownership and liens or encumbrances against the property.
CHANGE, CYCLE OF OR NEIGHBORHOOD CYCLE	This appraisal principle involves activity which goes from growth or integration to equilibrium to disintegration and perhaps to growth again.
CHAPTER 7	Bankruptcy with all debts canceled.
CHAPTER 13	Bankruptcy with a payment plan.

CHATTEL	A synonym for personal property. It comes from the word "cattle."
CHATTEL MORTGAGE	A loan secured by personal property.
CLOSED-END LOAN	A loan with a specific balance set at the beginning, and the balance cannot be increased during the term of the loan.
CLOSING	When any loan funds are received from the lender(s) and the applicable documents are recorded. This comes after the settlement.
CLOUD ON THE TITLE	A term that refers to any kind of lien or encumbrance against the title.
CO-BORROWER (CO-SIGNERS)	These persons are equally entitled to receive disclosures.
CODE OF ETHICS	Standards for ethical conduct which have been systematized for a group of professionals.
CODICIL	An addition or change to an existing will.
COLLATERAL	A term that refers to security used for a loan. It may be real or personal property.
COLOR OF TITLE	To all outward public appearance, or from a document that seems to be valid, the possessor of the property would seem to have ownership.
COMBINED LOAN TO VALUE RATIO (CLTV)	The ratio of all financing (first and junior mortgages) to the value of the property.
COMMERCIAL PROPERTY	A classification of real estate that includes income-producing property such as office buildings, gasoline stations, restaurants, shopping centers, hotels, and motels, parking lots, and stores.
COMMON AREA	Land or improvements in a condominium developments designated for the use and benefits of all residents, property owners, and tenants.

521

COMMUNICATION	The process of notifying the offeror that the offer has been accepted.
COMMUNITY PROPERTY	A form of ownership between husband and wife where each has an equal interest in property obtained during their marriage. The only way either can hold separate property is to obtain it before marriage, after the marriage is ended, or during the marriage by gift or inheritance.
COMPARATIVE MARKET ANALYSIS (CMA)	A method of valuing homes that looks not only at recent home sales but also at homes presently on the market plus homes that were listed but did not sell.
COMPENSATING FACTORS	A condition that allows an underwriter to overlook negative underwriting information.
COMPETENCY OR CAPACITY	The ability to understand the terms of a contract and to make a rational decision as to whether or not to enter into it.
COMPETITION	An appraisal principle: When a particular use of property is bringing a high return, others enter into the same business or purchase property for the same purpose.
COMPLAINT	Filing this document with the court initiates foreclosure under a mortgage.
COMPOUND INTEREST	Interest is paid on earned interest as well as on the principal. It is used in savings accounts.
CONDEMNATION ACTION	Process by which government exercises the power to transfer ownership of property from private to public use. See Eminent Domain
CONDOMINIUM	One owns the air space of one's own unit and an undivided interest in the common area.
CONDOMINIUM OWNERSHIP ACT	The act which governs ownership and related issues when one owns airspace and undivided interest in the common area.
CONFORMITY	An appraisal principle which states that because all homes in a particular area are harmonious in design and value, their value is sustained and tends to increase over time.

CONFORMING LOAN	See Conventional Conforming Loan.
CONFORMING LOAN LIMIT	The maximum loan amount permitted by Fannie Mae on a single family residence.
CONSIDERATION	The process wherein each party to a contract makes a sacrifice and each party receives a benefit. It is an essential element of any contract.
CONTRACTIONARY POLICY	Decreases the total money supply. This is designed to "cool" the economy by increasing interest rates which slows investment in an effort to control inflation.
CONTINGENCY	A provision in a contract that requires the completion of a certain act or the happening of a particular event before that contract is binding.
CONSTRUCTION LOAN	An open ended loan funded in installments as various portions of the work are completed.
CONSTRUCTIVE DELIVERY	The process of transferring a deed from the grantor to the grantee by recording the deed at the county recorder's office.
CONSTRUCTIVE EVICTION	When the landlord violates the terms of the lease by not keeping the property livable or habitable, the tenant can legally vacate the property and not be held liable for further rent payments.
CONSTRUCTIVE FRAUD	A party misrepresents innocently, with no evil intention, but that misrepresentation could have been avoided with reasonable care.
CONTINGENCY CLAUSE	Sometimes known as a "subject to" clause, it requires completion of certain acts before the contract is fully binding.
CONTRACT	An agreement between two or more parties to do or not to do certain things. It may be oral or in writing.
CONTRIBUTION	The appraisal principle which states that an improvement to a property must add its cost to the value.
CONVENTIONAL CONFORMING LOAN	A loan that does not exceed the monetary limits set by FNMA and FHLMC, and which is not an FHA or VA loan.

COOPERATING BROKER	A broker who assists another broker in the sale of real property. Usually, the cooperating broker is the (selling) broker who found the buyer who offers to buy a piece of property that is listed with another (listing) broker.
COOPERATIVE	A form of ownership in multiple unit housing where the owner purchases shares of stock in the entire development, then obtains exclusive use of a unit by means of a proprietary lease.
CORPORATION	A legal person. It cannot die or go to jail.
CORPOREAL	Something that is physical or tangible, such as land or buildings.
CORRELATION	See Reconciliation.
COST OR COST BASIS	What you paid for the product or property when you bought it.
COST APPROACH	An approach to appraisal which considers the price of resources necessary to build the same or a similar property. It is the only approach which places a separate value on the land.
COST PLUS	A contract where payment is for material and labor, with a profit factor added.
COST RECOVERY	An income tax deduction allowed on investment property to treat the improvements as though they will waste away in a certain number of years. It cannot be applied to raw land or a personal residence. Also known as depreciation.
COUNTER OFFER	A response to an offer wherein the offeree changes one or more of the terms of the contract, becomes the offeror, and sends the offer back to the original offeror.
COUNTY	This state jurisdiction differentiates base loan limits for conforming loans.
COVENANT AGAINST ENCUMBRANCES	This covenant in a deed assures the grantee that the title has no liens or encumbrances except those that have been revealed by the grantor.

COVENANT OF FURTHER ASSURANCE	In the event someone makes a claim against the property, the grantor has the full responsibility to defend the title against the claimant. This includes producing proper documents to substantiate the ownership of the grantee, and going to court if necessary.
COVENANT OF QUIET ENJOYMENT	In a deed, the guaranteed right of an owner or lessee legally in possession of property to uninterrupted use without interference from any third party claiming superior title.
COVENANT OF SEIZIN	This covenant in a deed guarantees the grantor holds title to the property and has the right to convey it to a grantee.
COVENANT OF WARRANTY FOREVER	If the grantor were to lose in defense of the title, this covenant guarantees payment for the defense of the title and for damages caused the grantee, including buying the property back from the grantee if necessary.
COVENANTS, CONDITIONS & RESTRICTIONS	See C C & R
CREDIT	An amount of money which will reduce what the buyer has to bring to closing, or increase the amount the seller gets at closing.
CUBIC FOOT METHOD	Under the Cost Replacement Approach, this method determines the cost per unit of volume and then multiplies it by the number of units of volume. It is most often used with warehouses.
DAMAGES	A money adjustment ordered by the court for actual losses suffered.
DEBIT	An amount of money which will increase what the buyer brings to close, or will reduce what the seller gets at closing.
DEBT RATIO	The sum of all contractual payments including hosing compared to gross income known as the back end ratio.
DEBT SERVICE	Loan payments of principle and interest.
DEDICATION	A private individual's gift of property for public use. It may be voluntary (giving land for a public park) or statutory (subdivider giving land for roads).

DEDUCTIONS	Items which the IRS allows to be subtracted from your gross taxable income in order to determine your taxable income.
DEED	The document that serves as evidence of ownership of real property, as well as the document of conveyance.
DEED IN LIEU OF FORECLOSURE	The defaulting borrower conveys title to the property to the lender. In return, the lender forgives the loan on the property.
DEFEASIBLE FEE ESTATE (DETER-MINABLE FEE ESTATE)	A fee simple estate which has conditions attached, the violation of which could cause the grantee to lose title. If written in the deed with the words "so long as," it automatically reverts back to the grantor or his heirs if the conditions are violated. It may also be referred to as "Fee Simple Qualified."
DEFEASANCE CLAUSE	A clause in most loans written in favor of the borrower. It requires the lender to re-convey all interest in the property after the loan has been paid off.
DEFERRED MAINTENANCE	When physical deterioration is repairable, but hasn't yet been taken care of.
DEFICIENCY JUDGMENT	A judgment obtained when a foreclosure sale fails to completely pay off a debt.
DELIVERY	The process of the grantor giving the deed to the grantee.
DEPT. OF HOUSING AND URBAN DEVELOPMENT (HUD)	A government entity which oversees mortgage lending, community planning and development, fair housing, public housing, and lead based paint compliance.
DEPARTMENT OF VETERANS' AFFAIRS (VA)	A government entity that oversees such issues and loans, health care, and education for those who have been in the military.
DEPRECIATION	A loss of value in real property, regardless of the reason for the loss. Also an accounting process used for investment property taxation, referred to by the IRS as cost recovery.
DESCENT	The laws by which the court determines ownership of property of a person who has died intestate, but who has heirs.

DESIGNATED AGENCY	The principal (buyer or seller) who is hiring an agent specifies exactly which person(s) will act as agent or subagent and exercise fiduciary care in representing the principal's best interest.
DEVISE	A gift of real property given in a will.
DEVISOR/DEVISEE	The individuals who give and receive gifts of real property in a will.
DISBURSEMENT AUTHORITY	Should be outlined in the agency agreement.
DISCOUNT POINTS	Money paid when a loan is initially obtained which is considered prepaid interest and permanently lowers the interest rate. Also known as a buy down.
DISCOUNT RATE	The rate charged by the Federal Reserve to member banks for money they borrow. It, along with reserve requirements, is one of the ways the Federal Reserve controls the economy.
DISCOUNTED LOAN OR NOTE	Selling a loan to the secondary money market for less than its face value. This increases the yield (profit) on the loan.
DOCUMENT RECEIPT	A confirmation by the buyer and seller that they received a copy with all signatures.
DOMESTIC PARTNER	This person is a committed in-home companion for at least one year.
DOMINANT TENEMENT	The name given to a property that encumbers a neighboring property with an easement.
DOUBLE COMMISSION	The seller pays a commission to the listing agent, as per their contract, and also a commission to the selling agent.
DOUBLE CONTRACT	The buyer and seller enter into a second sales contract in order to deceive the lender and enable the buyer to finance the purchase.
DUAL AGENT	When the agent is representing both principals in a transaction with their informed consent. (Also known as a limited agent.)

527

"DUE ON SALES" CLAUSES	An acceleration clause found in most mortgage loans, requiring the mortgagor to pay off the mortgage dept when the property is sold, resulting in automatic maturity of the note at the lender's option, effectively eliminating the possibility of the new buyer's assuming the mortgage unless the mortgagee permits the assumption.
DURESS OR UNDUE INFLUENCE	The use of force to obtain agreement. It can be physical or emotional.
DUTY OF CONFIDENTIALITY	The fiduciary obligation to not disclose information to unrepresented parties that would weaken the principal's negotiating position.
DUTY OF LOYALTY	The fiduciary obligation to act solely in the best interest of the principal.
DUTY OF REASONABLE CARE & DILIGENCE	The fiduciary duty to provide reasonable action and care to advance the priorities of the principal.
DUTY TO DISCLOSE	Licensees must disclose their status as licensees acting under an agency agreement in the first contact with a prospective tenant or tenants' agent.
EARNEST MONEY DEPOSIT	The deposit a buyer makes when submitting an offer to purchase real property. It shows he's serious in the offer and will serve as liquidated damages if he defaults on the contract.
EASEMENT	A non-possessory interest which one person has in land owned by another, allowing limited use or enjoyment of the owner's land. It may be referred to as a physical use or condition.
EASEMENT APPURTENANT	An easement which attaches to the land and/or the deed, and passes from owner to owner with the deed.
EASEMENT BY IMPLICATION	An unexpressed, but legally binding understanding regarding a right of way between the parties, created by their actions.

528

EASEMENT BY NECESSITY	Created by a court of law in situations where justice and need, not convenience, dictate the appropriateness of the easement; such as the case of land locked property.
EASEMENT BY PRESCRIPTION	An easement created by adverse use. The use must be adverse, hostile, open, notorious and continuous. This type of easement can be prevented by giving permission to the user, or by ordering the user to discontinue the use before the statutory period passes. (It requires 20 years in Utah.)
EASEMENT IN GROSS	An easement which is personal in nature and does not pass with the deed or the land. It runs with the persons who agreed to it for the term of their lives, or with the need for which it was created, such as a utility easement.
ECONOMIC LIFE	The period of time during which improvements give a return on investment. It is generally considered to be shorter than physical life.
ECONOMIC OR EXTERNAL OBSOLESCENCE	A form of depreciation caused by forces outside the property boundaries. They may be political or social factors. It is considered to be incurable.
EFFECTIVE AGE	An age placed on property for appraisal purposes, based on the condition of the property. It may be more or less that the actual chronological age.
EFFECTIVE INCOME	Net income that is predictable and eligible to be counted in the loan process.
EGRESS	Leaving a property by traveling across the servient tenement property.
ELEVENTH DISTRICT COST OF FUNDS INDEX (COFI)	An index produced by the Eleventh District of the Federal Home Loan Bank reflecting the weighted average cost of home mortgage loans made by member banks.
EMBLEMENTS	Crops nurtured in the year of the transfer or sale of the property. They are considered personal property.
EMINENT DOMAIN	The right of the government to take title, at fair market value, to land owned by a private individual.

EMPLYER ASSISTED HOUSING (EAH)	An eligible employer gift.
ENCROACHMENT	The unauthorized intrusion of a building, tree, or other improvements onto a neighbor's property.
ENCUMBRANCE	Anything which burdens the title to real property so as to restrict, limit, or otherwise affect an owner's rights.
ENFORCEABILITY	The issue of whether a contract dispute could be taken into the court to be settled.
ENVIRONMENTAL PROTECTION AGENCY	The government entity which deals with the impact of commercial, industrial and residential development on the environment.
EQUAL CREDIT OPPORTUNITY ACT OF 1974	Federal act which prohibits discrimination in financing, based on race, age, sex, or marital status.
EQUITABLE PERIOD OF REDEMPTION	In foreclosure, the period of time during which the borrower can reinstate the loan before the foreclosure sales takes place. It is sometimes referred to as equity of redemption.
EQUITABLE TITLE	The legal interest held in a property by the buyer between the time the contract is signed and conveying the actual deed.
EQUITY	The market value of a property minus the debts secured by the property.
ESCALATION CLAUSE	A clause written into a loan or lease that allows for payments to be increased at specified times by stated amounts.
ESCHEAT	This occurs when someone dies without a will, having no heirs.
ESCROW	A depository where a neutral third party is used to hold money or documents. When a mortgage lender is holding the funds on behalf of the borrower it is frequently called Impound Account or Reserve Account.
ESCROW ACCOUNT	A lender held account holding borrower funds for the property taxes and/or insurance.

ESTATE OR TENANCY FOR YEARS	A leasehold estate form of interest in property that has a predetermined start and termination date.
ESTOPPEL CERTIFICATE	A document provided by a lender which reveals all the terms of a loan as requested by the borrower or ordered by the court.
ESTOVERS	The right of a tenant to use natural resources on leased land, such as timber, water, etc. when required as necessities.
EVICTION	The legal process of removing a tenant from the premises for some breach of the lease.
EXECUTIVE DIRECTOR, DEPT. OF COMMERCE	The person who appoints the Director of the Utah Division of Real Estate.
EXCEPTIONS AND RESERVATIONS CLAUSE	In a deed, it indicates rights in the real property which will not be conveyed to the grantee and is another name for the habendum clause.
EXCHANGE	See Tax Deferred Exchange
EXCLUSIVE AGENCY LISTING	One broker is named as the exclusive agent of the seller, but the seller reserves the right to locate a buyer without paying a commission.
EXCLUSIVE RIGHT-TO-SELL LISTING	One principal broker is designated to represent the seller and receive a commission when the buyer is found, regardless of who finds the buyer.
EXECUTE	To put a contract into effect by signing it.
EXECUTED CONTRACT	A contract with all of the terms completed by all parties.
EXECUTOR	The title of a person named in a will to carry out the terms of the will after the death of the testator.
EXECUTORY CONTRACT	A contract that is not fully performed, but which is not in default.
EXPANSIONARY POLICY	Increases the total supply of money. It is used to combat high unemployment in a recession by lowering interest rates.

EXPRESS AGENCY	Agency created through words, written or oral, between the principal and the agent, such as a listing agreement.
EXTENDED COVERAGE TITLE INSURANCE	Covers claims both on and off the record. It includes a site visit to give protection against unrecorded liens and encumbrances, such as mechanic's liens, as well as defects in the land itself, such as unrecorded easements, encroachments, and information based on incorrect surveys. It can be obtained by private individuals.
FAIR, ISAAC AND COMPANY (FICO)	Mathematical scores developed by the Fair Isaac & Company and used by credit bureaus and lenders to evaluate the risk associated in lending money; scores range from 450 to 850; the lower the score, the higher the risk.
FAIR MARKET VALUE	What a willing buyer is willing to pay, and a willing seller is willing to accept, with neither of them under duress and the property has been on the market for sufficient time to verify its value.
FALSE DEVICES	A licensee shall not knowingly participate in any transaction in which a document is used which does not reflect the true terms of the transaction.
FAMILIAL STATUS	One of the protected classes under Fair Housing referring to families with children under 18.
FEDERAL CONSUMER CREDIT PROTECTION ACT	This act is also known as Truth In Lending Act (TILA).
FEDERAL FAIR HOUSING ACT OF 1866	This body of law stated no discrimination based on race in the sale or lease of real estate is allowed and all people are to be treated the same as white people.
FEDERAL FAIR HOUSING ACT OF 1968	Extended the Federal Fair Housing Act of 1866 by adding the prohibition of discrimination according to color, sex, religion, and natural or national origin. It specifically stated that no discrimination should take place relative to sale or rental of real estate, or real estate brokerage services.
FEDERAL FAIR HOUSING AMENDMENT ACT OF 1988	Added two new protected classes to Fair Housing: handicapped and familial status.

FEDERAL HOME LOAN MORTGAGE CORPORATION (FHLMC)	This organization was originally forms to provide funding for the savings and loan industry.
FEDERAL HOUSING ADMINISTRATION (FHA)	A department under HUD that administers and insures loans designed to help low income borrowers with limited cash resources to get into homes.
FEDERAL OPEN MARKET COMMITTEE (FOMC)	Consists of the members of the Board of Governors of the Federal Reserve System and five Reserve Bank presidents.
FEDERAL RESERVE BANK	The bankers' bank; it regulates the money supply by establishing discount rates (cost of money to lending institutions) and setting a reserve requirement (how much cash lenders must keep on hand).
FEDERAL RESERVE SYSTEM	The nation's central bank created by the Federal Reserve Act of 1913 to help stabilize the economy through the judicious handling of the money supply and credit available in this country, functioning through a seven-member Board of Governors and 12 Federal Reserve District Banks, by setting policies and working with privately owned commercial banks.
FEE SIMPLE, FEE ESTATE, FEE SIMPLE ABSOLUTE	The highest or most complete form of ownership that can be held under the law. The ownership rights go on forever.
FEE SIMPLE DEFEASIBLE	See "Defeasible Fee Estate." Also sometimes called "fee simple qualified."
FHA INSURED LOAN	Loans that are insured by the Federal Housing Administration that provide third-party lenders with protection against losses incurred in a foreclosure.
FHA LOAN	A government loan with a low down payment, insured by the borrower's payment of the Mortgage Insurance Premium (MIP).
FHA LOAN LIMITS	The maximum loan amount that is available in a given county.
FHA/VA ADDENDUM	This addendum would be used any time the buyer is going to apply for an FHA or VA loan to finance the purchase.

FHLMC (FREDDIE MAC)	Federal Home Loan Mortgage Corporation; a privately owned secondary money market player. It is federally regulated.
FIDUCIARY	The word which describes the responsibility of an agent toward the principal, involving trust, loyalty, confidence, care and diligence.
FINANCIAL INSTITUTION RECOVERY, REFORM AND ENFORCEMENT ACT (FIRREA)	A comprehensive law passed in 1989 to provide guidelines for the regulation of financial institutions; created the Savings Association Insurance Fraud (SAIF) and the Bank Insurance Fund (BIF). Restructured the Federal Deposit Insurance Corporation (FDIC), created the Appraisal Foundation, and requires the use of state-certified or state-licensed appraisers to appraise properties involving a federally insured or federally regulated industry.
FINE FOR VIOLATING SEC. 8 OF REPSA	$10,000 and/or 1 year in prison.
FIXED COST	A contract where the price is established up front and there is no allowance for overruns.
FIXED-RATE LOAN	A loan where the interest rate, the number of payments, and the amount of payments is established in advance and will not change over the life of the loan.
FIXED-RATE MORTGAGE	A fixed-rate loan secured by real property.
FIXTURE	That which is attached without losing its identity. It is always real property.
FLAT LEASE	The lessee makes periodic, equal rent payments.
FNMA (FANNIE MAE)	Federal National Mortgage Association, a major secondary money market player. It is privately owned, but Federally regulated.
FOR SALE BY OWNER (FSBO)	When a property is sold by an unlicensed owner of a property.

FORECLOSURE	The legal process a lender uses to recover the investment from a defaulting borrower where the loan was secured by the property.
FORMAL WILL	Most valid form of a will, usually prepared by an attorney. It is the least likely form of a will to be challenged.
FORFEITURE	In a default situation when the lender may repossess the property, this is the effect to the borrower.
FRANCHISE	The private right to operate a business using a designated trade name and the operating procedures of a parent company (the franchisor).
FRAUD	An act intended to deceive or misrepresent in order to gain some unfair or dishonest advantage over another and induce someone to give up something of value.
FREEHOLD ESTATE	An interest in property in which some form of ownership is held.
FRONT-END RATIO	The percentage limit a mortgage payment can be compared to the gross income of the borrower known as the Housing to Income Ratio.
FULLY AMORTIZED LOAN	A loan that requires payments of both principal and interest. When the last payment is made, the loan is retired.
FULLY DISCLOSED PRINCIPAL	The "other party" knows there is a principal, knows who it is, and that there is an agent.
FULLY-INDEXED RATE	A rate bases on the index plus the margin.
FUNCTIONAL OBSOLESCENCE	The item in question is working fine, but is not what people want in their homes any more. Examples are a poor floor plan, four bedrooms and one bath, inadequate insulation, insufficient electrical outlets, etc.
GENERAL AGENT	An agent hired by contract to use the agent's expertise to fulfill the objectives of the principal.
GENERAL OR FULL WARRANTY DEED	A deed that contains all five covenants and covers the period of time from the date of transfer back to the date of the patent.

GENERAL PARTNER	A partner who has full authority to make decisions, act for the partnership, and has full liability for the business dealings of the partnership.
GENERAL PARTNERSHIP	A partnership composed only of general partners.
GIFT DEED	A transfer of ownership made for love and affection. Creditors of the donor could still use the property for payment of the grantor's debts if it can be shown that the donor was insolvent and transferred the property to evade creditors.
GNMA (GINNIE MAE)	Government National Mortgage Association. A secondary money market player which is government owned and purchases loan pools of FHA and VA loans.
GOOD CONSIDERATION	Consideration given in the form of love, friendship, loyalty, etc.
GRADUATED LEASE	A lease where the rent will increase periodically in amounts specified in the lease, as contained in the escalation clause.
GRADUATED PAYMENT MORTGAGE (GPM)	Payments begin below the normal, fully amortized payment and are then increased for a set period of years. Some lead to negative amortization.
GRANT DEED	A type of deed used in some states which contains limited warranties. The grantor usually also provides title insurance.
GRANTEE	One who receives property or property rights from a grantor.
GRANTOR	One who conveys property or property rights to a grantee.
GROSS LEASE	The tenant pays a set amount of rent. From this rent, the lessor is required to pay some or all operating expenses.
GROSS OPERATING INCOME (GOI)	The total income received from an investment property after subtracting vacancies and lost rents.

GROSS RENT MULTIPLIER (GRM)	A "quick and dirty" estimate of value based only on a relationship between the value of the property and the gross rents. It is referred to as the GRM.
GROSS SCHEDULED INCOME (GSI)	What an investor would receive if there were no vacancies or lost rents.
GROSS-UP	To multiply tax exempt income by 125%.
GROUND LEASE	The landlord leases the land to the tenant, and the tenant builds improvements on the leased land.
GROWING EQUITY MORTGAGE	A loan where payments increase each year, thereby allowing the loan to be paid off many years sooner and a substantial amount of interest dollars to be saved.
GUARANTEED SALES	Includes, but is not limited to: a) any plan in which a seller's real estate is guaranteed to be sold or; b) a plan whereby a licensee will purchase the seller's real estate if it is not sold within the specified period of time.
HABENDUM CLAUSE	Known as the "to have and to hold clause," and sometimes as a "subject to" clause, it defines and limits the estate which the grantee will receive when the property is transferred.
HARD MONEY LOAN	Short-term mortgage loans which require high amounts of borrower equity in the collateral in exchange for limited and/or expedited underwriting.
HABITABILITY CLAUSE	If not actually written in the lease, there is an unwritten or implied warrant of this in every lease, which says the property is livable.
HAZARD OR HOMEOWNERS' INSURANCE	An insurance policy which indemnifies real property against loss resulting from physical damage to the property such as fire, vandalism, etc. The lender will require this insurance.
HIGHEST AND BEST USE	The appraisal principle which states that value should be based on the utilization of the property which will bring the greatest return to the owner. That use must be legal and feasible.

HOLDER OF LIFE ESTATE	The receiver of a life estate who has the property for the duration of the grantee's own life.
HOLDOVER TENANT	The lessee had an estate for years which has now terminated. The lessor accepted a rent check so now the tenant is on periodic tenancy basis.
HOLOGRAPHIC WILL	A handwritten will, which must be dated, written entirely in the handwriting of the testator, and does not need witnesses in order to be valid. It can pass both real and personal property.
HOME EQUITY LINE OF CREDIT (HELOC)	An open-ended loan which can be drawn from when needed, up to the credit limit, and uses available equity in a residence as collateral.
HOME OWNERS PROTECTION ACT (HPA)	The act that requires Private Mortgage Insurance (PMI) removal.
HOMEOWNERS ASSOCIATION (HOA)	A nonprofit association of homeowners organized pursuant to a declaration of restrictions of protective covenants for a subdivision, PUD, or condominium.
HOMEOWNERSHIP AND EQUITY PROTECTION ACT OF 1994 (HOEPA)	A law that requires lenders to make disclosures to the borrowers regarding the costs involved in high fee and high rate loans.
HYPOTHECATION	Using property as collateral or security for a debt without giving up possession of the property.
INDEMNIFICATION	Reimbursement of loss.
IMPLIED AGENCY	See Ostensible Agency.
IMPOUND, RESERVE OR ESCROW ACCOUNT	A trust account established to set aside funds for future needs relating to a parcel of real property. Those needs typically include such things as property tax and hazard insurance.
IMPROVEMENTS	A term that refers to any additions to the land made by man. It includes buildings, roads and utilities and landscaping.

INACTIVE LICENSE	A real estate license in inactive status.
INCOME OR CAPITALIZATION APPROACH	An appraisal approach based on the cash flow the property produces. It addresses the question, "How much will a potential investor pay for the cash flow?"
INCORPOREAL RIGHTS	Intangible or non-possessory rights in real property, such as easements, licenses, mining claims, etc.
INCURABLE DEPRECIATION	Physical deterioration that cannot be repaired in a cost-effective manner.
INDEPENDENT BROKER	Brokers who choose to NOT affiliate with any real estate franchise.
INDEX/ INDICES (plural)	In an ARM loan, a financial indicator which will have the margin added to it to create the adjusted interest rate.
INDEX LEASE	Rent payments are periodically adjusted based on an economic indicator, such as the consumer price index.
INGRESS	Entering by traveling across the servient tenement property.
INITIAL INTEREST RATE	The rate at which the first set of loan payments are calculated. This rate is also used to qualify the borrower for the loan requested. Do not confuse this rate with "Teaser Rates" which are an artificial rate used to market a loan product. "Teaser Rates" generally create negative amortization.
INJUNCTION	Legal action taken to enforce the restrictive covenants in the Uniform Declaration of Restrictions or to prevent a neighbor from encroaching.
INTEREST	The sum paid or accrued in return for the use of money.
INTEREST-ONLY LOAN	Straight note.
INTEREST RATE	Money paid during the term of a loan that is profit to the lender. It represents the return, or yield, on the lender's investment.

INTERMEDIATE THEORY	A combination of Title Theory and Lien Theory that allows the lender to sell the property in case of default, but does not allow it to keep any equity.
INTESTATE	The condition of a person who dies and leaves no will.
INVERSE CONDEMNATION	The legal process by which a private individual sues to have the property taken by eminent domain.
INVESTMENT PROPERTY	Property which is generating a cash flow, such as a strip mall or a single or multi-family rental property.
JOINT TENANCY	A form of concurrent ownership where all owners have equal rights of possession, equal interest, took title at the same time, there is one deed, and each owner has full rights of survivorship.
JOINT VENTURE	A "temporary" partnership between individuals and/or companies to accomplish a particular project or business activity.
JUDGMENT	The decision given by a court after a case has been heard.
JUDICIAL FORECLOSURE	A method of foreclosing on real property by means of a court-supervised sale.
JUMBO LOAN	A non-conforming conventional loan that exceeds the monetary limits set by FNMA and FHLMC.
JUNIOR LIENS or JUNIOR LOAN	Any lien or encumbrance that has a lower claim for payment than another lien or encumbrance. This condition is generally created by recording order. First recorded has higher priority over subsequently recorded liens. Two exceptions over this rule are property taxes which always are the most senior of liens and mechanics liens whose priority is not set by recording date but by beginning date of work.(see also mechanics lien).
KICKBACKS	An illegal referral fee, under RESPA, paid by a lender to a real estate agent for referring a borrower.
LAND CONTRACT, INSTALLMENT SALES CONTRACT, OR CONTRACT FOR DEED	A document wherein the lender (usually the seller) retains title to the property until the debt is paid. It is known in Utah as a Uniform Real Estate Contract.

LATERAL SUPPORT	The duty to give support to a neighbor's property, such as building a retaining wall.
LEAD BASE PAINT DISCLOSURE	For any property built before 1978 this form must be given to the seller.
LEASE	A contract for a less-than-freehold estate or right in real property. Rent is paid for the right of possession in someone else's property.
LEASE WITH OPTION TO PURCHASE	A lease contract which allows the lessee the right to purchase the property. Sometimes a portion of the rent will apply to the down payment if the right is exercised.
LEGAL NONCONFORMING USE	The right of an individual to continue a use of land contrary to current zoning regulations because the use existed prior to the establishment of the current zoning category.
LEGAL PURPOSE	The essential element of a contract that protects the public.
LESS THAN FREEHOLD	An estate or legal interest in real property that is not an ownership interest.
LETTER FORM REPORT	An appraisal report that provides a short, written statement giving the bare essentials of the appraisal.
LEVERAGE	Using as much of other people's money and as little of your own as possible in order to buy property.
LICENSE INTEREST	A limited, revocable interest in property. It grants a privilege, not a right, and is often an oral agreement granting a short term use of real property. Examples would include an owner allowing someone to hunt, boat, or fish on his property; or attendance at movie theaters and sporting events.
LIEN	An encumbrance for money against real property.
LIEN THEORY	A legal doctrine or theory of mortgage law, used in most states, which gives lenders an interest in the property and allows them to force the owner to sell the property to pay the debt in the event of default.

LIFE ESTATE	A form of freehold estate wherein the holder acts as though he owns the property so long as he lives.
LIFE ESTATE PUR AUTRE VIE	A life estate based on the life of a person other than the holder of the life estate.
LIFETIME CAP / RATE CAP	The highest rate allowed by the note agreement in an adjustable rate loan.
LIMITED PARTNER	A partner who has no authority to make decisions or act for the partnership. He is financially liable only for the amount of his investment.
LIMITED AGENT	See Dual Agent
LIMITED PARTNERSHIP	A partnership with at least one general partner and one limited partner. Beyond that, there can be as many general or limited partners as desired.
LIQUIDATED DAMAGES	In anticipation of a particular default, clauses are sometimes written into a contract to specify the default and its penalty.
LIS PENDENS	It gives constructive notice that an action affecting a particular parcel of property has been filed in court. The property can be sold, leased, or otherwise disposed of, but all transactions are subject to the outcome of the court action.
LISTING	An agency agreement between a seller and a principal broker. The owner authorizes the broker to place the property on the market and seek a ready, willing, and able buyer and agrees to pay consideration if the broker is successful.
LOAN FRAUD	A licensee shall not participate in a transaction in which a buyer enters into an agreement not disclosed to the lender, which, if disclosed, might affect the granting of the loan.
LOAN ORIGINATION FEE	A fee paid by the borrower to the originator for the originators service.
LOAN TO VALUE RATIO OR L-T-V-R	The amount of debt secured by the property compared to the worth of the property, expressed as a percentage.
LONDON INTER-BANK OFFER RATE (LIBOR)	An index for used with Adjustable Rate Mortgages which is an average of daily lending rates from several major London banks.

LOT, BLOCK, AND PLAT	A method of land description used for subdivisions, identifying the location of a particular parcel in the subdivision or tract.
MANAGEMENT CONTRACT	An employment contract between a property manager and an owner of investment property.
MANAGEMENT FEES	Percent of gross property income. A common method of computing property manager compensation is as a percentage of the total revenue collected.
MARKET DATA OR COMPARISON APPROACH	An appraisal approach that contrasts the subject property with other properties that have recently sold. Adjustments are made to account for variations between the subject property and the others.
MARKETABLE RECORD TITLE ACT	The law that allows the simplification and stabilization of title searches by allowing old liens and encumbrances to be removed after 40 years.
MARGIN	The percentage, established with the ARM loan, which will be added to the index to create the adjusted interest rate.
MAXIMUM LOAN AMOUNT	The maximum insurable FHA loan amount.
MECHANIC'S LIEN	A lien placed by a person who has integrated labor or materials into a property and has not been paid.
MEDIATION	A non-binding process of meeting with a disinterested third party to try to resolve a dispute between the two principals in the transaction or contract.
MERGER	The joining of two contiguous properties so as to extinguish a lesser right. For instance, this process can terminate an easement on land locked property.
MERIDIAN	A north-south line which intersects a baseline and creates a point from which land can be measured under the Government or rectangular survey method.
METES AND BOUNDS	A method of land description that uses measurements and monuments and utilizes angles.

MILE	5,280 linear feet.
MINERAL RIGHTS	Subsurface rights of an owner of real property which extend downward to the center of the earth. These rights are real property.
MINIMUM SERVICE REQUIREMENTS	Created in 2005 to ensure that the public would not be left to address sensitive situations such as contractual offer presentations and counter offers alone.
MONETARY POLICY	Refers to what the Federal Reserve does to influence the amount of money and credit available in the U.S. economy.
MONUMENT	A fixed surveyor's marker for a metes and bounds description. It can be natural or man-made and marks the corners of the property.
MORTGAGE	A document used to secure a loan. It is a judicial agreement, meaning if non-payment takes place, the holder of the promissory note can take it to court and the court will order the sheriff to foreclose.
MORTGAGE OR LOAN FRAUD	Is a broad term meant to describe various schemes to obtain money on terms that otherwise would not have been offered, if they were offered at all, if the lender had been aware of actual and/or truthful information.
MORTGAGE INSURANCE	Insurance required by a lender if the principal of the loan is above a set LTV. It covers the interests of the lender if there is default on the loan, and proceeds from foreclosure do not cover the amount owed. It can be added to an FHA loan.
MORTGAGE INSURANCE PREMIUM (MIP)	See Mortgage Insurance
MORTGAGEE	The lender who receives a mortgage as security for a loan or debt.
MORTGAGOR	A borrower who hypothecates property as security for a loan through the use of a promissory note and a mortgage.

MULTIPLE LISTING SERVICE (MLS)	A service in which member brokers pool their listings and offer cooperation and compensations to the other member brokers usually owned and operated by a local association of REALTORS', but not always.
MULTIPLE OFFERS	Occasionally there are more than one offer presented at once on the same property. The listing agent should be careful to not only treat each buyer and their agent fairly, but to also counsel with their seller appropriately.
MULTIPLE OFFER DISCLOSURE	Gives each buyer the options to submit their best offer by a deadline set by the seller.
MUTUAL AGREEMENT	The essential element of a contract achieved through the offer and acceptance process.
NARRATIVE REPORT	The longest form of appraisal report which uses a variety of supporting documentation.
NATIONAL ASSOCIATION OF REALTORS' (NAR)	The dominant real estate industry trade association in the United States.
NATURAL PERSON	An individual. The opposite of a legal person.
NEGATIVE (PASSIVE) INTENTIONAL FRAUD	When a person covertly hides facts, thus leading the other contracting party to believe certain things which are not true.
NEGATIVE OR REVERSE AMORTIZATION	A loan that requires payments of no principal and only part of the interest. The unpaid interest is added to the principal. This technique is used on some graduated payment mortgages.
NET LEASE	Tenants pay the landlord rent; and, in addition, also pay their portion of the operating expenses (such as utilities).
NET LISTING	An illegal listing wherein the seller identifies an acceptable amount for the property and everything above that figure will be commission to the agent.

545

NET OPERATING INCOME (NOI)	The profit that remains after the operating expenses have been subtracted from the gross effective income.
NON-CONFORMING LOANS	A loan that does not qualify for FNMA or FHLMC financing.
NON-ASSUMPTION CLAUSE	See Alienation Clause
NON-DISTURBANCE CLAUSE	A clause in a mortgage which protects the rights of the lessee if the property should be foreclosed by the lender upon the owner's default.
NON-HOMOGENEOUS	A term that means no two parcels of land are exactly alike.
NON-INVESTMENT PROPERTY	A property that has no cash flow; for example, your home or a vacant lot.
NON-RECOURSE LOAN	The terms of the loan stipulate that even if the lender receives less than the balance owed as a result of a foreclosure action, the debt is satisfied and the lender may not go after the borrower's personal assets.
NON-RESIDENT LICENSE	A real estate licensee from another state acquires this kind of a license to enable him/her to practice real estate in Utah.
NOTICE OF DEFAULT	The action filed to initiate foreclosure under a Trust Deed and Note.
NOTICE	Information that may be required by the terms of a contract.
NOTICE OF INTEREST	Holders of junior liens against a property would file this. If the senior lien holder foreclosed, they would be notified and could protect their interest.
NOTICE TO QUIT	The first step a lessor must take against a tenant before filing an Unlawful Detainer with the courts.
NOVATION	The substitution of a new party or a new obligation in a contract. This process requires the agreement of all original parties in the contract, but once it has been agreed to, the original obligatee is released from liability.

NUNCUPATIVE WILL	Oral will, written down by someone and witnessed by two non beneficiaries. It can only convey personal property.
OFFER	A promise by one party to act or perform in a specified manner provided the other party acts or performs in the manner requested.
ONE-TIME-CLOSE	This happens when a takeout loan closes with a construction loan.
OPEN END MORTGAGE	A loan which can be increased up to an agreed upon maximum, similar to the way a credit card works. It is often used for construction loans and home equity loans.
OPEN LISTING	A listing agreement that can be given to as many principal brokers, on the same property, as the seller desires. It is a non-exclusive listing.
OPEN MARKET OPERATION	Purchases and sales of US treasury and federal agency securities.
OPERATING BUDGET	A projection of the financial operation of an investment property.
OPTION CONTRACT	A contract wherein a seller agrees to sell property for a set amount at specified terms, if the buyer chooses to exercise that right to purchase during the contracted period of time. In return for the seller taking his property off the market, the buyer pays valuable, non-refundable consideration.
OPTIONEE	One who receives an option; a potential buyer who may or may not buy by the end of the term of the option.
OPTIONOR	One who gives an option; the potential seller.
OPTION ARM	An adjustable rate mortgage with optional payment terms. 1)fully amortized payment 2)accelerated payment 3)minimum payment 4)interest only payment.
"OR MORE" CLAUSE	See Prepayment Privilege
ORIGINATION FEE	A fee (profit) charged by the lender to initiate a loan.

OSTENSIBLE AGENCY	Agency which is created through the actions of the parties, rather than through an express agreement. Also called implied agency.
PAID OUTSIDE OF CLOSING (POC)	Fees paid by the borrower prior to settlement that will be disclosed on the HUD1 statement but will not be included in the totals to be paid at settlement.
PACKAGE MORTGAGE	A loan that uses both real and personal property as security.
PAR	The interest rate charged on a loan that requires no discount points be paid nor pays a yield spread premium. Rates above Par pay a yield spread premium. Rates below Par require the payment of discount points.
PAR RATE	The market interest rate for a mortgage loan that neither costs nor returns money to the borrower to originate the mortgage.
PAROLE EVIDENCE RULE	Prevents the admission into court of oral agreements reached prior or subsequent to the written contract and which contradict the terms in the written contract.
PARTIAL RELEASE CLAUSE	A loan clause which allows partial amounts of the total collateral to be excused in exchange for an agreed upon balloon payment.
PARTIALLY AMORTIZED LOAN	A loan requiring payments of both principal and interest, but when the final payment is made, a balloon payment is required to retire the loan.
PARTIALLY DISCLOSED PRINCIPAL	The "other party" knows who the agent is, knows there is a principal, but is not told who the principal is.
PARTICIPATION LOAN	A loan where the lender becomes an investor or owner in the project for which the money is being loaned.
PARTITION SUIT	A court process where property owned concurrently can be divided into distinct portions so each co-owner may hold his or her portion in severalty. The court may order the property sold.
PARTY WALL	A common wall between two properties, usually involving a zero lot line.

PATENT OR PUBLIC GRANT	The instrument issued when the property is first conveyed from public or government ownership to a private individual.
PATRIOT ACT DISCLOSURE	Notice that identity will be checked.
PAYMENT CAPS (PERIODIC CAP)	Adjustable rate mortgage adjustment limits. Shorthand notation frequently follows this pattern – 2/1/6. These caps are set by contract and never change. The caps limit the initial adjustment (x/-/-), each individual adjustment (-/x/-) and the maximum adjustment from the initial rate (-/-/x).
PERCENTAGE LEASE	A lease used in commercial leasing. The tenant pays a percent of the net or gross income derived from the use of the property, or the tenant may be paying a flat rate plus a stated percent of the gross or net income.
PERIODIC TENANCY (MONTH-TO-MONTH)	A lease which automatically renews itself. The period for legal notice is established by statute in each state, or can be agreed upon as one of the terms of the lease (15 days in Utah).
PERMANENT FINANCING	A long term loan that pays off the construction loan (Take-Out-Loan).
PERSONAL PROPERTY	The opposite of real property, it is moveable and destructible. Synonyms are chattel and personalty.
PERSONAL REPRESENTATIVE	A term used in Utah for the Administrator or Executor of a will.
PERSONALTY	A synonym for personal property. The opposite of "realty."
PHYSICAL DETERIORATION	A type of depreciation that occurs when something wears out and will no longer perform the function or give the service that was originally intended.
PHYSICAL LIFE	The time span during which an improvement is still standing though it no longer has economic life.
PLAIN LANGUAGE POLICY	Title insurance covering the borrower, which will cover mechanic's liens.

549

PLANNED UNIT DEVELOPMENT (PUD)	A nontraditional type of housing development designed to produce high density of dwellings, maximum use of open spaces, and greater flexibility for residential land and development; local government approval is required. The developer records a declaration of covenants and restriction and records as a subdivision plat reserving common areas to the members of the association but not to the general public and nonprofit community association is organized to provide for maintenance of the common area.
PLEDGE	The borrower gives up possession of the property being used as collateral for the loan (the way a pawn shop works).
PLOTTAGE	Combining two or more parcels of land with a resulting increase in total value.
POINT OF BEGINNING	In the Metes and Bounds method, this is the corner at which the boundary description starts.
POLICE POWER	The right of government, such as in zoning, to exercise control over private property without their consent and without compensation.
POSITIVE INTENTIONAL FRAUD	When a person deliberately and overtly deceives or misrepresents facts pertinent to a contract.
POTENTIAL SERVICING TRANSFER STATEMENT	Notice given at time of application and again at settlement that the lender intends to sell its servicing rights.
POWER OF ATTORNEY	What an attorney-in-fact holds which authorizes actions in behalf of another person, including signature authority.
POWER OF SALE (BARE, NAKED, LEGAL TITLE)	The authority (conveyed from the trustor to the trustee at the time the Trust Deed and Note are signed) to sell the property in the event of default.
PREPAYMENT PENALTY	This clause in a loan penalizes the borrower for paying off the loan earlier than agreed.

PREPAYMENT PRIVILEGE	This clause in a loan allows the borrower to pay the loan off early. The amount of the monthly payments can be increased, with all of the extra payment applying to the principal; refinance without penalty; or make balloon payments from time to time.
PRE-QUALIFICATION LETTER	A letter from the lender indicating that the borrowers loan application has been accepted subject to providing the collateral.
PRICE	The amount of money being asked for a product or property, or the amount it sells for.
PRIMARY MONEY OR MORTGAGE MARKET	Those who originate loans of any type, regardless of the priority of the loan, are in this financial market.
PRIME RATE	The interest rate that is charged a lender's most favored clients and is established by the major banks or lenders of America.
PRINCIPAL	The agent works for this person. This person is also sometimes referred to as a client.
PRINCIPAL BROKER	The broker who manages the offices and is responsible for supervising the activities of the licensed and unlicensed staff.
PRINCIPAL, INTEREST, TAXES, AND INSURANCE (PITI)	A mortgage payment which includes principal (funds that were borrowed), interest (the payment of rent for the amount borrowed), taxes (an amount to go into an escrow account for future payment of property taxes), and insurance (an amount to go into an escrow account for the future payment of hazard insurance).
PRIOR APPROPRIATION OR STATUTORY APPROPRIATION	The legal doctrine used in Utah for distribution of water based on the "first come, first served" idea.
PRIVATE MORTGAGE INSURANCE (PMI)	Insurance typically required on conventional loans that meet exceed 80% LTV.
PROCURING CAUSE DOCTRINE	A doctrine governing who gets the selling portion of the commission. It says the agent who set up an uninterrupted chain of events that led to the closing earned the commission.

PROMISSORY NOTE	The document given as evidence of the loan. It contains all information relative to the money: payment, term, interest rate, etc.
PROPERTY FLIPPING	Buying a property and selling as soon as possible.
PROPERTY MANAGEMENT	This activity occurs when a licensee manages investment property for the owner.
PROPERTY MANAGER	One who represents the interests of the owner of investment property. The property could be for residential or commercial purposes. This person must have a real estate license.

PROPERTY MGMT. TRUST ACCOUNT	Must be opened when a real estate brokerage is handling more than six property management accounts.
PROPERTY TAX	The tax levied by government against real estate. These taxes are due in Utah on November 30 and cover the full calendar year. They are also referred to as real property tax.
PROPRIETARY LEASE	Sometimes called an "owner's" lease. It is held by a person who owns shares in a stock cooperative. They own personal property which entitles them to this type of lease.
PRORATION	The process of computing the buyer's and seller's portion of an obligation owed by both, such as property tax.
PUFFING	Sales talk or exaggerated statements that reflect an obvious overstatement by the agent and are not considered misrepresentation or fraud.
PURCHASE MONEY MORTGAGE	A loan for a home purchase where the home being purchased is the security for the home loan. Examples are seller financing, and first and second mortgages.
QUANTITY SURVEY METHOD	The appraiser determines the cost of the materials; labor; management fees, and profit. These are used to determine the value of improvements when using the cost approach in appraisal.
QUASI-GOVERNMENTAL	An organization that looks and acts like government but is owned by private citizens. Examples include Freddie Mac or Fannie Mae.

QUIET ENJOYMENT	One of the rights in the "Bundle of Rights." The right of an owner or lessee to uninterrupted legal use of the property without interference or disturbance caused by defective title.
QUIET TITLE ACTION	A court action to determine the actual ownership of real property. This type of proceeding would be conducted to transfer title to an adverse possessor.
QUIT CLAIM DEED	A deed that conveys all interest in a property which the grantor may or may not have, and gives no warranties as to the condition of title. Its primary use is to remove clouds from the title.
RADON	Radioactive, colorless, odorless, tasteless noble gas, occurring naturally in our environment as the decay of radium.
RANGE	A vertical column of townships, counted east and west from the meridian in the Government or Rectangular Survey Method.
RATE LOCK PERIODS	The length of time the quoted interest rate will be guaranteed to the borrower.
RATE OF RETURN	Same as Capitalization Rate or Cap Rate.
RATE SHEET	A form used by lenders to inform mortgage loan originators of the par rate and the costs or credit paid for rates above and below the par rate.
REAL ESTATE PURCHASE CONTRACT	A State approved form which must be filled out by all licensees which is used when writing an offer to buy real property. When accepted, it becomes the sales agreement.
REAL ESTATE PURCHASE CONTRACT FOR NEW CONSTRUCTION	Similar to the Real Estate Purchase Contract, but this one is to be used solely when the property being purchased is a new home to be constructed or for which no Certificate of Occupancy has been issued.
REAL ESTATE SETTLEMENT PROCEDURES ACT (RESPA)	An act that is designed to protect the borrowers in real estate transactions through thorough disclosure of the costs of obtaining the loan. It is also known as Regulation X, and is different than Truth In Lending.

REAL PROPERTY	Land and appurtenances, air space to infinity, and the subsurface to the center of the earth.
REAPPRAISAL LEASE	A lease wherein the rent is determined by a periodic re-evaluation of the property's value.
RECONCILIATION	An appraiser should use as many of the approaches to appraising as possible. This technique synthesizes the results into a single estimate of value. It is sometimes called correlation.
RECONVEYANCE OF DEED	The document a lender uses to return all interest in the property after the debt has been satisfied under a Trust Deed and Note. This is in accordance with the defeasance clause.
RECORDING	A form of delivery of a deed, also known as constructive delivery or notice.
RECTANGULAR SURVEY METHOD	A method of land description that uses base and meridian lines, townships and sections. It is also referred to as the Government Survey Method.
REDLINING	The discriminatory practice of refusing to make loans in certain neighborhoods.
REFERRAL COMPANIES	These Brokerages are designed to house agents that do not wish to be a part of the local REALTOR° Board. Agents in these brokerages may still operate as any other Active Real Estate Agent, but without the benefits or the services and information of the Board of REALTORS°. These agents choose to refer contacts, clients or leads to agents in other Brokerages.
REFERRAL FEE	A fee paid for sending a customer to another for services.
REFINANCE	Obtaining a new loan, often at a lower interest rate, out of which the old loan is paid off.
REGULAR SALARIES EMPLOYEES	An individual not employed on a contract basis, which has withholding taken out of his/her paycheck by the employer.
REGULATION Z	See Truth in Lending.

REIT (REAL ESTATE INVESTMENT TRUST)	Its purpose is to avoid double taxation. It must have at least 100 members, and return at least 90% of the profits to the investors.
REJECTION	Terminates offer. When a Buyer or seller rejects an offer, they effectively terminate the offer. The offer is no longer alive.
RELEASE CLAUSE	When a blanket loan has been given, this clause will allow part of the property to be removed as security for the loan when certain requirements have been met, sometimes called a partial release clause.
REMAINDERMAN	The person who will receive the life estate when the current holder of the life estate dies. There can be more than one of these.
RESCISSION	As a remedy for fraud, or by agreement of the parties, all parties return to their original positions prior to the executing of the contract. It is also known as a "contract to end a contract."
RESERVE ACCOUNT	An account that holds borrower funds until hazard insurance premiums are paid.
RESIDENTIAL PROPERTY	Property used for housing. Includes single-family housing, condos, cooperatives, and apartment buildings.
RESIDUAL INCOME	An amount determined as the income available to make mortgage payments after other obligations have been considered. It is used instead of debt to income ratios in determining eligibility for VA loans.
RESIDUAL INCOME ANALYSIS	The VA method of determining the borrower's ability to pay the mortgage payment.
RETAIL MORTGAGE RATE	The interest rate on a loan which is charged to the consumer (borrower).
RETAIL MORTGAGE RATE SHEET	The published rates of a lender.

REVERSE ANNUITY MORTGAGE (RAM)	When the mortgagee makes regular monthly payments to the mortgagor. The payments create the loan. It is used for elderly people whose homes are paid off or nearly so. The debt is not repaid until they either sell the house or die.
REVOCATION OF LICENSE	The act of terminating, canceling or annulling a license.
RIGHT OF FIRST REFUSAL	A right given to a prospective purchaser to be able to meet the price and terms at which the owner is willing to sell the property to another party. Unlike an option, the seller is under no obligation to withdraw his property from the market.
RIGHT OF REVERSION	Future interest in real estate created by the grantor that provides for the property to revert to the grantor upon expiration of the interest.
ROOFTOP LEASE	This lease is used when the tenant only wants to rent the top of the building.
RULE OF DISCLOSURE	An agent's responsibility to reveal all material facts to a principal, including mistakes and misrepresentations. Indeed it might be said concerning the fiduciary relationship, what the agent knows, the principal knows.
RULE OF OBEDIENCE	An agent's responsibility to follow all instructions of the principal.
SAFETY CLAUSE	A clause in a listing contract that protects the listing broker from the seller's attempt to sell the property after the expiration of the listing to avoid paying a commission.
SALES AGENT	A real estate licensee who does not have a broker's license and must work under the supervision of the employing principal broker.
SALE AND LEASEBACK	An owner sells a property, then leases it back from the new owner. This could be a long or short term lease.
SATISFACTION OF MORTGAGE	The document used by the lender to reconvey all of his interest in a property, as required by the defeasance clause under a mortgage.
SEASONED FUNDS	Buyer funds held in an institution with deposit and balance records available for a period of time.

SEASONED LOAN	A loan with a payment history. This feature of a loan is preferred by the secondary money market.
SECOND FEET	One cubic foot of water flowing past a given point in one second of time.
SECONDARY MONEY OR MORTGAGE MARKET	Individuals or financial institutions that purchase existing loans.
SECTION	An area of land one mile square in the Government or Rectangular Survey Method. It contains 640 acres.
SELLER CONTRIBUTIONS	An allowable payment from the seller toward closing costs.
SELLER DISCLOSURES	The property's title and physical condition information required by the REPC to be given to the buyer by the seller.
SENIOR LIEN	Refers to first mortgages or trust deeds or the debt first recorded against the real property.
SERVICE PROPERTY	Property such as government buildings or churches which are used for public purposes and are non-profit.
SERVICE RELEASE PREMIUM (SRP)	A payment to the originating lender for the transfer of servicing obligations to a new loan servicer.
SERVICER	The entity that collects payments and manages the reserve account.
SERVIENT TENEMENT	The name given to a property encumbered by an easement appurtenant, such a landlocked situation.
SETTLEMENT	The date specified in the purchase contract when buyer and seller deliver any monies required, as cleared funds, to the settlement agent and sign the documents applicable to the transaction.
SEVERALTY	A form of ownership wherein an individual owns the property in sole ownership.

SEVERANCE	A process by which real property becomes personal property.
SHARED EQUITY MORTGAGE	The lender not only collects interest on the loan, but when the property is sold, the lender will receive a portion of the profits from the increase in the property's value since the time it was purchased.
SHERIFF'S DEED	The document given to the person who bid and bought property at a Sheriff's Sale. This document is not given until the statutory six-month period of redemption has passed.
SHERIFF'S SALE	The name of the event wherein a property is sold in foreclosure under a mortgage.
SHERMAN ANTITRUST ACT	A law designed to encourage competition and free enterprise by outlawing price fixing.
SHORT FORM OR CHECKLIST REPORT	An appraisal report that uses a standardized form wherein the appraiser checks boxes and fills in blanks. It is often required by a lending institutions.
SHORT SALE	A sale of secured real property that produces less money than is owned the lender; also called short pay, in that the lender releases its mortgage or trust deed so that the property can be sold free and clear to the new purchaser.
SIMPLE INTEREST	The type of interest that is computed on the unpaid principal balance.
SITUS	Personal preference for one location over another which affects the value of the property.
SPECIAL ASSESSMENT	A tax customarily imposed against only those parcels of property that will benefit from a proposed public improvement such as sidewalks, sewer, street lights, parks, etc.
SPECIAL PURPOSE PROPERTY	Property that doesn't fit one of the standard zoning classifications (residential, commercial, agricultural, etc.) is put in this general category.

SPECIAL WARRANTY DEED	This type of deed contains only two covenants: the covenant of seizing and the covenant against encumbrances. Furthermore, it only warrants the period of time that the grantor actually owned the property.
SPECIFIC PERFORMANCE	A legal remedy requiring a party to perform as agreed in the contract.
SPECIFIC, SPECIAL AGENT	An agent hired by contract to carry out specifically stated activities.
SPOT ZONING	The process involved when the zoning and planning commission changes the zoning of a single lot to be different from others surrounding it.
SQUARE FOOT METHOD	In this Cost Approach Method, the appraiser multiplies the value per unit of area times the number of units of area.
STANDARD COVERAGE TITLE INSURANCE	Title insurance which protects against losses arising from both recorded title claims, omissions and errors in public records, and from inadequate title search procedures. It does not protect from undisclosed and unrecorded claims against the title such as unrecorded mechanic's liens.
STANDARD SUPPLEMENTARY CLAUSES	UAR provided and recommended forms. Each clause is designed as an addendum to the REPC.
STATE APPROVED FORMS	The Division of Real Estate and the State Attorney General's office allow licensees to fill out these forms. They include the Real Estate Purchase Contract, its Addenda; the Real Estate Purchase Contract for Residential Construction; the All Inclusive Trust Deed and its Note; and the Uniform Real Estate Contract.
STATE CONSTRUCTION REGISTRY	This act took effect in November 2005. The property owner and the general contractor don't always know how many subcontractors, suppliers and laborers are involved in the project, or who they are. The State Construction Registry solves that problem.
STATE ENGINEER	In Utah, the entity to which one applies for water rights. It encompasses the Division of Water Rights.

559

STATUTE OF FRAUDS	The requirement that certain contracts must be in writing in order to be enforceable in court.
STATUTORY DEDICATION	When the developer is allowed by the city, county, or state to convey the streets, sidewalks, gutters, etc. for maintenance by the government.
STATUTORY MINIMUM DOWN PAYMENT	FHA 3%
STATUTORY PERIOD OF REDEMPTION	The period of time, following a foreclosure sale, wherein the mortgagor has the right of paying off all debts against the property, thus regaining ownership.
STEERING	The act of directing buyers to or away from certain geographical areas for the purpose of discriminating.
STIGMATIZED PROPERTY	The site or suspected site of a felony, or suicide; the dwelling of a person with infectious disease; or property that has been found to be contaminated.
STOCK COOPERATIVE or CO-OPS	Persons buy a stock interest in a building. This entitles them to a lease in one of the units, called a proprietary or "owner's" lease. Note: stock is personal property.
STRAIGHT NOTE	A loan that requires payments of interest only, sometimes called a term loan. Usually the entire principal is paid off in one balloon payment at the end of the loan.
STRAW BUYER	Someone who purchases property for another so as to conceal the identity of the real purchaser; a dummy purchaser; a nominee; a front.
SUBAGENT	Anyone who is assisting the agent (principal broker) in the agent's responsibilities. For instance, a sales agent or associate broker in the office, or principal broker with a co-broker agreement.
SUBDIVISION	Land divided into lots which may or may not include improvements such as water, utilities, curbs, gutters, and streets; but does not include buildings.

SUBJECT TO CLAUSE	This clause may be found in either a contract or a deed. In a contract, it is another name for the contingency clause. In a deed, it is another way of referring to the habendum or "to have and to hold" clause.
SUBLEASE	A lease given by the original lessee. The lessee remains fully liable to the lessor. The lessee pays rent to the lessor or landlord, and collects rent from the sub-lettee.
SUBORDINATION CLAUSE	The clause in a loan that can alter the priority of a loan.
SUBROGATION	The substitution of liability or rights, as in a title insurance policy.
SUBSTITUTION, PRINCIPLE OF	The appraisal principle which states that no prudent buyer will pay more than he has to get what he wants. This is the basic principle of the Market Data or Comparison approach to appraisal.
SUB-PRIME LOAN	Borrowers who do not qualify for conforming or A paper, but do qualify for B, C or D paper would get this kind of loan.
SUPPLY AND DEMAND	The principle of economics, as well as appraisal, which states that when there is an overabundance of a particular product, the price will go down; conversely, when there is a limited amount of that product, the price will go up.
SURVIVORSHIP	The surviving owner(s) automatically receives ownership of the deceased person's share. It takes precedence over a will.
TACKING	In adverse possession, this process allows consecutive periods of adverse possession by multiple adverse possessors to be added together to make up the required number of years.
TAKE-OUT LOAN	Once construction is completed and an appraisal obtained, this is a term referring to the permanent, long-term financing for the property.
TAX CREDIT	Items which the IRS allows you to subtract from the dollar amount of taxes due. There are very few of these allowed.
TAX DEFERRED EXCHANGE	An exchange of like for like properties. Tax on any capital gains is paid at a later date. Boot or debt reduction is taxable.

TAX SERVICE FEE	A fee to a third party vendor who confirms whether taxes are current and provides amount of taxes for credit at closing.
TEASER RATE	An introductory rate lower than the rate would have been if computed by adding the margin to the index on an adjustable rate loan.
TEMPORARY BUY DOWNS	An agreement that does not pay all the interest due and increases the loan amount.
TENANCY AT SUFFERANCE or ESTATE AT SUFFERANCE	The lease has expired and the lessee is now possessing the property illegally, having been given proper notice to vacate. It is similar to trespassing except that the lessee, at one time, held a legal lease.
TENANCY AT WILL or ESTATE AT WILL	A lease which requires little or no notice of termination. It is used in special circumstances wherein both the lessor and lessee agree that the lease can be terminated by either party. It is of uncertain duration.
TENANCY BY THE ENTIRETY	A form of ownership that can only be held by husband and wife, similar to joint tenancy, except that one party cannot sell or encumber the property without the approval of the spouse.
TENANCY FOR YEARS or ESTATE FOR YEARS	A lease which contains a termination date. Its term can be for any agreed-upon period of time. (It can be more or less than one year.)
TENANCY IN COMMON	A form of ownership where owners have full rights of possession, but each owner can have a different percent of ownership. Upon the death of one, that interest goes to the heirs.
TENANT IMPROVEMENTS	Common in commercial and industrial leasing. Every retail store has its own personality.
TENDER	Another term for the process of making or presenting an offer.
TESTATOR	The title of a person who makes a will.
THIRD PARTIES	A person such as the broker or escrow agent who is not party to a contract but who may be affected by it; one who is not a principal to the transaction.

THIRD PARTY DELIVERY	Delivery of the deed is accomplished by a disinterested party who has written, acknowledged instructions from the grantor. It is also called a deed in escrow.
TIER	The horizontal row of townships, counted north and south from the baseline in the Governmental or Rectangular Survey method.
TIME IS OF THE ESSENCE	The clause in a contract that means all dates are firm and non-performance by the date specified may create a voidable contract.
TITLE	An abstract term denoting ownership; not a document.
TITLE INSURANCE	Since an attorney's opinion does not offer the buyer financial protection if the title proves unsound, this can be purchased, giving varying degrees of financial protection relative to the condition of title of real property.
TITLE THEORY	A legal doctrine or theory of mortgage law used in a few states that allows the lender to take property as collateral for the debt by holding ownership of the property until the debt is paid.
TO AND THROUGH DOCTRINE	An approach which says the agent who first showed the property to the buyer earns the selling portion of the commission.
TOWNSHIP	The largest land area used in the rectangular or government survey system. It is six miles square.
TRADE FIXTURE	That which is considered legally attached to a business. It is always personal property.
TREASURY BILL INDEX (T-BILL)	An index that follows the risk free government lending market.
TRIGGER TERMS	Under Truth in Lending, if any number other than the APR or purchase price is used in advertising, all these other numbers must be disclosed.
TRUST DEED (OR DEED OF TRUST)	The document that provides for a non-judicial foreclosure process. It is used to secure a promissory note, by which a borrower hypothecates property as collateral for a debt or loan.

TRUSTEE	Since the courts are not being used in the case of a Trust Deed and Note, this person acts as an escrow agent to insure that the terms of the loan are carried out, and to initiate foreclosure if they are not.
TRUSTEE'S DEED	The document that is given to the individual who successfully bids at a foreclosure sale and purchases the foreclosed property. It conveys fee simple title immediately after the sale.
TRUSTEE'S SALE	The event where property is sold in foreclosure under a Trust Deed and Note.
TRUSTOR	The legal term given to one who hypothecates property as collateral for a loan, using a promissory note and trust deed.
TRUTH IN LENDING, OR FEDERAL CONSUMER CREDIT PROTECTION ACT(OR REGULATION Z)	An act created in Congress to protect consumers from being deceived about the costs of borrowing money. It requires full disclosure of the cost of borrowing money and regulates advertising of credit.
UNDERWRITER	The loan decision maker.
UNDISCLOSED PRINCIPAL	The "other party" thinks that the agent is the principal and sees no evidence of an agency relationship. It is usually illegal.
UNDUE INFLUENCE	Taking advantage of another person because you hold a unique position of trust, such as a doctor/patient, attorney/client, real estate agent/client relationship.
UNIFORM COMMERCIAL CODE	The body of law that regulates the transfer, or sale, of personal property, such as when one is selling a business (UCC).
UNIFORM DECLARATION OF RESTRICTIONS	The document that is used when a sub-divider or developer records a group of restrictive covenants on all of the lots in a subdivision.
UNIFORM REAL ESTATE CONTRACT	See All Inclusive Trust Deed.
UNIFORM RESIDENTIAL LANDLORD AND TENANT ACT	Federal legislation aimed at creating proper legal relationships between landlords or owners and tenants.

UNILATERAL CONTRACT	A contract wherein a promise is exchanged for a performance. Only one of the parties is initially bound, as when a reward is offered, for example, finding a lost animal.
UNIT-IN-PLACE METHOD	An appraisal method for determining the cost of improvements which takes a general approach. It is sometimes referred to as a sub-contractor approach and considers the cost of components, such as the concrete work, the framing, etc. or such items as extra light fixtures, kitchen or bathroom fixtures, etc.
UNIVERSAL AGENT	An agent hired to do all things for and in behalf of the principal.
UNSECURED LOAN	Loan which requires the debtors promise to pay as collateral.
UNLAWFUL DETAINER	The legal action a landlord brings against the tenant to evict when there is legal cause.
UPFRONT FUNDING FEE	A fee charged by the VA for funding the loan.
UPFRONT MORTGAGE INSURANCE PREMIUM (UFMIP)	An insurance premium charged by the FHA at closing.
URBAN RENEWAL	The procedure of condemning private property as a blighted area and having it torn down and rebuilt.
USURY	Interest rates above the legal rate, or statutory limit.
UTAH ASSOCIATION OF REALTORS° (UAR)	The dominant real estate industry trade association in Utah.
VA LOAN	A government loan that is guaranteed and does not require a down payment.
VALID CONTRACT	A contract that contains all the essential elements of a contract and therefore is binding on all parties.
VALUABLE CONSIDERATION	Consideration in the form of money, services, promises, or real or personal property.

565

VALUE	The power of a product, service, or property to command other goods or money in exchange. It is the present worth of future benefits arising out of ownership.
VARIANCE	The right of an individual to do something that violates current zoning regulations because the zoning and planning commission or Board of Adjustment granted that right.
VENDEE	One who buys or offers to buy.
VENDOR	One who sells or offers to sell.
VERTICAL LEASE	A lease for either air rights or subterranean rights (such as oil).
VOID CONTRACT	A contract that lacks one or more of the essential elements of a contract and therefore is not binding on any of the parties.
VOIDABLE CONTRACT	A contract wherein one of the parties can challenge one or more of the essential elements of the contract and therefore has the right to affirm or disaffirm the contract.
VOLUNTARY DEDICATION	When a private individual gives land as a gift for public use, such as land for a park, church, hospital, etc.
WALK-THROUGH INSPECTION	An optional visit by the buyer to check and approve the condition of the property and any repairs that have been made.
WASTE	When the owner of the property commits destructive acts on the property or fails to keep up with maintenance requirements.
WITH-DRAWL	An offer can be withdrawn any time prior to its acceptance. To withdraw an offer the buyer or seller should instruct their agent to write a written notice of cancellation.
WRAPAROUND LOAN	A loan that encompasses one or more existing loans.
WRIT OF EXECUTION	A court order directing an officer of the court to sell property of the defendant in order to satisfy a judgment.
WRIT OF RESTITUTION	In an Unlawful Detainer Action, the judge's order for the sheriff to evict a tenant and restore the premises to the lessor.

YIELD SPREAD PREMIUM (YSP)	The amount paid by a lender to mortgage for originating a loan with an interest rate above the par rate.
ZONE A	The zone designation that indicates a likelihood of flood and which is requires the purchase of flood insurance.
ZONING	A right of state governments to regulate the height, bulk and use of private property in order to protect the health, morals, welfare, and safety of the public; usually delegated to the local level.

568

Index

© Stringham Schools

Index

Index